Curriculum in Abundance

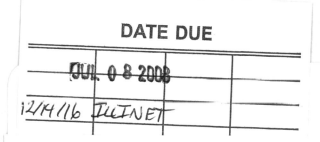

STUDIES IN CURRICULUM THEORY
William F. Pinar, Series Editor

For more information on titles in the Studies in Curriculum Theory series, please contact Lawrence Erlbaum Associates, Publishers, at **www.erlbaum.com**

Curriculum in Abundance

David W. Jardine
Sharon Friesen
Patricia Clifford
University of Calgary

2006

LAWRENCE ERLBAUM ASSOCIATES, PUBLISHERS
Mahwah, New Jersey   London

Lawrence Erlbaum Associates, Inc., Publishers
10 Industrial Avenue
Mahwah, New Jersey 07430
www.erlbaum.com

Cover design by Tomai Maridou

Library of Congress Cataloging-in-Publication Data

Jardine, David W.
   Curriculum in abundance / David W. Jardine, Sharon Friesen & Patricia Clifford.
      p.   cm. — (Studies in curriculum theory)
   Includes bibliographical references and index.
ISBN 0-8058-5601-3 (pbk. : alk. paper)
1. Education—Curricula.   I. Jardine, David William, 1950-   .
   II. Friesen, Sharon.   III. Clifford, Patricia (Patricia Anne)
   IV. Series.
LB1570.C88378 2006
375.006—dc22   2006000782

Books published by Lawrence Erlbaum Associates are printed on acid-free paper, and their bindings are chosen for strength and durability.

Printed in the United States of America
10   9   8   7   6   5   4   3   2   1

Contents

Foreword
The Lure That Pulls Flowerheads to Face the Sun

William F. Pinar

> [T]his heart of mine knows the world is alive and full of purpose.
>
> —*David W. Jardine*

This is, as David Jardine, Sharon Friesen, and Patricia Clifford acknowledge, "the oddest of texts to grasp".[1] Actually, the text isn't odd; it's the present day that is, and that makes this text seem odd. The present day is one of scarcity, demanding of us "sure-fire methods," the success of which is measured by standardized examinations, regularly administered. Such is, we are told, accountability. In the United States, politicians' calls for accountability seem reserved for the schools only. In the business sector—think of the Enron scandal, for instance—has anyone even heard of the word? Certainly this is a concept foreign to the Bush Administration. Complaints about the Bush Administration's incompetence in responding to the 2005 Hurricane Katrina disaster are dismissed as "blame-games." In such Orwellian times, David Jardine, Sharon Friesen, and Patricia Clifford dedicate this book

> to the teachers and children who are suffering in the confines of a form of schooling premised on scarcity and impoverishment, and to teachers and children who have taught the three of us so much about what an enlivening and pleasurably difficult thing teaching and learning can be in light of curriculum understood as abundance. (p. xxviii)

---

[1]Unless otherwise indicated, unnamed references are to the present text.

Pleasure in difficulty? The curriculum as abundance? In the present day, these phrases sound odd all right.

Language creates as it decodes reality. David, Sharon, and Patricia's vocabulary—drawn, in part, from Ivan Illich—functions likewise. "We therefore use the term *abundance*", they tell us, "because of what it invokes, what it provokes, what it allows, the questions it supports, the language it encourages, the images and hopes and desires it brings." As in post-structuralism,[2] language here is a passage to a world not evident in the present era of scarcity, but the world everywhere around us, in us, in classrooms.

This is hardly Jardine's first post-structuralist moment (see, e.g., Jardine, 1992d). His astonishing accomplishment has been grounded in phenomenology, and, more specifically, in radical hermeneutics, with its "decoding/creating" function always already restructuring its "original difficulty." In the present volume, phenomenology and post-structuralism become background to his and his colleagues' original point of view. Despite being distracted by scarcity, we are called to return to our original difficulty, asking: "What is our real work as teachers and students?" To answer, the authors report, "We have been drawing upon three interrelated disciplines in order to cultivate this imagining [of abundance]: (1) ecology, (2) contemporary threads of Buddhist philosophy, (3) hermeneutics." These traditions are not prerequisites for understanding *Curriculum in Abundance*, but serious students will return to these traditions. Such study will permit a fuller and more nuanced appreciation of the scale of the scholarly accomplishment of this book. In it, we discover "a great kinship between hermeneutics, ecology, and pedagogy."

TO THE THINGS THEMSELVES

> Understanding is thus not method: It is learning to dwell in the presence of this riveredge ... and, under such witness, becoming someone because of it.
> —*David W. Jardine*

The idea of abundance, we are told, emerged at the end of their last book, *Back to the Basics of Teaching and Learning*: *"Thinking the World Together"* (2003). In that text, Jardine, Friesen, and Clifford suggested that "what is in fact basic to a living discipline (and therefore a curricular inheritance entrusted to teachers and students in schools) is precisely its excessiveness" (p. xxvi). Acknowledging that this idea is unimaginable during regimes of scar-

---

[2]Post-structuralism is a movement in literary criticism and philosophy originating in France in the late 1960s. In no minor way derived from Martin Heidegger's *Being and Time* (1962), post-structuralism suggested that language is not a transparent medium that connects one directly with a "truth" or "reality" outside it but, rather, a structure or code whose elements derive their meaning from their contrast with one another and not from any explicit connection with an "outside"—in the present context, non relational—world. See Pinar, Reynolds, Slattery, and Taubman, 1995, chapter 9, for its history in curriculum studies.

city, Jardine explains in the Preface of this volume that "understanding curriculum in abundance requires thinking and experiencing that is substantive, material, bodily, earthly, located, specific" (p. xxiv). To be understood, the authors insist in chapter 1, it must be practiced: "We have argued ... for the ways in which our thinking must find its thoughtfulness through the worldly work, in the face of the testy case that will slow thought down and test its resolve, its strength, its patience, and its worth" (p. 18).

David, Sharon, and Patricia experienced and practiced this abundance in public-school classrooms. There they hear not only the voices of students and teachers. They hear the sound of our calling. In the midst of children's bustling about, David speaks, in the Preface, of hearing his ancestors calling to him: "I like the experience of having my attention drawn, of being whispered to, of having a *calling*" (p. xxiii). Having been called, we do not act as self-made men fantasize themselves, exploiting the world's "resources." Rather, we listen and we respond. This is no unilateral assertion, but a dialogical, relational gesture of acknowledgment: "What abundance requires of teachers and students is a much more cultivated, much more deliberate and intellectually sound sense of the nature and limits of our own agency" (p. 10). There is no politicized or psychologistic conception of agency here; indeed, this text underscores agency's passivity. Discussing the study of mathematics, the subject is described as a "living place, a living field of relations, and that to make our way into it requires a momentary sense of loss, of giving oneself over to *its* ways by 'letting'" (p. 66). Prospective and practicing teachers won't hear such advice in many methods courses.

Still speaking of mathematics in chapter 4, Jardine appreciates that teaching is a meditative practice. It is, as Ted Aoki understood, a mode of being. He can "participate in the open space of mathematics," David tells us, "when my breath settles down and steps out paces of walking meditation: breaths and steps symmetrical and measured, seeking equilibration, oxygen filling up the longing spaces in patterns chemical precisions that return with exhalation" (p. 85). This meditative sense of study—wherein an academic discipline seems simultaneously a spiritual discipline—calls us to go beyond issues of epistemology toward issues of ontology. "Epistemology has to do with issues of what it means *to know* something—rooted in the Greek term *episteme*, to know. Ontology has to do with what it means *to be* something—from the Greek *ontos*, to be" (p. 87). In my terms, academic study supports, indeed structures, self-formation; it recalls the German theory of *Bildung* (von Humbolt, 2000 [1793–1794]).

Self-formation occurs through movement, as if on a journey (see Kliebard, 2000 [1975]). Human experience has "the character of a journeying ... becoming someone along the way" (p. 271). That some "one" is hardly alone—the authors emphasize the relationality, the ecology, of human experience in the world—but there seems to me the suggestion of an apparently essential unified self, as least when they write: "Each variant *is* the original and therefore each stubborn particular must be read, somehow, in its wholeness, in its originary character. The simplest child's simplest utterance may itself be prophesy" (p. 86). A western word, prophesy is not prediction (certainly in no social scientific sense), but a revelation onto times "not yet," as Maxine Greene is so fond of saying. The simplest child's simplest utterance represents a call from beyond the apparently present moment in which we older creatures dwell, beyond yet not apart from it. Hongyu Wang (2004) suggested:

> The call from the stranger invites movement toward the beyond, but not beyond into absolute, essential, metaphysical truth. This movement toward the beyond is *with* the web of interconnections ... . Only through her efforts to reach *out* can the deep connections within be touched, felt, and transformed. In a third space. (p. 129)

That is, she suggested, a third space in which Western distinctions among past, present, and future blur. There, our situation becomes discernible, and we can hear prophets among us.

Surely David Jardine, Sharon Friesen, and Patricia Clifford are among them. Listening to them, "the dry and lifeless impoverishment of the curriculum guide version of the topic cracks open. A world begins to appear and we feel drawn into it" (p. 41). Under regimes of scarcity, responding to the call of the other is re-coded into "learning styles" wherein one "constructs" the world according to cognitive schema. For these authors, abundance is an ontological, not epistemological, fact. Responding to the call of the other requires, perhaps above all, the discernment of difference:

> [S]uggestions of multiplicity and diversity are not opulent educational *options* regarding how we might come to know topics that are in reality simple and manageable. Rather, multiplicity, diversity and abundance define the way in which things *are*, and therefore, the great array of the ways of traversing a place that students bring to the classroom is precisely what living things require if they are to be "adequately" understood in their abundance. (p. 88)

We may take epistemological paths to reach this place, but where we arrive is a living breathing place of being.

In this place—this curriculum—of abundance, not only people but ideas and images speak to us. "Images," we are told, "have a most peculiar sense of arrival. They seem to *arrive*, out of nowhere, often unexpectedly, with a clear feel of agency, of portend, of demand and deliberateness. This is phenomenologically undeniable" (p. 91). The world does not wait for us to act on it, silent, defenseless; instead, this world of abundance is a meaningful place, alive with purpose. This vibrant world provokes our awe and wonder: "First is the question posed, not *by us* but *to us*" (p. 91). A curriculum topic understood in abundance "pulls us into *its* question, *its* repose, *its* regard" (p. 91). I am reminded of Rita Irwin's (2003) depiction of aesthetic surrender to the labor of creation. Such devotion does not mean relinquishing agency, but, as the authors acknowledge: "What abundance requires of teachers and students is a much more cultivated, much more deliberate and intellectually sound sense of the nature and limits of our own agency" (p. 10).

This is a nuanced, situation-specific, relational conception of agency. It would seem to acknowledge that agency requires recognition of the particular situation—its horizons, its meaning—so that we may act with precision, care, and tact (van Manen, 1991). The agency of pedagogy demands, with the authors citing the work of Hans-Georg Gadamer, "deliberation" and "decision." The omnipresence—the worship—of technology does not alter this fact. "In fact," David, Sharon, and Patricia emphasize, "the new technologies are aggravating and highlighting the necessity for deliberation and decision, a necessity that, strangely enough, was *there all along*" (p. 51). Information does not obviate the necessity for ethical and intellectual judgment, as the authors are well aware: "Now that the Internet has broadened the boundaries of what we and our children *can* do, in our own work, the question of what we *should* do with these new arrivals arises anew" (p. 55). We find ourselves in the midst not only of plenty, we are in the midst of "too much," and the pedagogical point is how to listen and, then, to respond to the call that then discloses the situation and the questions it poses to us.

CURRICULUM IN ABUNDANCE

Where to start? As that previous paragraph implies, we have already started, we are already "thrown" into the abundance of the classroom, already "beached" on a shore simultaneously familiar and strange. We are always already in the midst of a situation, to which we listen, in which we act. "When teachers ask us where to start," David, Sharon, and Pat tell us, "our only answer can be that they have to come to understand that they have already started because they, as well as their students, are already living in an abundant world" (p. 98). Distracted by curriculum guides, we risk not seeing what—who—is in our midst, in whose midst we are. As Dwayne Huebner appreciated, the pedagogical question is also an ethical one: How are we to conduct ourselves?

Teaching within a curriculum of abundance cannot be reduced to technique. It is not tantamount to purchasing consumer goods from the shelf of curriculum topics, those "impossible, consumptive, isolated, never really satisfying bits and pieces [of the curriculum that] always leave us looking longingly for the last days when all will be redeemed and we can finally rest, assured" (p. 274). Teaching the curricular abundance around us is less a behavior we "do" than "a way we carry ourselves in the world, the way we come, through experience, to live in a world full of life, full of relations and obligations and address" (p. 100). It is a matter of ontology, not epistemology; ethics, not instrumental rationality; and ecology, not the exploitation of resources and assets.

Curriculum in abundance derives from "a deeply seated belief about how the world fits together in its deepest and most vigorous intellectual and spiritual possibilities" (p. 100). Dwelling within curriculum in abundance supports, then, modes of being in the world that enable us to experience the world, to recall the epigram with which I opened this foreword, as alive, indeed, purposeful. These modes of being do not just happen; they are not learning styles or pedagogy tools. "Experiencing the abundance of things must be cultivated" (p. 10) these experienced teachers point out. Moreover, "this process is often long and hard and full of its own dangers" (p. 10). Does living amidst abundance render one abundant: passionately and profoundly engaged with the living compelled to live in scarcity? Is this why, as David discloses in chapter 6, "it is a little too easy for me to become rather zealous about this issue" (p. 100)? Does abundance become

> quite literally a matter of life and death, of liveliness and deadliness, not only for myself but for the teachers and students I often witness laboring under the terrible burden of the belief in a world that doesn't fit together and that must therefore be doled out in well-monitored, well-managed, well-controlled packages, one lifeless fragment, one lifeless worksheet, one lifeless objective at a time[?] (p. 100)

Full of life, one discerns the death in one's midst. Following Serres (1983), Jacques Daignault has warned us that "to know is to kill" (1992, p. 199), "that running after rigorous demonstrations and after confirmations is a hunt: literally" (1992, p. 198). As we will see momentarily, "literally" is also a kind of hunt that haunts the schools.

Those quoted lines from Jacques Daignault ascribes agency to us, but Jardine and his co-authors—true to the experience of a world that is alive and purposeful—ascribe agency *to the world*, in this instance, to the curriculum. Curriculum guides would seem to be themselves the hunters. They are "defacing," precisely because they decline to recognize the faces of those who encounter them. Moreover, as we learn in Preamble 7, "they will not listen. They already know ahead of time anything worth saying. They only speak and those who approach must only listen" (p. 105). Curriculum guides ensure that "nothing happens" in the classroom that is not planned. There is little support for improvisation (Aoki, 2005 [1990]). Instead of music,

> we inundate our children with relentless streams of one activity after the other and excuse it by referring to their short "attention spans," never once suspecting that many of the things they are inundated with in schools are *not worthy of attention*, because they have been stripped of their imaginal topographies (their living "ecologies," we might say). (p. 274)

The employment of knowledge to monitor, control, and distribute the world's abundance not only engenders "defeat" and "bewilderment." It leads to "exhaustion, paranoia and, I suggest, eventually violence" (p. 101). It leads not only to psychological violence; it has led, on occasion, to spectacular school violence (see Webber, 2003).

A CURRICULUM OF SCARCITY

> There is no use hiding this fact: Once curriculum is experienced in abundance, sometimes continuing to live in some schools becomes unbearable.
>
> —*David W. Jardine, Sharon Friesen, Patricia Clifford*

The violence of the school system is a curricular issue as well, as Dwayne Huebner once pointed out during conversation at LSU just after the Columbine murders. By including this book in courses for prospective and practicing teachers, teacher educators can critique the culture of scarcity within the curriculum of teacher education. The subject should be included in the secondary school curriculum as well. Why would students be kept from studying what they themselves are undergoing and see around them? If teachers regain relative control of the curriculum they teach—a prerequisite, I argue, for practicing our profession—there are those who will choose to offer courses on violence, including school violence. Courses might be offered not only on the history and gender of violence, but on its educational institutionalization in curriculum guides.

In chapter 8, Jardine implies, wryly, that there is also violence in the theory of constructivism. "Charmed by constructivism," he opines, "we don't quite know how to deal with the fact that the orderliness and ways of the pine tree outside of my window have disappeared into appearances of my own ordering" (p. 129). Here he fells not only the savagery of solipsism, but the eeriness of equilibrium, at least as that concept has established itself as the center of gravity in developmentalism. David offers, in chapter 4, to invite "the old man home," but the invitation is, it appears, for a tongue-lashing, as he complains that, thanks in part to Piaget, development is construed as "a succession of structures oriented towards steadily increasing stability and inclusiveness" (p. 132). Despite its apparent biological underpinnings (see Doll, 1993), such confidence seems cultural and even compensatory.

It would seem to be colonial as well. There are several gestures of genius in this book, and this is, it seems to me, one of them. In chapter 8, David links developmentalism and "the images of maturity that it portends" to "the old colonialism." A culture of incalculable confidence would seem to serve as the bridge between the two. "With colonialism," Jardine explains,

> we were able to believe that we stood in the midst of the world as the best—the freest, the most reasonable, the most civilized. With developmentalism, we get a new twist on the modernist spirit of universality and necessity ... we are not just "the best" ... we are that *towards which* the world is heading in its progress toward maturity. (p. 134)

The old colonialism—and the culture it reflected and promoted—was also gendered and racialized (Stoler, 1995). David appreciates the simultaneity of historical events: "At the same time as the rise of objectivism in modern science, Europe underwent the systematic witch-burning purification quackery of crones who bore odd and bloody wisdoms in their breath and bones" (Jardine, 1997, p. 164). The culture of scarcity is gendered masculine; in racial terms, it is White.

The assault on the earth is also gendered and racialized; like C. A. Bowers, this text focuses on the culture of this violence. For him, the ecological catastrophe would seem to be, in part, a consequence of how we live, how we are educated. Like the critique offered here, Bowers (2006) also considered constructivism as a symptom and cause of this cultural problem. In chapter 9, David focuses on environmental education to make the point:

> I believe that "environmental education" should not be a subdivision of schooling, but should describe the way we educate *altogether*.... *All of the topics* entrusted to teachers and students in school can be understood as living fields, living inheritances, living places with ways and relations and interdependencies, *including* (but not restricted to) those topics that usually fall under "environmental education" currently in schools. (p. 144)

The social and curricular fragmentation a market economy of education institutionalizes accompanies and supports the exploitation and degradation of the biosphere. "What would happen," David asks, "if we imagined children, not as consumers and producers of constructed products of our own making, but as inhabitants in a world that is more abundant than I make of it" (p.147)?

The answer to that question is, in part, that we would devise not a fragmented, specialized curriculum to be "covered," not only traversed (in chapter 12, David plays with the idea of surfing, warning us that if we slow down we sink), but "covered over," its abundance buried deeper, it sometimes seems, than 6 feet under. (Curiously, that TV series testifies to this text's point that confronting death invigorates life.) "When the idea of scarcity insinuates itself into how we imagine the curriculum topics entrusted to teachers and students in schools, " David, Sharon, and Patricia point out "those topics become necessarily bounded in ways that make it possible to control, predict, assess, and monitor their production, distribution" (p. 4).

In unbinding curriculum topics and allowing them to circulate amidst the life in our classrooms, we create "an integrated curriculum that is a lived (in) place where we can "understand ... the full, living breadth of its Earthly interdependencies and kinships" (p. 174). This is no curriculum we can imagine as entrapping us in an ivory tower; it is a curriculum whose endless hair enables us to move. As we read in chapter 11, "An integrated understanding neither 'constructs' nor 'consumes' its object but delicately sustains that object while drawing from it; as ecology maintains, the living source must be protected so that we can return" (p. 174). At "home" we are not dispersed amidst the fragments scattered before us as "curriculum topics," bulletin boards, and sound bites, lacerating our uncovered skin.[3]

---

[3]Rather than being "skinned" by the curriculum, Dennis Sumara and Brent Davis (1998, p. 76) recommended "unskinning" the curriculum, "simultaneously removing and imposing boundaries."

Assault guarantees the inability to focus. Curricular fragmentation, David, Sharon, and Patricia appreciate, risks subjective fragmentation. The obsession with covering curriculum, with constructing knowledge (preferably "collaboratively" in groups) by constant activity, produces hyperactivity. Dispersed amidst curricular fragments, is it any surprise that, in David's phrase, "attention starts to skitter"? It is a circular and compounding process: "Skittering attention leads to the belief that the world is fragmentary." The ecological crisis is also a cultural crisis.

> It is fascinating to consider how, in these ecological desperate days, just as ecology is heralding the need for a continuity of attention and devotion, our schools are, in so many cases, full of attention deficits (itself wonderfully co-opted marketing term along with its dark twin, "paying attention"). (p. 181)

Embedded in the monetary images a business-model of education sells is an explicitly political discipline.

This political discipline—the indebting of attention—is not new of course: Foucault associates the rise of the disciplines with the end of monarchy (Ransom, 1997). One hundred years ago the American progressives were asserting the centrality of interest—and the apparent autonomy of attention such an educational concept implies—as key in the continuum between child and curriculum. Progressives' emphasis on the autonomy of attention occurs, Jonathan Crary (1999) pointed out, at a time when technologies and institutions, including the school, were being mobilized to command the attention of mass populations. Crary implies that the American progressives—Crary is thinking of William James in particular—were consciously contradicting the influential work of William B. Carpenter, work done in the 1870s in which attention is described as an element of subjectivity to be externally shaped and controlled:

> It is the aim of the Teacher to fix the attention of the Pupil upon objects which may have in themselves little or no attraction for it.... The habit of attention, at first purely automatic, gradually becomes, by judicious training, in great degree amenable to the Will of the Teacher, who encourages it by the suggestion of appropriate motives, whilst taking care not to overstrain the child's mind by too long dwelling upon one object. (Carpenter 1886, pp. 134–135; quoted in Crary 1999, p. 63)

In our time, we strain to keep the child's mind by covering curriculum topics quickly.

If we lose momentum as we surf along the surface of curriculum, Jardine points out, we're sunk. We lose our very being, and not only our subjective being, but, at the same time and predictably so, the biosphere in which we dwell. The warning signs are all around us—yes in global warming and in intensifying hurricanes, but also in our children. In particular, in chapter 12, Jardine thinks of the "ADD kids" as canaries in a mine shaft—warnings, portends, heralds, like the monstrous, transgressive child often is ... that airs have thinned and sustaining relations have been broken and need healing. Perhaps they are signs that education needs to become a form of ecological healing. (p. 182)

Like Crary's progressives 100 years ago, Jardine, Clifford, and Friesen are attempting to contradict—through education—the primary tendencies of our day.[4]

The primary of these is the political imposition of the business model accompanied by increased accountability and curricular fragmentation, all of which is accomplished through the uncritical acceptance of new technologies and their presumed centrality to teaching and learning. In the United States, technology—and the utopian fantasies marketed around it—functions politically to distract citizens from the political and cultural problems political conservatives' embrace of business and religion have only aggravated. Presumably, technological advancements will solve the educational problems that the political conservatives' assault on the poor and lower middle class has intensified.

Most directly in chapter 14, the authors question the new information communication technologies (ICTs), focusing our attention on why "we want information" and on what "we wish to communicate." These questions—why and what we want to know—are, indeed, curricular questions, and the authors appreciate that ICTs cannot answer them. Although "ICTs cannot help us with this, at the same time, they are radically transforming both what and how we think about curriculum topics themselves" (p. 205). Like Theodore Sizer (2004), this text focuses on the world youth already inhabit, pointing out that

Our students are already experiencing a world that is much richer, much more difficult and challenging, much more alluring and full of adventure than the version of the world made available in many classrooms. (p. 23)

For Sizer, this fact means the school building as the only or even primary site of education is antiquated. For David, Pat, and Sharon, this fact underscores the intergenerational character of public education: "Young and old thus deeply *belong together*" because "*inquiry is a necessarily intergenerational enterprise*" (p. 208). The educational point is for young and old to understand together and from their generationally situated subject positions the present "version of the world."

LIVING IN THE WORD

A culture of scarcity is a culture of literalism. It is no accident that biblical literalism—and the religious zealotry it reflects and supports—accompanies

---

[4]Recall that Madeleine Grumet (1988) postulated curriculum *as* contradiction.

political conservatism and consumer capitalism in contemporary America.[5] Abstract ideals become commodities: The American dream is no longer democracy but wealth, a fantasy compensating for those massive transfers of economic assets from the poor and lower middle classes to the upper classes during these last 40 years of Republican Party rule. Lives of literalism are so miserable for so many—misery intensified by the discrepancy between the fantasy and the reality of minimum wage jobs the market economy creates—that they flee to the American versions of the Taliban. Like the Taliban, U.S. religious fundamentalists and political conservatives (the so-called Christian Coalition, for instance), claim the moral high ground (no abortion, no gay marriage, no drugs) based on the literal Truth (God's word). It is an ideology of literalism.

Educationally, such literalism takes the form of curriculum guides to be covered as if they were so many Internal Revenue Service (IRS) or Revenue Canada income tax regulations and procedures. Indeed, the curriculum is to be audited (English, 1999). This is anti-intellectualism at its most extreme, accountability covering up political manipulation and scapegoating. Because the curriculum is alienated from those who study and teach it, is it any wonder millions suffer from "attention deficit disorder"? There is assessed learning but no study (Block, 2004), no pleasure, only misery:

> If, however, we begin within the scarcities of dryness and impoverishment of those very same curriculum guides, this will never necessarily lead us to the deep intellectual pleasures of learning, the deep intellectual pleasures to be had in our living in the world with children. The movement between the mandated curriculum and the disciplines and the beauties of the world it bespeaks is a one-way-street. (p. 227)

As the road sign announced at the start of our street in Baton Rouge, it is a Dead End.

What's in a sign? It is an indication of realities beyond itself, realities to which it points. Only in a culture of scarcity and literalism is the sign self-enclosed, pointing only to itself. As David, Patricia, and Sharon appreciate: "Literalism is indicative of precisely the sorts of closure regarding what can be said, written, spoken, heard or imagined that healthy, living systems do not display" (p. 160). The American Taliban claims eternal life for its adherents but displays none of the earthly kind, except through the occasional but regular sex scandal. Jardine prescribes inversion (I can't help but hear the 19th century echo) to medicate the sickness of literalism:

---

[5]There's a cup in this text, but it doesn't runneth over, and, moreover, it's Styrofoam. Jardine, in chapter 19, associates it, not with a morally bankrupt politicized Christianity, but, rather, with "a perfect example of a Cartesian Substance: something that is bereft of any relations." The essential, self-enclosed, socially isolated Christian "soul" is indeed bereft of earthly relations; it is with the loin-clad son on the cross and his ill-tempered irresponsible Father with "whom" the believer is, presumably, related, and then through "gracious submission."

> Let's invert this, then: Interpretive inquiry is directed toward the causing of dis-ease in such moments of closure. It is deliberately provocative, playful, audacious, and, too, petulant sometimes. But its provocations are on behalf of something: re-enlivening, finding the life in what has become morose. (Jardine, 1997, p. 165)

Such inverted inquiry may not be the second coming, but it holds the promise of resurrection after educational death.

Judaism, not Christianity, provides Jardine and Jennifer Batycky the imagery for our time of scarcity and literalism. They think of an empty chair, the place left vacant with bread and wine at the Seder table. We are waiting for Elijah to arrive. This empty chair does not

> bespeak someone who has *left* but someone who is *coming*.... This empty chair now stands for *a future which has yet to come*. The futurity represented by the empty chair is not a given, not "frozen" but "yet to be decided." What will become of me, what will become of this work I am producing—all this is still coming, is not yet settled, and no amount of hurry or anxiety or effort will outrun this eventuality. (p. 219)

David is speaking of himself, and of schools as well. Hurry and anxiety structure the culture of scarcity. In Malachi 4:5-6, we are promised: "Behold, I am going to send you Elijah the prophet before the great and terrible day of the Lord. And he will restore the hearts of the fathers to their children, and the hearts of the children to their fathers, lest I come and smite the land with a curse." Can you hear Elijah through the words of this sacred text, the book you are about to study?

Moving from an empty chair to emptiness, from Judaism to Buddhism, David tells us "the idea of abundance leads to a deep experience of the limitedness of human life, this life, my life." Paradoxically, this experience of limitation leads to fullness. The nearing of death intensifies one's remaining days. Collectively, the emptiness of the present enables us to experience the fullness the future portends. There is

> something the three of us have just recently named and can't quite follow up yet with any words—that this experience of the "letting go" of a topic out of its self-containedness and fragmentary and impoverished isolation—its "emptying" in the Buddhist sense, into the abundance of things—seems to ask us to experience a sort of death. (p. 268)

It is the death of that isolated ego that regimes of scarcity and literalism produce; it is a welcomed end to "the venerated Protestant-Eurocentric-Neo-North American Loneliness of Individuality, of one's self existing estranged of all its relations" (p. 267). Following, in the same sentence from chapter 19, David adds a compelling capsule summary of that accursed episteme: "(like some independent, immortal soul caught through some awful accident in the messy, bloody, dependent squalors of the flesh" (p. 268).

END BIT

> Perhaps the greatest and most fearsome is the moment of knowing I am this Earthbody *and nothing besides.*
>
> —*David W. Jardine*

Let us embrace the "dependent squalors of the flesh." God knows they are what drew me to New Orleans 20 years ago. The sin of Hurricane Katrina was not, as the televangelists were quick to proclaim, New Orleans'. The sin of Hurricane Katrina was the Bush Administration's. From the ineptitude that allowed the 9/11/01 attacks to occur, to the lies rationalizing the invasion of Iraq, to the ineptitude that produced the disaster following Katrina, the Bush Administration personifies and institutionalizes what Jardine and his colleagues name as a "self existing estranged of all its relations." Given its moral emptiness, it is no surprise, then, that the Bush Administration's *No Child Left Behind* legislation is designed to accomplish precisely that, to entrap teachers and students in a competitive culture of scarcity and literalism in which many children and teachers must be left behind. Like those stranded in a flooded city, huddled together on rooftops holding scribed signs "HELP US," children huddle in "youth cultures" where (no canaries here) they suffer no "attention deficit disorders."

Study *this* sacred text, dear reader. Allow yourself to experience "the lure that pulls these flowerheads to face the sun." Join David Jardine, Sharon Friesen, and Patricia Clifford as they are "pulled now, beyond ... wanting and doing, into an effort, these words, at airbubble rockcast riversinging" (p. 270). No false prophet he, Jardine, in chapter 19, invites us to join him, Sharon, and Patricia in acknowledging that, yes, educational experience involves suffering; it "involves opening ourselves to the open-ended sojourn of things, their ongoingness and fragilites and sometimes exhilarating, sometimes terrifying possibilities and fluidities" (p. 271). In the suffering of study we can experience redemption:

> [E]xperience is not something we *have*: It is something we undergo, and, to put it more intergenerationally, something we just might *endure*. It therefore has to do with duration, with what lasts, and therefore with what can be cultivated, taken care of: Experiences worthy of the name are not [only] interior mental events had by a self-same subject, but are more like places that hold memory, topographical endurances (like these riveredges) full of ancestry and mystery and a complex, unrepayable indebtedness. Full of dependencies, full of "it depends," full of dependents. And more, experience therefore links with my own abundance, what I can live with, which, in part, means where I need to be, in what "space," (in what relations) to endure. (p. 271)

It is not by refusing the squalors of the flesh, but by embracing them, embracing our worldliness, our being in the world, that we can experience *abundance*. We can experience abundance now, not in an after-life. It is here, even in classrooms, especially in classrooms, where we dwell in the curriculum of abundance that we can *live*, in *this* world, the world now being destroyed before our eyes.

The "hidden chapter" (Britzman, 2003) of *Curriculum in Abundance* is, I am suggesting, a political chapter. The clues, I submit, are everywhere, lodged among the ancestors, the prophets in our classrooms, the living knowledge disguised and degraded as curriculum topics. These clues point to an unwritten chapter on politics, a chapter calling us to outrage: moral, generational, professional. What has happened to the schools, what (for us Americans) has happened to our country, what is happening to the planet? Yes, it is a crime: a crime against children, against America, against life. Full of life, living amidst abundance in these terrible sites of scarcity, we might steady ourselves through study. So steadied and made strong, "[w]e must also," David, Sharon, and Patricia remind us,

> cultivate in ourselves the ability and the desire to adamantly refuse some inheritances, those that toy with impossibility and despoil our ability to dwell in the suffering of things.... We must refuse the leveling that violates the deeply ecopedagogical repose of things. (p. 277)

We must face the sun. Join us.

Preface
"What Happens to Us Over
and Above Our Wanting and Doing"

This had to be the preface title for this book. We cite this passage from Hans-Georg Gadamer's *Truth and Method* (1989, p. xxviii) *23 times* in this collection of essays. Must be a clue of some sort.

This is the oddest of texts to grasp in these days of overwhelming interest, in education, in activities, methods, sure-fire classroom materials and tests, these days, too, of great declarations of unfulfilled ideals: "no child left behind," sung with trumpets. Gadamer insists that he is not interested in *what we do* or *what we ought to do,* but with *what happens to us,* what, so to speak, befalls us. Gadamerian hermeneutics is not about method or conscious intent or experience, or about ideal portrayals of what ought to be, but about something that happens when we understand, a rattling of air between my own individuality and agency and hopes and desires, and the great blood bath I'm standing in the midst of and to which I owe something of my life, my living. Language, history, ancestry, interweaving, often contradicting lines of thought and expression, blistering images, cultural, political, economic, aesthetic, and spiritual tides that carry us and sometimes drag us down, and, too, the sweet pathologies of being just this person and no other, with family, home, friends, work, and surroundings just like this.

In these school days of hyperactivity, my age might be showing. I'm much more in love now with happening upon the slow pull of things. I like the experience of having my attention drawn, of being whispered to, of having a *calling.* I really like taking time to smell those lower branch yellowy tomato leaves as I break them off to let the sun at the reddening fruit.

That smell.

That smell, smelled slowly, is at the center of all things. It's like that red wheel barrow that William Carlos Williams (1991, p. 224) writes about. Here, an ordinarily insignificant object is portrayed with such spacious clarity that the insight becomes unavoidable: Somehow, *everything* depends on this red wheelbarrow he's spotted upturned in the rain amidst white chickens. Somehow, from out of a mindfulness to *this*, the particular object before us, in its very particularity, becomes like a sacred place where the whole Earth comes to nestle in relations of deep interdependency:

> This is one of the secrets of ecological mindfulness. To understand what is right in front of us in an ecologically sane, integrated way is to somehow see this particular thing *in place*, located in a patterned nest of interdependencies without which it would not be what it is. Differently put, "understanding 'the whole'" involves paying attention to *this* "in its wholeness." (Jardine, 2000, p. 70)

This is a brief hint at what we mean by "curriculum in abundance."

Having the time and comfort and space to experience the curriculum topics entrusted to schools in this way must seem like quite an opulent luxury or a naive theoretical/poetic fantasy. From within the current confines of schooling and how it images itself and its work, curriculum in abundance must seem like little more than a meaningless idea, an empty phrase. It can't compete in a world full of images of old women draped in flags against the floods and sweet New Orleans sinking.

All we can do at this point is attest to the fact that this book is based on years of having witnessed how it is that we can, right in the midst of the agonies of this world, cultivate this way of experiencing things in ourselves and in our students *in real, ordinary, everyday classrooms*. The events—the happenstances, one might say—described in this book did not happen in "model classrooms." Why? Because models are inevitably thin, anorexic, heavenly, insubstantial, idealized, blank-faced, and unattainable. We are suggesting that understanding curriculum in abundance requires thinking and experiencing that is substantive, material, bodily, earthly, located, specific. We cannot present readers with a broad, general, "here's how you do it" text. Why? Because such happenstances always have a face, and they are not the product of an anonymous, reproducible methodology (one that can be handed over to anyone and practiced by anyone). It causes no end of initial grief to teachers and students we work with to suggest that "something awakens our interest—that is really what comes first!" (Gadamer, 2001, p. 50), but we've found that this is the way to proceed. When students or teachers or student teachers ask questions about the classroom, or when graduate students ask about how to do hermeneutic research, our first question always is "What is the topic?" Only *then*, in the face of the fact that, so to speak, it is *this* smell, can an interpretation that is truly abundant and generous begin. Only in the face of the "stubborn particulars of grace" (Wallace, 1987) can hermeneutics be prevented from becoming just one more theoretical display.

Not everything works, every student does not get caught up in the sway of what is happening in the same way, to the same extent, or for every venture. This is a truth that we must simply accept and learn to live with however much we might rail against it, again and again, however often we have our hearts broken as teachers. But even though this is the case, in a classroom where curriculum is understood and practiced in abundance, even "ordinary" is better than it was, because at least all the students get to live in the presence of work being done that is beyond the scarce pale of schooling. I've experienced this often, that it is all right, sometimes, to live in the presence of people who know what they are doing even if, for now at least, I do not. There is some relief to be had in realizing that the worlds I venture into in classrooms are not dependent on my understanding for their life.

Even though understanding curriculum in abundance is not the product of an anonymous, reproducible methodology, it does have a way to it. However, this way is only understandable if it is practiced. And, as such, it is only understandable to the extent that the one practicing it slowly becomes practiced in it. There is no anonymity here. Bluntly put, you *become someone* (not just anyone) as a consequence of how you carry yourself in the world. With practice, you can become more experienced in experiencing things in their abundance. It takes, well, practice, just like everybody says about teaching. The result of this practice is not an increasing sense of "seen it all before." On the contrary, as Gadamer suggests, the result of becoming more experienced is that you become more sensitive to the happenstances that new experiences might bring. Even though hermeneutics is interested in "what happens to us over and above our wanting and doing," you can get better at allowing and taking pedagogical and spiritual pleasure in such happenstance, and at taking care of what is being asked of you in such moments.

I'm just about to go back to the weird work of practicum supervision, and I find, as years progress, that this work is almost intellectually and spiritually unbearable. *Right there before my eyes,* a young girl will take us all back to the Origins of geometry. *Just there,* the threshold into the communicating that words can do will open its yaw for the first time, and a child will *read.* As Roberto Calasso (1993) suggested, at such moments, the variant is the original. Or as Gadamer's hermeneutics allows, the new variant adds itself to what we heretofore understood the original to be. The beginning of something, its origin, its "basics," is not some past event, but a repast. This child's learning to read, for example, is no mere anecdotal event even though, of course, that is exactly what it is. Some of my colleagues, who find no intellectual interest in classrooms unless they are conducting a "research project" in one, find this all rather bewildering.

We hope that this book will be of service to teachers and students as a way to begin experiencing differently what is happening in classrooms. There is a great relief and pleasure to be had in this image of curriculum in abundance. There is great relief to be had in realizing that the curriculum topics entrusted to teachers and students in schools don't need to be simply covered. They can also be loved and cherished and *experienced*. We know full well that this is terribly hard work, even to imagine this possibility. But schools are already hard work and the course that labor has taken—scarcity, panic, acceleration, impoverishment—is wearing thin and getting worse. Too many wonderful teachers whom we know have had to simply quit. There is no use hiding this fact: Once curriculum is experienced in abundance, sometimes continuing to live in some schools becomes unbearable.

WHAT FOLLOWS AND WHERE IT'S BEEN

Sharon and Pat and I have been working together for about 15 years, and this book is a collection of work from all across that time span. The image of abundance has been, for us, a way to gather these papers together and rethink what our work has brought us to. There are two related origins to this gathering.

First, the idea of abundance emerged at the tail end of our last book, *Back to the Basics of Teaching and Learning: "Thinking the World Together"* (Jardine, P. Clifford, & Friesen, 2003). In that text we were exploring how it may be that what is in fact "basic" to a living discipline (and therefore a curricular inheritance entrusted to teachers and students in schools) is precisely its excessiveness. This idea is unimaginable under regimes of scarcity. However, we suggested there something that is vital to our current work on curriculum in abundance:

> When any of us think of those things in the world that we dearly love—the music of Duke Ellington, the contours of a powerful novel and how it envelops us if we give ourselves over to it, the exquisite architectures of mathematical geometries, the old histories and stories of this place, the rows of garden plants that need our attention and devotion and care, varieties of birds and their songs, the perfect sound of an engine that works well, the pull of ice under a pair of skates, and on and on—we understand something in our relation to these things about how excessiveness might be basic to such love. We do not seek these things out and explore them again and again simply for the profit that we might gain in exchanging what we have found for something *else*. What we have found, in exploring and coming to understanding, to learn to live well with these things is not an arms-length commodity but has become part of who we are, and how we carry ourselves in the world. We love them and we love what becomes of us in our dedication to them. And, paradoxically, the more we understand of them, the better—richer, more intriguing, more complex, more ambiguous and full and multiple of questions— *they* become and the more we realize that gobbling them up into a knowing that we can commodify, possess, and exchange is not only undesirable. It is impossible. We realize, in such knowing, that the living character of the things we love will, of necessity, outstrip our own necessarily finite and limited experience and exploration. (p. 208)

Coming to know, as is the great and terrible task of schooling, can be imagined as *adding to* the abundance of the world, not diminishing it.

The second happenstance that led us to gather these papers under the image of abundance was a simple yet telling experience that Pat had when working with a group of elementary school teachers. She read with them a brief, unpublished paper that now forms chapter 6 of this collection, and she was struck by how refreshing and liberating these teachers found this idea to be. The very idea that we can *treat* our task as teachers in this light—the very idea that they had been heretofore unwittingly and unintentionally *treating* that task under the shadow of scarcity—broke a deep spell, a weird slumber. But let us be clear here. This sense of "breaking a spell" did not make their lives any easier or simpler. In fact, coming to experience that shadow-spell and its dulling and deadening effects can be quite unbearable when one has to return to the confines of some schools. We work in a great many classrooms in which breathtaking work is being done, in which great hardships are fought and overcome. But we know, too, that the pall of scarcity is widely cast. Getting a glimpse of the fact that things could be different—could be *better* and *more intellectually genuine* for teachers and students alike—can make living and working in a school where that pall is still drawn simply intolerable.

In the chapters that follow, we deal with curriculum and teaching topics such as mathematics (chaps. 1, 3, 5, and 13), features of the science curriculum (chaps. 2 and 8), environmental education (chaps. 8, 9, 11, 12, 13, and 18), the social studies curriculum (chap. 7), various aspects of language arts (chap. 18) and the arts curriculum (chaps. 15 and 17). We deal, also, with issues arising from inviting student teachers and practicing teachers into the idea of curriculum as abundant (chaps. 6 and 7, plus most of the preambles). Two chapters (2 and 14) deal specifically with the issue of the arrival of information and communications technologies into the classroom, and the effects that this has on the nature of the work that can be done. Three other chapters (4, 8, and 9) explore the philosophical underpinnings of constructivism and the dilemmas it poses to thinking about curriculum in abundance. All of the chapters (but most explicitly chap. 10) provide images of how to conduct interpretive research in the classroom.

Rather than providing more detailed summaries at this juncture, we preface each individual chapter with a preamble. Each preamble takes up certain themes of curriculum in abundance found in the introduction and weaves these themes into the chapter that follows it.

ACKNOWLEDGMENTS

Many acknowledgments. One of Anh Linh's shapes graces the cover of this book. Eric Jardine did a great job of editing a draft of this manuscript and asking just the right questions at just the right time. As we have experienced before, the folks at Lawrence Erlbaum Associates sure do know how to take care of cranky writers and their work and their goofy repetitions of the same questions over and over again. Their encouragement and help has been invaluable. Our coauthors have graced us with their work and their words: James C. Field, Brent Novodvorski, Bruce Johnson, Lessa Fawcett, Jennifer Batycky, Annette LaGrange, and Hanne Kisling-Saunders.

Dr. William Pinar has graciously agreed to write the Foreword to this book. It is well known and worth saying loud and long that without his tireless, long-standing efforts and unwavering support, this field of curriculum would be a much impoverished place. This book, and much of the success that I have had as a scholar, would not have happened in the first place without his generous heart. Now that he has moved to the University of British Columbia, the only task left is to train him well in using "eh?" properly in a sentence. This will be very difficult, but we will try our best.

This book is a bit of a companion to our early text, *Back to the Basics of Teaching and Learning: "Thinking the World Together"* (Jardine et al., 2003), and we'd like to end our acknowledgments as we did there. This book is dedicated to the teachers and children who are suffering in the confines of a form of schooling premised on scarcity and impoverishment, and to the teachers and children who have taught the three of us so much about what an enlivening and pleasurably difficult thing teaching and learning can be in light of curriculum understood in abundance.

—*David W. Jardine, Bragg Creek (Alberta, September 2005)*

Introduction

> Where is our comfort but in the free, uninvolved and finally mysterious beauty and grace of this world that we did not make, that has no price, that is not our work? Where is our sanity but here? Where is our pleasure but in working and resting kindly in the presence of this world?
>
> —Wendell Berry (*The Profit in Work's Pleasure*, 1989, p. 21)

A SECRET MEETING WITH PYTHAGORAS' GHOST

A few years ago, on a bitterly cold Alberta winter day, near enough to winter solstice that the sun was very low up here, at 52 degrees North Latitude, I (D.J.)[1] was out on an elementary school playground with a 12-year-old boy. We had just been inside in a classroom of around 60 students, quarreling in lovely, heated ways, about dropping perpendiculars and bisecting angles with only compasses, pencils, and straight-edges in hand (see chaps. 1 and 5). I was still reeling a bit from the moment at which a group of students turned their page of work on angle-bisection sideways and discovered that the problem of dropping perpendiculars was already somehow solved. Even more disorienting, one girl suggested something that I had never exactly imagined before: that dropping a perpendicular was basically little more than bisecting a 180-degree angle. As soon as she said this, I knew that I had already heard this before, years ago, in my own schooling, but it had, as has so much of those times, faded into forgetfulness and irrelevance.

---

[1] Many of the chapters in this book are coauthored. In each such chapter, the term "we" refers to "the authors" unless otherwise designated. When a single voice is used in such chapters, the authors are identified after the first use of the term "I."

That girl's breakthrough of insight broke through layers of my own experience, layers of my own education, of its successes and failures, its remembering and forgetting. It also helped recast other students' questions and worries, helped us all navigate our way around this already well-worked, already deeply cultivated place. It helped us all experience this place as a place that had a character and integrity and design and history and ancestry *of its own*. Perhaps even more extraordinary was that we could experience how our own efforts belonged here, too, alongside these vanished others whose work we were taking up as our own. Our efforts in this place were not isolated and alone, nor is this place simply a manipulable thing that is at our beck and call. We have *come upon something* that we did not simply make up, something that stands there "beyond our wanting and doing" (Gadamer, 1989, p. xxviii). This thing is, shall we say, *abundant*. We were learning what it meant to work in the midst of such abundance, with an eye to *what is being asked of us by this place* as much as with an eye to *what we might ask of it*. All these lovely conversations and questions and examples in this mathematics classroom counted as one more of the sort of humiliation that makes teaching unendingly intellectually and spiritually worthwhile, difficult and, frankly, fun.

In the middle of all of that sweaty mathematical work, we had been invoking and reinvoking the ghost of Pythagoras, his secret cult, his great geometrical insights and his unfashionable trousers. We had been finding our way in this old, ancestral world of relations and work and insight and betrayal and knowledge, secret and public. We all experienced, in different ways and to differing degrees and with different images and work involved, a great sense of common strength (common fortitude, "comfort," one might say) that came from realizing that we were here together, and that our work was not simply interior, psychological work, but public work, out in the open, in the "common wealth" and, of inner necessity, in the witness and care of others—those here in the classroom, and Pythagoras, too, and all the other hands that have handed this work to us. As Bronwen Wallace (1987, pp. 47–48) shows, such things betray and witness the flesh of more than just the hands that made them. In the work of coming to know this world, we are not alone, each "left to our own devices" (Arendt 1969, p. 196). We were here *together* in this place, in this abundant (ad)venture of understanding and cultivation, each of us making our own unique way, but each of us bound together in the diverse work of a common place: this place, geometry, the great and sometimes troubled human inheritance of the measures of space.

Left to my own devices, I may have never turned that angle-bisection solution on its side and seen it gifts.

All this work with teachers and students and images and ideas and markers and paper and conversations and heated arguments lasted weeks, as well it could, given the amazing complexities of this world into which we had ventured. In fact, you could reasonably say that that conversation is still going on, after a fashion, here, in a book about curriculum. It certainly makes sense, in this instance, what Hans-Georg Gadamer (1983) has suggested about the character of understanding: "Understanding is an adventure and, like any adventure, it always involves some risk" (p. 141). To come to an understanding of the rich places, the rich topographies, the rich topics that have been entrusted to teachers and students in our schools (those that are listed in such an orderly, dull, unimaginative fashion in our curriculum guides for the various subject areas and grade levels), we must venture into such places and risk being transformed, risk changing, risk learning more than we might have originally anticipated or hoped or desired or planned for. We—students and teachers alike—risk becoming *educated*. Even more wonderfully mysterious is the fact that the Pythagorean theorem, too, is at risk in such ventures. If its allures are not taken up by the young, it will atrophy. What seems like such deadly dull formula in the realms of schooling *needs* to be taken on and understood anew if it is to remain a living part of a living discipline.

Back out on that cold noon-hour playground, a 12-year-old boy from this Grade 6 mathematics class was facing south, with his toes touching the end of the shadow of a pine tree directly south of where he was standing. I can only vaguely recount what he said. He talked about having been out here on this playground in the summer, and the shadows had been so short because of how high the sun was, and now, the shadows were so long and the sun was so low. He was recognizing, in part, the great arc of seasons, somehow, but then he said something that still haunts me to this day: "But Pythagoras says that something is still *the same* ..."

CURRICULUM TOPICS TREATED AS REGIMES OF SCARCITY

Schools are not especially amenable to the great abundance that overflows from this boy's comment on a winter playground. In fact, recent literature on curriculum, teaching, and learning speaks of the predominance of precisely the opposite: ideas of scarcity and lack as the terrible, exhausting engine of contemporary education (e.g., Peters & Humes, 2003; Prakash, 2004). Ivan Illich (1972, 1973; Illich & Cayley, 1992) speaks eloquently of how the institutionalization of education in the 20th century insinuated into students and educators alike the idea that knowledge was a scarce commodity and therefore that the shape of education must be one of a competition for this limited resource. Moreover, access to this limited resource is itself limited to the very institution that imagined its scarcity in the first place: *schools,* as places that have come to emulate images of the market economy. This is the great lesson we first learned from Illich 35 years ago, with the first appearance of his *Deschooling Society* (1972) in 1970.

The roots of such an image of knowledge as a commodity that operates under "regimes of scarcity" (Illich & Cayley, 1992, p. 118) is, Illich suggests, long-standing:

Commenting on the *Politics* of Aristotle, [Karl] Polanyi [e.g., 2001] shows that the technique of marketing, in which the value of a good is made to depend on demand and supply ... is a Greek invention of the Early fourth century B.C. I then found increasing evidence that the conceptual space within which *paideia* acquired a meaning was defined about the same time. (Illich 1992, p. 165–166)

Central to this conceptual space was the idea of scarcity: "Educational rituals reflected, reinforced and actually created belief in the value of learning pursued under conditions of scarcity" (Illich, 1992, p. 165). Such a pursuit has dire consequences for education. Schools "have been transformed into huge zero-sum games, monolithic delivery systems in which every gain for one turns into a loss or burden for another, while true satisfaction is denied to both" (Illich, 1996, p. 27). Despite contemporary critiques of the idea of an "economy" in which knowledge is a scarce commodity (see, e.g., Stiglitz, 1999, 2002), traces of this regime remain at work in schools.

When the idea of scarcity insinuates itself into how we imagine the curriculum topics entrusted to teachers and students in schools, those topics become necessarily bounded in ways that make it possible to control, predict, assess, and monitor their production distribution, consumption, dispensation, and accumulation. This is how a scarce resource appears in a market economy. The Pythagorean theorem, for example, becomes stripped of its abundance of unmonitorable and uncontrollable relations, possibilities, and unguarded appearances. It becomes reduced to its manageable and monitorable surface features. Under this regime, to understand the Pythagorean theorem means to memorize its formula and to be able to correctly apply it to mathematics problems on demand in an examination. Understanding thus becomes equated with "possession" and "dissemination." Under the assumption of scarcity, curriculum topics must be broken down and doled out in carefully monitored, zero-sum exchanges. Such curricular fragments become thus identified, as we have previously explored (see Jardine et al., 2003), with "the basics" in education.

The correct application of the formula for the Pythagorean theorem can be "objectively" determined. The same is not true of that playground shadow conversation. We cannot especially assess its current or future exchange value. As a consequence, saying that it is of great worth takes on the appearance of being merely "subjective." My assessment of its worth as a consequence of many years of experience in such matters becomes suspect. It becomes a mere anecdote about certain students' and teachers' subjective experiences, and no longer visible as an opening up of the abundances of the topic at hand.

But something awful has happened here. It is not visible as an opening into the topic at hand because, under regimes of scarcity, the topic has been rendered into something that *has no openings or abundance*. It is, rather bounded and fully known: "In a right angled triangle, the square of the hypotenuse is equal to the sum of the squares of the other two sides" (see Preamble 1).

Long and heated classroom conversations over the abundance of relations found in any particular curriculum topic are thus marginalized as "out of bounds." They are the frills and extras that one might do if there is time, but, as with so much in school, *there is never enough time*. In fact, in schools, time itself becomes experienced as scarce precisely as a consequence of the low-level panic that is produced by imagining curriculum topics as themselves as sequentially doled out and assessed under the regime of scarcity (see Jardine et al. 2003, pp. 11–36). As Wendell Berry (1983) suggests, for this way of being in the world of the classroom, "time is always running out" (p. 76). And not just this. The whole of educational discourse becomes pervaded by a sense of scarcity, lack, and "never enough." Consider how common is this litany: If only we had more time, or more teacher's aides, or more computers, or faster Internet connections, or more research on even more "multiple intelligences" (Gardner, 2000), and so on, perhaps we could "manage" (a telling term, etymologically linked to being able to "keep things in hand"). Perhaps, as has happened in the Calgary, Alberta, area, we imagine that we simply need more specialized schools to outrun the ever-expanding sense of students' needs: a girl's school, a sports school, a science school, a "traditional" school, and so on. All this does, of course, is leave behind in the public school system a further sense of aggravation, another "lack," one more sense of scarcity with all its ensuant panic. By "inducing [such] little panics … [we] can be made to buy virtually anything that is 'attractively packaged'" (W. Berry, 1986, p. 24). We can't help but think here of how much of the marketing of educational materials preys upon such panic and its (actually never satiable) relief (see chap. 12).

The terrible, commonplace, response to this situation is one we have witnessed countless times: an exhausting *acceleration* (Glieck, 2000; see chap. 12) that is ravaging teachers and students alike. Of course, under a regime of scarcity, there is no possible acceleration that will result in a sense of "enough." Once knowledge is understood as a scarce commodity to be consumed, satisfaction of the desire to consume is not only not *sought*, it is not *desirable*. Once we concede, wittingly or otherwise, to education understood under a regime of scarcity, *the desire for more must be maintained if the ravenous sway of scarcity is to be maintained*. What is lost in this equation, however, is that the idea of scarcity produces and sustains a particular *sort* of desire, a particular *version* of what would constitute "more" or "enough." We can't let in-bounds the abundance of relations and ghosts that hover around the Pythagorean theorem, which would certainly result in a sense of "plenty." Why? Precisely because this abundance represents, from within the scarcity bounds of schooling, something unmonitorable and uncontrollable, something a little too wild and woolly (see chaps. 11 and 19), even a little dangerous perhaps. Scores of teachers and student teachers we have worked with attest to this phenomenon. Imagined from within the bounds of scarcity, abundance becomes near-monstrous (see Preamble 7 and chap. 7).

As with any new way of imagining education, the regime of scarcity had the effect, initially, of giving rise to a certain level of productivity in educational circles. Early in the 20th century, it was productive to imagine education along the lines of an industrial assembly line, where tasks were portioned out, outcomes could be easily measured, and troubles could be easily identified and fixed. However, we believe that this way of imagining education has reached what Illich identified as the point of "counterproductivity" (Cayley, in Illich & Cayley, 1992, p. 110). There is a certain point where any system operating under the regime of scarcity begins to aggravate and, in fact, *create* the troubles for which it was meant to be the solution. He demonstrates that in the field of medicine, for example, we are now experiencing how hospitals are the breeding grounds of "superbugs." In transportation, he presents a startling fact: The faster that air travel becomes, the *more* time we spend traveling this way. Moreover, "up to a certain speed and density automobiles may expand mobility, but beyond this threshold society becomes their prisoner" (Cayley, in Illich & Cayley, 1992, p. 15) and we spend more and more time caught immobile in our cars. The more we accelerate, the more we experience "time consuming acceleration" (Illich, 2000, p. 31).

In the field of education in particular, we have witnessed, over and over again in our conversations with students, teachers, administrators, and parents, that the idea of scarcity and lack have produced a counterproductive exhaustion, sense of defeat, cynicism, panic, and regret. Something perhaps even worse has occurred that is harder to name and harder to prove. Because the idea of a regime of scarcity has its home in economic theory, it is perhaps no coincidence that a great deal of the talk in schools these days is about the scarcity of funding and about children being frighteningly named as our greatest natural resource. In this milieu, trying to even articulate how that playground conversation was potentially a way into great abundance seems hopelessly naive and quaint.

CURRICULUM IN ABUNDANCE

> The key issue is ... the removal of the shadow thrown by economic structures onto the cultural domain. For this purpose we need to learn how to speak in a disciplined way ... choosing words that do not surreptitiously drag in assumptions of scarcity. (Illich, 1992, p. 45)

> If this were done ... education could become one of the rare fields that attempts to clarify one of the least recognized and most characteristic aspects of our age: the survival, even at the heart of highly developed societies ... of patterns of action that have successfully resisted colonization by the regime of scarcity. (Illich, 1992, p. 118)

As with any dominant discourse, the sway of the idea of regimes of scarcity tends to define how alternatives to it are to be understood. Any talk of abundance is commonly understood as nothing more than a failure to understand "the real world" of schools and the troubles they face. Moreover, any examples wherein this idea of abundance might be demonstrated to be successfully at work in an actual classroom are themselves marginalized: "I could do it if I had *those* kids, or *that* administrator, or if I was teaching in *that* part of town, or if I didn't have Provincial Exams to contend with," and so on. The abundance of that playground conversation is also easily marginalized in another, much more pernicious and well-meant way: That boy is deemed precocious or gifted (see chap. 15). Such psycho-pathologizing of the abundance of the topic into the exceptional where-withal of the individual child has the effect of leaving in place the discourse of scarcity and depositing the abundant excess of that conversation into the safe haven of that child's interiority. This has the effect of preventing the arrival of abundance from disturbing the bounds of schooling. That boy's disturbing insight into this terrible agony of human life itself—the monstrous question of what stays the same, what lasts, what remains, in the face of the turning of seasons?—becomes exceptional, "abnormal" (see chap. 7 and Preamble 7; see also Jardine et al., 2003, pp. 41–52). That playground conversation doesn't give us a glimpse of how this curriculum topic is full of an abundant wealth. It simply tell us that that child is special.

Education is full of such hedges. Abundance can always be ignored, pathologized, deemed an extra, naive, quaint, frilly, unnecessary, not possible here or now or in this grade or with these kids or in this part of town, and so on. We are suggesting that it isn't the part of town that causes this. We've seen it work in "that" part of town ("one of *those* schools," as a local official put it here in Calgary [see Preamble 1]). It is in the nature of educational discourse insofar as it is premised on what it is possible to imagine and articulate under regimes of scarcity. This is what is meant by the dominance of this way of thinking.

That is why we have found it fruitful to step out of the orbit of educational discourse in order, as Illich (1992) suggested, to "learn how to speak in a disciplined way" (p. 45) about what imagining curriculum in abundance might mean for students and teachers in school. We have been drawing upon three interrelated disciplines in order to cultivate this imagining:

1. From the discipline of ecology (e.g., Abram, 1996; W. Berry 1983, 1986, 1989; Jardine, 2000; Orr, 1992; Snyder, 1977, 1980; see in particular chaps. 9, 11, 12, 13, and 19) we adopt the idea that any seemingly isolated thing on earth in fact is the nestling point of vast, living abundance of relations, generations, ancestries, and bloodlines. Understanding the places we inhabit therefore requires of us a sense of obligation, belonging, work, commitment, pleasure, patience, and love. From here, we suggest that curriculum topics can be imagined in a similar way. Understanding the living "place"—the topos, the topic—of the Pythagorean theorem means working in this place, learning from the others, here and gone, who have worked here too, and thus coming to know its ways,

its interrelations and interdependencies, its signs and its seasons. Understood ecologically knowledge itself is understood differently. "Our knowledge of the world instructs us first of all that the world is greater than our knowledge of it. To those who rejoice in abundance and intricacy, this is a source of joy. To those ... who hope for knowledge equal to (capable of controlling) the world, it is a source of unremitting defeat and bewilderment" (W. Berry, 1983, p. 56). The adventure of coming to understand is thus a matter of rejoicing in the abundance and intricacy of the world, entering into its living questions, living debates, living inheritances. And this adventure is intimately available to all, each in their own measure, even though, as Illich (1972) suggests, schools are designed to convince us otherwise. Waiting on school(ed) knowledge as a way of monitoring, controlling, and doling out this abundance leads to a sense of defeat and bewilderment (see Jardine & Abram, 2001). And simply wanting to not be left behind in the panic to get such school(ed) knowledge is no solution but merely serves to aggravate matters. Ecologically imagined, we also understand that the work of this curricular topic, or topography or place not only has gone on before us, but it will go on after us, too. Under this image, understanding the curriculum topics entrusted to schools is, as we have explored elsewhere (Jardine et al., 2003, pp. 115–128), an intergenerational project, not just a pathological one handed to an isolated individual.

2. From contemporary threads of Buddhist philosophy, we take seriously what seems at first like a rather "otherworldly" position: "Within each dust mote is vast abundance" (Hongzhi, 1991, p. 14). We take this to mean that things are most genuinely understood insofar as they grasped in their abundant interdependence with all things (in Sanskrit, *pratitya-samutpada*, often translated as "dependent co-arising") (see especially chaps. 5, 12, and 19). Each curriculum topic we explore, then, is full of abundant relations, threads in a great net of interdependence. The Pythagorean theorem does not *exist* in isolation. As Ludwig Wittgenstein (1968, pp. 32–33) suggests, we can *give* it a boundary to some curriculum topic, perhaps for the purposes of mastering its application on an upcoming exam, but it *exists* only *in* the abundance of all its relations. This opens up a whole field of exploration of boundaries and borders and their transgression, of insiders and outsiders and of how, as Lewis Hyde (1983) contends, "given ... abundance, scarcity must be a function of boundaries" (p. 23) and how, therefore, abundance is somehow linked to the idea of the gift (see Jardine et al., 2003, pp. 207–221).

3. From hermeneutics, especially the work of Hans-Georg Gadamer (1989), we have learned that the living traditions of the human inheritance (writing, reading, chemistry, literature, geometry, language, biology, cultures and their long and contested histories and geographies) are characterized, not as inert, finished, bounded, isolated, commodified, and manageable objects, but as living, contested, still-ongoing human projects.

Such matters are not objects we produce and consume, but are inheritances to which we belong and in which we have been raised and in light of which our schools have some intergenerational, not especially uncontested purpose and desire. To understand them, then, is to find ways to "get in on the conversation" (Smith, 1999c). Our conversations, inside and outside of the classroom, have the effect of "keep[ing] the object, in all its possibilities, fluid" (Gadamer, 1989, p. 330) because, hermeneutically understood, the object under consideration (this or that curriculum topic) *is* its possibilities, its fluidity, its living overflow into an as-yet-unforeclosed future (see Smith, 2000, for a terribly disturbing discussion of how education often pursues a sense of a "frozen future" that is no future at all). This does not mean that this topic is chaotic or out of control (as might be imagined under a regime of scarcity). It means, simply, that it is a living part of the living human inheritance. It is, by its very nature, susceptible to being questioned anew, applied differently, cultivated otherwise. To understand any topic, then, is to open up its living abundance, to seek out its susceptibility. By treating these topics entrusted to us in schools in their abundance, we necessarily "keep [them] open for the future" (Gadamer, 1989, p. 340; see especially Preamble 15 and chap. 15) because, without such openness, these topics lose their living character.

These three ways of understanding abundance hold true even for our use of the word "abundance" itself. It, too, has this interdependent, abundant characteristic found in these three traditions of work: "Every word breaks forth as if from a center and is related to a whole, through which alone it is a word. Every word causes the whole of the language to which it belongs to resonate" (Gadamer, 1989, p. 458). We therefore use the term "abundance" because of what it invokes, what it provokes, what it allows, the questions it supports, the language it encourages, the images and hopes and desires it brings. As with our previous work (Jardine et al., 2003), we follow the suggestion of Lewis Hyde (1983): "The way we treat a thing can sometimes change its nature" (p. xiii). Therefore, we want to ask these sorts of questions. How might the idea of abundance change how we are able to think about the curriculum topics entrusted to schools? About what is our real work as teachers and students? About classroom practice and its shape and pace and organization?

We believe that treating the curriculum topics entrusted to schools under the image of abundance rather than scarcity has a profound effect on how we teach, what learning means, what the role of students and teachers is, how knowledge itself is imagined. Going back to that boy's pondering of tree shadows, it is impossible to imagine a response that would be able to outrun its abundance once and for all, but this does not result in a panicked feeling of "lack" or "not enough." In fact, something like the reverse occurs. We can take a certain comfort in the fact that its abundance outruns us, and, in understanding this, we understand this topic out from under the regime of scarcity.

So long as it is not placed in the object-world of producing and marketing, [that Pythagorean conversation:] draws us entirely outside of ourselves and imposes its own presence on us. [It] no longer has the character of an object that stands over against us; we are no longer able to approach this like an object of knowledge, grasping, measuring and controlling. Rather than meeting us in our world, it is much more a world into which we ourselves are drawn. (Gadamer, 1994, pp. 191–192)

We can thus experience the world of Pythagoras' ghost as part of "conversation that we ourselves *are*" (Gadamer, 1989, p. 378). More simply put, the Pythagorean theorem is precisely *not* a fixed and finished object ripe for measuring and controlling, but is, rather, part of an ongoing conversation, still "in play," still "open to question" in our human inheritance. And, "as in love, our satisfaction sets us at ease because we know that somehow its use at once assures its plenty" (Hyde, 1983, p. 22). There is anything but panic here. There is no lack.

Of course, abundance is *not simply and straightforwardly a property of certain classroom events*. Students (and teachers) must gradually learn how to experience the abundance of things. Experiencing the abundance of things must be cultivated, and this process is often long and hard and full of its own dangers. Abundance, we suggest, is a *practice* that not only takes abundant time, but takes living and working in a classroom context that exemplifies and embodies such abundance. What is hidden here and what we hope to demonstrate in the chapters that follow is what happens when students' and teachers' conversations and questions and dilemmas were *treated with abundance* by being *treated as abundant*. That boy's musings on Pythagoras, or that girl's spontaneous insight of how lines can be treated as 180-degree angles were *treated* as openings (from the Greek *poros*, also the root of the word "opportunity") into the abundance of possibilities that is the living world of mathematics. That living world is, of necessity, full of further questions, like mine: "Why does the intersection of two small arcs of two different *circles* give you the point of angle bisection and the point to which a perpendicular can be dropped? All this seemed to be about lines and angles. Now it seems to be about circles."

I still haven't quite figured out this one.

Something shifts under the image of abundance. And, as Paul Feyerabend (1999) clearly notes, faced with the abundance of things, we can easily become simply paralyzed. What abundance requires of teachers and students is a much more cultivated, much more deliberate and intellectually sound sense of the nature and limits of our own agency. In the face of abundance, we are called upon to act carefully and vigorously. We are called upon to *venture*. We are, of necessity, involved, because without active involvement, we will be overwhelmed. The good news is that, treated with abundance, curriculum topics become vivid, alluring, interesting, provocative and, a word rarely use in relations to schooling, *pleasurable*. And, more than this, as living parts of the living human inheritance, the curriculum topics entrusted to schools *require* our attention and our work and our care for their well-being, for their "furtherance" (Gadamer, 1989, p. xxiv).

Imagine this: Understood in abundance, it is not simply that "kids need math." As a living discipline, mathematics needs "the next generation" to "set it right anew" (Arendt, 1969, p. 192).

Preamble 1: From Scarcity to Impoverishment

Every simple need to which an institutional answer is found permits the invention of a new class of poor and a new definition of poverty. Poverty [comes to] refer to those who have fallen behind an advertised idea of consumption in some important respect.

—Ivan Illich (*Deschooling Society,* 1972, p. 4)

Once we begin to think and speak about our curriculum inheritance in terms of regimes of scarcity, schools do not simply provide restricted access to, say, the Pythagorean theorem, or to the other curriculum topics that are entrusted to teachers and students. Not only does the institution of school create a new type of poverty—underachieving children, those who don't have the means for continued access to education, those who are, in the contemporary buzz-words of the day, "left behind." It has the power to spellbind our ability to question many of the unspoken effects of schooling itself, effects that shape and limit the questions that can be legitimately asked and answered about the theory and practice of schooling. Many urgent and heartfelt educational concerns and questions often unwittingly *leave in place* what school has to offer and then work on how to ensure that no child is left behind in the taking up of such schooled offerings.

But something has *already been left behind* in such questioning. As Illich notes (1972, p. 4), the very institutional transformation of education under regimes of scarcity does not simply involve a "translation" of the rich, generous, and contentious inheritance of human thought that has been entrusted to schools. Schools not only require a translation of our curriculum inheritance into the sort of manageable and assessable objects that they are able to

control, monitor, manage, dispense, and assess. Such a translation necessarily involves a "degradation" (p. 2).

What has surreptitiously occurred is that not only do regimes of scarcity
create a new type of poverty—those "left behind" in education. Under such
regimes, the curriculum topics entrusted to schools become *impoverished*.
What we mean here is this. A regime of scarcity can only be maintained to
the extent that that which is deemed scarce is the sort of thing whose avail-
ability can be efficiently and effectively "controlled, predicted and manipulated" (Habermas, 1973, p. 133). Only to the extent that the Pythagorean
theorem, for example, becomes reduced and restricted to the efficient
memorization of its formula and the monitorable application of this formula on tests—only to that extent does it form part of the work of schooling
based on scarcity. As such, the potent, troublesome, and compelling insights that might be had if we follow up that playground conversation about
tree shadows and their constancy and change over the seasons—all this
might be deemed a wonderful thing to pursue, but it cannot properly and
warrantably "count" within the boundaries of schooling.

Therefore—and here is the most terrifying turn—the Pythagorean theorem, for example, becomes understood to *be* nothing more than that which
can "count." The conversations and questions and philosophical speculations become frills, unaccountable, unassessable, unwarrantable "extras."
What has happened here is that, at its heart, the pernicious idea of scarcity
has come to define what is basic and necessary and essential and relevant to
understanding the various curriculum topics that schools have inherited.
Scarcity comes to define "the basics" (see Jardine et al., 2003).

In this way, that which one might receive if one is *not* left behind in
school has itself already become impoverished under the regime of scarcity, such that *not* being left behind means being caught up in an intellectually and spiritually weak version of the world, stripped of its ancestries and
histories, of its rootedness, in Pythagoras' case, in ancient Greek worlds of
secret cults and secret knowledge, its tethers to the rope stretchers of ancient Egypt who would resurvey the lands after the yearly flooding of the
Nile. Lost is the warrant of ancient conversations about what changes and
what remains the same in the passing of seasons and still contested place of
the seeming "absoluteness" and "uncontestability" of mathematics in this
ancestry (and this even though we are still easily spellbound by, and often
silently beholden to, anyone who can produce "statistics" or "data" or "evidence" that is mathematically based).

Lost, too, are the great and beautiful geometries that unfold from Pythagoras' work, as we see in detail in the chapter that follows.

It is clear from these hints that when we try to imagine what curriculum
in abundance might mean, it is not as if we might now have an abundance
of that which was once scarce—with our current example, lots of opportunities and time to memorize the formula for the Pythagorean theorem,
lots of "real world" examples upon which to practice its correct applica-

tion, lots of access to computers programmed with self-correcting practice sheets geared to individual students' learning needs in this particular area, lots of examinations to test students' knowledge, lots of resources on how to help students get better marks in such matters, better ways to monitor the results of our teaching and testing, clearer guidelines on how to assess teachers' competencies at producing successful student outcomes, rank-ordering schools according to their achievement results, and so on. One doesn't begin to happen upon curriculum in abundance by simply monitoring and testing more and therefore, in this already impoverished sense, getting more "results."

Something else happens when we begin to treat curriculum in abundance. We do not now have an abundance of what was once scarce. Rather, we have to take on an honorable and not especially venerated venture. We have to learn how to begin to undo the curricular degradation that scarcity has engendered in our understanding of the curriculum topics entrusted to schools.

And so we introduce Anh Linh, who came upon the inner geometries of the Pythagorean theorem, and the risks that she, her classmates, and her teachers undertook ("understanding is an adventure and, like any adventure, it always involves some risk" [Gadamer 1983, p. 141]). This was a large class of over 60 Grade 9 students in what is recognized, in Calgary, Alberta, as one of the most "troubled" schools in the district—most "left behind" the regimes of schooling, one might say. As a caveat, however, we have to add one more note of preamble. When Anh Linh and her fellow students were allowed to explore the abundant and generous territories that surround Pythagoras and his cult and the shapes that blossom from its secrecies, these students were able to "practice" this theorem in robust and *mathematically* vital ways. In fact, the overall statistical performance of this group of 60 Grade 9 students on provincially mandated mathematics examinations improved dramatically over previous year's results—a startling fact to many, especially because local education officials, in the local newspaper, called this setting "one of *those* schools."

This is one of the great effects of treating curriculum in abundance: From rich explorations of the abundance found in Pythagoras, it became *more* likely that the students would do well when asked to restrict themselves, on the exams, to the correct application of the Pythagorean theorem to various real-world examples. We contend that, had they *started* with such a restricted mandate, the ghost of Pythagoras would have never shown up. We contend, therefore, that suggesting that such rich explorations are a luxury or a frill and that we need to slavishly "teach to the [upcoming Provincial] test" for our students to be properly prepared, are, in fact, nothing more than signs of the spellbinding, paranoid, frightened character that regimes of scarcity produce and sustain—powerful, deadening, dispiriting, panic-inducing *mythologies* about "the real world" of schooling.

And so, an example from the real world of schooling.

Chapter 1

Anh Linh's Shapes

Sharon Friesen
Patricia Clifford
David W. Jardine

> *The light dove, cleaving the air in her free flight, and feeling its resistance, might imagine that its flight would be still easier in empty space.*
>
> —Immanuel Kant (1964/1787, from the "Introduction"
> to his *Critique of Pure Reason*)

This passage was originally written as a way to begin a critique of those forms of philosophical idealism that speculatively shun the resistance and troubles and lessons of the world, lessons that might, in their resistance to the flights of reason, help shape and strengthen and measure our philosophizing. It was written by Immanuel Kant as a critique of the perceived constructive freedom of human thinking (see chap. 8). Our constructs are not enough until they feel the resistance of "application."

This invocation of an Earthly measure is not meant as an embarrassment to philosophizing per se, but as a reminder that the sense of reasonableness that our lives require—we think especially of the lives of teachers and students in school classrooms—require of reason that it maintain a sense of proportion, of properness, of having to work itself out here, and here, in the midst of the frail conditions of human existence.

We are especially taken with this image of the dove and its flight in two nearly contradictory ways. First of all, we have encountered countless situations in which constructivist, postmodernist, or "chaos theory" theorizing in education becomes so speculative that, as practicing teachers faced with the exigencies of everyday life, we become unable to recognize our own troubles in their philosophical flights. We have argued, with varying success, for the ways in which our thinking must find its thoughtfulness *through* the worldly work, *in the face of* the testy case that will slow thought down and test its resolve, its strength, its patience and its worth. Student-teachers especially ask such questions in ways that are vital. They understand the *idea* behind curriculum as abundance but have trouble imagining how it might actually work itself out in the face of the at-first mundane tasks they face—teaching "commas" to Grade 5, or the rules for using capital letters in Grade 3.

Second, however, we also find the opposite trouble appearing. When we delve into attempting to describe and explore the stubborn particulars of classroom life, classroom conversation, and the substantively abundant relations nestled in various curriculum mandates, no amount of detail seems to be adequate to its living thoughtfulness and it is all too easy to get lost in the thickets of particularity. The ordinary events of everyday life have an excessiveness and abundance that, of necessity, outruns interpretation and articulation.

In fact, thickening the dove's air is as troublesome as the desire for no resistance at all. So, we search for that tenuous balance, one deep in the heart of our very mortality—to say what we have seen, to think and speculate and soar, and to live well with the obligations that education puts us under, with this student, here, now, Anh Linh and her shapes.

THE STORY BEGINS WITH ANH LINH AT WORK

> "It's a poor sort of memory that only works backwards," the Queen remarked. (Lewis Carroll, *Through the Looking-Glass*)

She sits at the end of one of the tables in our classroom. Her long dark hair falls onto her paper as she methodically calculates then meticulously measures each new line. Placing her ruler across the two points that she has calculated and measured, she ever so carefully draws the first light pencil line. Then checking to ensure the accuracy of the line, Anh Linh draws the second, now darker line over the first line. She removes the ruler from the paper and critically analyzes her work. "Good, it's good," she seems to say. And then she repeats the process, recursively adding the next and then the next line to the geometrical drawing.

Sometimes a smile of intense satisfaction crosses her face. Sometimes fellow students come by to inquire about her work. "Wow Anh Linh, that is so beautiful," they say as they admire the emerging form. Anh Linh smiles and then goes back to calculating, measuring, and drawing. Each line is precise. Each calculation is exact. Pat and I also watch Anh Linh as she works on this construction. Images of Basle's (1583) *Margarita philosophica* (in Lawlor, 1982, p. 7) come to mind in which geometry is depicted as a contemplative practice, "personified by an elegant and refined woman, for geometry functions as an intuitive, synthesizing, creative, yet exact activity of mind associated with the feminine principle" (Lawlor, 1982, p. 7; see Fig. 1.1).

Deeply immersed in the traditions of geometrical ways of knowing and doing that have "arisen within our human space through human activity"

FIG. 1.1. Margarita philosophica.

(Husserl, 1970, p. 355), Anh Linh has come upon "an inner logic so profound that every critical piece of it [contains] the information necessary to reconstruct the whole" (Palmer, 1998, p. 123).

IT ALSO BEGINS WITH THE PYTHAGOREAN THEOREM

Pat and I learned the stories of the mystical Pythagoras and his disciples when we first set out on this journey together in our irregularly shaped classroom with 50-some children from Grades 1 and 2. Now here we were, once again telling the secrets of these early mathematicians and their quest to unite numbers and shapes to 50-some Grade 8 children. These students were just as enchanted by the stories of these ancient radicals as the younger children had been. "Good mathematics ultimately comes from and returns to good stories—and the questions that bug you" (Casey & Fellows, 1993, p. 1)—stories that have the power to open an engaging mathematical space in which compelling mathematical explorations invite and entice both the novice and the expert mathematician (Friesen & Stone, 1996). In this space, right-angle triangles are so much more than finding the length of the hypotenuse using the handy formula—a theorem that stills bears the Pythagorean name.

Invoking a 3-4-5 triangle and unfolding its beauty and simplicity necessitates the story of a man, an outcaste. How else can we let the students know that this simple formula carries with it the weight of history? It stands the test of time. It still stands as a pillar in trigonometry. This act of measurement is a fundamental one that reaches back to Ancient Egypt. Using a rope knotted into 12 sections stretched out to form a 3-4-5 triangle, rope stretchers reclaimed and reestablished the boundaries of land and set order to the watery chaos created by the annual flooding of the Nile.

Reaching back in time, the Pythagorean theorem is one of the earliest theorems to known ancient civilizations. There is evidence that the Babylonians knew about this proportional relationship some 1,000 years before Pythagoras (Siefe, 2000, p. 29). *Plimpton 322,* a Babylonian mathematical tablet that dates back to 1900 BC, contains a table of Pythagorean triples—3-4-5, 5-12-13, 7-24-25 and so on. The *Chou-pei,* an ancient Chinese text, also provides evidence that the Chinese knew about the Pythagorean theorem many years before Pythagoras discovered and proved it (Joseph, 1991).

AND IT BEGINS WITH AN EXPLORATION ...

"Draw a right-angle triangle. Any sized right-angle triangle. Using only triangles that are similar to and/or congruent with your original, I want you to explore the properties of right-angle triangles."

My instructions were very simple. The story had already charmed the students and generously bounded the territory of the exploration. I provided these few directions to start our mathematical journey, and then we all began.

What a strange place to be teaching like *this*. We were in the heart of East Calgary. These students scored in the lowest quartile in the entire province. Our colleagues told us that what these students needed were "the basics" (see Jardine et al., 2003).

"Make them memorize their basic facts."

"Give them real-life problems. You know problems like calculating how much change they need to give someone. Or how much money they will need to earn to buy groceries. Or how much material they will need to purchase in order to make the items that their customers desire."

We seldom entered into the exhaustive debates that these well-intended comments opened. What if this is not the way that mathematics *exists,* as objects either produced or consumed, either individually or collectively? Having endured 7 years of *consuming* and *producing* mathematics, these students were very clear about their regard for this image of math. *"We HATE math."* *"It's boring." "We are never going to need it." "We'll just get a calculator."* These students who were bored and turned off almost from their earliest days in school, who could not (or would not) read, who knew far too little mathematics, who would stop taking science as soon as they could get away with it, who dropped out of school at worrisome rates. It is with these students that we now taught like this.

IT ALSO BEGAN THE YEAR BEFORE ...

It began last year. Having made the decision to move to this school, Pat and I knew that if we were to make a difference to these students, we would have to work with them for longer than 1 year. And we would need to keep them together for long blocks of uninterrupted time throughout the day. And we would also need to teach them all the core academic subjects. This seems like a strange request when everything about the structure of junior high school works against this type of organization, this type of connection and connectedness. But the administrators were receptive and supportive of our request, eager to see what differences this would make to how these students learned.

We needed this type of structure in all the core academic subjects, and in mathematics we needed it to break free from the spell that mathematics is about the quick method, the quick answer, the one right algorithm, the boring repetitive math that they hated. We wanted to connect students meaningfully with the discipline of mathematics in all its wondrous complexity rather than reducing it to more memorized formulas and computation or more real-life problems of consumption and production. We knew that "to decide whether a math statement is true, it is not sufficient to reduce the statement to marks on paper and to study the behaviour of the marks. Except in trivial cases, you can decide the truth of a statement only by studying its meaning and its context in the larger work of mathematical ideas" (Dyson, 1996, p. 801). What we wanted to do was to present the idea that mathematics contained a landscape of possibilities.

"By teaching this way, we do not abandon the ethic that drives us to cover the field—we honor it more deeply" (Palmer, 1998, p. 123). We learn how to "inhabit" such a mathematical landscape. Teaching in this way requires nurturing. The cultivation of this place is not simply a recapitulation of the old, like plowing the same old furrow again and again. "Teaching from the microcosm, we exercise responsibility toward both the subject and our students by refusing merely to send data 'bites' down the intellectual food chain" (Palmer, 1998, p. 123). We were working more like the rope stretchers of ancient Egypt taking time and care to bring order to the newly fertile landscape so that we might find ways to draw new boundaries upon fertile ground. At times we would take out our string with the 12 evenly spaced knots and draw out 3-4-5 triangles. At other times, changing our perspective, we would open our rope stretcher's triangle revealing a circle with 12 evenly spaced knots linking us to the perfect, endless infinite and to time itself. "By diving deep into the particularity, these students [were] developing an understanding of the whole" (Palmer, 1998, p. 123). Working in this way with these students, we began to show them that the cultivation of mathematics necessitates the creation of the new in the midst of the old. Such cultivation requires creation and re-creation. It is a fruitful space, a space that "bears" something, births something and contains the conditions to take care of what is thus "birthed."

In this space, with these students, we asked:

> What if mathematics is much more a world into which we ourselves are drawn, a world which we do not and cannot "own," but must rather somehow "inhabit" in order to understand it? What if we cannot own mathematics (either individually or collectively), not because it is some object independent of us and our (individual or collective) ownerships, but because *it is not an object at all*? What if, instead of production and consumption, the *world* of mathematics (as a *living, breathing, contested, human discipline* that has been handed to us) needs our memory, our care, our intelligence, our work, the "continuity of [our] attention and devotion" (W. Berry, 1986, p. 32) and understanding if it is to remain hale and healthy and whole? (see chap. 5)

Deeply committed to finding new approaches, we struggled to find ways to help our students "inhabit" mathematics. From our first beginnings we worked with mathematical explorations—the stories and fruitful spaces that they opened knowing that working in this way would "bear" something if we cared properly for it. A full year had now elapsed and we were seeing some of the fruits of our care. It was a full year ago that I told these students the story of four spiders that started crawling from four corners of a 6-meter-by-6-meter square. As I remember, each spider began to pursue the spider on its right, moving toward the center of the square at a constant rate of 1 centimeter per second. I embellished the story as I went along so that the students would be intrigued by the exploration that the story opened. Would these spiders ever meet, and if so how long would it take and what would their paths look like (Holding, 1991, p. 119; Pappas, 1989, p. 228)? Through this exploration I intended to introduce the students to the ideas of area, ratio, similarity, and limits.

The students, however, became entranced by the pursuit curve—the path that an object takes when pursuing another object. They couldn't believe their eyes that these straight lines produced curves. We never did calculate the time it would take the spiders to meet. Instead, the beautiful curve that emerged as the students worked so captivated them that they spent their time drawing and redrawing the path produced by the four spiders. Beauty and wonder are not attributes that any students, especially these students, would associate with mathematics. However, here they were, describing these four congruent logarithmic spirals as beautiful, awesome, magical.

IN THE PRESENCE OF THE PAST: ANH LINH, THE PYTHAGOREAN THEOREM, THE EXPLORATION, THE YEAR BEFORE ...

Now, 1 full year later, Anh Linh called forward the pursuit curve and the beautiful logarithmic spiral as she explored the 3-4-5 triangle. However, she was not content to stay within the confines of the exploration. She began the exploration by creating a series of right-angle triangles much like Fig. 1.2. From these sketches she drew this logarithmic spiral. As Pat and I gazed upon this incredible piece of work, each point meticulously measured, each line precisely drawn, we could barely believe that this work came from a 12-year-old child.

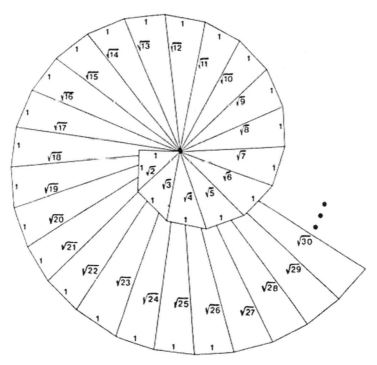

FIG. 1.2. Spiral using right-angle triangles.

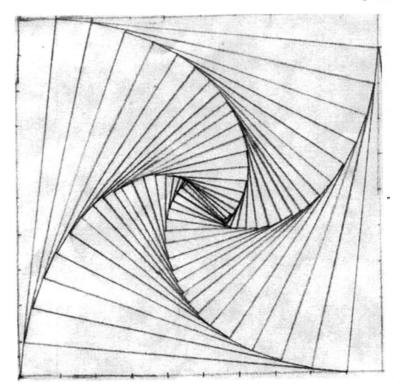

FIG. 1.3.   Anh Linh's spiral.

Anh Linh was on to something else (see Fig. 1.3). There was something in
the spiral that still called to her, something still unresolved. She wrote:

> I began with right angle triangles. I saw a spiral when I started to put them to-
> gether. I knew this shape. I remembered the spider's path. I saw the spider's
> path in the right angle triangles and I wanted to know if these were the same.
> I thought that my shapes might be similar in some way. I wasn't sure in what
> way they would be similar. I wanted to see what would happen.

The path formed by the pursuit curve that she had experienced last year
had a similarity known as self-similarity. By rotation, the curve can be made
to match any scaled copy of itself. In Fig. 1.4 I have shown how the angle between the radius from the origin and the tangent to the curve is constant.

This curve is known as the logarithmic spiral, the equiangular spiral, and
the growth spiral. Growing larger, this spiral exhibits expansive growth in
the form of seashells and hurricanes. It results from the play of a square with
the transcendental ratio—1.6180339 …

Getting lost in the exploration, Anh Linh decided to create another logarithmic spiral next to the one that she had just created (see Fig. 1.5).

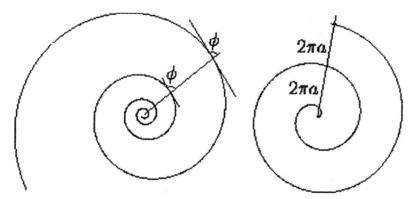

FIG. 1.4.   Angle between the radius from the origin and the tangent to the curve is constant.

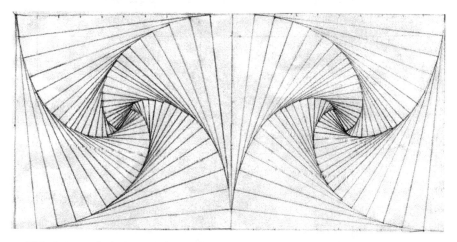

FIG. 1.5.   Anh Linh's reflected spirals.

As Anh Linh continued with her exploration, we all became intrigued with the natural forms this shape reminded us of and we started to examine naturally occurring logarithmic spirals (see Figs. 1.6 and 1.7).

Sometimes what at first seems unrelated, not similar, on closer inspection bears family resemblance. This shape was deeply familiar—a figure that the "Greek mathematicians called the *gnomon* and the type of growth based upon it. A gnomon is any figure which, when added to an original figure, leaves the resultant figure similar to the original" (Lawlor, 1982, p. 64; see Fig. 1.8). "This method of figuring the gnomon shows its relationship to the Pythagorean formula $a^2 + b^2 = c^2$. Shown here is the gnomonic increase from the square surface area of 4 to the square of 5, where the gnomon of the larger square 5 is equal to 1/4 of the initial square of 4" (Lawlor, 1982, p. 65).

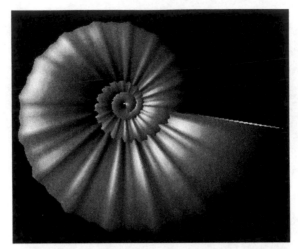

FIG. 1.6.   Natural spiral—1 (http://www.notam.uio.no/%EoyviFndha/loga.html).
Our thanks to Oyvind Hammer, National History Museum, University of Oslo, for
permission to use these images.

FIG. 1.7.   Natural spiral—2 (http://www.notam.uio.no/%Eoyvindha/loga.html).
Our thanks to Oyvind Hammer, National History Museum, University of Oslo, for
permission to use these images.

Anh Linh's quest to understand these dynamic spirals continued. When we
saw her drawing of four tessellated, symmetrical patterns, we were awed. To
produce such a stunning beautiful piece of work by hand certainly required
contemplation and exactitude beyond what we could have ever hoped for.
And for us, this would have been enough, but not for Anh Linh (see Fig. 1.9).

She continued to ask questions of this beautiful form and its symmetry,
and each new question led us all deeper into this exploration. Spiral doo-
dles started to appear all over the classroom—on notebooks, scraps of pa-

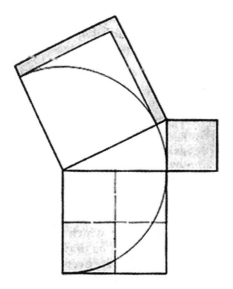

FIG. 1.8. Relationship between Gnomon and Pythagorean formula.

FIG. 1.9. Anh Linh's rotated spirals.

per, borders on assignments. Some students started to create a variety of spirals using the Logo program we had in the classroom. They learned the power of variables. Creating the following set of commands:

```
TO POLYGON :SIDE :ANGLE :AMT

IF :SIDE>300 [STOP]

FD :SIDE

RT :ANGLE

POLYGON (:SIDE + :AMT) :ANGLE :AMT

END
```

produced the spiral in Fig. 1.10.

Our work with Logo led us into the area of recursion and iteration—fractals. We saw a level of care, concern, and questioning that we had never before witnessed in this group of students. Their fractals were exquisite. Each calculation and line was exact. The students understood that the slightest

FIG. 1.10.   Logo-created spiral—student work.

variation would dramatically affect the outcome. (See Figs. 1.11 and 1.12.) We were experiencing what it meant to create mathematics. We were beginning to understand how creating new mathematics begins with asking questions. Sometimes a question that is easy to ask is impossible to answer. Sometimes a question that sounds difficult turns out to be something you already know, just dressed up to look different. Sometimes the question leads,

FIG. 1.11.   Sierpinski triangle—student work.

FIG. 1.12.   Sierpinski triangle—student work.

not to an answer, but to another question. And for these questions, the answers are not in the back of the book. It's the posing of questions that kept calling us on to new possibilities, wondering what might be around the next corner, helping us to understand that mathematics is not finished, it's work in progress, it's a *living, breathing, contested, human discipline* that has been handed to us (see chap. 5).

WORKING IN 3D

Working on the two-dimensional plane was intriguing and engaging, but what about 3D? Our questions were quite playful as we started, "I wonder what would happen if ..." "I wonder if the symmetries that we had found on the 2D plane would hold as we tiled them onto the surfaces of a solid."

We decided to begin by tiling the surfaces of regular solids known as Platonic solids: tetrahedron, icosahedron, dodecahedron, octahedron, and cube with the various symmetrical designs that we had constructed. What better place to try out our emerging understandings than on such perfectly symmetrical solids. Each of our geometric models began as a flat design. We not only had to determine the shapes of the sides we needed to construct in order to create the transition from the two-dimensional net to the three-dimensional solid, we also needed to figure out how to place our designs on the two-dimensional plane so they it would be perfectly symmetrical in three dimensions. The two-dimensional pattern gives few clues as to what you will see and feel when it takes shape in three dimensions. "The flat designs represent the possibility of infinite repetition but only a fragment of this infinity can be captured on a sheet of paper. On the surface of a three-dimensional object, infinite repetition of design can be realized with only a finite number of figures—the pattern on a solid has neither beginning nor end" (Schattschneider & Walker, 1982, p. 16). Creating the nets for each of the solids was fairly challenging, but determining how to draw the designs onto the surfaces so that when the edges came together the illusion of infinity was produced, was exigent. "Contrary to the impression given by most textbooks, the discovery of new forms and new ideas is rarely the product of the predictable evolution" (Schattschneider & Walker, 1982, p. 8).

After many attempts the students' solids began to take shape (see Figs. 1.13–1.15).

But it was Anh Linh who really pushed our thinking. It was Anh Linh and her love for the logarithmic spiral that pushed us to the frontiers of mathematics itself.

Starting with the cube, Anh Linh drew the curves on each of the six faces. Upon assembling the cube she discovered that the designs did not flow. The symmetry was broken. How could symmetry be lost on this perfectly symmetrical solid? (See Fig. 1.16.)

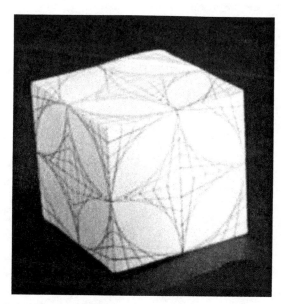

FIG. 1.13. Cube—student work.

FIG. 1.14. Icosahedron—student work.

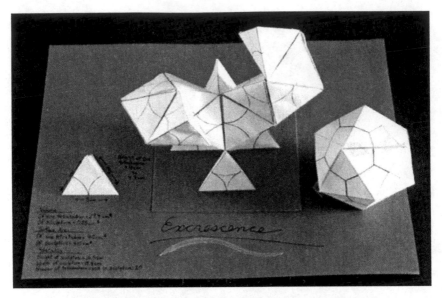

FIG. 1.15.   Excrescense—student work.

FIG. 1.16.   Anh Linh's cube.

Believing that she had made an error, she drew another cube. This time she transformed the spirals by reflecting them. However, upon putting the net together, she discovered that the problem was not solved. The pattern of the curve had broken the symmetry of the perfectly symmetrical cube—Greek symbol of earth. The act of reflection had not solved the problem. How could that be? What would work? "I want to find out why the symmetry breaks," Anh Linh wrote. *"I am going to see if I can make the symmetry work on any of the other solids. If I can, then maybe I will know why it doesn't work on the cube."*

Creating the curves on four equilateral triangles, Anh Linh started on her consuming quest to understand more about symmetry. She created the tetrahedron—the symbol of fire (see Fig. 1.17).

It didn't work. The symmetry didn't hold. Anh Linh wrote: "In this shape I noticed that the pattern [curves of pursuit] didn't match on all the faces. The symmetry breaks along the edge. I also found out that you can use the curve of pursuit on any platonic solid. I didn't know that when I started."

Intrigued by her new discovery and undaunted by her disappointment, Anh Linh took on the challenge of the octahedron—the symbol of air (see Fig. 1.18).

Once again, working on the two-dimensional equilateral triangles, Anh Linh meticulously measured and drew what we all now called "Anh Linh's curves." Magic—*"It was like magical,"* Anh Linh later wrote. As Anh Linh folded the edges of these eight equilateral triangles together, form and design came together, symmetry held, and infinity emerged from the finite. (See Fig. 1.19.)

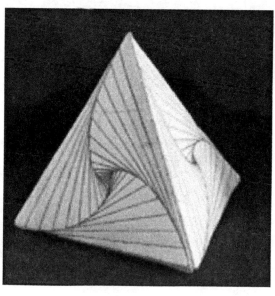

FIG. 1.17.   Anh Linh's tetrahedron.

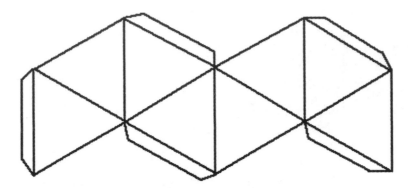

FIG. 1.18.   Octahedron net.

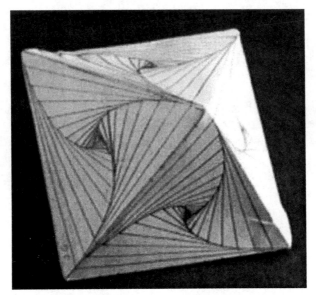

FIG. 1.19.   Anh Linh's octahedron.

What was it about the octahedron that was different from the tetrahedron or the cube? Everyone in the classroom was now involved in Anh Linh's problem—including Pat and me. Was there a solution? *"If there is, I don't know it,"* Anh Linh wrote. *"There might be an easy way to figure this out, but I don't know it. I will draw an icosahedron. It's faces are also triangles."*

For Anh Linh, as for all of us, we thought that the solution might be in the shape of the faces themselves. The tetrahedron did not work. But it was small—it had only four faces. Perhaps there was something in the number of faces. The octahedron had eight faces. Why should the symmetry hold with eight faces and not with four faces? They were both even numbers. But so was six for that matter—the number of faces on the cube. The solution had to be in the shape. Maybe there was something in the shape of the triangle that held the key to this problem. It had three vertices. The cube had four. Maybe there was something in that. Maybe there was something in the odd and the even. Like the ancient Pythagoras, we went looking for a connection between shapes and numbers.

Anh Linh continued drawing. Her next shape was the beautiful, perfectly symmetrical solid icosahedron, representing the Greek symbol for water. Upon each of its 20 identical equilateral triangle surfaces, Anh Linh drew the logarithmic spiral (see Fig. 1.20).

As she brought each of the five vertices of the solid together, she discovered, as did we all, that symmetry was lost. But why? There had to be a solution.

It would be easy to conclude that we were just involved in solving the problem posed by Anh Linh's shapes. But that is not really what was happening—at least not all that was happening. Mathematics is not just a problem-solving activity. We were involved in something far more fundamental—far more "basic" to mathematics. We were caught up in a generative act "the central activity being *making* new mathematics" (Wilensky, 1996). It was consuming for all of us. We noticed the students puzzling with the various shapes, trying to put them together in different ways, trying the dodecahedron, looking again at previously failed symmetries whenever they found breaks in their normal day-to-day studies. Pat and I puzzled along with them. While driving home from school one day along the busy, accident-riddled Deerfoot freeway I had a flash of insight. I

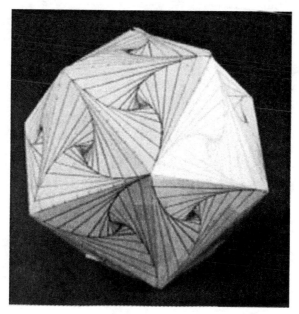

FIG. 1.20. Anh Linh's icoshaedron.

suddenly knew a direction to take that might hold the key to Anh Linh's shapes. I pulled over to the side of the road and frantically dug through my books for a piece of paper and a pen or a pencil. That's it. Flatten the shape. Step on it. Make a graph. Not the normal school-type graph (a statistical graph), but a network, that type of graph.

We had been playing with networks earlier in the year. I had read the students the story *Superperson Saves the Monster* (Casey & Fellows, 1993, p. 51). It is a zany story about three characters: Gertrude the goose, Monster, and Superperson. Now suddenly on this freeway, driving home from school this story seemed to somehow hold the key to Anh Linh's shapes. "Sometimes ideas are often born unexpectedly—from complexity, contradiction, and, more than anything else, perspective" (Negroponte, 1996).

"Look at the vertices," Anh Linh's shapes seemed to call. As I flattened each of the shapes, about their vertex points, I noticed that the vertices and edges came together in a pattern of odds and evens. The tetrahedron—three, the cube—three, the octahedron—four, the icosahedron—five. There it was. I could hardly wait to get back to school the next day. I needed to let the class know that the Superperson story might hold the key. Upon revisiting the story, the students saw it too. "I don't think I need to make a decahedron," wrote Anh Linh. "It has an odd number of edges at the vertices."

I still had some reservations. How could we be sure that we were right? I packed up all of Anh Linh's shapes and took them to a mathematician at the university. I told him the story of Anh Linh's shapes and showed him how we had come to a solution. *"Does this make sense to you, Albert?"* I asked.

"Let's see." Albert drew a number of sketches on the chalkboard in his office. *"Yes, I believe you and your class are on to something,"* he said. *"The direction you have chosen seems to be a good one."*

"But are we right?" I wanted to know.

"I don't know," he said. *"But it looks like you are in an exciting and productive place. This is all new mathematics. There are people here who know more than I do about this area. You are creating mathematics."*

We began our exploration with Euclidean geometry but as we searched for a solution to the problem of determining symmetry we found ourselves in a very different space—a geometrical space that had more questions than answers. It seemed as though we had left the deeply familiar Euclidean geometry behind and were pushing at the very frontiers of mathematics itself—graph theory. It was an exploration that drew us in. It pulled us into *its* question, *its* repose, *its* regard. Therefore, first is the question posed, not *by* us but *to us*. We were consumed by the questions that kept presenting themselves, that kept calling to us from Anh Linh's shapes.

Where was Pythagoras? Did we leave him behind? Or are we in a place that required Pythagoras? Were we standing in the long and twisted entrails of all the interdependencies that gave rise to what was being manifest, just here, just now? Did Pythagoras, in his explorations and eccentricity, know he was preparing a place that could give "birth" to this new mathematics? A place that could support Anh Linh's quest? A place large enough for all her classmates and her teachers? A place that required us all and all of us? Mathematics *is*, in some sensible sense, all the actual human, bodily work that is required if it is to remain hale and healthy, if it is to continue as a living practice that we desire to pass on, in some form, to our children.

Preamble 2: Signs of Abundance

As we saw both in chapter 1 and in our Introduction, the Pythagorean theorem—one of the myriad of curriculum topics entrusted to students and teachers in schools—is far more than a meager formula to be memorized and correctly applied. As with any curriculum topic, it is surrounded by a rich abundance of relations and ancestries and real, living questions. It is full of histories and conversations and debates and contestations and cultural and linguistic inheritances. It is complex and often beautiful and not always easy and simple. Yet, at times, under the shadows of playground trees, the simplicity and clarity and freshness of the questions it induces can be breathtaking. Understanding it this way—in its abundance—is no meager undertaking. As the topic of understanding becomes less and less impoverished, so too does the character of understanding become richer and more complex, diverse, and intellectually sound.

Chapter 1 reminds us of something we already knew: The Pythagorean theorem is part of a *living discipline* despite how it often appears in the classroom. It is precisely this character of a living discipline that is occluded by regimes of scarcity and their consequent impoverishment of our ability to imagine and understand the curriculum topics entrusted to us as teachers. We use the term occluded here, but not "erased." As Hans-Georg Gadamer (1989) suggests, such living disciplines and traditions of work and thinking and imagining, with all their complex, abundant conversations, controversies, contentions, images, ideas, and presumptions, continue to operate in our lives and our livings, even if their living character is left unnoticed in education's understanding of such matters under regimes of scarcity. For the most part, such occluded matters are simply taken for granted, pushed into the background and forgotten. The abundance of a particular curriculum topic is thereby presumed (after all, without all that teeming work of handing it down to us it would never appear as something to "cover" in schools), but this presumption is left undisturbed.

However, Gadamer (1989) also suggests that this occlusion has consequences for our ability to understand such matters in their abundance: "It is impossible to make ourselves aware of [these abundant, living ancestries, relations, inheritances and presumptions, these] ... prejudice[s] while [they] are constantly operating unnoticed, but only when [they] are, so to speak, provoked. Understanding begins when something addresses us" (p. 299). If it is impossible to make ourselves aware of such matters to the extent that they remain unnoticed, how can we begin to notice such matters? How can we begin to experience and understand the hitherto unnoticed nature of curriculum in abundance? Or, as many teachers and student teachers have asked us, where do you start?

One wonderful hint comes from the end of Gadamer's text: "Understanding begins *when something addresses us.*" This suggestion has two interrelated moments, the first is deeply experiential, immediate, and aesthetic, and the second sets forth for those interested in curriculum in abundance a deeply pedagogical, interpretive task.

There is an immediate, sensuous, easily recognizable, commonplace *experience* that provides a way to begin noticing, that provides a place to start. We can get a glimpse of this experiential and aesthetic phenomenon by sketching out the bare bones of the chapter that follows. Students were exploring a science curriculum topic on the difference between natural structures and human-made structures. After the students had ample opportunities to begin exploring the rich and troublesome ins and outs of this topic, one student declared that he wanted to use Dolly the sheep as his example, but that he wasn't sure whether Dolly was a human-made structure or a natural one.

This small classroom anecdote usually raises a smile or a nod of recognition and pleasure from those who hear it. It's funny, mildly amusing, somehow pleasurable and reassuring, the sort of anecdotal "teacher story" that educators love to tell each other and that has become commonplace in a great deal of research in education. With this we fully agree, and the pleasures to be had in the recounting of such tales is a vital component of sustaining us as teachers.

However, we suggest that such anecdotes and our responses to them are much more than this. *They are signs of the heretofore unnoticed presence of abundance.* This is a difficult experience to describe but is, as we have suggested, a very commonplace experience. In recounting and recalling such anecdotes, what we are experiencing is a sense of something *happening*, something *arriving*, something starting to open up, something stirring, becoming enlivened, lively. We feel a sense of vertigo, of movement (see Jardine et al., 2003, pp. 207–222). Such stories *strike* us, somehow—they have, so to speak, an aesthetic appeal that overflows our expectations. This aesthetic appeal has an important characteristic that is often overlooked: Such appeals are not experienced as subjective responses to, say, Anh Linh's shapes or a comment about Dolly the sheep. Rather, such matters are experienced as "impos[ing their] own presence on us. Rather than meeting us in our world, [they are] much more ... world[s] into which we ourselves are drawn" (Gadamer, 1994, pp. 191–192). It is as if the world in which we are working—this world of science curricula and classrooms and teaching and learning, or the world of Pythagorean geometries—becomes full of portend, full of as-yet-unexplored possibility and potency that allure us, draw us into their workings and ways:

> This sounds rather arcane, but it simply points to a commonplace experience: those moments when we know that "something is going on," ([*im Spiele ist*] Gadamer, 1989, p. 104), "something is happening" ([*sich abspielt*], p. 104), something is "at play," here, in this place and it has something to ask *of me* beyond what I might imagine asking of it. Rich and memorable experiences ask things of us, and, as such, they are characterizable as "more a passion than an action. A question *presses itself upon us*" (Gadamer, 1989, p. 366, our emphasis). (Jardine et al., 2003, p. 86)

On the face of it, this "Dolly the sheep" anecdote indicates that there might be much more to that original science curriculum mandate than appeared at first blush--there might be great and ancient and living and troublesome things operating heretofore unnoticed. Suddenly, perhaps even only momentarily, the dry and lifeless impoverishment of the curriculum guide version of the topic cracks open. A world begins to appear and we feel draw into it.

This sort of aesthetic experience is, in fact, very ordinary. A child's comment during a classroom conversation seems to erupt with possibilities, a piece of student's work takes our breath away, a citation from an essay or a book "speaks" to us and draws us out into new, unforseen terrains of thinking and imagining. Both students and teachers live in the world this way. Things "hit us," "speak to us," "strike us," "charm us," "provoke us."

Part of this aesthetic experience is thus rather disturbing, as one might well imagine when that which has been operating unnoticed starts to appear. The ground feels a bit like it's shifting and we can feel overwhelmed by what seems like "a chaos of possibilities" (Hillman, 1987, p. 154). In the face of such an "embarrassment of ... riches"(Turner, 1987, p. 18), the obviousness and commonplaceness of the original curriculum mandate seem to "waver and tremble" (Caputo, 1987, p. 7). What seemed to be just one more thing that needed to be covered in the classroom jumps up and bites (see Preamble 7 and chap. 7).

It is at this juncture that Gadamer's injunctions regarding the task posed to understanding become vital. He suggests that understanding *begins* by being struck by such arrivals, but if we are to take care of such arrivals, if we are to *understand* them (see Wilde, 1996, for a wonderful exploration of the link between care and understanding), we must now think about what is being asked of us in such moments of address. Such moments provoke us in a most literal way: They call us out (L. *vocare*) of our state of unnoticing and lay claim to our time and attention. There is rich and difficult intellectual work to be done, to find out what is at play in this world into which we have been aesthetically invited, this world in which students and teachers alike are living. Thus, such incidents have provocative power: They *call for* thinking (Heidegger, 1968), they ask for the work of teaching and learning.

In the chapter that follows, it was necessary for the author to surround this Dolly anecdote with a form of interpretive *work* aimed simply and squarely thus: What is it that is at work in this anecdote about Dolly the sheep? Who are the ancestors and ghosts that are in play here, that make this curriculum topic so fulsome and rich and relevant in our world, that make that original, commonplace anecdote so telling and amusing and true? More straightforwardly put, why is this topic in the curriculum guide in the first place? Why would it have been entrusted to us as something worthy of our attention and important to take up? And, perhaps most fascinating of all, why is that we now seem to understand the deep and provocative power of this curriculum mandate only *after* Dolly arrived?

This substantive, intellectually challenging work ahead is precisely the work of the classroom, the work of teachers and students alike, each in their own measure. It is not an intellectual game that teachers can play alone. It is, rather, a "playground" into which both students and teachers must find their ways. It is only in such work that we can deal with the possibilities of being overwhelmed by the abundant claims of Dolly the sheep.

Chapter 2

Eight Pedagogical Preambles on Dolly the Sheep[1]

David W. Jardine

PREAMBLE I

It followed her to school one day

Which was against the rules

It made the children laugh and play

To see a lamb at school. (second stanza of "Mary Had a Little Lamb")

Cloning ... is only a pathetic attempt to make sheep predictable. But this is an affront to reality. As any shepherd would know, the scientist who thinks he has made sheep predictable has only made himself eligible to be outsmarted. (Wendell Berry, from *Thy Life's a Miracle*, 1999)

PREAMBLE II

As Carolus Linnaeus wrote in the preface to a late edition of *Systema Naturae: Creationis telluris est gloria Dei ex opere Naturae per Hominem solum*—The Earth's creation is the glory of God, as seen from the works of Nature by Man alone. The study of nature would reveal the Divine Order of God's creation, and it was the naturalist's task to construct a "natural classification" that would reveal this Order in the universe. (Carl Linnaeus, 1707–1778)

Nearly two centuries ago, in this room, on this floor, Thomas Jefferson and a trusted aide spread out a magnificent map—a map Jefferson had long prayed he would get to see in his lifetime. The aide was Meriwether Lewis and the map was the product of his courageous expedition across the American frontier, all the way to the Pacific. It was a map that defined the contours and forever expanded the frontiers of our continent and our imagination.

---

[1]Reprinted from "Eight pedagogical preambles on Dolly the sheep" by D. Jardine, 2003, *Interchange: A Quarterly Review of Education, 34* (4), pp. 440–456. Copyright © 2003 by Kluwer Academic Publishers. Reprinted with kind permission from Springer Science and Business Media.

Today, the world is joining us here in the East Room to behold a map of even greater significance. We are here to celebrate the completion of the first survey of the entire human genome. Without a doubt, this is the most important, most wondrous map ever produced by humankind. Today's announcement represents more than just an epic-making triumph of science and reason. After all, when Galileo discovered he could use the tools of mathematics and mechanics to understand the motion of celestial bodies, he felt, in the words of one eminent researcher, "that he had learned the language in which God created the universe." Today, we are learning the language in which God created life. We are gaining ever more awe for the complexity, the beauty, the wonder of God's most divine and sacred gift. With this profound new knowledge, humankind is on the verge of gaining immense, new power to heal. Genome science will have a real impact on all our lives—and even more, on the lives of our children. (Remarks by the President, ... 2000)

We are currently living right in the midst of a grand new mytho-theological project: the complete mapping of human DNA in the Human Genome Project (HGP). This project and its permutations and "progressions" and the teeming lists of arguments and consequences (claimed, presumed, feared, seen and unforeseen)—from Dolly the sheep to genetically modified pigs ripe for xenotransplantation, to genetically modified organisms (GMOs), to the horribly named and newly (Canadian) patented "oncomouse"—is proceeding at such a rapid rate that it is impossible to make this sentence seem up-to-date on the latest news.

This characteristic is the first of many mytho-theological markers: a headlong and giddy and sensational and confident eschatological rush toward the future, toward the last days when all will be fulfilled, when we will somehow be done with this burden of suffering and continuance, and can finally rest, assured.

This characteristic also marks another one. *Questioning* this rush seems so unseemly, so quaint and out-of-date in the face of the always-as-yet-to-be-fulfilled up-to-dateness of our hopes and dreams coming true. How could we dare question all this? After all, as a recent *Time* magazine (July 31, 2000) cover declared in bold face "This Rice Could Save a Million Kids a Year" and then added parenthetically in smaller-case letters "... but protesters believe such genetically modified foods are bad for us and our planet. Here's why."

Just imagine! A million kids a year!

Oh, and did I say "recent"?

Apologies, because, again as a marker of the character of this grand project we find ourselves caught up in, "recency" has oddly either disappeared or become the equivalent of condensed imaginal and spatio-temporal immediacy, a sort of still Eternity of "*now*-what?"s. Therefore, only near-panic preambles are possible, because it always seems as if the real topic, its real warrant, its real significance, is just about to arrive, as if the real questions that we should have already long-since asked are just about to come pressing upon us, "accelerated" (Jardine, 2000; see chap. 12), "faster" (Glieck, 2000), as if the future is moving toward us as much as we are moving toward it, as if *we* are caught in *its* sights (in academia, in its *cites*—think of how terribly difficult it is to keep up these days with the latest "posts") and are helplessly becoming what *it* demands of *us*, rather than the reverse, as if we are always and already and ahead-of-time captured standing stockstill in the headlight glare of the next as-yet-to-arrive headline.

Caught in the rush of the news: Read as a plural, this is a perfect image of one of the faces of pedagogy, caught in the rush of the news, the children, what Hannah Arendt (1969, p. 236, my emphasis) tellingly called an *onslaught*.

PREAMBLE III

> The first test-tube baby to be genetically selected so that his cells can be harvested to save his critically ill sister has been born to an American couple. Adam Nash was conceived after tests to ensure that his cells were suitable for a life-saving transplant for his six-year-old sister, Molly. Adam is the first baby to be born from an embryo that has been screened for anything other than genetic abnormalities. Cells from Adam's umbilical cord were injected into Molly's blood at Fairview-University Hospital in Minneapolis.
>
> "Molly has been holding Adam in her lap," Linda [Nash, Molly and Adam's mother] told the Washington Post.
>
> "It was the most awesome, monumental experience of our life, yet it was so simple. You'd think there'd be thunderbolts and lightning, but it was calm." "Test Tube Tech May Save Child," (Reuters, 2000)

But Jack Scarisbrick, of the anti-abortion charity Life, said the use of PGD (preimplantation genetic diagnosis) was morally repugnant: "Scrutinizing human beings and discarding those which are found to be inferior is incompatible with the respect we should show to all human life. Its proper place is in the barnyard" (Henderson, 2000, p. A2).

This whole, roiling rush of related phenomena is, of course, not *deliberately* a mytho-theological project—despite Linda Nash's unintended Germanic Christmas gods-talk of *Donner und Blitzen*, of "thunderbolts and lightning"—but is, rather, an inevitable extension of work in the biological sciences that extends back through the eugenic blood-sciences that underwrote racial theories earlier this century, and back, from there, to the great "Father of Taxonomy," Carolus Linnaeus (1707–1778), whose work, the enormous *Systema Naturae* (with its own bloodlines traceable back to the work of Aristotle before him), unfolded the whole of creation into the grand typologies of Kingdoms and Genera and Species and Subspecies and Families and Kinship Relations and other relations of Kind, that are still taught, in supplemented and modified forms, in our schools.

When we move downward into the (binomial, in Linnaeus' case) naming of these typologies in the One Universal Language of Latin (into which, as was commonplace, Carole Linne translated his own name to Linnaeus, which means, oddly enough given his life's work, "lines") we finally come upon mythological and theological groundwaters: echoes of images of the

Great Chain of Being, images of the orderly and ordered issuance of all things from the one great act of Creation, and countless examples of the perennial human hope of being able to map the proximity and distance of any thing to the Origin from which it emerged and to which it owes its Being.

The Human (and, of course, less fantastically, other animal) Genome Project(s) can therefore be understood as standing in a long, shared, and contested ancestry, even though, of course, as a science, it necessarily denies, claims ignorance of, but most commonly simply ignores such placement. As a science, it must, of necessity, simply understand itself as naming what is the case, given the methods and conceptual "ground plan of nature" (Heidegger, 1977, p. 23) that underwrites it.

But still, for those of us not simply spellbound by science's indigenous advances, the echoes are not only undeniable but oddly meaningful, oddly audible in the meant-to-be straightforward newspaper claims and newscast comments with which we have been inundated: Soon, in all of this, we will have the Great Blueprint of the One Great Creation. Even to the extent that contemporary science is no longer enamored of or interested in whether there is anything of God's glory to be found here—thunders, lightnings, and the great and given and unquestionable separation of humanity from the mangy and mangery ways of Jack Scarisbrick's "barnyard"—nevertheless, the theological ring is clear and the theological clamor that has arisen is equally evident.

PREAMBLE IV

> Technoscience ["dense nodes of human and nonhuman actors that are brought into alliance by the material, social, and semiotic technologies through which what will count as nature and as matters of fact get constituted" (p. 51)] designates a condensation of space and time, a speeding up and concentrating of effects in the webs of knowledge and power. In what gets politely called modernity … accelerated production of natural knowledge pervasively structures commerce, industry, healing, community, war, sex, literacy, entertainment and worship. (Haraway, 1997, p. 51)

Here is the mark of another old tale in all these constellating and condensing structures. Despite the ways in which we have become full of a sense of the future, of urgency, of news and newness, of innovation far beyond what might have ever been previously imagined, still, there is housed here a disturbingly old and familiar hubris, a disturbingly old and familiar confidence. Unlike (but *exactly like*) other such architectonic efforts, we believe, once again, an old and often-told tale: *This* time, *somehow*, we've "got it." Unlike previous similar claims or confidences (and, at the same time, *precisely identical to previous claims and confidences*), we imagine that *this* time, as an effort of objective science, we've broken the "real" code of our being human (and, of course, the "real" codes of our *not* being the sheep and pigs we manipulate, except, of course, for Adam Nash and his rich and salvational umbilical cord).

Such talk has become commonplace this time, with this project, as it has become so commonplace so often before. Moreover, *this* time, we feel that we will fulfill the desire for the last days and end up with a *complete* map. But, more than this, we will not only have a map of what makes us human beings *in general*. We are on the verge of a complete map that will allow us, in the (although difficult to discover, never subtle or mysterious) differentiations of DNA, to locate the uniqueness and difference of any and all individuals. In such grand mapping, *just this person*—**you**—will be identifiably and predictably different from any other, and, at the same time, such difference and identifiability and predictability will be able to be encoded and submerged into a great, transcendent "[gene] pool" in which we all belong together as humans.

Here, again, age-old stories in which identity and difference, the one and the many, the individual and the general, the idea and its manifestations, the essential and the accidental, the origin(al) and the copy, are believed to be on the verge of being finally resolved.

PREAMBLE V

Having the ability and desire to know, how and what should we learn? And, having learned, how and for what should we use what we know? One thing we do know is that better solutions than ours have at times been made by people with much less information than we have. We know, too, from the study of agriculture, that the same information, tools and techniques that in one farmer's hands will ruin land, in another's will save and improve it. This is not a recommendation of ignorance. To know nothing is, after all, no more possible than to know enough. I am only proposing that knowledge, like everything else, has its place, and that we need urgently now to put it in its place. (W. Berry, 1983, pp. 54–55)

Here, again, is another old story about our fiery confidence in our own knowing, in its nature, its limits and place in living our lives well. Compare:

[It is incorrect to presume] that the human prerogative is unlimited, that we *must* do whatever we have the power to do. What is lacking [in such a presumption] is the idea that humans have a place and that this place is limited by responsibility on the one hand and by humility on the other. (Berry, 1983, p. 55)

And:

If the application of science were simply the problem of how, with the help of science, we might do everything we can do, then it is certainly not such application that we need as humans who are responsible for the future. For science as such will never prevent us from doing anything we are able to do. The future of humanity, however, demands that we do not simply do everything we can. (Gadamer, 1977, pp. 196–197)

And again:

> Addressing an international conference on transplantation techniques, the Pope said respect for human life should be the guiding principle in determining the boundary of scientific experimentation.
>
> "Every medical procedure performed on the human person is subject to limits: not just the limits of what is technically possible, but also limits determined by respect for human nature itself," the 80-year-old pontiff said in a rare public address.
>
> "What is technically possible is not for that reason alone morally admissible," he said. (Baker, 2000, p. A20)

And yet, of course—thunderbolts and lightning be damned—we must do everything we can to save Molly, to save a million kids a year (!), to raise pigs to be harvested for organ xenotransplantation into humans in such dire need that death hovers (this written just as a colleague of mine died on the operating table for want of an aorta not ruined by the years).

But death hovers now just like it has always hovered. However (and here is a deep agony right in the heart of the "progress" of technoscience), now that we *can, not* doing what we can becomes a *refusal to do what we can*. (We didn't have to refuse [or accept] before because we *couldn't*: again an old story, because we've *always* had to accept or refuse, because there has *always* been something we *can* do that we decide, warrantably and fairly or otherwise, that we *shouldn't*.) Thus the very knowledge we intended and hoped would save us from the agonies of our being human ends up—and with a mere glance at human history, this ought not be a great surprise—*creating* as much agony as it was meant to overcome, for *now*, we might have to refuse what we *can* do because we *shouldn't do it* (*whatever* this might turn out to mean, because, as what we *can* do expands, boundary issues of what we *ought* do are constantly reaggravated).

And so we turn to the technosciences whose intricacies and thrilling advances have so vigorously expanded the bounds of what we can do. We ask for help in curbing our rush, help in considering the rupturous cascade we face and, of course: "Science will not do us this favour. It will continue along its own path with an inner necessity beyond its control, and it will produce more and more breathtaking knowledge and controlling power. It can be no other way" (Gadamer, 1977, p. 10). It *cannot* do us this favor. It *should not be expected to*, and it is precisely this blurry expectation that makes these matters so ripe.

Because when we read John Paul II's declaration, that "what is technically possible is not for that reason alone morally admissible," we can all retreat from this terrible burden and endlessly fight over who is to say what is morally admissible and perhaps, in the end, become exhausted and simply withdraw from the issue of such admissibility. But if we do this, if we withdraw into epistemological timidity ("who is to say?"), by default, the technically possible becomes "the good."

Which, of course, marks off again another mytho-theological characteristic of these Dolly events. We start losing track of how to say "no" and how to get those enamored by such technical advances to take "no" for an answer.

PREAMBLE VI

Science education contributes to this overall aim of education in several ways:

- first, by providing learning experiences that help students understand and interpret the world in which they live

- second, by developing knowledge, skills and attitudes that support the intelligent and responsible application of science and technology

- third, by developing a foundation of knowledge, skills and attitudes that support further study of the sciences.

To achieve these purposes, the Junior High Science Program provides a broad range of learning experiences in the biological, physical and earth sciences.

Specific Learner Expectations

Concepts

1. Design can be observed in both natural and manufactured materials.

Students will be expected to:

- identify patterns of organization in natural materials

- identify patterns of organization in manufactured materials

- recognize similarities between natural and manufactured structures. (*Alberta Junior High Science Curriculum Guide*, Revised 1990)

This series of preambles first began a couple of years ago in a Grade 7 class taught by Patricia Clifford and Sharon Friesen. The students had been given a generous, wide berth in exploring the (mandated *Alberta Science Curriculum*) question of natural and manufactured structures. Choose a natural and a manufactured structure and explore them, their similarities, differences, designs, purposes, aesthetics, shapes, strengths, character, conflicts.

So I stumble in one morning and Pat corners me and warns me that one student, Richard, wants to talk, as soon as possible. With Sharon and Pat's encouragement, Richard was someone who had come to trust me to take his philosophical ventures seriously. What occurred turned out to be one of those wonderful moments that sometimes happen in classrooms, where a student has come to know, consciously or not, that the question they have is for you and no one else.

Of course, too, Richard is, as Pat put it, sometimes a bit like a cat with a chewed-up mole, who sneaks into the house and plops it on your shoe and casually sashays away, grinning as only cats can.

What happened next was almost too simple.

"I want to do Dolly the sheep for my 'structures' project. But I can't figure it out. Is she a natural structure, or a manufactured one?"

Suddenly, unexpectedly, beyond the watchful monitor of schooling, a curriculum guide distinction that was supposed to be a "given"—"natural and manufactured structures"—is no longer a given. Having Richard's question about Dolly the sheep arrive at school one day turned out to be against the rules, against the rule-governed and well-defined curriculum guidelines that had already been laid out, and it did indeed make for laughter and an odd feel of "play" in what was once a tight and well-bounded lesson topic.

But yet again, this "against the rules" turned out to be also *on behalf of the rules* and their continued urgency and life. Suddenly, the previously seemingly given rules of natural and manufactured structures began to "waver and tremble" (Caputo, 1987, p. 7) in the face of Dolly's unexpected arrival.

Richard had surely, if only momentarily, broken loose from the confines of schooled knowledge. But more than this, he acted as a herald, bringing back to us from a sojourn in the world great and joyous and disturbing news, that this seemingly calcified and dry-ruled distinction was no longer so. It was no longer closed and done and given, but was now, once again, open to question. And here's the real humiliation: We get a momentary, fleeting glimpse that this distinction, as part of the shared and contested traditions we have been living out (*one thread of which* is the schooled version of biology and zoology) *has never been a "given."* It has *always been open*, in spite of the seemingly confident textbooks or the feigned confidences of provincial or state testing.

After all, the very idea that some structures are considered "natural" contains multiple silent voices. It hides sidelong affronts to the idea of the Earth as God's *ens creatum,* God's, so to speak, "manufacture." Understanding the "nature" of something, understanding its "natural" structure, used to mean understanding it *as* a creation, not for the purposes of controlling, predicting, and manipulating its causes and effects, but for witnessing the Glory of God. *This* is the great debate that the sciences once had with the Church: that a pretense to knowledge-as-human-manufacture-and-control is eventually insane because it necessarily forgets its own limits (a point made, too, by ecology and a long-standing point always made by Wisdom Traditions: that knowledge and its allures are always *the problem we face as humans,* not the means of our salvation from being human).

And what of the intricate twiggyness of an oriole's nest that is also certainly beyond *human* manufacture—natural? themselves manufactured? Or is our human manufacturing wrought in God's image (even though we ourselves are also not just creators-in-God's-image but also *ens creata:* created creatures who also create) whereas the manufacturings of orioles are not? Hang on! With Dolly, we become created creatures who now also create other creatures (like Dolly and oncomouse and Adam Nash) who themselves create offspring (or umbilical body parts) of our determining. Yikes!

And yet all these damn troubles have been hiding there *all along,* long before and in spite of Dolly's sweet and unanticipated appearance.

Differently put, then, with Richard's herald, what was once a deadly curriculum requirement suddenly became *really interesting,* a *real intellectual challenge,* a *real, worldly, vital, yet-to-be-decided phenomenon.* It finally became a *genuinely scientific quandary,* and no longer simply one of those fake and feigned, profoundly nonscientific "experiments" that form a great part of "science curriculum" whose outcome is already understood by teachers and students alike. And, perhaps most important, there was now nothing in the world that could protect us from the insight that we had found ourselves caught in the sites of a question the genuine posing of which would mean that our lives, our world, and the decisions that we will have to henceforth make in and about ourselves and that world, would be irretrievably different.

This is how far such an interpretive move moves. As Hans-Georg Gadamer (1989) puts it, interpretation "breaks open the *being* of the object" (p. 30) under consideration. That is, understood interpretively, this originally seemingly innocent distinction between natural and manufactured structures *is* its openness to the future. Perhaps understanding this distinction (as is the mandate we are entrusted with by the *Alberta Science Curriculum Guide*) is precisely to understand this distinction *in its openness to the future.* Perhaps understanding involves "keeping the world open" (Eliade, 1968, p. 139) to a sense that the reality of all these matters handed to us as teachers and students is always and irreparably "yet to be decided" (Gadamer, 1989, p. 361) and that to understand the "yet-to-be-decidedness" of something is to understand its reality.

PREAMBLE VII

In a decision that will allow patents for all genetically modified animals—except human beings—the Federal Court of Appeal yesterday agreed to grant Harvard University a Canadian patent for a modified mouse. The court's declaration that animals can be classified as "inventions" under Canada's Patent Act also reignited calls for a parliamentary review of the 1869 legislation in view of modern bio-ethical questions. Justice Marshall Rothstein signaled that courts should keep an open mind to rapid changes in technology. "The language of patent law is broad and general and is to be given wide scope because inventions are, necessarily, unanticipated and unforeseeable" he wrote. (Chwialkowska, 2000, p. A1)

Opportunities are not plain, clean gifts; they trail dark and chaotic attachments to their unknown backgrounds, luring us further. One insight leads to another; one invention suggests another variation—more and more seems to pass through the hole, and more and more we find ourselves drawn out into a chaos of possibilities (Hillman, 1987, p. 154).

PREAMBLE VIII

> "This [Canadian patent decision] applies to any kind of animal from which
> you can get a sperm and egg," said David Morrow, the lawyer who repre-
> sented Harvard University. "But the court made it quite clear that this does
> not open the door to human beings." (Chwialkowski, 2000, p. A6)

Speaking of opening doors, speaking of old tales often told, speaking of
however unintentionally invoking these images and histories:

> Warnings were sounded today over the Pandora's Box opened by scientists
> who have cultivated human "master" cells, paving the way to growing any
> type of human tissue in the laboratory. The breakthrough, described as the
> most dramatic since the birth of Dolly the sheep clone, could herald a revolu-
> tion in medicine, transplant surgery and genetic engineering. ("Critics
> Sound Alarm Over 'Master Cell' Technology," 2000)

Pandora and the confident belief in which doors may be safely opened and
which not, as if our actions are not open to a future that is itself yet-to-be-decided. Look what other images show up, again full of unintended Old Testament mixed-metaphors:

> When it comes to biotechnology, Joy Morrow, an Ottawa lawyer with biotech
> clients, has heard all the hyperbole. Pink elephants. Two-headed fish. "You
> name it," she laughs. Critics of biotechnology have long argued that if corpo-
> rations such as Harvard University can patent a genetically engineered
> mouse, then the world can expect a Noah's Ark full of freakish new creatures
> to follow. (Evanson, 2000, p. A6)

Thus inevitably linked to this whole matter is a panoply of monsters. And
speaking of hyperbole, the monster was always sent in order to teach, in order to warn (*monere*), in order to demonstrate.

So what is the real monster here?

TEMPORARY END BIT: "THE COMMODIFICATION
AND OBJECTIFICATION OF LIFE"

> I had been struck by a remark of Bergson that appeared to give me a guiding
> thread for the start of my philosophico-biological studies. This was his sur-
> prise at the disappearance of the problem of "kinds" in favour of the problem
> of laws. (Piaget 1965, p. 6)

> The problem as it appears to me, is that we are using the wrong language.
> The language we use to speak of the world and its creatures, including our-
> selves, has gained a certain analytical power (along with a lot of expertish
> pomp) but has lost the power to designate *what* is being analyzed or convey
> any respect or care or affection or devotion towards it. Cloning, to use the
> most obvious example, is not a way to improve sheep. On the contrary, it is
> a way to stall the sheep's lineage and make it unimprovable. (W. Berry,
> 1999, p. 4)

Once we move from the *question of kinds* to the *question of laws*, we move away from conditions of kinship and kindness and affection and indigenous relationship and interdependence, to lawlike conditions of monitoring and control and prediction. And, once the outcomes of the manipulation and application of such laws become commodified and commercialized, we have the reordering of things under the auspices of ownership:

> "We work with transgenic salmon and we have a patent on a gene in the fish," said Dr. Garth Fletcher, [A/F Protein Canada] company president. "Although the animal isn't patented, if you have a fish with our gene in it, then we own it." (Evanson, 2000, p. A6)

> "This decision goes far beyond the [onco]mouse," said Michelle Swenarchuk, a lawyer for the Canadian Environmental Law Association, which intervened in the case to argue against the patent. They warned against "the commodification and objectification of life." (Chwialkowska, 2000, p. A6)

Now here is one such monstrous spin, one that Carolus Linnaeus could not have imagined. Linnaeus still strangely believed what we have so much trouble believing, that his search for the great mappings and great lines and lineages were up against something *that was not his.*

Knowledge, in such a case, did not mean "ownership."

But this spells how well we are living out the logic of the great Kantian move, so well suggested by George Grant (1998): "[Immanuel] Kant's dictum 'the mind makes the object' were the words of blessing spoken at the wedding of knowing and production, and should be remembered when we contemplate what is common throughout the world" (p. 1). Here is the great monstrosity: We have a recasting of the grand typologies of Kingdoms and Genera and Species and Subspecies and Families and Kinship Relations and other relations of Kind into relationships of provisional and revocable *Ownership.*

We thus see again a tale where nothing is new except the particular object of attention. The Great Plan is not something we are up against, but something we own (like Meriwether Lewis' well-mapped continent, with no hint of indigenouness beyond our owning), something that has become part of the free-market economy. Let's push this: What Dolly's arrival might finally let us see is that the Great Plan *is* the free-market economy, and *that* Great Plan now has the Great Genetic Map under its unforgiving gaze.

The Great Genetic Map maps something that *is* a commodity. Things become commodities in becoming known.

Hence, John Gray's (1998) description of the movements of economic globalization ring eerily familiar in the present context: "The permanent revolution of the free market denies any authority to the past. It nullifies precedent, it snaps the threads of memory and scatters local knowledge. By privileging individual choice over the common good, it makes relationships revocable and provisional" (pp. 35–36). And, once this occurs, all public relationships are seen to be, not relationships of kind, or of affection, or of place or locality or loyalty or blood obligation, but rather revocable monetary ones whose only obligation is zero-sumness. Once the indigenous communities of relations and kinds are thus destroyed and replaced with commodified relationships of law, issues of monitoring, management, and potential incarceration (zero-tolerance) come to predominate the public (one might say, "public school") realm (Gray, 1998, p. 32). Any attempt to interrupt, for example, the discussion of genetic manipulation with concerns that are other than those of ownership are immediately deemed as belonging to "special interests."

So we get again the great inversion we've seen so often in such mytho-theological projects: The life and lives that give life to the Great Plan become unworthy of its grace unless those lives submit to its revisioning.

After all, we *are* our genetic makeup, aren't we? Surely we are just as much as we are also the customers and clients of each other.

TECHNOLOGICAL ADDENDUM

"No learned or mastered technique can save us from the task of deliberation and decision" (Gadamer, 1983, p. 113). Thomas Jefferson apparently took great pleasure in Meriwether Lewis' map of what the American imagination *can* do henceforth settled, but the expansion it foretold never disturbed the question of whether it *should* occur. No learned or mastered technique can save us from the task of deliberation and decision. However, learned and mastered techniques can all too easily make us believe that the question of deliberation and decision is either unnecessary or obvious.

Recall from earlier that President Clinton cited the "our" of "*our* continent" and "*our* imagination" without qualm or hesitation as if such expansions did not also diminish those for whom this continent was already home and not in need of such beneficent revisioning mappings.

No learned or mastered technique can save us from the task of deliberation and decision, except that this is precisely what learned and mastered techniques seem to do: save us.

Consider: It's no accident that many of the references in this chapter were found online, any more than it is an accident that Richard came upon Dolly and her ways with such ease because of Internet access. It should be said that Richard never completed his science project, at least not in a way commensurate with how it began. He's the sort of kid who loves the vertigo rush of the Idea and hardly ever sees the need to form and fashion a work out of the rough particularities needed to carry it out.

The pedagogical point here is luscious and strange. With the arrival of new technologies into our classrooms, technical questions of "how do they work?" are the least of our worries. The great worry is that these technologies allow our children to "skip school" and bring back into its once-seemingly-secure confines questions that pierce right at the heart of our knowing, what it is for, how its legitimacies might be judged, and so on. The task of pedagogy is now oddly beyond us like it always should have been. No learned or mastered technique can save us from the task of deliberation and decision. In fact, the new technologies are aggravating and highlight the necessity for deliberation and decision, a necessity that, strangely enough, was *there all along*

The incarceration will no longer hold. We will have to learn to face the effacing of what always seemed, but never was, a given.

But here, too, no technique will save us. Now that the Internet has broadened the boundaries of what we and our children *can* do, in our own work, the question of what we *should* do with these new arrivals arises anew. What should we do *now*, as the latest news tells of Dolly's arthritis? Funny how old this news has become as I read this now. Part of the abundant nature of knowledge is that I cannot imagine how strange or how ordinary all this will seem so soon.

Preamble 3:
On Play and Abundance

Animals under various forms of threat—the continuous presence of predators, lack of adequate food, drought, and the like—tend to play less and less. They tend, quite naturally, to revert to those kinds of activities that will aid them in gaining comparative control over their environment, activities that involve little or no risk. They revert, so to speak, to what is tried and true, what is most familiar. (Jardine, 2000, p. 123)

Scarcity is the prototypical certainty: a condition we constantly reproduce by our fervent belief in it. (Cayley, 1992, p. 23)

War tends to make cultures alike whereas peace is that condition under which each culture flourishes in its own incomparable way. From this, it follows that peace cannot be exported; it is inevitably corrupted by transfer, its attempted export means war. (Illich, 1992, p. 17)

War, which makes cultures alike, is all too often used by historians as the framework or skeleton of their narratives. The peaceful enjoyment of that which is not scarce [that which is not under threat, embattled] ... is left in a zone of deep shadow. (Illich, 1992, p. 19)

These are fairly haunting words, and we would be wrong to believe that they are uniquely resonant in these "post-9/11" times. This is an old story. It has long since framed the narrative of education and of our ability to imagine what curriculum might be.

Under regimes of scarcity, options narrow, room for movement is denied, unavailable, even feared. There is little play in the line(s). Things become taut, stretched to the limit, overburdened, heavy and skittery at the same time. We become "on edge." Under various forms of threat, we begin to scout the borders and boundaries for incursions. We become wary, hunkered down. We become more and more concerned with security, accountability, monitoring, and management. But, more than this, the field *within which* security can occur itself retracts—our living space becomes less generous, less forgiving, less variegated, less open to interpretation, shall we say, because generosity, forgiveness, and variegation might, under threat, be potentially harmful to security, even fatal. The interpretation of things that is allowed is the one established from *within* that which has been bounded.

As we've heard so many teachers and student teachers say, with great and terrible warrant, "It's about survival out there." And so, the rich and play-filled fields within which we might deeply desire to wander at our leisure (*schola*, the root of "school" and "scholar") become "out of bounds." The side trails and old ways in which we might come upon seasonal tree shadows, or patterned and constructed mathematical handiworks, or the gambolling arrival of Dolly the sheep must not only be foregone. They seem like little more than Romantic fantasies of a bygone era, child dreams. This is, in the language of schools, *the trenches*. The Pythagorean theorem, for the sake of survival, must be stripped to the manageable and monitorable application of the formula to various presecured and precleared test cases. Only thus is it safe. Dolly the sheep becomes just a silly example of an individual student's exuberance, which might be tolerable were there not so much to cover, so little time, so few resources. As a consequence, and as Illich suggested regarding war, we become more alike when we are deemed to "understand" the Pythagorean theorem under such a siege. Under the siege of scarcity the criteria of natural and human-made structures becomes unilateral—unquestionably *the same* for all. Questioning what is thus unilaterally understood is terrifying. Curriculum, schooling, teaching, learning, children, knowledge, accountability, obligation, good work, thoughtfulness, character, insiders, outsiders, discipline—all of this becomes cast under the pall of what David Smith (1999c) chillingly named "monstrous states of siege" (p. 140). The only peace that is possible is enforced, unilateral, imposed pacification.

"Left in peace" (Illich, 1992, p. 16), however, tree shadows appear.

Left in peace, we can overhear the words (and not just from the young) "Come on, let's play."

Any teacher or parent knows the depth and beauty and pedagogical power of the energies that can be released by such an invitation. An invitation to play is an invitation into a "horizon of ... still undecided future possibilities" (Gadamer, 1989, p. 112). The invitation "let's" opens up "a world into which we ourselves are drawn" (Gadamer, 1994, p. 192), a world whose abundance goes beyond our own agency and knowledge and experience. From the point of view of scarcity, such an invitation or draw feels like an invitation to chaos. It is not. It is a sign that the living character of knowledge is precisely that, living, full of inheritances and movement and as-yet-undecided questions. Mathematicians know about such a "draw" even though "school-math," under the auspices of scarcity, may have forgotten this territory. As the work of both Johan Huizinga and Hans-Georg Gadamer demonstrates so vividly, play, *Spiel,* is not a chaotic, unbounded space, but is full of character, full of characters. It is an open wisdom and open way in the world. That boy with his toes on tree shadows knew, as we mentioned in Preamble 2, that "something is going on (*im Spiele ist*), something is happening (*sich abspielt*)" (Gadamer, 1989, p. 104). He was, so to speak, "onto" something, he (and, too, Anh Linh and Richard) was being drawn into an abundant and venturous play space *(Spielraum)*, but that space was full of ancestors, ghosts, inheritances, bloodlines, comforts, faces, dates and names and kindred spirits, ongoing contestations, and conversations that are still happening. It is precisely this sense of entering a world larger than ourselves that portends the freedom and ease experienced in playing. We are, so to speak, released from our own subjectivity, our own concerns, our own limits, and find ourselves taken up into a world of possibilities and we can deeply experience our own agency in the midst of such matters. Elementary school students have shown us, over and over again, how invigorated they become in knowing that this *Spiel* that they have come upon is real.

It is possible, therefore, to imagine Dolly the sheep's arrival at school one day (see chap. 2) or the hovering of Pythagoras' ghost (see the Introduction and chap. 1) as precisely this sort of invitation—to enter into what is "in play," to enter into what is possible, living, and unforeseen in this science curriculum mandate regarding structures and their origins, or in the blossoming consequences of Pythagorean theorem in tree shadows or the construction of two- and three-dimensional shapes. It is possible, therefore, to imagine the work of teaching as the work of exploring what it is that is so abundantly inviting regarding a particular curriculum topic and practicing the art of such invitation here, now, with these children. Because, of course, the students we face will have something to say about the nature, limits, and efficacy of that invitation. They will also have something to say about where they might want to go in order to follow up such invitations. They just might want to do Dolly the sheep. Whatever choice the next child makes, teachers have to be able—dare we use this language?—to make a good pedagogical judgment about that choice. The only way to do this is for teachers to become experienced in the places into which we invite our students. You can't experience "I want to do Dolly the sheep" as a compelling, scientifically powerful and challenging choice if you don't know much about such matters. It takes experience to be able to experience the "play" in such a choice of project topics.

Thus, to ask "What is it that is 'in play' in this or that curriculum topic?" is to ask after its abundance, and to let Anh Linh continue as long as she did with her exploration of two- and three-dimensional shapes is to place pedagogical hope in such abundance and to constantly draw out its deeply geometrical, ancestral *Spiel*. "To play" is somehow "to let."

"Let's play!"

"Let's" means we have to let go of the stringencies portended by scarcity. It's not about survival.

So who would have thought that such a playful invitation not only appears in, but is, in fact, fundamental and basic and central to, of all things, Grade 9 algebra.

Chapter 3

"Let Eric's Age Be 'X'": A Brief Mathematical Phenomenology

David W. Jardine

I

Eric's family has three members: Eric, his father David, and his mother Gail. David is 2 years older than three times as old as Eric. Gail is 17 years older than the difference between David's age and Eric's age. Altogether, they have lived 111 years. How old are Eric and his family members?

Many of us—myself included—must first stop hyperventilating before we can even read on. Mathematics (so-called) "story problems" such as the one just cited represent a precisely identifiable and recognizable form of panic, urgency, and bewilderment that is an oddly shared experience of schooling in North America, Europe, and, through the beneficent dispensations of these centers of educational imagination, worldwide. And, if this simple example is not enough to exhaust and set the teeth on edge, consider:

David, here are some variations on the theme of Eric's father:

1. Person A is now some # times as old as person B. In some # years, person A will be some # times as old as person B will be then. Find their present ages.

2. Person A is some # years old and person B is some # years old. How many years ago was Person A some # times as old as Person B?

3. Person A is some # years older than person B. In some # years, Person A will be some # times as old as person B will be then. What are their present ages?

4. Person A is some # times as old as person B. Some # years ago, person A was some # times as old as person B was then. Find their present ages.

5. Person A is now some # years old and person B is some # years old. In how many years will person A be some # times as old as person B?

6. The sum of person A's age and person B's age is some # year(s). In some # year(s) from now, person A's age will be some # times person B's age some # years ago. Find their present ages.

7. Eric's father is some # times as old as Eric. In some # years, Eric's father will be some # times as old as Eric. What are their ages?

8. Some # year(s) ago, Person A was some # times as old as Person B is now. Some # years ago, Person A was some # times as old as Person B will be in some # years. How old are they now?

9. In some # year(s), some # times Person A's age will be some # less than Person B's age now. Person B's age in some # years will be some # times what Person A's age was some # years ago. Find their ages now.

10. A person has two friends. The person's age is some # times the sum of the friend's ages. Some # years from now, the person's age will be some # times the age of the youngest friend, and it will be some # times the sum of the friend's ages. Find their ages now.

11. The square of a person's age is some # less than some # times his age. How old is the person? (Friesen, 2003)

These odd pedaeo-mathematical formations have become the butt of many a joke. In fact, Gary Larson, in his now-retired *The Far Side* comic strip, has, in two different cartoons, given us a glimpse of just how broad and grand are such panics. In one cartoon, Hell's Library is a shelf-full of story-problem books; and in another, a great, final question that Saint Peter seeks an answer to as our final test on the way through the gates of Heaven begins something like this: "Jane leaves the train station heading west...."

Heaven and Hell, indeed. Such story problems are reported to be the beginning of the end for many of the hundreds of student teachers I have taught in courses on "Elementary School Curriculum Methods." Many times in these classes, simply putting the word "mathematics" on the chalkboard in the university classroom has brought tears. There is perhaps no mere coincidence here, these invocations of Heaven and Hell—the terrible sense of *demand*, of something being desperately at stake and feeling totally helpless, almost *guilty*, in the face of all this.

How can we deny feeling spotted, witnessed, called out, by such questions? Even in reading the first few words of this story problem, things tighten, ears plug, and there grows an unbearable sense of fixity, immobility and incompetence—almost unworthiness. There is something experientially unique here. We don't confront simply a lack of knowledge. Nor do we confront a question that is simply and easily a matter of indifference. Consider.

Even in the confines of an important examination, when I am asked "What is the capital of Canada?" I realize that, even if I don't know the correct answer ("Ottawa," for those of you who can't bear the suspense), I do experience a sense, so to speak, of possible, if not actual, "recourse." I *could* find out, I *could* have remembered, even though I haven't actually done either in time for this question's arrival. There is thus some "room" around my not-knowing the answer, some sense of space and possibility, however dire may be the consequences of my having not pursued this possibility in this examination instance.

Experientially, with a question like "How old are Eric and his family members?" *there is no experience of recourse,* there is, it seems, no "way." Differently put, there is no way in the world I can begin to answer this question because I no longer experience myself as in the world: I am singled out by this question, isolated, alone, without worldly recourse, support, or sustenance. There is no experience of recourse (for those of us panicking) because the question itself is *precisely about recourse* and the response required is *precisely the opposite, experientially, of the spot I find myself now in*—this place of enclosure, paranoia, demand, immobility, singularity, personal culpability, and, so to speak, "stuckness."

Here is the terrible problem: Mathematically speaking, in order to even *begin* answering this question, and right in the middle of this stuckness, I must somehow *give myself recourse* in order to proceed.

II

In order to proceed beyond this place of great and traumatic demand, a place of great holding-on and hesitancy and withdrawal, I must first somehow *let.*

I must, in a great act of intervention, a great act of agency and confidence and determination, "*Let* Eric's age be 'x'."

It is vital, first of all, to glimpse the experience of agency here. At first, I experience that all the agency seems to be issuing from this question, not upon it. The question seems to bear down upon me, demanding, asking, and as the force of such bearing increases, my experience of my own forbearance and agency in fact decreases. I experience what many who despise mathematics experience as its *horror,* and many who love mathematics experience as its *relief.* What is meant here is this.

Over and over again, in elementary mathematics methods classes, the answer to what is despised and what is loved is the same: *There already is a hidden solution copresent in this question.*

Those who despise mathematics find this hidden copresence unbearable: There already is an answer and I don't have it and can't find the recourse to it and it knows of my weakness and sits there in judgment, already perfect, already complete and answered. Things are therefore not well, I am unable, disabled, stuck.

Those who love mathematics find *the very same copresence* a relief: There already is an answer and I don't have it and therefore, my own agency is not experienced as at stake here. If I proceed carefully, I already know that things will be fine, more strongly put, that things are already fine without my own findings.

It is important to note, however, that in the case cited previously, when those at ease with mathematics easily "Let Eric's age be 'x,'" this is not just an act of agency and confidence and determination. It is an act of humility and acceptance: I must let what I do not know, what I have not yet determined, stand there *as* indeterminate. When I let Eric's age be "x," I let my own troubles stand as yet-to-be-determined (an as-yet-to-be-determined "x" [Jardine et al., 2003, pp. 133–136]), but when I let my troubles stand as yet-to-be-determined, I let them stand out into the confluence of (themselves yet-to-be-determined) *mathematical* determinations. My troubles become disburdened from their terrible proximity to me and my agency and ability. These aren't *my* troubles. They are *mathematical troubles*. My at-first seemingly personal troubles find a world through such indeterminacy. They are let loose into the *world* of mathematics, a world to which I now belong, a world that can take care of my troubles, a place where those troubles can be worked *out*, not just worked *on*.

Thus, phenomenologically, right in the midst of a heralding act of agency ("letting"), I also forgo my agency at the very same time. By "letting (Eric's age be 'x')," I act and also at once let go of my self as the *topic* of such action. I get "myself" out of the line of sight.

By letting Eric's age be "x," I *create* an indeterminacy whose value will remain constant ("x" will, in this territory, always be the very self-same "x") but whose value is as-yet unknown. To know the way to proceed, I must trust the constancy of something undetermined, unknown except in this one sense: "x" is what it is and will not betray this self-identity, even though I do not know *what* it self-identically *is*. A very strange sort of exploration thus arises: This "x" will be "x," and I am able, around this point of undeterminedness, to uncover a whole world of relations. And, in uncovering this world of relations, I will, slowly and purposefully, discover what this undetermined "x" is. By turning away from it, I return to it. But only if I "let."

If I let Eric's age be "x," what begins is a sense of yet-to-be-determined *interrelatedness*: Suddenly, David's age and Gail's age both become equally as-yet-undetermined, but they are both now *related* to the indeterminateness of Eric's age. Thus it begins, an issuance of interrelatedness from this "let."

III

Let Eric's age be "x."

David's age is three times Eric's age (x) plus two years: $3x + 2$.

Gail's age is the difference between David's age $(3x + 2)$ and Eric's age (x) plus 17 years: $(3x + 2) - (x) + 17 = 2x + 2 + 17 = 2x + 19$.

So now, having "let," Eric's age (x) plus David's age (3x + 2) plus Gail's age (2x + 19), totaling 111 years, becomes thus:

$$x + 3x + 2 + 2x + 19 + = 111$$

Therefore:

$$6x + 21 = 111$$

Therefore:

$$6x = 90$$

Therefore:

$$x = 15.$$

And, therefore, reading this backward through the question: Eric (= "x") is 15 years old, David is three times this plus 2 years (47) and Gail is twice this plus 19 years (49).
And:

$$15 + 47 + 49 = 111.$$

Tracing the movement of determination, then, we have this. We let Eric's age be "x," and from this, produced definitions of the undetermined value of David's and Gail's ages (3x + 2 and 2x + 19, respectively). The open space of indeterminancy of "x" thus had to come to define *all of the undetermined factors,* Eric's, David's, and Gail's ages. We all gathered together in our indeterminancy around a common factor, some common "x" that is yet to be determined. We then related the total of these three undetermined quantities to a known quantity (111) and then determined "x." Suddenly, then, all three ages were understandable, because the undetermined "x" around which all three undetermined ages were gathered is now determined. Set forth a let. Gather all undetermined things around what has been thus let. Relate this gathering to something determined. Determine the original let and its gathered dispensation.

IV

Of course! It all seems so easy *after* the event of "letting." Once we "let," the whole matter unwinds. But we must remember, here, the pre-"letting" terrors: Right at the moment when many students feel most threatened, we ask them to give themselves play space, give themselves room, give themselves a break, relax. We ask them to forgive, to let go, right in their moment of vulnerability and fear:

> Animals under various forms of threat—the continuous presence of preda-
> tors, lack of adequate food, drought, and the like—tend to play less and less.
> They tend, quite naturally, to revert to those kinds of activities that will aid
> them in gaining comparative control over their environment, activities that
> involve little or no risk. They revert, so to speak, to what is tried and true,
> what is most familiar. (Jardine, 2000, p. 123)

This brief phenomenology points to how, in the movement of withdrawal, reversion, and retreat, it is so easy to lose the very recourse that mathematics often requires: a worldly recourse, a recourse into a world of relations that has its own *Spiel*, its own life beyond the paranoid enclosures of a threatened subjectivity:

> This sounds rather arcane, but it simply points to a commonplace experi-
> ence: those moments when we know that "something is going on," ([*im Spiele
> ist*] Gadamer, 1989, p. 104), "something is happening" ([*sich abspielt*], p. 104),
> something is "at play," here, in this place and it has something to ask *of me* be-
> yond what I might imagine asking of it. Rich and memorable experiences ask
> things of us, and, as such, they are characterizable as "more a passion than an
> action. A question *presses itself upon us*" (1989, p. 366, our emphasis). Such ex-
> periences-as-sojourns-to-a-place take the form of a "momentary loss of self"
> (Gadamer, 1977, p. 51). (Jardine et al., 2003, p. 86)

It is, in this case, "letting" that lets this sojourn begin. But, as this passage suggests, those students who are easily terrorized by mathematics may have a point: It does require understanding that mathematics is a living place, a living field of relations, and that to make our way into it requires a momentary sense of loss, of giving oneself over to *its* ways by "letting."

V

"Momentary loss of self?" Hardly. In the panic felt over the presentation of "story problems," I fully understand that the real topic of the problem is *me* and *whether I know what to do* and *whether I am going to succeed*. Story problems are thus not *mathematical problems*. They are pedagogical tests. As soon as we see this problem, we know right away that we are not doing mathematics. Rather, we are in school.

VI

The term "story" here itself requires phenomenological investigation, for here, "story" becomes an in-fact-irrelevant "carrier" for a mathematical phenomenon in relation to which the story is, in fact, not only dull and unin-teresting but *irrelevant*. After all, if you want to know how old Eric is, ask me and I'll tell you, if it is any of your business, and why do you want to know, anyway? Anyone who reads that original problem knows full well that the example is not relevant. The example is simply a "site" at which to practice and master a certain mathematical way of thinking. Eric's age is not important except as an example of something in relation to which Eric and his age are irrelevant. And we know this right away. This isn't about Eric. So we are asked to "see through" the surface story to its underlying form or mechanism, a form or mechanism that is also at work in "Jane leaves the train station heading West...." This is what it means, in mathematics class, to "understand" the story of Eric and his age. Thus, a paradox.

We use the example of Eric or Jane in order to give the mathematical phenomenon body and shape and concreteness, but the insight required in the face of these two examples is precisely one of overcoming such embodiment, shapeliness, and concreteness—seeing through to the mathematical operations. A deeper paradox is this. We use the Eric and Jane examples in order to make the problem "relevant to the students" when students know full well that the examples are irrelevant and that the pretense to relevance is precisely that and nothing more.

END BIT

There is, however, a much more interesting, much more *mathematical* story at work here, a story that is profoundly mathematically relevant. It's a story about "letting."

This story is traceable in many high school mathematics textbooks. When we read the lists of questions of this sort, they begin with statements like "Let Eric's age be 'x'" as part of the question asked. Then, slowly, these statements disappear *as if* it has now become obvious that you, the reader, must "let."

What am I doing when I "let"? How do you know what to "let"? There is a great tale at work here, with great figures and faces, great agencies and desires, great needs. Much more interesting than Eric and his age, or Jane and her train station.

And, of course, and by the way, it would be most sensible, when confronted with questions of Eric and his age, to just ask him or his parents.

Preamble 4:
Do They or Don't They?

During my (D. J.) PhD dissertation defense, a member of the examining committee was becoming very frustrated with the ways in which I seemed to be evading his straightforward questions. This frustration had been evident in his margin notes to the copy of the text he had read months before: He wrote of "spinning webs" and of "demons" bent on deception. Very interesting language from someone who now wanted straightforward answers to straightforward questions. but the origin of such images is understandable, as we shall see.

The dissertation was an interpretive reading of the work of Jean Piaget, a topic I've since returned to in great detail (Jardine, 2006). Out of this committee member's frustration came the seemingly straightforward demand: "I want a yes or no answer. Do children go through stages of cognitive development, or don't they? Yes or no?"

The question seemed to issue from a place of great seriousness and concern, and, at first, it seemed as if being able to answer "yes" or "no" was a sign of great thoughtfulness and knowledgeability. The answer I gave felt hesitant and unsure of itself, almost embarrassed by its own timidity in the face of such apparent strength of purpose and pursuit.

My answer was, of course, rather long and convoluted and was clearly prone to the accusation that it avoided the question altogether. It involved exploring the fact that images of stages and progress were not simply empirical descriptions of states of objective affairs but were inevitably great and troublesome inheritances, great imaginal territories, full of old blood and great precedents that go far beyond the ken of the yes-or-no findings of empirical investigation. Empirical investigations of the stages of cognitive development in children (like those pursued by Jean Piaget) *seemed to* require putting aside all of this weird abundance, all these old tales, these complex webs, and only speaking about those matters that follow from the methods of that logico-mathematically based empirical pursuit (see chap. 9). Piaget's pursuits appeared to be a matter of getting down to business—the business of what is "really" going on (as far as can be determined by the methods of objective science and within the limits that these methods entailed). I wanted to show how these ghosts and ancestries, seemingly banished by the methods of genetic epistemology, were still at work in Jean Piaget's work, especially before his work landed in North America and was subjected to a purifying purge of its imaginal character. (Under the influence of American psychology, Piaget and his followers simply stopped talking to children and set up, instead, "experiments" that just required "observation.")

Both the presumption-laden conversations he had with children and the great Greco-European intellectual atmosphere that surrounded the erupting human sciences at the beginning of the 20th century slowly came to seem like great invasions and defilements of the objectivity of Piaget's work and the work of his followers. It was like some border had been breeched, like some methodological purity had been suddenly contaminated by the appearance of invasive little demons, spinning webs bent on deception.

In retrospect, that dissertation wasn't really that good, but this delicious question—"do they or don't they?"—still haunts. In our abundant human inheritance, images of stages, progress, and development hold a great sway in our imagination. To the extent that such images are limited to empirical questions of their objective application, development, for example, becomes impoverished. Instead of its vivid invocation of great ancestries, it becomes a way in which, for example, to control and manage schooled affairs. With reading, for example, many elementary schools end up having files full of little developmentally color-coded "readers," each of which has been specifically designed to developmentally follow the others, but no one of which contains a story that is actually worth reading. "Development" and "stages" have come to mean, in practice, that we present children with sequenced mathematics worksheets, each geared to the development and practice of an isolated skill (adding, subtracting, adding two-digit numbers, and so on) when in fact, in the world of mathematics, no such isolation actually exists. In both these cases, the world of language and the world of mathematics are subjected to what could be called a *developmental breakdown*, the very sort of breakdown that is requisite of the sort of control and management required by regimes of scarcity. Reading and mathematics become scarce commodities that have to be doled out in proper measure to children who are themselves premeasured as having a sequence of developmental needs.

In this way, our understanding of the great contributions of Jean Piaget's work—the abundant worlds of development, progress, recapitulation, and the search for origins that it invokes as a living part of our human inheritance—becomes impoverished by the question "do they or don't they?" Piaget's work becomes lean territory and teachers become ravenous for the next set of promised developmentally appropriate materials.

In the midst of Piagetian theory itself, however, lies great abundance, an abundance that outstrips the paucity of the question of "do they or don't they?" Treated interpretively, Piaget's work reveals great inheritances, great arcs of thought. Just like the innocent invocation of Dolly the sheep, what comes out to play outplays us, and it is in this that we take great pedagogical pleasure, as we would in any great tale.

The chapter that follows follows one such *Spiel,* and it is as old as the hills—the great desire for origins, for the beginning, for, as we might say in education, "the basics."

Chapter 4

Welcoming the Old Man Home: Meditations on Jean Piaget, Interpretation, and the "Nostalgia for the 'Original'"

David W. Jardine

> *No sooner have you grabbed hold of it than myth opens out into a fan of a thousand segments. Here the variant is the origin. In each of these diverging stories all the others are reflected, all brush by us like folds of the same cloth. If, out of some perversity of tradition, only one version of some mythical event has come down to us, it is like a body without a shadow, and we must do our best to trace out that invisible shadow.*
>
> —Roberto Calasso (*The Marriage of Cadmus and Harmony*, 1993)

I

Jean Piaget's work has long since entered the grain of pedagogy and it has taken on a soft patina—it has aged, softened, become more forgiving, less full of the harsh, bright certainties requisite of "the concepts and categories of established science" (Inhelder, 1969, p. 23). Through its aging, this work has assumed the character of a tale told, a commonplace and kindly response to the question "What's the story about children and growing up and our task as teachers?" Through their aging, the images and figures from Piaget's work have come form what we now see as the commonplace story of children and classrooms.

The "fact" that children go through stages and that one must be sensitive to "where the child is at," the expectation that individual children will be at "different levels of development" in a class, the related idea of the importance of (developmentally) appropriate materials and curricular expectations, the commonplaceness of talk of "developmentally appropriate practice," the belief that young children learn through the concrete and active manipulation of objects (a thread of "hands on learning"): All of these beliefs about and insights into the nature of children and pedagogy suggest the breadth of Piaget's legacy. These tales also have a life and a vigor independent of the empirical verifiability of various features of his theories (and all the quarrels between Piaget's friends and enemies that result). They form a sort of cosmology—constellations of fundamental tales about how pedagogy might be formed and fashioned, how life is between the old and the young, the movement between them, and the permutations and transformations in the worlds they mutually inhabit.

But as Roberto Calasso (1993) suggests, such tales are haunted by invisible shadows: "Stories never live alone. They are part of a family which we must trace back and forth" (p. 13). To trace these invisible shadows, we must avoid taking Piaget's work at face value and free ourselves of the questions that, as a "scientific" enterprise, drive Piaget's work itself—questions regarding the correspondence of his and his followers' claims to name and sequence objective affairs in the world. Rather, we must read his work as a cluster of odd, occluded signs that point a way in to an underworld of multifarious interweaving tales to which Piaget's work bears a "kinship" or "family resemblance" (Wittgenstein, 1968, pp. 32, 38). To be understood interpretively rather than literally, Piaget's work must be placed back into all its relations.

Jean Piaget does, of course, provide us with tales of the young and their rites of passage, tales of stages and transitions, tales of continuities and discontinuities in the journey of one's life, tales of quests for "the origin" (1952) or "the beginning," or of "genesis" (1968). He describes our need to repeat such quests if our lives are to have meaning with tales of "life" (1965) or "spirit" (1977) caught in the circular-reactive-instinctual animality of the flesh and struggling for release, tales of "missions" (1977) and "destinies" (1952), tales of space (with Inhelder, 1998), time (1969), memory and identity (1971b), dreams (1962) and reality (1971b) and stars and suns (1974a).

This can be murky territory, especially if one grows accustomed to the harsh rational brightness of educational philosophy, rooted as it tends to be in modernist dreams of clarity and mathematical precision that have lost their earthly beginnings. In his way, Piaget asks us to walk this terrain: His earlier works (1971b, 1972, 1974a, 1974b) are full of the rich tales that children tell that, if we take them seriously, complement our own tales and give them depth, dimensionality, direction, and hope. But, sad to say, Piaget tends finally to turn on these tales under the compulsion of an early 20th-century version of "objective science." These lovely tales of dreams coming from the night, dreams that are not in me because I am in them (Piaget, 1974a), turn out, under the lens of science, to be "exceedingly suggestive deformations of true conceptions" (p. 50).

What we need here is a sort of interpretive courage. We could simply turn our backs on the old man and his tongue-clucking reprimands of the young. We could dismiss him for his objectivist condescension. Or we could, as interpretation requires, read his work more generously than he might read it himself. We could, in short, do our best to welcome the old man home.

If we enter this imaginal, interpretive territory and refuse to let the patriarchal voice silence or demean all its kin *and* refuse to turn our backs on the tales the old man might be telling in spite of himself and his angers, Piaget's work takes on a strange allure. It evokes a dark, instinctual memory of near-forgotten words and worlds. We feel an odd shock of recognition: We have heard these tales before.

Tracing such invisible shadows requires the deliteralizing (Hillman, 1989) movement of interpretation—an opening up of texts to the multifarious voices and figures and possibilities and relations hushed within them. Through such interpretive work, we can slowly discern kinships we had forgotten and recollect family ties and resemblances once severed, dispersed, or denied. Interpretation thus moves against the diaspora implicit in literalism—that is, the separating and scattering of ambiguous kinships and family resemblances that occur when we claim for any one tale the status of "the literal" or "original" so that all others become mere ghosts, ignorable in favor of the one true voice.

Interpretation works against this modernist and vaguely Platonic notion of "originality," this monotheistic, monological idea in which the variant is no longer the original but is only a dim-witted remembrance. Interpretation, as Thompson (1981) noted, requires that we "ignore the orthodox who labour so patiently trying to eliminate the apocryphal variants from the one true text. For us a legend or a *midrash* may be a greater opening to the archetypical world than the overly refined redactions of the urban priestly intelligentsia. There is no one true version of which all the others are but copies or distortions. Every version belongs to the myth" (pp. 11–12). Or, as Trin Minh-ha (1994) suggested: "For scarcely has an important event been experienced before men, always eager to act as theoretical policemen, begin to speak out, to formulate theoretical epilogues, and to break the silence ... here silence is precisely the sum of the voices of everyone, the equivalent of the sum of our collective breathing" (p. 24).

Accordingly in interpretive work, the only "one true version" of a tale, the only "original," is all the versions, each brushing by each of the others like folds of the same cloth, the same weave, the same original text. Each version of a tale must be read into and out of all of the others. Thus each version makes every other fuller and more complete and healthy and saner than it might have been alone.

But another twist is essential to understanding interpretive work: "The whole" (e.g., "the whole idea of an 'origin' and the quest for it") is never given (Gadamer, 1989), never fully or finally "present" and therefore never fully or finally utterable, describable, nameable, or knowable. This "absence" (one might call it) does not reflect simply the nested complexities involved—the task of reading every particular in and out of every other is already impossible. It is not occur simply because I, too, bear many of these versions in my very breath, so that the reading I pursue always bears the traces of just here, just this fragile life and no other.

Both of these reasons might suffice for a postmodern critique of givenness or presence, but this is still too halting a reading of the absence hermeneutics requires. In hermeneutics, the whole is never given because new "stubborn particulars" (Jardine, 1995; Wallace, 1987) continually arrive in the world. Hermeneutics and the absence it courts is thus inevitably linked to "the fact of natality" (Arendt, 1969) and is from there immediately linked to the character of pedagogy itself, waiting as pedagogy does at the moments of arrival, to see how the new will evoke the ancestors in ways irretrievably different than they would have been without just this child, just that voice, just that little revelatory citation.

"The original" in its wholeness is always just arriving and with each variation has always just arrived. This paradoxical formulation is necessary because, despite the relentless arrivals, *this* tale about "the origin" and *that one*, interpretively taken up, are, too, "the original tale of 'the origin,'" graciously adding themselves to what we will now understand the whole matter to have always been about. All these three moves—the impossibility of reading each into each, the presence of my hands in this writing, and the arrival of the young—constitute the hermeneutic dance of a part and a whole never fully given. Baffled by this absence and caught, as well, in a faith in its promise, hermeneutics too is full of a "nostalgia for the original."

But here is the difficult work and the shocking admission. Even William Irwin Thompson's previously cited "overly refined redactions of the urban priestly intelligentsia," even Trin Minh-Ha's utterances of "theoretical policemen" are themselves *midrashim*, even if they refuse to understand themselves as such, even if precisely these ones deny the generative arrival of new voices.

Even when Piaget himself speaks against such a generous relation to all his relations, and suggests that "a single truth alone is acceptable when we are dealing with knowledge in the strictest sense" (1965, pp. 216–217), we can avoid the problem of accepting or rejecting this claim. We can resist his attempt to draw us helplessly into this old philosophical argument and its angers. Rather, Piaget's claim about the singularity of truth itself bears the darker, more difficult "truth" of similitude: The claim aligns his work with many old monologics, monotheisms, and fundamentalisms, each claiming for itself ethical or epistemological precedence and thus representational power (J. Clifford, 1986) over all the rest. Piaget's claim regarding the singular character of truth thus has a multivocal, interpretive "truth" to it: This, too, is an old story we have often heard before.

II

Why pursue such a reading of Piaget?

Taken literally, Piagetian talk of "the origin" and all his claims to objectivistic exclusivity become a "perversity of tradition" (Calasso, 1993). Literally cast, his theory loses its sense of place and relation, having pushed away all the other voices as superfluous or contaminative or immature or deformed or underdeveloped. Bereft of such familial relations, it becomes disproportionate or monstrous (Jardine, 1994c; see Preamble 7 and chap. 7) or, like an alcoholic father, violent and fearsome, hating all its relations for not living up to some queer image of the true and its singularity. The child's tales or tales from other times and places—see Piaget's (1968) bewildering and enticing paralleling of ontogeny and phylogeny—become little more than objects to be submitted to the will of a develop mental discourse in which the child remains unable to participate fully without eventual ridicule, itself a perfect parallel of the colonial ridicule of "primitive" cultures (Jardine, 1992b; Nandy, 1987). Understood literally, Inhelder's (1969) "the concepts and categories of established science" do not seriously require the continuing presence of the child's versions of the world and their various articulations except as a dim-witted remembrance of how its own one true version finally safely arrived to replace them all with what Piaget (1973) called their "perfection" (p. 7) in the machinations of objective science.

Taken interpretively, Piaget's work becomes returned to the full range of all the intergenerational voices that have also spoken of sun and moon and stars. We find ourselves inhabiting an ecological and imaginal space generous enough to include ourselves and our children, our Earth, and those many voices that read our lives back to us in ways we could not by ourselves. In such an interpretive space, Piaget's work comes to stand in the midst of and in the witnessing presence of all other versions and voices, and the old man must face all his relations and all the generations that have brought him here. To be welcomed home, the old man needs to learn to listen and not just ceaselessly speak.

Loosing the centrifugal hold of literalism might thus allow the tales that engulf us and that form us "beyond our wanting and doing" (Gadamer, 1989, p. xxviii) to become more open and generous, to take themselves less seriously, and therefore, to let us appreciate their humanity, humility, and humor. It might allow us to see other tales as our kin and our own tales as full of relations. It might allow for relations of generosity and kindness to emerge, rather than the degeneration and violence inherent in "a single truth alone."

As it turns out—and this may be painful—Jean Piaget is one of us, however contested and difficult this "us" may be.

III

[At the end of the nineteenth century] all Western historiography was obsessed with the quest of *origins*. "Origin and development" of something became almost a cliche. Great scholars wrote about the origin of language, of human societies, of art, of institutions, of the Indo-Aryan races, and so on. Suffice it to say that this search for the origins of human institutions and cultural creations prolongs and completes the naturalist's quest for the origin of the species, the biologist's dream of grasping the origin of life, the geologist's and astronomer's endeavour to understand the origin of the Earth and the Universe. One can decipher here the same nostalgia for the "primordial" and the "original." (Eliade, 1968, p. 44)

We can read the work of Jean Piaget as a grand reiteration of an old tale—a profound "nostalgia for the original" that typifies countless efforts throughout the text and texture of human life. "Returning to the origin"—for example, the *Origins of Intelligence in Children* (Piaget, 1952)—expresses every spiritual tradition in swirling, contested ways. We feel it in the blur of new faces at the beginning of the school year, in the passing of the winter solstice and the return of light, in a display of Hanukkah candles, or in the spectacle of a bloody new baby rebirthing the Earth again. But we find another old tale buried here too in Jean Piaget's answer to the question of origins. Consider the following passages from his very early work (written around 1915, first published in English translation, 1977) entitled *The Mission of the Idea:*

The good is life. Life is a force which penetrates matter, organizes it, introduces harmony, love. Everywhere life brings harmony, solidarity in the new and vaster units that it creates. Life is good, but the individual pursuing his self-interest renders it bad. Every individual instinctively, unconsciously serves its species, serves life. But self-interest may lead the individual to keep for himself some of the vital energy which he might bring to others. One day intelligence appeared, illuminated life, opened new domains to mankind, and through him God thought to attain His ends. But here again self-interest appeared, now armed with reason. Life is threatened, instinct evolves and is transformed into a sacred feeling which sets man on the right path again, and brings him back to God. But man, having tasted of the fruits of the tree of life, remains caught in this conflict between self-interest and renunciation. (pp. 29–31)

This wonderful image of "life" as the Origin that collects us all appears throughout Piaget's work if, that is, we allow ourselves to understand his work interpretively. But a complex nest of relations to interpretation exists here (just when we thought we might have been able to straightforwardly venture into Piaget's work itself). "Life-as-originative" in Piaget's theory is not simply an "object" of hermeneutic interpretation. Rather, the idea of life-as-originative percolates up through Edmund Husserl's (1970) work and the phenomenological concepts of "lived experience" and "life world" that underwrite much contemporary curriculum theory discourse. This phenomenological figuring of human life also informs, in a different version, the work of Hans-Georg Gadamer, one of the originators of contemporary hermeneutics.

Gadamer's *Truth and Method* (1989) both provides an hermeneutic exploration of this eighteenth- and nineteenth-century phenomenon of life and helps us see why Jean Piaget (1965) would evoke Henri Bergson's *elan vital* as an origin of his own work in genetic epistemology (p. 6). We get a sense, as well, that this phenomenon of life, like phenomenology itself (Jardine, 1992e), is also a *source* for hermeneutics found in the evocation of Hermes as a flighty young boy (Smith, 1999c), full of life and vigor and fecundity (Gadamer, 1989; Jardine, 1992a), who portends generative boundary breaching as the origin of understanding and therefore of pedagogy. (Incidentally, Coyote, the figure of folklore who teaches but never learns, also skirts boundaries [P. Clifford, Friesen, & Jardine, 2003]. Here, again, the variant is the original. It is not that Coyote *is* Hermes [or isn't—this isn't a matter of "do they or don't they"]; rather, "this is a story about that, this is *like* that" [J. Clifford, 1986]. The relations are of likeness and kind, family resemblances.)

We must try again to draw a bit closer.

What is first and generative and originary in Piaget's (1952) work is less a set of structures or categories, than a set of vital functions: assimilation, accommodation, and equilibration. Thus the structures evident in the life of the developing child are hardly fixed and unchanging from birth; rather, they are "the products of a continuous activity which is immanent in them and of which they constitute the sequential moments of crystallization" (p. 388). The developmental sequence of structures in Piaget's work is a sequence of plateaus of equilibrium and stability in the organization of the functions of assimilation and accommodation. Structures are thus like plateaus of alert and active calmness, places where I might be held up in grace by all my relations. The movement "life itself" is, moreover, defined as a "progressive equilibrium" (p. 7).

Piaget's invariant, functional a priori of "life itself" (1952, p. 19) remains continuous throughout development and throughout the changes of structure or developmental level. In fact, he (1971a) claimed that "the essential fact concerning this functioning is its absolute continuity" (p. 140). He also uses the terms "functional identity," "functional analogy," "functional invariants," and "functional correspondence" to describe these continuities (1952, 1971a). In all my Earthly relations, he said, life is "necessary and irreducible" (1952, p. 3), and the whole of things, in all its variations, participates (by "identity," "correspondence," "analogy," or "absolute continuity"—each one of these describing as it does a relation between variant and origin) in this necessity. Additionally, this functional a priori of assimilation, accommodation, and equilibration gives direction to those alterations of structure, making them more than a series of random changes. Children do not simply *change;* they *develop.* As Piaget (1952) observes:

[This functional a priori] orients the whole of the successive structures which the mind will then work out in contact with reality. It will thus play the role that [Kant] assigned to the *a priori:* that is to say, it [the *functional a priori*] will impose on the structures certain necessary and irreducible conditions. Only the mistake has sometimes been made of regarding the *a priori* as consisting in structures existing ready-made from the beginning of development, whereas if the functional invariant of thought is at work in the most primitive stages, it is only little by little that it impresses itself on consciousness due to the elaboration of structures which are increasingly adapted *to the function itself.* (p. 3)

At each stage of development, we impose the schemata or structures we possess upon our experience and organize it accordingly. As Piaget (1971b) put it, we impose cosmos on the chaos of experience (p. xii). Over the course of this influx of experience, elements of that experience will resist being schematized by the structures thus far developed and will cause a "disequilibration" in those structures. In other words, we will fail to assimilate some incoming experience into already existing structures, nor will we be able to accommodate it to already existing structures. Piaget (1973) saw such dis-equilibration as leading to an adaptive recrystallization of the functions of assimilation and accommodation into a more inclusive and more stable organization and structure. He (1952) stressed however, that "From the simplest of reflexes to the systematic intelligence, the same method of operation seems to continue through all the stages, thus establishing a complete continuity between increasingly complex structures. But this functional continuity in no way excludes a transformation of the structures" (p. 153). Once again, throughout all the variations and transformations of structures, "complete continuity" becomes an evocation of the origin.

Another turn appears here, however. If we carefully reread the previous two extended passages from 1952, we see that the sequential development of structures becomes better and better adapted, not to the Earth and all its relations, but to the inevitabilities of adaptation itself. That is to say, the life functions of assimilation, accommodation, and equilibration are *a priori,* and the best adapted structures (stablest and most inclusive and thus the calmest and most equilibrated) are the ones best adapted "to the functioning itself." The variations in our understanding of, say, the sun and the moon and the stars are oriented toward better and better adaptation to the inevitable "organizing activity inherent in life itself" (p. 19).

Now one might naively hope that such an adaptation would be deeply ecological in character, involving a generous and loving embrace of the functioning of life in all its variations and relations. But again, for Piaget (1965), all these versions are oriented toward "a single truth alone," (pp. 216–217) one tale that tells the truth of all such tellings. Thus, even though Piaget could recognize the nebulous beginnings of science in the children he studied, science cannot hear those tales as serious counterpoints to its own, because it is *its own* version, which is singularly best adapted to describe what is with some objectivity and "truth." Children's (or "primitives'") evocations of animism and evocations of a world full of agencies and potentialities and powers beyond my own cannot be understood in genetic epistemology to be true. Belief in such an animate world can be only an object of an (scientific) investigation whose contours alone house the "single truth." "Animism" is simply a "belief" that primitives (children or otherwise) hold. Genetic epistemology often assumes children's beliefs to "fail." As Gadamer (1989) noted, they lose their power of address and their power to claim us and place us into question; they become "another's opinion" (p. 294). All this occurs in spite of that fact that animism too, and in its own irreplaceable way, fully contains the origin by being an expression of the absolutely continuous functioning of "life itself."

IV

One can trace how, in order to heal an ailing science that had lost sight of its origins, Piaget and Inhelder (1969) sought out "life itself" in the form of a return to the child: "The child explains the man as well as and often better than the man explains the child" (p. ix). The child thus holds, in Piaget's work as in the work of so many others, a restorative image of healing or making whole again (Eliade, 1968). Here we have what one could see as an identification of "the origin" with the chronologically *first*. In his *Origins of Intelligence in Children* (1952), Piaget made clear that what he meant by origins was a return to the biological emergence of intelligence in the life of the child. Distinguishable from efforts to ground science in its self-referential methodologies or its own epistemological premises, Piaget (1970a) asked "How, in *reality*, is science possible?" (p. 731). Genetic epistemology is a response to the question of how we can start our lives as squalling infants and in the course of development become capable of logic and mathematics. It is an attempt, in this sense, to ground our lives as adults in all our relations and kin.

Of course, what Piaget found in the thoughts and dreams and words of children was "life itself," but in typically inchoate form. As Eliade (1968) said, in the child we find life itself at its most "amorphous and chaotic," helpless and vulnerable to constant disequilibration: "Vital sciences stress especially the precariousness and imperfection of the beginnings. For them, it is process, becoming, evolution that gradually corrects the difficulty and poverty of the 'beginnings'" (p. 78). What Piaget found is what so many fairy tales play upon: the image of the helpless child (that wonderful biblical image of "life itself") trapped in the bulrushes or stable, in the wilderness of the body and the bloodiness of the flesh. We see children's experience this way as "immediate and momentary" (1973, p. 101) or, at the level of infancy, "episodic" (1952) (which could help one define some images of postmodernism as infantile).

Piaget (1974a) even vaguely evokes images of children as monsters (Jardine, 1994c), suggesting that their tales often amount to odd "deformations" of the truth (p. 50), that children often become "duped" (1972, p. 141), and they can become "victims of illusion" (p. 141), where the tales they tell become "traps into which [they] consistently fall" (1974a, p. 73) to the extent that "the whole perspective of childhood is falsified" (1972, p. 197).

Thus it is possible and, we might say, necessary to Piaget's faith in the redemptive quality of science to invert this picture. We might see development as "life itself" caught in the animalities of the flesh and struggling for release. Life functioning is, so to speak, "caught" in the body such that the operations of this "absolute" are encumbered by the fragile limitations of embodiment. The origin barely visible in the blood and piss of childhood.

We might therefore conceive of development as a continual process of shedding the embodied factors that house the functional a priori (that is, that house "the absolute") in a tenuous, unstable state. As I have observed elsewhere (Jardine, 1992e), the stages thus proceed "upward" away from the difficulty and poverty of the beginnings (the difficulty and poverty of the body, one might say) toward a gradual self-realization inherent in logic and mathematics, where the knowing subject and the subject known are identical:

> Formal logic is perfectly "equilibrated" since the structures of thought and language in terms of which we do logic and the object of such doing *are precisely the same*. Formal logic "proceeds by the application of perfectly explicit rules, these rules being, of course, the very ones that define the structure under consideration" (Piaget, 1970, p. 15). In formal logic, the frontiers of discourse and the frontiers of the object of discourse are identical. The lines that have been drawn are identical, because the matters under consideration have become matters of method (that is, matters regarding the ideal, formalized *operation* of discourse itself). (p. 69)

In this sense, we might view logic and mathematics as the moments at which "life itself," in its pure functioning "comes to." They become conceivable as fulfilments in their way of a "tendency towards an all-embracing equilibrium aimed at the assimilation of the whole of reality" (Piaget, 1973, p. 9).

It becomes clear then why Piaget (1977) might parallel the work of science with a form of "renunciation" (p. 30). It becomes clear, as well, why we find constructivism so alluring. Consider, with Eliade (1968), "the exceptional value attributed to *knowledge of origins*. For the man of archaic societies, that is, knowledge of the origin of each thing ... confers a kind of magical mastery over it; he knows where to find it and how to make it reappear in the future" (p. 76). If we consider the functioning of "life itself" to be the origin of our "construction of reality" (1971b), clearly, understanding the operations that construct reality "confers a kind of magical master over" the whole of those things thus constructed (this is why Piaget's theory might be conceived as modernist, because there is, here, the inherent belief in the possibility of a full *presentation* of the "essence" of things in the representation of the schemata and functions in terms of which there *are* things at all [see chap. 9]). And if logic and mathematics show themselves to be the pure expression of such mastery, science and its ways become something we are "destined to master" (p. 372) because such mastery will fulfil the age-old dream of dominion over the Earth some of us have been granted through a developmentally sequenced mastery over the "origins" of the truth of all things (i e , a master over the methods of science that constitute the "perfection" of the originary functional a priori). Development becomes conceivable, then, as a dual movement of a progressive "renunciation" (1977) of the sins of the flesh and a correlative progressive "conquest of things" (1952, p. 363) through a conquest and mastery of the functional conditions under which such things are constructed in the first place.

V

It is hard to pull out of this movement in Piaget's work and it is hard to avoid this "rage for order" (Jardine, 1992b) and the rage it can easily produce when we spin it out like this. So be it; there are other ways.

What if we were to conceive of development not as a line but as an open field of relations each portion of which requires the generous copresence of all the others in order to be comprehensible, healthy, and sane?

Instead of developmentally portioning off animism and artificialism and the dream images coming in the night (Piaget, 1962, 1974a, 1974b) from the "true conceptions" gleaned from a crass literalism, what if we read these in relation to each other and understood them to be mutually articulating?

What if, in parallel fashion, we gave up the need to portion off the young from the old, the teacher from the child, the established from the new, and brought them back together in a space large enough to embrace them all and the real, difficult work that goes on "in between"? (As Hans-Georg Gadamer (1989) suggests, interpretation always works in such a "between.")

What if all the variants come forward, heralding each other, requiring each other? Piaget might be able to help. We could take passages like these more generously than Piaget (1952) may have been able to take them himself:

> Intelligence finds itself entangled in a network of relations between the organism and the environment. Intelligence does not therefore appear as a power of reflection independent of the particular position which the organism occupies in the universe but is linked, from the very outset, by biological apriorities. It is not at all an independent absolute, but is a relationship among others between organism and environment. (p. 19)

To be what it is, intelligence must find itself "among others," not isolated in its own operations (and simply subjecting others to those operations, rendering the world its object and thus silencing the voices that might thus "object") but back "in relation." Perhaps the understanding of the world requisite of logico-mathematical operations becomes equilibrated, not as a closed system that turns all others into its object (as occurs in genetic epistemology as a logico-mathematically based, "scientific" enterprise), but as a way-among-others whose articulations it requires if it is to understand its own. In fact, this latter idea could *almost* provide a definition of genetic epistemology except that genetic epistemology does not require the broad copresence of an imaginal, interpretive space large enough to embrace, say, both mechanical causality and animism. It requires simply the sequential replacement of one (animism) with the other (mechanical causality)—that is, the replacement of falsehood with truth.

Understood interpretively, animism is more than simply a precursor one somehow developmentally overcomes. It is, rather, a relative one might (but, of course, need not necessarily) learn to live with generously and well. In other words, children are right here with us; as are Native North American tales of Coyote's spirit haunting the world; as are hermeneutic flights of fancy; as are the forms and figures of the texts I read, haunted as they are with spooks and spirits and long-dead ancestors wrapped up in a single word (imagine how haunted even the word "child" is, hiding ancient cosmologies and ancestral bloodlines); as are the demonological agencies of the dream; as is this heart of mine that knows the world is alive and full of purpose.

One effect of a return to origins is what Mircea Eliade (1968) called "keeping the world open" (p. 139). Here, returning to the origin is returning to the moment of the world opening. Perhaps, as Piaget suggested, "keeping the world open" involves the infusion of "life itself" into all the articulations of human and Earthly life. Perhaps, as Piaget never quite suggested, this copresence of life is the space within which we can meet our kin. Or as hermeneutics puts it, we meet our kin in the world-of-relations that goes beyond any of us and houses us in shared and contested ways, for good or ill.

Consider the following excerpt from an older work of Piaget's: "The self-conserving tendency of the organization of life is the origin of the principle of identity, from which the principle of non-contradiction can be deduced" (Piaget, 1972, p. 48). Just as surely as the self-conserving tendency of life is the origin of the mathematical principle of identity, so too is the mathematical principle of identity the origin of our image of the self-conserving tendency of life. Here, the variant is the original. Each reflects in each and each is understood better with the other nearby. Understood interpretively, each is full of life itself, each is the origin, and neither need be understood to be true at the expense of the other. In fact, *each* becomes true only in the *space* opened by granting the address and claim and possible truth of the other.

With this simple example of the principle of identity, we can envisage the conduct of, say, the mathematics classroom, as standing in deep Earthly relations to all its kin. All efforts directed toward the formation of identity and self-identity, all quests to find oneself as oneself and to find out what something itself is, its inherent character, are wrapped up together here. The fan opens into a thousand segments here, and issues of borders and boundaries and structures and limits and edginess and what all this has to do with understanding the world in a deep, truthful manner, fly up like sparks (Merleau-Ponty, 1964, p. xxi).

The healing of logico-mathematics is not had by despising the legacies it has wrought. It is had by placing it back into all its relations and kin (almost like the project of genetic epistemology). Thus, even though (self-)identity defines the whole of mathematics as a closed system of operations (Piaget, 1970b, pp. 7–8), that self-identical, self-referential, self-regulatory ("Life is essentially auto-regulation" [Piaget, 1971a, p. 27]) whole is always already akin to the body and breath and blood. Its closure, before so harsh and unforgiving (Jardine, 1994a), is vaguely recognizable now. We've heard this tale before, and I somehow participate in the open space of mathematics when my breath settles down and steps out paces of walking meditation: breaths and steps symmetrical and measured, seeking equilibration, oxygen filling up the longing spaces in patterns, chemical precisions that return with exhalation.

Stop.

END BIT

> If we provide enough room for restlessness so that it might function within the space, then the energy ceases to be restless because it can trust itself fundamentally. Meditation is giving a huge, luscious meadow to a restless cow. The cow might be restless for a while in its huge meadow, but at some stage, because there is so much space, the restlessness becomes irrelevant. (Trungpa, 1988, pp. 48–49)

Roberto Calasso almost trivializes his image of the myth as a fan of a thousand segments by saying "no sooner have you grabbed hold of it than myth opens." This is often not what occurs. Often, such opening takes its own sweet time, frustrating efforts of movement, frustrating writing, frustrating teaching. It is hard, hard work to develop an interpretive ear for how versions and origins interplay.

For this large, imaginal space to open, often time is required, often the slow slugwork over academic references, and reading and underlining and repeating and remembering and imitating and writing and speaking and listening and failing and writing and speaking and listening again. Interpretive work takes time and it requires, not a method that can be adopted by anyone with anonymous technical skill, but rather patience and the slow accretions of age and experience. Differently put: I've hated this old man for years, which spoke as much to my deafness as his.

So when one of her students follows her around the room after mathematics class imploring "But Ms. Friesen, the numbers can't just keep going on forever," it takes a certain discipline to hear the truth leaping in this single comment, to hear the opening, to hear the way, to hear how such a statement clears an open, generous, difficult, pleasurable, compelling space of genuine questions, generative possibilities. It takes time and discipline to hear how this comment helps keep open the world of mathematics, helps keep open, too, teacher and child alike, both now out in an open place of relations that is spacious and will allow the restlessness to become irrelevant. The fan unfolds only on the premise that we are somehow immersed in the world of relations of which this comment is a variant original and in which this comment arrives full of rich address, full of rich relations.

We have to be able to hear in this child's comment Zeno moaning relief that the world turns again, and that the nostalgia for the origin in the stopping of numbers *somewhere*—in God, in infinity—has not been lost.

This is not just some vague meditative notion of "attunement," but also long hours of thought, long hours of working through the deadly calcifications of mathematics that we bear in our sweaty palms, working on keeping open the world (of mathematics). Mathematics must become interpretable again, that is, full of life. And suddenly, the leap, suddenly seeing how the mathematical principle of identity (as itself a beautiful answer to the nostalgia for origins) underwrites the giggles of musical chairs and how musical chairs reenacts an old mathematical cosmology. Real, exhilarating work.

There is something amiss here. The first flush of this onrush of possibilities loosed by interpretation is hyperactivity and attention deficit disorder. At first, it seems like what is required of us in the invocation of the origin is a brainstorming flurry—abundance as engorging. It falsely seems that the only true tale involves doing everything, and therefore involves, like so many elementary schools, plunging in to a headlong rush of ever-accelerating "activities." This, too, is part of the giddy rush of some readings of postmodernism: adrenalized surfing panics, surface thrills, and the licentious playing of surface images.

No. We must learn to stick with *just this*. Recall. Each variant *is* the original and therefore each stubborn particular must be read, somehow, in its wholeness, in its originary character. The simplest child's simplest utterance may itself be prophecy.

Preamble 5:
On Ontology and Epistemology

It is not at all a question of a mere subjective variety of conceptions, but of [a topic's]
own possibilities of being that emerge as it explicates itself, as it were, in a variety of
its aspects.

—Gadamer (1989, p. 118)

The following chapter proposes that part of the difficulty in making the transition from understanding curriculum topics under regimes of scarcity to understanding them "in abundance" goes beyond issues of epistemology towards issues of ontology. What is meant here is this.

Epistemology has to do with issues of what it means *to know* something—rooted in the Greek term *episteme*, to know. Ontology has to do with what it means *to be* something—from the Greek *ontos*, to be. If we believe that a topic *is* simple and straightforward and manageable and controllable, suggesting that there is an abundance of ways of *knowing*, it becomes imaginable as subsequent to its *being* simple. Abundance is conceived as, so to speak, "after the fact" of something *being* simple. Differently put, the topic we might deal with in a classroom *is* simple, even though student may "bring" to it "a subjective variety of conceptions." Abundance becomes considered to be accidental to the way things actually *are*. It becomes subjectivized, or, one might say, epistemologized—there is an abundancy to our "ways of knowing," even though *what is known* is simple. There are "multiple intelligences" (Gardner, 2000), but we've become timid in suggesting that *the matters under consideration* are multiple and therefore lend themselves, somehow, to multiple ways of taking up such matters. This all seems epistemologically naive.

This is what regimes of scarcity have promoted in educational circles, that things *are* simple and monitorable and manageable and that the suggestion of multiplicity, diversity, and abundance is, in consequence, an opulent educational *option* that we might need to pursue in order to help the diversity of our student populations to come to know this (in fact simple and scarce) topic. Abundance and diversity become drained out of the topics and become signs, rather, of the pathological variety of "learning styles" we each bring with us to the classroom.

We are suggesting something different—that the topics entrusted to schools *are* abundant, and, therefore, suggestions of multiplicity and diversity are not opulent educational *options* regarding how we might come to know topics that are in reality simple and manageable. Rather, multiplicity, diversity, and abundance define the way in which things *are,* and therefore, the great array of the ways of traversing a place that students bring to the classroom *is precisely what living things require if they are to be "adequately" understood in their abundance.*

In short, abundance is an ontological issue, not an epistemological one.

We understand the conundrum here, one well-heeled in our postmodern times. Any claim as to what things *are* is understood to be foundationalist, fundamentalist, positivist, exclusionary, unreflective, and dangerous. And yet, those very postmodern claims claim for themselves the desire to keep things open to diversity and multiplicity and to the inherited complicities of grand and small narratives. All we are suggesting is that such a postmodern urge is correct: Things *are* abundant, nonfoundationally fluid, and inherently complex, with all the difficulty, contestation, dangers, and pleasure this entails. This is what Gadamer (1989) meant when he talked of interpretation "breaking open the being [ontology] of the object" (p. 362). Interpretation doesn't simply provide multiple ways of complicating a topic that *is* simple. Rather, interpretation transforms what it means to *be* a topic—to be is to be-in-abundance (see chap. 19).

And so, as is so often the case with interpretive work, we ran into this issue in two ways—right in the midst of an elementary school mathematics classroom, and right in the midst of reading a book on the nature of writing and poetry that contained this explosive image from Buddhist ontology—"behind each jewel are three thousand sweating horses." Behind each seemingly scarce and impoverished curriculum topic is great abundance.

Chapter 5

"Behind Each Jewel Are Three Thousand Sweating Horses": Meditations on the Ontology of Mathematics and Mathematics Education[1]

David W. Jardine
Sharon Friesen
Patricia Clifford

PREAMBLE

> [What if mathematics, or poetry, or the taxonomies of biology, or any other of the pieces of the world entrusted to us as teachers] no longer has the character of an object that stands over and against us? We are no longer able to approach this like an object of knowledge, grasping, measuring, and controlling. Rather than meeting us in our world, it is much more a world into which we ourselves are drawn. [It] possesses its own worldliness and, thus, the centre of its own Being so long as it is not placed into the object-world of producing and marketing. The Being of this thing cannot be accessed by objectively measuring and estimating; rather, the totality of a lived context has entered into and is present in the thing. And we belong to it as well. Our orientation to it is always something like our orientation to an inheritance that this thing belongs to, be it from a stranger's life or from our own. (Gadamer, 1994, pp. 191–192)

What possible good could come from a meditation on the *ontology* of mathematics and mathematics education?

Our answer to this question is simple to state, even though its practical educational consequences are enormous. Currently, the only discourses

---

[1]Reprinted from "Behind each jewel are three thousand sweating horses," by D. Jardine, S. Friesen, and P. Clifford, 2003, *Curriculum Intertext: Place/Language/Pedagogy* (pp. 39–50), edited by E. HasebeLudt and W. Hurren, Copyright © 2003 by Peter Lang Publishing. Reprinted with permission.

available in mathematics education are those of consumption or production. Becoming involved in mathematics, therefore, means becoming either a producer or a consumer. Mathematics, therefore, is something produced or consumed. One either "makes meaning" of it oneself, or the meaning made by another is imposed "from outside" and simply "swallowed" because of the "authority" (which always means "power") of the maker.

Or, we "socially construct." That is, we are *all* producers and consumers of knowledge, and the whole known world is at the formative disposal of our knowing. Thus a thread of European history and the collapse of epistemology into the market begins: "[Immanuel] Kant's dictum 'the mind makes the object' were the words of blessing spoken at the wedding of knowing and production, and should be remembered when we contemplate what is common throughout the world" (Grant, 1998, p. 1). "Accordingly, the spontaneity of understanding becomes the formative principle of receptive matter, and in one stroke we have the old mythology of an intellect which glues and rigs together the world's matter with its own forms" (Heidegger, 1985, p. 73). And, accordingly too, the Earth becomes a passive, malleable (and eventually disposable) "resource" for our consumptive and productive manipulation, and the term "math manipulatives" carries no irony or hesitation.

And children become "our greatest natural resource" with little thought given to what we've done to the rest of those things we've considered merely sources for our consumption and satisfaction, with no Being of their own, no reserve or character beyond our desire, our "wanting and doing" (Gadamer, 1989, p. xxviii).

But what if this is not the way that mathematics *exists*, as object either produced or consumed, either individually or collectively? What if it somehow *is* differently than the economies of production and consumption, either individual or collective, can handle? What if the options of production and consumption (along with their consort images of ownership and the commodified exchange of objects between "individuals" whose only "world" is now "the market" [Jardine et al., 2003, pp. 211–222]) turn upon the same ontological ground and are therefore not especially options at all? What if, therefore, the epistemological quarrels over "production versus consumption" (and those over "individual versus collective") that have been exhausting us, instead conceal a deeper, more dangerous debate that has been thus far successfully avoided?

What if mathematics is much more a world into which we ourselves are drawn, a world that we do not and cannot "own," but must rather somehow "inhabit" in order to understand it? What if we cannot own mathematics (either individually or collectively), not because it is some object independent of us and our (individual or collective) ownerships, but *because it is not an object at all*? What if, instead of production and consumption, the *world* of mathematics (as a living, breathing, contested, human discipline that has been handed to us) needs our memory, our care, our intelligence, our work, the "continuity of [our] attention and devotion" (W. Berry, 1986, p. 32) and understanding if it is to remain hale and healthy and whole?

I

> [Images] announce themselves, bear witness to their presence: "Look, here we are." They regard us beyond how we may regard them, our perspectives, what we intend with them, and how we dispose of them. (Hillman, 1982, p. 77)

> Catch only what you've thrown yourself, all is mere skill and little gain. (from a poem by Rainer Maria Rilke, cited as the frontispiece to Gadamer, 1989)

Images have a most peculiar sense of arrival. They seem to *arrive*, out of nowhere, often unexpectedly, with a clear feel of agency, of portend, of demand and deliberateness. This is phenomenologically undeniable. During the act of writing, of composing, of setting forth an idea in the already-imaginal (not simply signifying and signing [Gadamer, 1989, pp. 405, 412–418]) realm of words, images can, sometimes, become catalytic moments of experience, finally, it feels, saying what was silent, gathering what was dispersed, drawing us into the ways of a world of relations that has the center of its own Being beyond our "wanting and doing" (Gadamer, 1989, p. xxviii). "Every word [-as-image, not -as-sign (Gadamer, 1989, pp. 405, 412–418)] breaks forth *as if* from a center. Every word causes the whole of the language to which it belongs to resonate and the whole world-view that underlies it to appear" (Gadamer, 1989, p. 458, our emphasis). As signs, words re-present. They are mere stand-ins for the real thing, pointers to elsewhere.

As images, the real thing presents itself "in" words.

The title of this chapter is cited in Jane Hirschfield's wonderful work *Nine Gates: Entering the Mind of Poetry* (1997, p. 43). When we happened upon it, the first question was how to take care of it. This is because its arrival is first and foremost experienced as a claim made upon me (Gadamer, 1989, pp. 126–127, 297), an address spoken to me and for me (Gadamer, 1989, pp. 290, 295, 299).

This image we simply stumbled upon seemed to *require something of us*, seemed to require our attention and devotion and love and care and cultivation.

"Look. Here I am" (Hillman, 1982, p. 77).

The trouble always is, of course, that *the image itself* contains many, most, maybe all of the answers to the questions its demand provokes.

It pulls us into *its* question, *its* repose, *its* regard.

Therefore, first is the question posed, not *by us* but *to us*. Good questions must be first *posed* (Gadamer, 1989, p. 363) and the writing that follows necessarily belies the writers' own emerging composure (an "exaggerated" [Gadamer, 1989, p. 115] reading of Gadamer's reading of *Bildung* [p. 9]) in the face of such questions.

And, too, if things go well, the writers and the readers might get a wee glimpse of the composure of the thing written about, its "repose" (Gadamer, 1977, p. 227) its *"Da,"* (Gadamer, 1994, pp. 22–25), its "standing-in-itself" (Gadamer, 1977, p. 226), again, over and above our "wanting and doing" (Gadamer, 1989, p. xxviii).

II

"Behind each jewel are three thousand sweating horses." This is an image from Zen Buddhism that invokes the tale of Indra's Jewelled Net from the *Avataska Sutra:*

> Far away in the heavenly abode of the great god Indra, there is a wonderful net that has been hung by some cunning artificer in such a manner that it stretches out infinitely in all directions. In accordance with the extravagant tastes of deities, the artificer has hung a single glittering jewel in each "eye" of the net, and since the net itself is infinite in all dimensions, the jewels are infinite in number. There hang the jewels, glittering like stars of the first magnitude, a wonderful sight to behold. If we now arbitrarily select one of these jewels for inspection and look closely at it, we will discover that in its polished surface there are reflected all the other jewels in the net, infinite in number, not only that, but each of the jewels reflected in this one jewel is also reflecting all the other jewels, so that there is an infinite reflecting process occurring. (cited in Loy, 1993, p. 481)

This image of Indra's Net invokes an ontological claim: that things *are* their interdependencies with all things, and, therefore, to deeply understand any thing, we must understand it as *being itself* only in the midst of all its relations. Each thing, therefore, must be understood and experienced, not as some self-contained, self-existing substance ("a substance is that which requires nothing except itself in order to exist" [Descartes, 1640/1955, p. 255]), but as empty (*sunya*) of any self-existence (*svabhava*) apart from such living relatedness.

Each thing thus *is,* so to speak, what it *is not* while still remaining itself (Nishitani, 1982). This is a thing's reposing "in itself." It *is* the long and twisted entrails of all the interdependencies that gave rise to its being manifest just here, just now.

It *is* all the rains, all the breaths, that passed it along.

Each thing thus *is* all the codependent arisings that brought it here, and to understand this particular thing is to understand its standing in an "inheritance that it belongs to" (Gadamer, 1994, p. 192). Each thing, therefore, is not simply its own, isolated, subsequently-in-relation self, but is itself a center of a "totality of a lived context" (Gadamer, 1994, p. 191). This totality has "entered into and its present in the thing" (Gadamer, 1994, p. 192).

"And we belong to it as well" (Gadamer 1994, p. 192).

"Thus in each dust mote is vast abundance" (Hongzhi, 1991, p. 14).

This inexhaustible emptying-out-into-all-their-relations is the deeply Earthly "repose" of things. They "stand-in-themselves," not by standing cut off from all things, but by standing *as* an opening, a portal, a way, an "e-vent," into a world of relations. This seemingly isolated object or word or glance, or even the seemingly most ordinary of classroom events (Jardine, 2000) *is* all of its relations.

As Martin Heidegger (1962) might have put it, even ordinary things sometimes "world," if we care to sit with them and wait a bit. Again, as Hans-Georg Gadamer (1994) says in his lovely essays on his great teacher's thought, "there is a totality of a lived-context [a 'world'] present in the thing" (p. 192).

But this image of "sweating horses" does something more than simply invoke Indra's Net. It plays with the sense of ornateness and visionariness that Indra's Net entails—bright jewels, tapestries, heavenly arcs of space and time and vast, heady infinities, and great, swarming *ideas* of interconnectedness, interdependency, interpenetration, recursiveness, and dependent coorigination (*pratitya-samutpada*).

"Behind each jewel are three thousand sweating horses" disrupts the charming, entrancing, composure of such delicious visions of "relatedness." Roaring behind each jewel, now, are not infinite refracted jewel-like visions, but *something coming at us,* something full of piss and blood and sweat, something crashing, stampeding, rough, vigorous, dangerous, full of life and death and the agonies in between, something animate that's spotted us beyond our spotting it, *demanding* attention.

III

The point to the doctrine of interdependence is that things exist *only* in interdependence, for things do not exist in their own right. In Buddhism, this manner of existence is called "emptiness." Buddhism says that things are empty in the sense that they are absolutely lacking in a self-essence by virtue of which things would have independent existence. (Cook, 1989, p. 225)

Lacking in self-essence resembles social and historical constitution, understands individual things as constituted by their relations to other things and especially to groups, families, species, and kinds. Emptiness resists the autonomy of the individual [which now appears] uniquely European American. (Ross, 1999, pp. 213–214)

We came across the title of this chapter in the midst of a series of Grade 7 mathematics conversations, 60 students, two teachers, and a university researcher, over the course of several weeks. This was an ordinary classroom in an ordinary school undergoing what turned out to be, for all of us, an extraordinary experience.

All of us (students, teachers, and researchers) were deeply embroiled in heated talk and the heated display of differing mathematical explorations and differing mathematics solutions gathered around angles and their bisection, compasses and their workings, circles and their arcs and cords, and all the frustrating beauty of the dropping of perpendiculars. Living in the midst of these conversations day after day, this seemed like real, vigorous, embodied work, and mathematics seemed like a living, breathing discipline that drew us all in to an old, rich, Earthy place, a "topography" (Gadamer, 1989, p. 21): the deeply interrelated, interdependent, fertile (Gadamer, 1989, p. 32) terrains of geometry. Here, the sweating horses: arguments and frustrations and returns, pulling together and pulling apart the long and convoluted work of long-standing relations. And here, too, the sudden condensations of insight, moments of clarity, as they twisted pages sideways with breathtaking yells and smiles, took the pens over from each other, insisting on one more thing, one more thing.

Standing at one table. Four boys pushing a large piece of newsprint between them, set with the task, with a straight-edge and compass alone, to drop a perpendicular line from a point to a line below it. We all know this one, and one student pressed ahead of us with moves we all recognized.

With the compass draw an arc through the line with the point as its center. From each of the two points where the arc intersects the line, make two marks below the line. Use the straight-edge to connect the original point with the intersection of the two marks. This new line is perpendicular to the original line.

All of us at this one table knew, *beyond a shadow of doubt*, that this solution was correct. But, equally, none of us knew *at all* why it might be correct.

One boy insisted with an insistence that we all recognized in ourselves "That's just how you *do* it, OK?"

"But how do you know it's not hitting the line at, like, 89 degrees and not 90?" This simple question brought the whole sweaty roil to a halt all over again. We ended up in an odd place, stuck, almost dazzled by our own clarity and assurance, unable, at least initially, to "break open the being of the object" (Gadamer, 1989, p. 382). Many of us in this classroom had, over the year, talked about that odd feeling of having learned, having *memorized* a procedure and knowing how to *do* it beyond question or hesitation, and yet suffering the terrible silence and feeling of being stuck with it, a feeling of cold and deathly immobility if anyone should have the audacity to ask a question about 89 degrees instead of 90.

All of us at this table did agree, however, that knowing this sort of flat, clear, mindless, unmoving way of understanding a procedure, unsurrounded and unsustained by the heated, tangled movements of relatedness that gives it life, was not adequate. Here, in this classroom, we had come to understand that these arcs and lines and points, this compass movement and the circles it hints at first through and then below the line all belong properly here together, together along with the ghosts of Pythagoras and Euclid and the whole cascade of memory and work that brought all this down to us. This "belonging together" is where this procedure actually *lives* as something sensible, something sane, something understandable in its living movement as a historically, humanly constituted inheritance to which our lives already and inevitably bear unvoiced obligations.

"That's just how you do it" mistakes what that procedure actually *is*. It is an uprising from this terrain of circles and lines and arcs, an uprising and a naming and an ordering and a setting-forth. As such, it is not a *substitute* for that terrain, but an imaginal coming-to-presence of it, a jewel-like condensation of the messy vigor of that terrain. Without this terrain and the risks that are involved in traversing it, that procedure remains merely memorizable. Within this terrain and our travels, it becomes memorable, like an old tale told by those who've been here before and have huddled us around a fire in the darkness to whisper. It is not a command, as we might often experience mathematical procedures. It is a telling of where we have been, places we have witnessed *for ourselves*. We already know the roiling life of which this tale tells.

So one of the boys completed the circle that intersected the line in two places, and completed into circles the crisscrossing arcs below the line, ending us up, now, with a beautiful figure, reposing, full of the *Vesica Piscis* that we've since discovered (Friesen 2000; Lawlor, 1982; see chap. 1), a wee long-lost geopoetic ancestor caught kicking around in Greek sands.

"OK. I'm 49 years old and it never occurred to me that that crosshatch below the line was parts of two circles." What did I think they were? Did I think about them *at all?* I expect the latter is important: I rarely *thought* about mathematics in the way I was witnessing here, in this classroom. I'd only rarely felt this living movement of understanding, this sense, in this case with geometry, of being in on its being what it is.

So over this diagram, one student said "Oh boy. *Now* what?!" with a wonderful, weary sense of pleasure and exhaustion, but also this lovely, palpable sense of mathematical reality.

IV

What man has to learn through suffering is not this or that particular thing, but insights into the limitations of humanity, into the absoluteness of the barrier that separates man from the divine. (Gadamer, 1989, p. 357)

[We] belong to the text [we] are reading. The line of meaning that the text manifests ... always and necessarily breaks off in an open indeterminacy. [We] can, indeed [we] must accept the fact that future generations will understand differently. (Gadamer, 1989, p. 340)

Mathematics *is*, in some sensible sense, all the actual, human, bodily work that is required if it is to remain hale and healthy, if it is to continue as a living practice that we desire to pass on, in some form, to our children.

"Every experience worthy of the name involves suffering" (Gadamer, 1989, p. 356). Thus, experience is not something we *possess* (like some commodifiable object) but something we *endure*, something we *undergo*. For mathematics to be deeply experienced, it must be drawn back into its suffering, its undergoing, its movement of becoming what it is, its living coming-to-presence, rather than its foreclosing *being* present. It *is* its "passing on." It *is* a fragile and finite and deeply human enterprise. This is the horrible mortality-insight of interdependency, that the seeming self-sufficiency of any seemingly isolated, self-referential object breaks outward into cascading interdependencies with all the ways it has arrived here, seeming so. "Future generations will understand differently." Mathematics *is* its being different in the future.

To understand mathematics out from under the stultifying ontology of produced and consumed objects is to enter into the living movement of its "furtherance" (Gadamer, 1989, p. xxiv). Or, differently put, to understand geometry is to help keep it "open for the future" (Gadamer, 1989, p. 340). That is, to understand geometry is to keep it susceptible to being taken up and transformed anew and, it must be emphasized, to keep ourselves open to being transformed in our traversing its terrain and meeting our own ancestors in that terrain. In such a sojourn, we risk becoming someone who bears the marks of having undergone such an adventure. We run the risk of coming to bear the marks of becoming *experienced* in mathematics in that wonderfully ecological sense that both Martin Heidegger (1962) and Hans-Georg Gadamer (1989) have identified as coming to "know your way around."

Given the dazzling allure of its rules and axioms and procedures, who would have imagined that, right at the heart of what once seemed to be the most cold and unforgiving and punishing of disciplines, is a generative, pedagogic heart? Who would have imagined that geometry *is* all the risk and pleasure and stubborn, sweaty work that brought it safely here to us?

"Behind each jewel are three thousand sweating horses."

Preamble 6:
Getting Over the Great Humiliation

A common lament of teachers and student teachers as they begin to glimpse what is in store for them and their students when they face the prospects of curriculum in abundance, is that they don't know enough, that they feel weak and helpless and unprepared and incapable. It certainly feels like this for us every time we hit upon a new topic—one more humiliation, one more opportunity to be flabbergasted by the fact that we've ended up this old and never knew something that now yawns open-jawed in the path ahead.

Many teachers have become accustomed to having full charge over what they do as a sign of their ability and worth. Teaching is thus understood as an act of outrunning the abundance of any possible classroom event with a thorough knowledge of the topic, such that no student's question is left unanticipated. We all know, as educators, what a hopeless enterprise this is, and how well textbook publishers prey upon the insatiable panic that ensues from it.

What happens in the face of talk of curriculum in abundance is a whole other sort of initial panic. It is a feeling of, well, almost paranoia—that things are not only "going on" behind the scenes or under the surface, but have long since being going on, even if we don't know it or experience it. A common and, we suggest, unavoidable experience that flows from abundance is an experience of repeated humiliation: I don't know anything about Linnaeus, or about Pythagoras or the Human Genome Project or about the great topographies of angle bisection or the dropping of perpendiculars. I've never known about the search for origins in the late 19th century. Once I move away, for example, from the well-wrought and well-known rules of angle bisection, I'm lost in what feels like a wilderness, wilds I've never been asked to traverse and, in many cases, never knew were there.

I don't know enough to continue. Very often, at the very threshold of abundance, some teachers (and we certainly include ourselves in this number on many an occasion) understandably recoil—as noted earlier, under various forms of threat, we tend to play less and less, and tend to see the prospect of play as a threat to security.

It is at this juncture that it is vital to understand that part of coming to experience curriculum in abundance requires slowly turning this humiliation into precisely our comfort. And, as is not surprising, this slow turning has to happen again and again.

This turn reminds us of a peculiar phenomenon that occurs in many of our elementary mathematics curriculum methods classes. The reasons given for loving mathematics and hating mathematics are very often *the same*. Those who hate mathematics often say that they know there is an answer and they can't find it and they are panicking and full of anxiety. Those who love mathematics often say that they know there is an answer and therefore they can relax, because the exploration that is about to ensue is not dependent on their knowing, but only on taking up the adventure and being careful. Knowledge will come as they become more and more experienced with the ways of this heretofore unexplored territory.

To understand what is meant by curriculum in abundance, it is important to realize that the lines and threads we've unraveled thus far were, in each case, as much a *consequence* of pursuing the abundance of particular curriculum topics, both inside and outside the classroom, as they were a *precondition* of those pursuits. That is to say, in order to follow, say, Anh Linh's shapes, we had to know some things about the abundant topographies within which those shapes were allowed to appear in the classroom. However, and *at the very same time*, in order to know about those topographies, it became necessary to *follow* the invitation wrought by Anh Linh and the shapes that emerged in her work. In order to cultivate a sense of abundance in the classroom, teachers need to prepare themselves for the unprepared.

For now, we have to let this paradox simply stand: Knowing about the abundance of this or that curriculum topic is both the *goal* of teaching and learning as well as the *precondition* of teaching and learning. Perhaps we should say that presuming abundance is a precondition. The language here becomes difficult to sort out. "Dolly the sheep" was experienced as abundant before its abundance was exactly "known." And the process of coming to know its abundance made that experience of abundance *increase*. The only real advice we pass on to student teachers at such junctures is that any curriculum topic with which they are entrusted is full of ghosts, even if they have yet to begin a venture into their presence. When teachers ask us where to start, our only answer can be that they have to come to understand that they have already started because they, as well as their students, are already living in an abundant world.

Chapter 6

Abundance and the Limits of Teacher Knowledge

David W. Jardine

> *Within each dust mote is vast abundance.*
>
> —Hongzhi (1991, p. 14)

> *To see a world in a grain of sand and heaven in a wild flower, to hold infinity in the palm of our hand and eternity in an hour.*
>
> —William Blake

It is always somewhat humbling to see what sorts of things might make the difference in a conversation about how to conduct a rich, generous inquiry in a classroom, one based on a sense of vivid abundance and intellectual love. I have been lecturing for 8 months, on a weekly basis, to a large group of first-year student teachers about the character of such inquiries—bringing forth dozens of examples, talking in great detail about the philosophies behind inquiry, and so on.

At the end of a recent lecture, I offhandedly said, "So, later this week, when you are in the bar and you lift up that beer glass and see that water ring on the table, you will know that you live in the midst of a vast abundance—condensations, specific humidities, evaporation, the capacities of different airs to hold moistures. In fact, the whole of Alberta's aridness conspires to form that ring."

Sure enough, it was *this* example that finally made the difference and caused a sort of great release in the experience of a group of student teachers. It was (how embarrassing!) *this* example that broke open something: The world fits together in great patterns, great architectures, great ancestries and blood-lines, great contestations and debates, and these fits are alive and constantly being formed and re-formed, remembered and lost.

So, a premise of classroom inquiry based on a sense of abundance is this: Whenever you come upon even the seemingly most trivial of things, it can be experienced, or taken up, or read, or treated as a way into the ways of the world. Thus, Zen Master Hongzhi's words or those of William Blake do not point to some other-worldly, mystical, or strange phenomenon (although it can be a quite disorienting experience as well). They point, in fact, Earth-ward, to a deeply bodily, deeply experiential, deeply aesthetic fact to which we have been blinded by our culture of fragmentation and isolation (Jardine et al., 2003). This is why classroom inquiries based on the idea of abundance can be spoken of as something more than simply a "teaching technique among others." It is, rather, a way we carry ourselves in the world, the way we come, through experience, to live in a world full of life, full of relation's and obligations and address. It is a deeply seated belief about how the world fits together in its deepest and most vigorous intellectual and spiritual possibilities. It is also perhaps why it is a little too easy for me to become rather zealous about this issue because, for me, it is quite literally a matter of life and death, of liveliness and deadliness, not only for myself but for the teachers and students I often witness laboring under the terrible burden of the belief in a world that doesn't fit together and that must therefore be doled out in well-monitored, well-managed, well-controlled packages, one lifeless fragment, one lifeless worksheet, one lifeless objective at a time.

There is a rub here that is vital to understanding what difference inquiry is pointing toward and it requires a wee story. Years ago, I became friends with someone who knew how to think this way—generously, interpretively, full of adventure and thoughtfulness. For ages after we met, I experienced this: As long as he kept talking, I understood what this way of thinking was like and could understand the topic of our conversation in generous ways that were thrilling to experience. *As soon as he stopped talking, the whole thing fell apart!* Whenever I tried, initially, to think this way all by myself, I hit a wall. I initially thought that this was simply an issue of *my lack of knowledge* and my student teachers have since expressed the same thing to me: "You know a lot of stuff, we don't" so the issue for them became one of trying to accumulate knowledge about anything and everything as fast as possible ("Where should we start?" or "What should I read first?"—coupled with "Until I know a lot more, I'm not going to even attempt an inquiry" and "Maybe I'll stick with the more standard stuff when I begin teaching until I get more experience"). Of course, as we all have experienced, this means you'll never attempt an inquiry premised on abundance because this sense of *knowing enough* never occurs. Having enough knowledge to outrun abundance would simply provide abundance to be an illusion.

This understandable enamorment with "knowledge" actually hides something about the nature of inquiry. Here is another simple example I used in my lectures. When you pass a globe in your school library and you see the Tropic of Cancer inscribed on it, you can rest assured that *it does* mean something, *it has* come from somewhere, *it already holds* a history and voices and faces and feuds, *even if you don't know it*. Thus, the rest and assurance that comes with interpretive inquiry doesn't come from having already stuffed oneself full of knowledge but from, as Gadamer (1989) put it, "entrusting ourselves to what we are investigating to guide us safely in the quest" (p. 378). It comes from an *ontological assurance* about the abundance of things (see chap. 5), an abundance that is not dependent on my knowledge of that abundance.

"Our knowledge of the world instructs us first of all that the world is greater than our knowledge of it. To those who rejoice in abundance and intricacy, this is a source of joy. To those … who hope for knowledge equal to (capable of controlling) the world, it is a source of unremitting defeat and bewilderment" (W. Berry, 1983, p. 56). As Wendell Berry goes on to suggest, this is not a call for ignorance and it does not mean that shunning knowledge is preferable or even especially possible. It means, simply, that the adventure of inquiry is a matter of rejoicing in the abundance and intricacy of the world, entering into its living questions, living debates, living inheritances. And this adventure is available to all, each in their own measure (even though, as has been the case with many of us and our children, that adventure may rarely be available *in school*). Waiting on knowledge as a way of monitoring, controlling, and doling out this abundance leads to more than a sense of defeat and bewilderment. It leads, as every religious and spiritual tradition has suggested, to exhaustion, paranoia and, I suggest, eventually violence (see Jardine, 2000).

Preamble 7:
Monsters in Abundance[1]

> Aghast we cover our faces, confused between expressions of disgust or nervous laughter. What a surprise ... who could have imagined ... such horror. One word sputters to our lips: "Monster." The choice of word is instructive. Etymologically it is related to *demonstrate* and *remonstrate,* and ultimately comes from the Latin *monstrum,* an omen portending the will of the gods, which is itself linked to the word *monere,* to warn. Monsters ... teach lessons. (Chua-Eoan, 1991, p. 27)

Monsters have always had a compelling place in education. We are all familiar with how commonplace they are in children's stories. Monsters show up in children's books, as Chua-Eoan suggests, not simply to startle and to scare, but also to let somebody know something, to require someone to face something from beyond their mettle. They tell us that a limit has been reached or breached, or that from this point onward, things will have to be different. They live in a liminal space (Turner, 1987), outside but still right at the edge of town, or just off the path on a journey, or right at home in the closet or under the bed.

Elementary school teachers know all about this delicious imaginal territory. Monsters are linked with abundance, excess, and overflow, because their arrival summons me to go beyond the places in which I've already settled and to learn more, see more, be tried more. Monsters are therefore intimates in education. Traces of their appearance are experienced every year in the perennial onrush of new faces, new students, what Hannah Arendt called "the onslaught of the new" (Arendt, 1969). "In spite of all our con-

---

[1] With Brent Novodvorski.

certed efforts to 'teach them a lesson,' the young simply keep coming, standing before us, ripping open ever anew what we have taken for be 'established knowledge' and putting us and the world and the curriculum … into question again and again" (Jardine, 1998, p. 129). It is for this reason that, in our previous work (see Jardine, 1998, pp. 123–134) and in the chapter that follows, it makes a weird sort of sense to speak about "the monstrous child" in ways that are not simply negative or demeaning.

Hidden here is a sense in which the monster is not only identifiable with a transgression of some limit (see Foucault, 1999, p. 63). More than this, "there is monstrosity only when the confusion comes up against, overturns or disturbs … the law" (p. 63). "Monstrosity *calls law into question* and disables it. Law must either question its own foundations, or its practice, or fall silent, or abdicate, or appeal to another reference system or invent a casuistry" (p. 64, our emphasis). Like Richard and his invocation of Dolly the sheep, the rules set out in the curriculum guide were not simply transgressed or broken ("it was against the rules"). They were overturned and, in such overturning, they were oddly rescued from their own lifelessness. The monster thus is essential to the life of the commonplace and ordinary, saving it again and again from its own sleep, its own unreflectiveness, its own calcification. If we begin to unearth the archaic ancestries of this image of the monster, we find that they are sometimes linked somehow to the child (see Bordo, 1988; Miller, 1989; Warner, 2000), wild and wilful, and, as in Jean Piaget's work, full of originary, purifying, revivifying, and salvational energies (see chaps. 4 and 8; see also Jardine, 1992a; Jardine et al., 2003, pp. 55–70).

As we have seen, however, the sort of overflow and excessiveness and abundance portended by the appearance of monsters is not tolerable from within regimes of scarcity. Under such a regime, the troublesome child, the unrelenting or unexpected question, the surprise twist of meaning, the previously unforeseen turning of a geometrical drawing out of which springs monstrous mathematical insight—such matters become feared because there is no time, not enough resources, and so on. The monster becomes something to be avoided and excess and overflow are considered mere wildness and abandon and threat (see Preamble 3 and chap. 3). This describes all too well the terribly embattled sense we have of contemporary schools. If we no longer have room for the arrival of the monster and its lessons, its teachings, many psychiatric speculations will tell us that the monster, thus spurned, will, of necessity, return and do whatever is necessary to, if necessary, *force* attention to its message. The monstrosity will become enlarged by our ignoring of it.

As with the phenomenon of play (see Preamble 3 and chap. 3; see also Jardine, 1988, 2000, pp. 115–132) and with many of the curriculum topics entrusted to schools, under regimes of scarcity, the abundance and excess and overflow that the monster portends are degraded and, one might say, de-potentiated. The monster loses its ability to disturb us and tell us something from beyond the sway of what we already know. In contemporary education, the monster becomes transformed into "the abnormal" (see Jardine et al., 2003, pp. 41–52).

"The abnormal individual is essentially an everyday monster, a monster that has become commonplace ... a pale monster" (Foucault, 1999, p 57) The abnormal is named, measured, and controlled by normality. That is, this pale monster only appears insofar as it has been tethered to normality, and therefore defined by its proximity to or distance from the normal, the known, the expected, the standard, the ordinary. Any "abnormality" that is not thus tetherable is left monstrous. The eager or shadowed face of the "troubled child" in the classroom is understood along radiating gradients in his or her proximity to the normal, to "standards." Their troublesome face is thus defaced, "normalized" by being rendered abnormal. Curriculum guides provide one such set of gradients. These gradients are defacing because, in the face of what comes to meet them, they are not moved. They will not listen. They already know ahead of time anything worth saying. They only speak and those who approach must only listen.

The monster thus becomes "the individual to be corrected" (Foucault, 1999, p. 57)—either "taught a lesson" ("for their own good" [Miller, 1989]) and therefore rendered more normal, or generously accommodated through individual program plans and special-needs interventions. In this way, schools enter into "a kind of game between incorrigibility and rectifiability" (Foucault, 1999, p. 58) and schools then become justified in their actions in light of their ability to be that institution that serves this function. Hence, also, the game of "deficits" (an interesting word in light of education's love affair with regimes of scarcity), wherein, as Illich (1972) has well-noted and as we have discussed in Preamble 1, "every simple need to which an institutional answer is found permits the invention of a new class of poor and a new definition of poverty. Poverty [comes to] refer to those who have fallen behind an advertised idea of consumption in some important respect" (p. 4).

And so the monster, the one from outside, the one with a lesson to teach us, becomes someone already inside, already accommodated for and anticipated. Monstrosity is thus a threat to the limits of normality, a however brief transgression, a breach, an overflow, an excess, an abundance. Abnormality, on the other hand, is, paradoxically, a comfort to and strengthening of the limits of normality. One might even say abnormality condones the deepening entrenchment of the codes of monitoring that normality offers. And, because such security measures are expected of normality, what occurs is that normality itself becomes narrower, takes less chances, and builds higher walls, all in the name, in schools at least, of Standards. Here again we have the movement of impoverishment.

However, once schooling settles itself into this calm and reassuring regime, what occurs, especially with student teachers on the verge of entering this feigned calmness, are strange visions of monstrous children.

Chapter 7

"Disproportion, Monstrousness, and Mystery": Ecological and Ethical Reflections on the Initiation of Student Teachers Into the Community of Education[1]

David W. Jardine
James C. Field

In his essay "The Liminal Period in Rites of Passage," Victor Turner (1987) describes a phenomenon common to initiation ceremonies. Initiation rites often require that the familiar world that has housed and sustained the initiate be disassembled into its component parts. Each part of the familiar world becomes represented in a mask painted in unfamiliar colors. The features of the mask are usually distended and disproportionate, often monstrously depicted. The reason for this monstrous depiction is that the familiar feature of the world has been severed from its place. It no longer fits where one would normally expect it to fit and therefore loses all sense of "proportion." It stands out; it is out of place. The initiate is thrown into a position of "ambiguity and paradox, a confusion of all customary categories" (p. 7), because the initiate, too, is out of place and loses a sense of proportion. The initiate no longer feels at home and no longer has the reliable, familiar guideposts to keep things in perspective: "What is the point of this exaggeration amounting sometimes to caricature? It seems that to enlarge or diminish or discolour in this way is a primordial mode of abstraction. The outstanding exaggerated feature is made into an object of reflection" (p. 13). In this way, "much of the grotesqueness and monstrosity ... may be seen to be aimed not so much at ter-

---

[1]Reprinted from *Teaching and Teacher Education, Vol 8*, No 1, D. Jardine and J. Field, "Disproportion, Monstrousness, and Mystery," pp. 301–310, Copyright © 1992, with permission from Elsevier.

rorizing or bemusing the neophytes ... as at making them vividly and rapidly aware of what may be called the 'factors' of their culture" (p. 14).

After the "liminal period" (Turner, 1987, p. 6) is over, initiates are required to return home. This return to the familiar world is a vital part of the initiation ceremony. The "promiscuous intermingling and juxtaposing of the categories of events, experience and knowledge" (Turner, 1987, p. 15), all allowed "with a pedagogic intent" (Turner, 1987, p. 15), is brought back to the familiar world from which the initiate began. "The neophytes return ... with more alert faculties perhaps, and enhanced knowledge of how things work, but they ... are shown that ways of acting and thinking [too far] alternative to those laid down by the deities or ancestors are ultimately unworkable and may have disastrous consequences" (Turner, 1987, p. 15).

There is, thus, a deeply ethical character to such matters, for they involve initiating the neophytes into the *ethos* of their community, and invigorating that *ethos* through the ushering in of the young. The neophytes are required by the community, not simply to replicate already established ways of acting and thinking, but to rejuvenate and regenerate the old by infusing it with new blood (itself a common feature of initiation ceremonies) and thereby transforming the community by being themselves transformed into the community. "Undoing, dissolution, decomposition are accompanied by processes of growth, transformation, and the reformulation of old elements into new patterns" (Turner, 1987, p. 9). Young and old thus deeply *belong together*.

However, the initiation process and the disassembling of the familiar world attempts to show the initiate that, even in such reformulation of old elements into new patterns, "this liberty has ... limits" (Turner, 1987, p. 15). Certain matters *pertain* regarding what houses and sustains the familiar world of the community. These pertinent matters have a mysterious character, because they do not enter into the new patterns except as a limit condition. The patterns of the cosmos that sustain our familiar world go beyond the patterns we have made *in* our familiar world, and even though those patterns of the cosmos may bear a kinship to our world, they are not *ours* to tamper with except with a sense of delicacy and propriety. We must be careful not to violate the unseen patterns that sustain and house our community. More simply put, in such ceremonies, the initiate comes to realize that we do not make all the patterns (W. Berry, 1987, p. 3) and that our knowledge about and power over the world is limited in ways that go beyond our knowing. We can no longer be self-centered—centered on what we explicitly know and experience. We are always and already part of a community that is larger than us and that community is part of an Earth that houses it.

There is, thus, a deeply *ecological* character to these rites of passage, for they involve initiating the neophyte into a sense of awe regarding the mysterious ways of the cosmos that houses us. They involve initiating the neophyte into certain humility and attentiveness to the long-standing ways of things, known by those who have come before ("the ancestors") and not invented or made by us ("the deities"). Returning home to the familiar world thus entails realizing that that familiar world is deeply embedded in patterns, powers, and potentialities that are beyond us and that can be violated if our actions are not careful.

"THE TORPEDO'S TOUCH" REVISITED

In teaching we are too often persuaded to be gentle, fearing that we shall damage our children if we immerse them in dissonance and perplexity. We may argue that the young need not be torpified, but on the contrary require clarity, structure, simplification, reward. But perhaps it is we who fear the perplexity and disorder that for them is already intrinsic to life.

To be educated is to know what depths await us underneath the surface of things, whatever those things may be. To shield our children from life's inevitable perplexities is to leave them at the mercy of their ignorance and to deny them the wonder that is the basis of everything we know. (Thomas, 1985, p. 222)

The phenomenon of initiation suggests ways of understanding the dissonance and perplexity that we often confront in the simplest of instances in our work with student teachers. Consider the following statement made by an undergraduate student in an Early Childhood Education (ECE) Curriculum class.

This student was part of a third-year university class of approximately 25 students who were all facing an upcoming first practicum experience in a Grade 1, 2, or 3 classroom with much trepidation and excitement. This class ordinarily deals with the broad area of the integrated curriculum and focuses on the specific areas of Language Arts, Mathematics, Science, and Social Studies. The following statement erupted in class just days prior to the beginning of her practicum, and out of context with what had been going in the class thus far. We had been discussing the broad features of the Social Studies Curriculum Guide (issues of self-identity, family, neighborhood, community) in small groups and considering activities and themes that would be appropriate to various grade levels. When the instructor began to collect ideas from the various groups, one student said (with a tone of mild anger and fear) "I have *absolutely no idea* how to teach Social Studies to Grade 3. I wouldn't know where to begin."

This statement was uttered in a disproportionately horrified voice by a woman already reasonably well versed in curriculum matters. Her voice was full of a long-familiar anxiety that one comes to expect in teaching practicum courses. For this student, facing a first practicum produced an effect akin to "the torpedo's touch": It revealed the fragility and inherent ambiguities of what she could claim to know. More than this, taken-for-granted factors of the world—long-familiar issues of community, questions of self-identity, family identity, questions of other cultures, and the understanding and tolerance of difference, all dealt with in the Grade 3 Social Studies Curriculum Guide she had been reading and discussing with colleagues—had suddenly become grotesque and monstrous. She spoke as if a horrible mask had erupted out of the darkness around the communal fire.

In response to this revelation of fragility, she did not become vividly aware of what may be called the factors of her culture. She did not wonder at the depths that awaited her "underneath the [familiar] surface of things." She was not "exhilarated yet perplexed" (Thomas, 1985, p. 222). She was full of panic and desperation. She was confronted with the "abyss" (p. 222) of having, as she put it, absolutely no idea what to do with this once familiar feature of her world. It now seemed monstrous, out of place, no longer pertaining to her and what she already lived.

In response to her implicit question, a wonderful exercise that has become commonplace in the Calgary Board of Education was suggested as a way to begin opening up this space of the study of the social with children. Have each child go home that night and ask their elders what the oldest object is in the house. Where did it come from? Who gave it to you? Why did you keep it? How did it get to Calgary? and so on.

A whole range of possibilities was sketched out in the class, not in order to give a sharp and precise answer to the student's original query, but to show how her query fit into an already working network of integral patterns and relationships. From her "monstrous" experience of the Social Studies Curriculum (an experience that forced all of us in the class to reflect on one of the factors that pertains in the community of teaching) we attempted to return home to a more ordinary, familiar world, full of threads of connection that extended far beyond what we explicitly know. We seemed to have stumbled upon a mysterious, reliable pattern in the midst of which we and the children we might teach are already living. This class demonstrated that the student teacher could therefore begin teaching Social Studies to Grade 3 by recognizing how it is that she and the children had *already begun,* living lives *already* full of rich and relevant experiences. She could begin by reflectively recovering from these rich and relevant experiences *the very sorts of things* that need to be covered in Social Studies and from here, reliable patterns and similarities could be spun out that might eventually cover the curriculum quite literally as a whole. It is important to emphasize, then, that this particular example of old objects found in your house had an effect that was far more than simply providing an interesting idea for a lesson plan. Simply providing one more thing to "try with the kids" can often compound the original feeling of being overwhelmed and adrift. The breakthrough that occurred here had to do with recognizing that the ordinary and familiar world is full of pedagogical recourse.

The student's response to these suggestions was full of the "shock of recognition": "Oh yeah, right, I see. I can do that!" Clearly, for her, these suggestions were not new information. In fact, once the issues of the Grade 3 Social Studies curriculum were brought home and fitted back into their place in our lives, she was taken aback by how *familiar* this whole matter was. Things were back in proportion, back in perspective, because the living linkages of the Social Studies curriculum to her life and the life of the community (including the children she might teach) had been rethreaded, reinvigorated.

THE AMBIGUITIES OF "INTIMATE KNOWING" AND TURN TO LITERALISM

This student teacher could begin by recognizing that she and the children had *already begun,* and the class proceeded to help students reflect on the network of interrelationships that was already at work in their lives and the lives of the children they might teach. One of the things at work here is the phenomenon of familiar, intimate knowing. Terminology for this phenomenon has become part of everyday discourse in education: We know more than we can say; we are more than we know; we *are* in ways that are not knowing. We *live* in an implicit understanding of the factors that house and sustain us. This is why the student underwent a shock of recognition when the class discussion began. She somehow *already knew* what we were talking about, even though she could not imagine how her own implicit, intimate knowledge could serve to answer her own question of where to begin.

The philosophical legacy for the phenomenon of implicit, intimate knowing is daunting: Plato's (1968) theory of a heavenly life in which eternal ideas are always already understood and need only to be recollected; Jean Piaget's (1971b) reflective-abstractive reconstruction of what is already known in an implicit, concrete, embodied way; Edmund Husserl's (1970) phenomenological explication of a prereflective life already lived; Martin Heidegger's (1962) attention to the understanding of Being in which we already dwell; M. Polanyi's (1967) tacit knowing and the in-dwelling of understanding; Merleau-Ponty's (1971) flesh of the world up out of which things come to meet us; Gadamer's (1989) reflective recollection of the hidden themes and stories and contours and signs that weave and interweave the lives we already find ourselves living. This philosophical legacy has come to infuse education through the works of Schon (1983, 1987), Connelly and Clandinin (1988), Greene (1988), Berthoff (1981), and countless others.

One of the perplexing things about intimate knowing is that, even though it is deeply reliable, it is not literal and discursive. Intimate knowing is not explicit, clear, univocal, and certain. Instead it is, in its very familiarity and reliability, implicit, ambiguous, multivocal, and full of the "perplexity and disorder that is already intrinsic to life" (Thomas, 1985, p. 222). These perplexities and disorders of everyday life are not monstrous but simply indicative of its generative, lively nature.

However, under the pressure of her upcoming practicum experience (this was for her, as for many students in this class, the first time they have ever been responsible for a classroom of children; for those with some experience in this regard, it was the first *evaluated* round of teaching), the inherent ambiguities of this student's intimate knowing became suddenly visible.

She suddenly realized that there *is* something irremediably risk-laden, perplexing, and disorderly about raising questions of self-identity, family, community, and tolerance with thirty-five 8- and 9-year-old children. This topic *does* extend beyond our knowledge and control. *Before we know it and can control it,* this topic *already* makes a claim on us and each of the children we might teach in different yet interrelated, reliably patterned ways. These claims are not univocal and clear, but multivocal and ambiguous, each bearing a kinship to the other, but each unable to be straightened out once and for all into a fixed set of rules. As every experienced teacher knows, when the next group of children arrive, issues of self-identity, community, and tolerance will have lost none of their perplexity and dissonance. In fact, the experience of inherent perplexity and dissonance can be taken as signs of "the depths that surge below ... the surface of things" (Thomas, 1985, p. 222): In its perplexity and dissonance, this topic *comes alive* and breaks open into its deep, reliable, living patterns. Long, explicit, discursive lists of *exactly* how to teach this or that, so often demanded by our prepracticum students (and so often provided by textbooks), will not save us from finding ourselves right in the midst of this inherent perplexity and dissonance. In fact, those lists are often misused by beginning student teachers to attempt to ensure that *nothing happens* during the lesson that is not controlled and planned. They are often misused to unintentionally take the life out of teaching. It is here that a dangerous turn can sometimes occur. If intimate knowing becomes torn out of those familiar contexts that would kindly sustain its lively, ambiguous nature, the essential and unavoidable perplexities of intimate knowing can become distended beyond recognition. (We cannot help but think of a statement we have heard every year from one or two prepracticum students: "What will I do if a child *asks me a question?*" uttered in pure, disproportionate panic.) These perplexities are not taken to be signs of the depths that surge below the surface. They are, instead, taken quite literally to be monstrous *mistakes* that can be fixed by transforming that which is implicit, ambiguous, and multivocal into long, explicit, discursive lists of objective information.

With such transformations, the depths that surge below are flattened out into literal surfaces that can (so it is hoped by beginning practicum students) be easily manipulated and controlled:

> The increasing literalism at work in the demands of our undergraduates ("Tell me exactly what it is you want in this assignment") reflects somehow a shaping of the imagination away from an ability to think analogically, metaphorically, poetically. [We become] indifferent to the full play of possibilities inherent in human discourse, a disposition which underwrites dogmatism. (Smith, 1999a, p. 111)

Students (and, of course, many teachers and administrators and parents and researchers) begin to demand "clarity, structure, simplification, reward" (Thomas, 1985, p. 222). Such increasing literalism points to a deep disruption of our familiarity with the world or being at home in the world. It points as well to a particular *solution* to this disruption.

Increasing literalism involves an attempt to *replace* intimate knowing with clear, explicit knowledge, methodically produced. Such replacement not only shifts the conception of reliable knowing from intimate to explicit. It also shifts the conception of what lies *outside* of the boundaries of what we know from mysteriously yet reliably patterned to chaotic and out of control. Attempting to turn students from incessant demands for explicit knowledge back into reflecting and relying upon what they already intimately know, any suggestion of "homecoming" (Weinsheimer, 1985, p. 5) is understood as nothing less than an invitation to chaos. Their desire for secure, explicit knowledge (perhaps produced, in part, by the insecurity of facing the upcoming practicum experience) has thus already prefigured what an alternative to it can be.

It is no coincidence, then, that student teachers become fixated on questions of management and control, because they cannot envisage something *they* do not control as anything but *out of control*. No pattern, no order already pertains. Following this, to begin teaching Social Studies to Grade 3 can thus quickly devolve into issues of classroom management once the pertaining pattern and inherent discipline of the topic have been severed that might already link it to our lives and the lives of the children we teach.

"FAMISHING THE CRAVING FOR HOMECOMING"

> Method is a response to the condition of being no longer at home in the world. To be at home means to belong, to live in surroundings that are familiar, self-evident and unobtrusive. Its contrary consists in a schism between past and present, I and others, self and world. Method derives from this sense of living among objects to which one no longer belongs. (Weinsheimer, 1985, p. 4)

This student's sense of having absolutely no idea how to teach Social Studies to Grade 3 became, in our class, the occasion to reflect deeply on the factors at work in the lives of 8- and 9-year-old children and the assumptions and implications of what we teach them. The suggestions given to the aforementioned student attempted to turn her back from her monstrous vision into what she already knew, back in to the familiar or "familial" sense of belonging with children in a world that already makes (an albeit multivocal and often perplexing) sense. Ludwig Wittgenstein (1968) described this sort of knowing constitutive of everyday life as operating in terms of "a complicated network of similarities, overlapping and criss-crossing" (p. 32). This network is made up of relations of "kinship" (p. 48) or "family resemblance" (p. 32) that bespeak both a way of knowing and a way that things fit together.

One of the interesting things about Wittgenstein's metaphors of "family resemblance" and "kinship" is not only that these metaphors bespeak a certain ambiguity of interrelationship that cannot be resolved once and for all in explicit, univocal terms. These metaphors also pertain to our ambiguous and irresolvable relationships with children:

> If we forget that we dwell *with* children in the deep resonances of language and experience, we can forget our kinship with children. In becoming estranged from our kinship with children (with the fact that they are our "kind"), they can become our strange and silent objects, ones that have nothing of their own to say, ones we must now instruct without feeling the need to listen to the unvoiced experiences they have already undergone. (Jardine, 1990, p. 185)

The anxieties of an upcoming practicum experience can constitute precisely such an estrangement or schism in the deep "kinship system" of everyday life (the one that binds us all, in our example of Social Studies, to issues of self-identity, community, understanding, and tolerance difference, etc.). But instead of forcing us to reflect on our familiarity with the world and recover a deeper sense of the factors at work in teaching, such anxieties can disaffect us from our familiar knowing. These anxieties can break the familial bonds that make, for example, issues of self-identity precisely the sort of thing adults speak to children about and are concerned about themselves. It can make us feel that we somehow do not already belong with children, living in the midst of such ordinary, albeit perplexing, matters of everyday life.

In such estrangement, the world is no longer familiar/familial but strange, full of separate objects that stand over and against us. The issue of self-identity, for example, becomes an inert, strange, distant *topic* in a curriculum guide, not a living part of our lives with children. "One's world devolves into the material of knowledge" (Weinsheimer, 1985, p. 5).

From this disruption or loss of being at home with things evolves a series of correlative movements that gradually transform our familiarity with the world into relations between a *knowing subject* and an *object*. Central to this movement is an increasing focus on *method:*

> Method aims to redeem this loss [of being at home] by substituting itself for the kind of understanding that is not reflective knowledge because it understands everything in advance by belonging to it, before knowing and its methodical regulation come into play. But the paradox of the substitute is [that] method famishes the very craving for homecoming that it is designed to satisfy. (Weinsheimer, 1985, p. 5)

In response to the anxiety of facing her upcoming practicum, the student was no longer comfortably at home with what she already knew. What she knows "doesn't work right, or fit into its usual relationships, or possess its usual significance. From one's surprise or frustration at this sudden unintelligibility derive both the first and third person. Subject and object separate and precipitate out simultaneously" (Weinsheimer, 1985, p. 5). The subject, separated from the "primordial unity of being at home in the world" (Weinsheimer, 1985, p. 5) no longer understands. The student has absolutely no idea how to teach Social Studies and what is now an object (Social Studies) no longer fits or belongs in the midst of the student's familiar world. It stands out of place as something "thrown before" her (an object), and she stands before it, unknowing, herself displaced from what she intimately knew.

The final moment in this movement of estrangement is the posing of "cognitive remedies for these twin defects" (Weinsheimer, 1985, p. 5) of an object that does not fit and a subject that does not know. These remedies are *not* directed toward recovering that original familiarity with the world that could provide a reliable set of rich experiences held in common with children from which to proceed. Rather:

> The object is disassembled, the rules of its functioning are ascertained, and then it is reconstructed according to those rules; so, also, knowledge is analyzed, its rules are determined, and finally it is redeployed as method. The purpose of both remedies is to prevent unanticipated future breakdowns by means of breaking down even further the flawed entity and then synthesizing it artificially. (Weinsheimer, 1985, p. 6)

Thus, the ambiguity and multivocity of the "family resemblances" that constitute our being at home in the world are reconceptualized as flaws that must be fixed before we can proceed. The familiar world is disassembled (as happens in the case of initiation rites), but it is not reassembled by returning home. Rather, it is *artificially reassembled* by means of an explicit, univocal method that *demands* univocity and explicitness from what is now not its familiar home but its object. The world, thus, becomes our "artifact." It becomes under our control (so we believe) by becoming, not the home that sustains and embraces us, but by becoming an object of a method whose explicit purpose is the control, prediction, and manipulation (Habermas, 1973) of that object.

Method (and its correlative of explicit, objective knowledge) is deployed in response to not feeling at home. Ironically, however, method (and its correlative of explicit, objective knowledge) does not simply "famish the craving for homecoming" (Weinsheimer, 1985, p. 5). It *creates and increases the sense of not being at home* because being at home, with all its living perplexities and ambiguities, is precisely what method is designed to *replace* by rendering that home into an object purged of its perplexities and ambiguities, purged, that is, of its life.

"HOMECOMING" AND "PATTERNED MYSTERY"
AS ETHICAL AND ECOLOGICAL PHENOMENA

> The acquisition of knowledge always involves the revelation of ignorance— almost *is* the revelation of ignorance. Our knowledge of the world instructs us first of all that the world is greater than our knowledge of it. To those who re-

joice in ... abundance and intricacy ..., this is a source of joy. To those would-be solvers of the "human problem," who hope for knowledge equal to (capable of controlling) the world, it is a source of unremitting defeat and bewilderment. One thing we do know, that we dare not forget, is that better so-. lutions than ours have at times been made by people with much less information than we have. We know, too that the same information that in one [person's] hands will ruin land, in another's will save and improve it. (W. Berry, 1983, p. 65)

There are no explicit, univocal, discursive rules that will allow us to "artificially produce" the actual, living vibrancy and potency of raising questions of self-identity and family history with thirty-five 8- and 9-year-old children. Such a situation has a lot of "give" or "play" in it, a lot of resilience and risk that cannot be fixed by univocal rules. It is full of abundance and intricacy. Most telling is that better solutions than ours as to how to handle such a situation have been made by people with much less information (about child development, teaching strategies, various curricular models, classroom management techniques, lesson planning, and so on). After all, when children arrive after this assignment with stories about how their family has no old possessions because their family home burned down or because they fled as refugees from war and death, there is no way to manage this situation other than with care and love and attention.

The student teacher's question about Social Studies, therefore, is not one of a simple lack of information (although this may have contributed to her dilemma, it was clear once the class began its reflections that she possessed a wealth of unrecognized information). At issue is the problem of whether we can allow ourselves to return home, and begin to trust and more deeply understand the sustaining patterns that *already pertain* and that bind our lives and the lives of our children to topics we wish to teach. At issue is how we can let go of the belief that we can and must control and predict all possible events through the accumulation of more and more explicit, objective information and that such "letting go" is *not* an invitation to chaos. Rather:

> Some truth meets the eye; some does not. We are up against mystery. To call this mystery "randomness" or "chance" or "fluke" is to take charge of it on behalf of those who do not respect pattern. To call the unknown "random" is to plant the flag by which to colonize and exploit the known. To call the unknown by its right name, "mystery," is to suggest that we had better respect the possibility of a larger, unseen pattern that can be damaged or destroyed and with it, the smaller patterns. (W. Berry, 1987, p. 4)

Our actions must therefore become delicate and careful and attentive to what crackles beyond and beneath the boundaries of what we explicitly know. This is good advice to someone confronted with the prospect of teaching thirty-five 8- and 9-year-old children who each have a profound stake in questions of self-identity, understanding, and tolerating difference, and each of whom are implicated in relations of kinship into a larger, unseen pattern that binds us all to these issues.

Put the other way around, such action on the basis of mystery has a certain quiet confidence that what surges underneath the surface of things is reliable, *even if* we do not explicitly know what it entails. A good teacher seems to understand this, that children and adults and questions of, for example, self-identity and understanding and tolerating difference deeply *belong together* in intimate, ambiguous ways. Attempting to act only on the basis of what we explicitly know can result in panic, and monstrous visions of chaos. We must relearn that "the ancient program is the right one: 'Act on the basis of ignorance'" (W. Berry, 1987, p. 4).

At issue here is more than a student teacher simply misjudging the extent and nature of her knowledge and the knowledge of the children she teaches. We are not dealing with a simple epistemological miscue, but with a deeply ethical and ecological issue that was in part illustrated by the ensuing class discussion that this student teacher's comments evoked.

This notion of "patterned mystery" is an ethical issue in the following sense. Tearing apart the kinships that bind together the lives of adult and child and replacing them with clear and univocal relations between a subject and an object is tearing apart a deep, mutual *ethos* (so evident in the returning home of the initiate). Object relations *need not pertain:* Both subject and object could be what they are without being related, because they are conceived as separate in the first place. Saying that the relations between adult and child are relations of kinship is to say that *adult and child cannot be what they are without each other.* Each not only mutually articulates the other but, without the regenerative eruption of the new in the midst of the old—without the inextricable "belonging together of adult and child" (Misgeld, 1985, p. 188; see also Jardine & Misgeld, 1989)—human understanding, human *life,* quite literally could not continue.

This is an ecological issue in that the deep kindred sense that binds adult to child also binds both of these to the Earth in relations of "kind." Tearing apart the fabrics that sustain us in the name of explicit knowledge betrays the worst sort of hubris and bespeaks the ecological rumblings we now hear in the distance. Without recognizing and paying careful attention to "that anciently perceived likeness between all creatures and the earth of which they are made" (W. Berry, 1983, p. 76), we begin to act only on the explicit knowledge that we have, irrespective of any sense that there might *already* be an existent order that pertains and that binds us beyond what we explicitly know. As mentioned in the examples we spun out in our class, issues of understanding similarities and differences betray a "kinship" that we have with all life and begin to show that our concerns are perhaps more "global," more "whole" than we had anticipated. Without such an eye to long-standing and "anciently perceived likenesses" (*precisely* the sorts of things, to use Turner's, 1987, terms, "laid down by the deities or ancestors," p. 15) we find ourselves in a position of potentially violated and unseen, mysterious orderliness in the name of objective knowing. However, "no matter what distinctions we draw, the connections, the dependencies, remain. To damage the Earth is to damage your children" (W. Berry, 1986, p. 57).

Speaking on behalf of intimate knowledge and the notion of being up against mystery is not necessarily speaking against explicit, objective knowledge. Such explicit knowledge surely has an appropriateness and place in the task of teaching. However, raising the questions of appropriateness and place raises the question of how such knowledge "fits." It raises questions of the pursuit of objective knowledge with a sense of propriety. Having such a sense of propriety entails having reflected upon the factors that are at work in the community of teaching and that bind the lives of children and adults together and bind these lives to the life of the Earth. It means having considered questions of "place." But considering questions of place and the ways in which objective knowing might be fitting require *precisely that deep sense of being at home that objective knowledge is wont to replace*. Explicit, objective knowledge certainly has its place (as does all the information student teachers received about child development, about teaching strategies, about classroom management techniques, about lesson planning, and so on). But raising questions of the place of what we objectively know requires more than objective knowledge. It requires raising the ethical and ecological issue of how to act delicately and carefully and considerately in response to the mysterious patterns that house and embrace us. Thus, as most student teachers come to realize, objective knowledge and long, explicit, discursive lists of information about teaching and children are of little use without a sort of reflective "homecoming" in which the issues of the *ethos* of the community of teaching are raised and in which the *living* character of curriculum demands can be addressed.

POSTSCRIPT

> It is not only that young people expect a genuine responsiveness from their elders, but also a certain direct authenticity, a sense of that deep human resonance so easily suppressed under the smooth human-relations jargon teachers typically learn in college. Young people want to know whether, under the cool and calm of efficient teaching and excellent time-on-task ratios, life itself has a chance, or whether the surface is all there is. (Smith, 1999c, p. 139)

To loop back to the beginning of our chapter, there is a sort of initiatory character to student teacher education. Our task is not simply to inculcate student teachers with information for, in the inevitable stress of a practicum setting, no amount of explicit, discursive information feels like enough. The demands to tell them exactly what to do in every situation such that nothing will go wrong will not be satiated by having them gorge themselves on a glut of information. There is something they must go through and endure: an inevitable, painful process of being required to reflect upon the factors that house and sustain the community of teaching that they are entering, and this process has come to form part of the ECE class we teach, as well as other elementary-school-level "methods" courses. These courses are ordinarily taught separately from practicum/practical considerations of the entrance of student teachers into the community of teaching. They are ordinarily engorged with information, and have little time for reflection and the recovery of any deep sense of the initiatory character of students' experiences. Part of this initiatory process—perhaps an inevitable part—is the monstrous, disproportionate visions that we so often encounter in our work with student teachers.

As teacher educators, we are caught up in the delicate, agonizing balance between, on the one hand, ushering "new blood" into the community of teaching and thus ensuring its regeneration and, on the other hand, being wary that the patterns that pertain (which bind our lives to the lives of children and the life of the Earth) are not violated simply in the name of novelty or by allowing the new student teacher a certain freedom. The task of teacher education is therefore deeply ethical and ecological: We are asked to help student teachers reflect upon the reliable, ambiguous, mysterious "factors" that house and sustain their lives and the lives of the children they will teach.

More pointedly put, the task of teacher education is to help student teachers themselves to see the deeply ethical and ecological character of what *they* do and what *their* responsibility will henceforth be. They themselves are charged with taking on the agonizing balance between, on the one hand, ushering children into the world and being open to the new, ebullient regenerativity that children bring with them, and, on the other hand, being wary and protective and careful of the patterns that pertain.

Preamble 8: "Catch Only What You've Thrown Yourself, All Is Mere Skill and Little Gain"

Catch only what you've thrown yourself, all is
mere skill and little gain.
—Rainer Maria Rilke, cited as the frontispiece of Hans-Georg
Gadamer's *Truth and Method* (1989)

The next two chapters take on what has become a popular contemporary epistemological gloss in educational circles: constructivism. In light of our discussion of the idea of a regime of scarcity and its origins and consequences, constructivism begins to reveal some disturbing beginnings that are, for the most part, left out of any discussion of our pedagogical love affair with constructivism. It also begins to reveal some even more disturbing contemporary political parallels.

In its ancestral origins (Immanuel Kant, 1704–1824, and, more familiar to educators, Jean Piaget, 1896–1980) constructivism signals the end of abundance. It is linked, as George Grant (1998) suggested, with the "marriage of knowledge and production" (p. 1) and thereby, as many authors have witnessed, to the rise of modern capitalism (see Illich, 1972, 1973, 1992; Illich & Cayley, 1992; Jardine, 2006, K. Polanyi, 2001; Smith, 2000, 2003) and thereby with the conceptual imaginary of "scarcity."

When knowledge becomes imagined as the constructed production of an individual, all that that individual can catch, to paraphrase Rilke, is what he or she has tossed. The idea that the world might overcome my constructions and draw me out of my constructive complacency becomes jeopardized.

Constructivism imagines managing the abundance of things in light of its own forms, its own ideas and beliefs by means of reconstructing anything that comes to meet it into what it already understands.

Knowledge becomes *privatized* (the constructions produced by an individual child [or by a particular cultural group]; see Jardine, P. Clifford, & Friesen, 1999) and *commodified* into a product. As a consequence, knowledge is in jeopardy of losing its worldly measure. It is in jeopardy of becoming the producing subject's private property. As a private property, knowledge is becoming equated with opinion. "I think this" is becoming a full and adequate public accounting of oneself.

Constructivism is born into and productive of an atmosphere in which propaganda can work very effectively and in which complacency makes no difference. If you believe that all you can do is have your own opinion, you won't even pursue anything beyond your opinion because that "beyond" is, of course, constructed by you anyway. Taken to such an hallucinogenic extreme, constructivism loses any sense of referent. It is premised upon "mere skill and little gain" because it can catch only what it has thrown itself.

In such a world, speaking of abundance makes no sense, because any sense of overflow and excess beyond what I might construct is always already constructed by me as "beyond." When what I can experience must of necessity take on the constituted, constructed, and produced form that I give it, I'm necessarily blocked from being in touch with anything "beyond me," beyond, that is, my sphere of production. Abundance is impossible. Worse yet (as contended in the following chapter and as seen already previously), abundance becomes wild and fearsome, monstrous, an alien threat. That there might be others that think differently that my constructs of them, that there might be things in the world that could be thought differently and that might overflow and outrun my experiences of them—this is "where the wild things are" (Sendak, 1988; see Preamble 7 and chap. 7) and where, in times of scarcity, we dare not venture.

Chapter 8

Cutting Nature's Leading Strings: A Cautionary Tale About Constructivism

David W. Jardine

> *Accordingly, the spontaneity of understanding becomes the formative principle of receptive matter, and in one stroke we have the old mythology of an intellect which glues and rigs together the world's matter with its own forms.*
> —Martin Heidegger (*The History of the Concept of Time*, 1985, p. 70)

> *No sooner have you grabbed hold of it than myth opens out into a fan of a thousand segments. Here the variant is the origin. In each of these diverging stories all the others are reflected, all brush by us like folds of the same cloth. If, out of some perversity of tradition, only one version of some mythical event has come down to us, it is like a body without a shadow, and we must do our best to trace out that invisible shadow.*
> —Roberto Calasso (*The Marriage of Cadmus and Harmony*, 1993, p. 133)

Immanuel Kant's *Critique of Pure Reason* (1787/1983) is precisely such a mythical event, containing precisely such invisible shadows in the ways that it has come down to us. It has become silently epoch making in our ability to imagine the nature and limits of knowledge, especially in the realm of educational theory and practice, and most pointedly in regard to issues of environmental education and ecological awareness and experience. The particular educational import of Kant's work is manifest, *via* the work of Jean Piaget, in the now-popular educational idea of "constructivism" and its educational consort, "development."

This chapter is intended as a cautionary tale to those in education who, like me, have been quite charmed by constructivism and the sense of interrelatedness and interdependence and epistemological intimacy that it seems to portend. I am not going to review the myriad folds and forms that constructivism has taken in contemporary thought. Rather, as a cautionary tale, this tale is populated by ancestors, by ghosts, by powerful images and ideas that, I suggest, have been occluded by constructivism's myriad contemporary appearances, but that still have power and potency behind the scenes of our experiences and intentionalities and hopes for the breakthroughs wrought by this still-fresh way of thinking.

Constructivism has become potent and powerful in our educational imagination but, as with so many cautionary tales, we find that our strength is also our weakness, our freedom is very often also our limit.

"A LIGHT BROKE UPON THE STUDENTS OF NATURE"

> *The brighter the light, the darker the shadow.*
> —Robert Bly (*A Little Book on the Human Shadow*, 1988, p. 1)

> *A light broke upon the students of nature. They learned that reason has insight only into that which it produces after a plan of its own, and that it must not allow itself to be kept, as it were, in nature's leading-strings, but must itself show the way with principles of judgement based on fixed laws, constraining nature to give answer to questions of reason's own determining. Reason ... must approach nature in order to be taught by it. It must not, however, do so in the character of a pupil who listens to everything the teacher chooses to say, but of an appointed judge who compels the witnesses to answer questions which he had himself formulated. While reason must seek in nature, not fictitiously ascribe to it, whatever has to be learnt, if learnt at all, only from nature, it must adopt as its guide, in so seeking, that which it has itself put into nature.*
> —Immanuel Kant (*Critique of Pure Reason*, 1964, p. 20)

Immanuel Kant's *Critique of Pure Reason* was, as its title suggests, intended as a *critique*, that is, as a *setting of the limits* of human reason, finding its borders or boundaries, its liminal edges. Kant was profoundly concerned about the potentiality for human reason to overstep its boundaries, to overreach its capabilities, and about the terrible dangers that follow from such overstepping. It is precisely this potentiality for overstepping that has fallen into shadow in much of the contemporary love affair with constructivism.

The roots of this potentiality can be simply stated, but its consequences are immeasurable. In knowing objects, we cast them into relationship with our ways of knowing. Therefore, we can never know things themselves (what Kant names the *Ding-an-sich*, the thing "in itself" or "in its indigenous nature independently of its admixture with us") because the act of knowing is the act of knowing-the-thing-only-in-relation-to-our-ways-of-knowing. In knowing things in the world, we inevitably, and to some mysterious extent, see our own face reflected there (in passing, consider the echoes of Genesis, and God's face reflected in the as-yet unformed waters that are then formed by His utterance, as well as the tale of Narcissus and his enrapture with his own reflection—both analogies to the charms and shadows of constructivism).

Briefly glimpsed here is Kant's admonishment: Things-in-themselves escape the potential tyrannies of being cast into a relation with human reason. Independently of human reason, things themselves, Kant allows, "conform to laws of their own" (Kant, 1787/1964, p. 178). But this skips too far ahead in the tale. Why would Kant consider that being cast into a relation with human reason might be potentially tyrannical?

The previously cited passage from Kant's *Critique* gives us two clues to follow, two folds of "the same cloth" (*textus*, the same weave, the same text) to explicate that are of especial interest to educators:

- Human understanding is a *demand* that is properly wielded free from nature's leading strings and earthly constraints
- The path to this freedom of human understanding is the road to *maturity*.

From these themes emerges a new figure in this cautionary tale, one much closer to the hearts and minds of educators: Jean Piaget.

THEME 1: HUMAN REASON AS A DEMAND

The first telling theme for educators in Immanuel Kant's epoch-making *Critique of Pure Reason* is the conceiving of knowledge as an active, constructive, orderly, and ordering, *demand made upon things*. "To know," henceforth, is no longer understood as merely and simply and passively receiving information from an object (think of all those old "filling an empty vessel" images of education, or ones of "writing on a blank tablet," a *tabula rasa*). Knowledge is not a matter of resting in the presence of things and learning their ways through tough experience that must be suffered or undergone (see Gadamer's, 1989, work on *Erfahrung*—a term that translates as "experience" but that contains the roots both of a journey [*Fahren*] and of ancestry [*Vorfahren*]). Rather, "to know" is to demand that *the world* suffer our acts of knowing: To know is "to impose structure," "to (give) order(s)," "to demand," "to determine," "to make," "to produce," "to create"—in popular contemporary educational parlance, "to construct."

To know is to *act* (in definable, determinable ways) and such action is not simply one that is taken or exercised "upon," say, this orderly pine tree outside of my window. Rather, such action is *productive of order*. Differently put, once things are cast into a relationship with human reason, the order of those things is *produced* by reason's demand: "The order and regularity in [what] we call *nature*, we ourselves introduce. We could never find [such orderliness and regularity] ... had not we ourselves, or the nature of our mind, originally set them there" (Kant, 1787/1964, p. 147). In the popular parlance of constructivism, we "construct" an understanding of things through acts and ideas that are formative of what we understand things to be. The patterns "of" that pine tree (I now parenthesize "of" because this the precise nature of this ascription to the tree is now in limbo) are, somehow or other, "human constructs." In knowing the pine tree, we don't know the pine tree and *its* patterns, but only the outcomes of what we make of it. The tree as known and experienced becomes our product—an epoch-making and ecologically traumatic "marriage of knowledge and production" (Grant, 1998, p. 1) in which things as known become commodities in what then becomes, in our time, a "knowledge economy." We become like little gods, the world (as far as we know) becomes our creation and we become its order-wielding center.

Here is where our ecological consciousness begins to stir in the shadow of Kantianism and its constructivist offspring. As conceived by and inherited from Immanuel Kant, human reason is a *synthesizing* faculty that, in the act of knowing something in the world, *actively constructs orderliness out of the chaos of experience* in accordance with human reason's own structures, reason's own forms, reason's own categories (over a century later, Jean Piaget, 1971b, would call this "imposing cosmos on the chaos of experience," p. xii). *To be an object in the world,* according to Kant, means *to have been constructed as an object* according to human reason's criteria of "objectivity." In short, "we make all the patterns" (W. Berry, 1987, p. 5).

The origin of this idea in Kant's work is very simple. He began by examining the type of knowledge that is at work in logic, mathematics, and Euclidean geometry and determined that such knowledge cannot be *derived from empirical experience.* Any knowledge thus derived can only lead to *empirical generalizations* whose status is always and necessarily *probable.* However, Kant noted that in logic, mathematics, and Euclidean geometry there is a type of knowledge at work that is not probable but rather universal and necessary—the grammar of logical deduction, the rules of geometrical calculation, the structures of mathematical reasoning (in short, "the categories and concepts of established science" [Inhelder, 1969, p. 23]—those very concepts and categories that, not especially incidentally, define the work of "environmental science"). He therefore deduced (in the section of the *Critique of Pure Reason* called the "Transcendental Deduction") that, by its very nature, human thinking has universal and necessary forms, necessary and unavoidable categories or structures or, if you will (and following Jean Piaget), schematic ways of operating. And, because thinking has such universal and necessary structures independently of and not derived from any contact with things in the world (a priori), thinking *about something in the world* (say, that pine tree outside of the window) necessarily becomes an act wherein the thing that is thought *about* must submit to the a priori forms of thought that think about it. These a priori forms are not born out of an intimacy with earthly things (this is not their "origin"; see chap. 4), but are essential conditions that human reason sets down ahead of time. These forms are, in this sense, right in line with the Enlightenment ideas of autonomy, freedom, and independence.

Ergo, in its infancy, one of the occluded origins of constructivism.

What occurs in Kant's work at this juncture is that a great divide opens up, a divide in the nature of nature itself: "That nature should direct itself [in] conformity to law[s imposed by human reason], sounds very strange and absurd. But consider that *this* nature is not a thing in itself but is merely an aggregate of appearances, so many representations of the mind" (Kant, 1787/1964, p. 140). A divide opens up between nature "itself" (whatever this might now mean. Something unspoilt by our demands? Edenic perhaps, lost through the acquisition of knowledge as Genesis suggests?), and the *appearance* of nature in human experience and knowledge, insofar as that appearance meets the conditions set out in advance and demanded by human agency:

> The question arises how it can be conceivable that nature should have to proceed in accordance with [a priori] categories which ... are not derived from it and do not mold themselves on its pattern? The solution of this seeming enigma is as follows. Things in themselves would necessarily, apart from any understanding that knows them, conform to laws of their own. But appearances are only representations of things that are unknown as regards what they may be in themselves. As mere representations, they are subject to no law of connection save that which the connecting faculty [the categorical, structural, constructive demands of human reason are synthetic in character, that is, they are ways that things are brought together in thinking, synthesized, connected, melded from chaos into cosmos] prescribes. (Kant, 1787/1964, p. 178)

In short, and only in regard to things as humanly experienced and known, not things in themselves, human reason is that faculty that *makes* all the connections, all the patterns, all essential forms and shapes of knowable things. And, insofar as human reason sets the conditions under which any thing might be experienced and known, it makes sense, now, to say that "the *a priori* conditions of a possible experience in general are at the same time conditions of the possibility of objects of experience" (Kant, 1787/1964, p. 138). Nature as experienced and known becomes a closed system with humanity at its center, holding, in advance and universally and necessarily, the conditions under which this nature can appear. And, more troublesome, we become effectively cut off from Nature "itself," as witnessed in the chilling words of Arthur Schopenhauer in *The World as Will and Representation* (1963), originally published in the mid-19th century:

> "The world is my representation": This is a truth valid with reference to every living and knowing being, although man alone can bring it into reflective, abstract consciousness. If he really does so, philosophical discernment has dawned on him. It then becomes clear and certain to him that he does not know a sun and an earth, but only an eye that sees a sun, a hand that feels an earth; that the world around him is there only as representation, in other words, only in reference to another thing, namely, that which represents, and this is himself. (p. 63)

Or, in the much more innocent and light-hearted parlance of constructivism (a parlance that has, in most quarters, given up the Kantian idea of universal and necessary categories or constructs and has, shall we say, psychologized, or perhaps democratized and individualized the idea of construction) I somehow "bring" to my experiences my own background and perspectives and constructs and can therefore only speak of things in the world—like that pine tree outside the window—"from my own perspective."

It was Kant's great and honorable intention to pronounce this light that had broken upon the students of nature regarding human reason as precisely a *humiliation* of its scope and power. Human reason is shown in his work to be *incapable* of thinking beyond its own constructions and therefore *incapable* of finding the measure of those things that come to meet us in our experience except through its own petulant demands.

Unfortunately, however, Immanuel Kant's imagining of human reason as a demand has a great and terrible consonance with the spirit of the times in which this imagining emerged, right at the height of *colonialism*. Kant's work (and thus one of the great ancestors of constructivism) resonates with the colonial spirit. Issuing from Europe at this time was the unshakeable belief that "we" (a great and contentious identifier) have in hand the conditions of reasonableness, of civility and culture and morality and so on, and it is our duty, in traversing the so-called New World, to demand that that world live up to these conditions that we have deployed a priori (see Smith, 2003).

Let's be clear-eyed, here. Kant's epoch-making imagining of human reason as a universal and necessary (a priori) demand made upon the world is perfectly in line with the spirit of colonialism. To the extent that we believe that we have come upon the essential character of reasonableness, civility, culture, morality, and so on, we demand these things of the world(s) we encounter in order to draw that heretofore uncivilized, disorderly, primitive, savage, world up into its truth, the truth that we have already secured a priori. We demand that the world submit to European invasion and colonization—can we bear this?—*for its own good* (see Miller, 1989).

And so, the shadow. We (who cleave to the essence of human civility, freedom and reasonableness) are *the best in the world* and the world is spread out in an array of proximity to and distance from such a center of moralizing, demanding, issuance, a center whose deafness regarding what is said *to* it is a sign of its strength. We can begin to grasp, here, the ancestry of George W. Bush's recent, but by no means novel, hallucination of a "crescent of democracy stretching from Morocco to Bahrain" created by the export of an array of American a prioris: freedom, democracy, individuality, the free market, liberty, and so on.

This is a glimpse of a constructivism that has lost its limit, lost its measure, and that finds its measure only in itself. As Jean Piaget put it a century and a half after Immanuel Kant, it is a measure that is "self-sufficient and alone guarantee[s] [its] own reflection" (Piaget, 1965, p. 225).

Of course, none of this was Kant's intent, but this simply indicates that admissions of good intentions are rather inadequate to understanding our current crises. Kant meant to show that Reason's self-containedness in a world of its own making marked out its helplessness and weakness and its need to be supplemented with a deeply moral and earthly sense of the appropriateness of its application. For us, here, charmed by constructivism, we don't quite know how to deal with the fact that the orderliness and ways of the pine tree outside of my window have disappeared into appearances of my own ordering.

THEME 2: IMMATURITY, MATURITY, AND THE DEVELOPMENTAL STEPCHILD OF CONSTRUCTIVISM

We need to begin unfolding this second theme by recalling the passage from Immanuel Kant's *Critique of Pure Reason*, wherein a light broke upon the students of nature. Certainly, as this passage indicates, we can learn things from the world and must not fictitiously ascribe things to it. However, the things that can and must be learned from the world are necessarily *accidental features of the world,* not *essential* features. Why? Because the essence of things (as known and experienced) is an issuance of Reason itself, "put into" nature by Reason's synthesizing, patterning, constructing agency. The universal and necessary forms that things can take is known a priori. Or, as the saying goes with constructivism, I can only talk about the object under consideration in light of my own constructs in terms of which I experience or filter or form or fashion or determine or make up or shape or determine or schematize or ... and so on.

But there is another theme here that is much more immediate in the minds of educators. In *The Critique,* and also from a later essay titled "What is Enlightenment?" (1983, originally published in 1794), Kant consistently links up the refusal to use your own Reason (and its ordering demands) with *immaturity.* We catch sight of this in the previously cited passage when Kant asks us to sever our dependence on "Nature's leading-strings" (our infantile, dependent, immature "apron strings," if you will) and cleave only to those demands produced by Reason itself. Acting in accord with the a priori demands of us maturity, and Kant's clarion call to pursue Enlightenment is full of implied images of adult and child:

> *Enlightenment is man's emergence from his self-imposed immaturity. Immaturity* is the inability to use one's understanding without guidance from another. This immaturity is *self-imposed* when its cause lies not in a lack of understanding, but in a lack of resolve and courage to use it without guidance from another. *Sapere Aude!*: "Have courage to use your own understanding!"—that is the motto of the Enlightenment. (Kant, 1794/1983, p. 41)

The Enlightenment image of Reason, then, is pictured as the way in which humanity has overcome its immaturity, its primitiveness, its animality and wildness ("leading-strings" names a cord used to lead and train animals), its dependence ("leading-strings" were use to teach children to stand and walk).

JEAN PIAGET AND THE "SPIRIT OF KANTIANISM"

> One can feel very close to the spirit of Kantianism (and I believe I am close to it). [However] the necessity characteristic of the syntheses [Kant's *a priori* categories of Reason are the universal and necessary ways that experience is "knit together" by Reason. They are "synthesizing." They are "syntheses"] becomes [in Jean Piaget's work] a *terminus ad quem* and ceases to be [as in Immanuel Kant's work] a *terminus a quo.* (Piaget, 1965, p. 57)

Jean Piaget's work shares this characteristic with the work of Immanuel Kant: Jean Piaget believes that human reason is an active, organizing, structuring *demand made upon the world.* However, typical adult human reasoning as manifest in the Kantian a priori categories, and its handmaiden disciplines, logic and mathematics, are only a late-arriving set of structures and ordering demands in the course of both the development of the species (*phylogeny*) and the recapitulatory development of the individual (*ontogeny;* see Jardine, 2006, for an elaboration of these ideas).

In Piaget's work, the Kantian categories are not the point *from which* knowledge emerges (*terminus ad quo*), but the *point to* which knowledge develops (*terminus ad quem*). The Kantian categories emerge as humans mature. In Piaget's work, responding to the Enlightenment call that we "grow up" is not a matter of courage and resolve but is, rather, a matter of *the natural course of human development.* For Piaget, humans naturally tend toward the maturity of the demands of reason. Piaget thus tethers together the light that broke upon the students of nature with the burgeoning theme of progress that was rampant in the late 19th and early 20th century (see Jardine, 2006, for more on this theme).

Now if the Kantian categories emerge as humans mature, how can they be understood as a universal and necessary demand made upon things? In Piaget's work, it seems that "the concepts and categories of established science" (Inhelder, 1969, p. 23) are simply a demand made by *adults* (and, as many critiques have offered, European, especially male, adults at that). It is here that the brilliant insight of Jean Piaget emerges and that the lifeblood of contemporary constructivism takes further shape and consequence.

According to Piaget, the demanding, structuring, constructing, organizing, ordering character of human life is totalized. *All of human life*—from the frail actions of a newborn infant, to a child bursting bubbles and laughing, to the pristine and abstract intricacies of a mathematician's scrawls—*has the character of such a demand*:

> *Every relation* between the living being and its environment [not just those in logic and mathematics and the logic of objectivity characteristic of the concepts and categories and methods of established science] has this particular

characteristic: the former, instead of submitting passively to the latter, modifies it by imposing on it a certain structure of its own. (Piaget, 1952, p. 118, my emphasis)

And, in a breathtaking ecological insight, the same is true *for all beings*—the chickadees swooping out of the branches of that pine tree outside the window, the nuthatches upside down on its trunk, that tree itself, *all living things* have the character of active, living, formative, demanding, ordering, organizing engagement in the world. Or, as Piaget puts it, there is a "self-organizing principle *inherent in life itself*" (Piaget, 1952, p. 19, my emphasis), and this inherent principle defines the living being as an active agent who "imposes structure" on the things with which it interacts. This way of operating on the world is, according to Piaget, "the fundamental reality about living things" (Piaget, 1971a, p. 347) and not simply a characteristic of the Kantian categories.

So what is it, then, that makes the realms of logic, mathematics, and Euclidean geometry (the great realms of Kant's a priori in his *Critique of Pure Reason*) seem universal and necessary when, in fact, they only emerge slowly over the course of human development? Here is the great turn in this cautionary tale. In Jean Piaget's work, it is not a particular set of constructs that are a priori. Rather, it is the "self-organizing principle inherent in life itself" that is a priori. What is a priori is not this or that set of constructs, but the inevitability, in all living beings, of the *functioning* of constructing (captured in Piaget's terms assimilation, accommodation, and equilibration).

Therefore, according to Piaget, this a priori functioning (not the structures or categories or forms peculiar to this or that living being at this or that stage of development or maturing) becomes that in relation to which the development or maturity of humanity occurs.

> [The functioning of "life itself"] orients the whole of the successive structures which the mind will then work out in contact with reality [culminating in the structures peculiar to the mature adult]. It will thus play the role that [Immanuel Kant] assigned to the *a priori:* that is to say, [this functional a priori] will impose on the structures [characteristics of each stage of development under consideration] a certain necessary and irreducible condition. Only the mistake has sometimes been made [for example, in the work of Immanuel Kant] of regarding the *a priori* as consisting in structures existing ready-made from the beginning of development, whereas if the functional invariant of thought is at work in the most primitive stages, it is only little by little that it impresses itself on consciousness due to the elaboration of structures which are increasingly adapted to the function itself. (Piaget, 1952, p. 3)

Structures or constructs or categories or forms or orders must now be thought of, not as fixed and finished demands, but rather:

> [They must be thought of as] a particular form of equilibrium, more or less stable within its restricted field and losing its stability on reaching the limits

of the field. But these structures, forming different levels, are to be regarded
as succeeding one another according to the law of development, such that
each one brings about a more inclusive and stable equilibrium for the processes that emerge from the preceding level. (Piaget, 1973, p. 7)

Development, now understood as a succession of structures oriented toward
steadily increasing stability and inclusiveness, *"tends towards an all-embracing
equilibrium by aiming at the assimilation of the whole of reality"* (Piaget, 1973, p.
9). Life, according to Piaget (and in light of age-old mythopoetic narratives
[see Jardine, 2006]), is *teleologically oriented* toward a particular end: an
all-embracing equilibrium.

It will be of no surprise that it is precisely a version of the Kantian categories
that constitutes this "all-embracing equilibrium" (Piaget, 1973, p. 9). Formal
logic and mathematics, which underwrite the methods of operation in established science (and, by the way, the so-called environmental sciences as well),
are understood by Jean Piaget to embody the functional a priori inherent in
"life itself." The functional a priori is embodied in the *functioning* of objective
science, its methods. As long as we cleave to the methods of objective science
and its products, we cleave to the inherent ordering character of life itself.

Therefore, development is not a process of slowly adapting, to use the
Kantian terminology, to things themselves, but is, rather, a process of becoming better and better adapted to *the inevitable a priori functioning of adaptation itself.* Development (the maturity alluded to in Kant's work) is
oriented, therefore, toward better and better adaptation to the inevitable
"organizing activity inherent in life itself" (Piaget, 1952, p. 19). The pecu-
liarity of the Kantian categories is that they constitute "an extension and
perfection of all adaptive processes" (Piaget, 1973, p. 7) insofar as they are
perfectly adapted to this organizing activity. In this way, the Kantian categories take on the appearance of universality and necessity (take on the appearance of being a priori) at the end of development because they are
perfect expressions of that which *is* universal and necessary. "The progress
of reason doubtless consists in an increasingly advanced awareness of the organizing activity inherent in life itself" (Piaget, 1952, p. 19). At its developmental end, such an awareness is an "all-embracing assimilatory schemata
tending to encompassing the whole of reality" (Piaget, 1973, p. 9) because it
is an awareness of that very organizing activity (which, in maturing, becomes
"that very method") in terms of which reality itself is constituted. At the
highest level of development we have the methods of logico-mathematical
knowledge that underwrite objective science, which is, in essence, a knowledge of the constructive and organizational operations of knowledge itself,
knowledge, that is, of the *functioning* that has been going on all along. When
we reach the level of formal logic and theoretical mathematics, however,
perfect equilibrium is attained because, in these sciences (which are crystal-
lized in the *methods* of established science) we "proceed by the application of
perfectly explicit rules, these rules being, of course, the very ones that de-

fine the structure under consideration" (Piaget, 1970, p. 15). That is to say, at the level of logic and mathematics, the rules for *doing* the operations of logic and mathematics are precisely the rules *upon which* one operates. Logic and mathematics are thus perfectly equilibrated (i.e., perfectly adapted to the inevitable process of adaptation itself), for there is no longer any difference between *the operator* (the subject who *does* logic and mathematics operates only in accord with the rules requisite of logic and mathematics—what Piaget calls an anonymous epistemic subject who operates identically to *any* subject who does logic and mathematics, in accord only with the general and abstract "processes common to all subjects" [Piaget, 1965, p. 108]), *the operations* we perform (logical and mathematical operations) and *that upon which we are operating* (things insofar as they have been constructed into possible objects of objective science, things, therefore, insofar as they follow the rules of logic and mathematics).

In sum, it is human reason as manifest in the methods of objective science that operates in line with the organizing functioning inherent in life itself, and this defines the autonomy, independence, and maturity hinted at in Immanuel Kant's Enlightenment clarion. Therefore, anything known under the auspices of this way of knowing is known for what it essentially is, because the questions posed to that thing are posed in line with what we know its essence to already be: the organizing functioning inherent in life itself (which is now embodied in the concepts and categories of established science). The circle is now closed and objective science finds its measure only in itself.

"THE SAVAGE CHILDHOOD OF THE HUMAN RACE"

This surely isn't the place to even attempt to lay out all of the threads tangled here. For now, I offer only a sketch, another monster in this cautionary tale.

We have all witnessed how the language of "development" has come to be used in our understanding of the diversity of cultures and peoples in the world. We know how well the language of development follows from the logic of colonialism, just as Jean Piaget's developmental theory follows the "spirit of Kantianism."

We know full well of this history. For example, we know how, under the British Empire, the diversity of the Commonwealth was spread before the Crown as a wonderful, rich array of comparatively uncivilized, underdeveloped, less reasonable, less cultured, less "mature" places. We know, from, for example, the work of Nandy (1987), how those subjected to colonial rule were systematically and deliberately characterized as "children."

Once again, this cautionary tale demands both exaggeration and bluntness. Developmental sequences are set out only by those who consider themselves to be "developed." You don't map out a sequence in order to find that you are "[the] third [world]," only to show what you already believed, that you are "number one."

It is thus that developmentalism and the images of maturity that it portends that add a profound new element to the old colonialism. With colonialism, we were able to believe that we stood in the midst of the world as the best—the freest, the most reasonable, the most civilized. With developmentalism, we get a new twist on the modernist spirit of universality and necessity (recall, Kant's criteria for the a priori): We are not just "the best" amongst others in the world. We are that toward which the world is heading in its progress toward maturity. We are its natural *end*, and the failures of the world to continue to (naturally) develop into what we already are must be dealt with preemptively.

Just in case this seems to have gotten a bit out of hand, consider the following excerpt from an interview with David Frum, a Canadian who was the author of George Bush's recent "axis of evil" speech. David Frum was speaking with Evan Solomon, one of the hosts of the Canadian Broadcasting Company's (CBC) television program *Sunday Morning*. Frum was attempting to lay out his vision of the place of recent and future American preemptive actions in the Middle East, and images of childhood, adolescence, and adulthood—images of development—appear:

> *Evan Solomon:* It this a prescription for American imperialism? Is this the new empire? I know that you think it is a beneficent empire ...
>
> *David Frum:* No, no, absolutely not. This is the adolescence of the human race. This is the moment when human beings are making the transition from a world governed by violence to a world governed by law. Just as the North Atlantic is governed by law, we hope that some day the whole world will look like that. But the instrument whereby humanity is going to make that transition from the savage childhood of the human race to law-abiding adulthood is through the instrument of American power. It is America who is going to ... maybe someday it will be somebody else's ... maybe someday it will be India's job, a while ago it was Britain's, but today it is America's power that is going to spread the realm of law and civilization and democracy. (Frum & Solomon, 2004)

Our self-understanding is thus not simply that we are *the most developed*, but that we (and, again, I leave this contentious signifier undefined) are *the destiny of the world*. Our interventions in the world are thus aimed at bringing out in others what we already know their inevitable destiny to be.

And though they may petulantly and peevishly resist, it is their salvation we offer, or, otherwise, their sacrifice (see Smith, in press, for a brilliantly terrifying exploration of this theme).

END BIT

In his 1772 lectures on philosophical anthropology at the University of Konigsberg, Kant proclaimed that the American Indians "are incapable of civilization." He described them as having "no motive force, for they are without affection and passion. They are not drawn to one another by love, and are thus unfruitful. They hardly speak at all, never caress one another, care about nothing, and are lazy." In a note in his lecture he foreshadowed two long centuries of racist thought in Germany when he wrote that the Indians "are incapable of governing themselves" and are "destined for extermination." (Weatherford, 1988, p. 127)

And this from a man who never in his life left Konigsberg.

I'm not going to try to find my way out of this cautionary tale in this context, partially because, of course, the tale it tells is in some sense true. We all do find our way in the world in accord with our ways in the world. And still, somehow, I want to note the familiar springtime change in the call of those Mountain Chickadees in a way that at least attempts to rest in the integrity of *their* ways and not just in the outcomes of my own construction.

Part of the gift of constructivism is a deep and troublesome recognition of our complicity in our knowing, in our experiencing. This gift portends a deep humiliation and a clearer understanding of the necessity of patience and forgiveness and love.

I'm going to leave this tale now only with the most meager of morals. My strength, my power, my potency, is also my weakness, and only in recognition of this lacuna comes the possibility of the cultivation of humility, of real humanity. That I construct the world only in light of my own experiences names my terrible loneliness and frailty and vulnerability and dependence. It names how my own life is not adequate to my living in this world.

For now, I simply concede how inadequate is this moral to the tale it concludes.

Preamble 9: Stepping Away From the Marriage of Knowledge and Production

Constructivism is certainly well meaning and it has had the effect of demanding that educators realize that those they face in the classroom may be making different sense of what occurs than they presume. It has, on the face of it, the potential to disturb our complacency and open us up to the abundant array of possibilities that outstrip our presumptions. This is the most horrifying of insights for new student teachers—that your students *think about you*.

However, such a monstrous child (see Preamble 7, chap. 7, and Jardine, 1994c) can, under the dull-minded application of Jean Piaget's work, become hamstrung along a developmental sequence and we can dull the effects of their appearance by means of the very constructivism that allowed them to first appear. That is why Jean Piaget's work is so pivotal, because, as with any pivotal thinker, he opened educational discourse to something unforeseen that was then, through the beneficent work of his followers, colonized and de-potentiated into terrible little developmental readers and sequenced curriculum guides (see Jardine, 2006). As with any pivotal thinker, at first, a great imaginal territory is opened up, full of portent, but such matters are soon quelled and we produce, so often in education, contemptible "educational activities" that have drained the life out of what we love.

A version of the previous chapter was presented at the American Educational Research Association meetings on environmental education, with the gracious invitation of Bob Jickling, the editor of the *Canadian Journal of Environmental Education*. I (D.J.) was fortunate to have thoughtful responses to that paper by Bob Johnson and Leesa Fawcett, and Bob Jickling encouraged the three of us to write it up. What follows is that conversation.

Chapter 9

Further Thoughts on "Cutting Nature's Leading Strings": A Conversation

Bruce Johnson
Leesa Fawcett
David W. Jardine

David Jardine (DJ): This conversation is a follow-up, both to the paper published in this issue of *CJEE* and to the AERA session of the same name from April 2005. I want to extend many thanks to all concerned. Having the time and forum for such talks is rare and I'm so thankful to Bob Jickling for the conference invitation and the chance to continue things here. I also want to thank Bruce Johnson (*BJ*) and Leesa Fawcett (*LF*), both for the careful responses they provided at AERA, and for the great questions that follow (*italicized*). Thinking about them has certainly helped lift my head out of the great gray of winter.

BJ: I preface with three qualifiers that I hope will help readers interpret my questions. First, I am much more concerned with and grounded in practice than I am in philosophy. Second, from a very practical standpoint, namely the desire for humans to be able to continue to live on our planet, I believe that there are rights and wrongs in how we relate to the natural world. Third, in my view, the purpose of education is change.

If, in the Kantian view, the way we know the world is determined (constrained) by our a priori mental structures, then is our job in education to work on the a priori structures? If the most common a priori structures (or worldviews or perceptions) in Western societies are anthropocentric and lead to destructive relationships with the natural world, is what we are doing, or should be doing, really helping people to reconstruct more ecocentric a priori systems within themselves?

DJ: I'm not sure if the working out of any a priori system doesn't simply further entrench the narcissism and egocentricity that constructivism feeds upon. Let me worry this for a bit.

Constructivism begins, I think, with the premise of the Cartesian separation of subjectivity from the world. Pursuing a more "ecocentric" set of a priori categories in terms of which I construct the world still leaving us with a world constructed and produced by a category wielding subjectivity. It leaves us with the world produced by humanity (which is why constructivism can be understood to be very urban epistemology).

I think that it is vital to simply step away from this whole line of thought. How do we do this? Well, wouldn't it be nice if there was an easy answer to that! Let me try a beginning in the classroom, because like you, Bruce, I am interested in how the sort of imaginal shift we are seeking works itself out in the classroom, in practical, lived terms.

When we take an example like the Pythagorean theorem, say, as a particular curriculum topic entrusted to teachers and students in schools, hermeneutics suggests that we do not begin with the belief that this phenomenon is an object over which I wish to have constructive command. Rather, we (students and teachers) can begin by thinking of the Pythagorean theorem as part of the contested, vivid human inheritance *to which we belong*. Rather than it being understood as an object that belongs to me because it is produced by my epistemological productivity or constructivity, it can be just as easily understood as an ancestry, a bloodline, an ancient tale that has been handed to us by one of our kin and into whose inheritance we have been born(e).

Here is another set of, I think, deeply ecological images that come from the hermeneutic tradition. The Pythagorean theorem (to continue this example) can be understood as a *topic*—that is, a topography, a place, a territory full of life and ways and memories and tales told and ventures, both ancient and still to be had. By beginning like this, we begin with a view of human subjectivity as belonging and living in a multifarious, contested, ancient world. Understanding begins, therefore, not with constructs that are then applied to things, but with belonging, obligation, inheritance, contestation, concern, interdependence, a sense of place, the possibility of love and heartbreak and discovery. Certainly, in entering such a place, I bring with me my presumptions, previous constructs and experiences, but I realize that I must be quite wary of such matters. This place reads the nature and limits of my experiences and constructs back to me in ways that I cannot do by myself and from within the limits of those constructs. Producing things only in my own image doesn't bode well for education, for becoming experienced in the ways of the places we inhabit.

Starting off this way subverts the Cartesian/constructivist logic and, you know, it just might start to hint at a sort of "ecocentric a priori." With you, Bob, I'll declare that I, too, believe that there are rights and wrongs in how we live and in what we ask of our kids. I'll declare this: Any topic of the human inheritance that is entrusted to teachers and children in schools is full of abundant relations, full of ancient tales and wisdoms, full of contestation and life and difficulty, and to the extent that we break apart and fragment that living world, and dole it out as lifeless objects over which we are to have nothing but constructivist dominance and command, to that extent, we are pursuing both a pedagogical and ecological disaster. How's that for a priori? The problem remains, however, that the very idea of an a priori has become, post-Kant, something *wielded* by a subjectivity. I'm concerned, then, about wielding this "ecocentric a priori" as a weapon of dominance or humiliation. Every time in human history that someone has trumpeted having in hand the universal and necessary truth (i.e., the a priori), it has turned out to be very bad news for anyone or anything that will not submit to that truth. In the abstract (in the a priori if you will) ecology can sound as imperialistic and as shrill as any other clarion call. I don't trust myself at this juncture and I become cautious and worried all over again.

BJ: If, the Piagetian view, the a priori structures are the logical result of a maturation process (development or "becoming better and better adapted to the inevitable"), then we end up with an anthropocentric worldview because it is inevitable. But is it really inevitable or simply most likely because of the ways in which our societies are structured?

DJ: I believe it is the latter and that you've hit upon something really important in these questions. In a very early work, Piaget explicitly says that he is not interested in the child's developmental construction of reality, but in the child's developmental construction of reality *as reality is understood and constructed by the objective sciences*. Piaget is only interested in how children come to "master science" and he believed quite adamantly that the mastery of science is the a priori mastery of the world, because logic and mathematics (the undergirding of science) *construct* the world into an object for science.

When Piaget's talks about this as a sort of psycho-biological inevitability, I believe that this is nothing more (and nothing less, indeed) than a voicing of a deeply seated, Eurocentric belief in the inevitable progress and ever-widening dominance of objective science (a dominance we are now surrounded by, especially given its technological consorts). This is an old Enlightenment ideal of human reason as the crown jewel of creation itself and an even older Greek belief in mathematics as the crowning jewel of human endeavor—and therefore a tale about how we are bound to fall under its (presumed) inevitability if we want to be understood as reasonable and civilized. Piaget's work is therefore part of the very Enlightenment project that the hermeneutic tradition (and some traditions that more directly inform our understanding of ecological awareness) wishes to critique.

The sort of fragmentation and logics of domination that are essential to the objective sciences and their logico-mathematical research methodologies hold a powerful sway, and these methodologies have transformed education profoundly. The topics entrusted to teachers and students in schools have been transformed from living inheritances, living places, into fragmented and inert objects that can be easily managed and assess and whose dispensation in schools can be measured and monitored. But there is nothing either natural nor inevitable about this. I've seen and written about classrooms that proceed quite differently, with an eye to a much more ecological understanding, even, say, of the Pythagorean theorem.

BJ: We are left with a rather sad moral, "That I construct the world in light of my own experiences names my terrible loneliness. It names how my own life is not adequate to my living in this world." Rather, that I construct the world in light of my own experiences fills me with hope. If education is about providing experiences, then maybe those experiences can help people construct a world in which we live with rather than on top of the earth's systems of life.

Perhaps I should have said that my constructing the world in light of my own experiences names my finitude and limits and humiliation. It names what I must transcend if I am to come to know anything other than my own image reflected in the constructs I wield. This is where I find that the hope lies, that in the classroom, students and teachers can learn to come out and play in fields of work, bodies of work, places that are abundant and that will take good care of them. My hope is that I won't live my life stuck with myself, but can, quite literally, live *out* my life. I always think of Wendell Berry at such a juncture: "Where is our comfort but in the free, uninvolved and finally mysterious beauty and grace of this world that we did not make, that has no price, that is not our work? Where is our sanity but here? Where is our pleasure but in working and resting kindly in the presence of this world?" (1989, p. 21).

LF: I found this paper generative in many ways. Here are snippets of my thoughts to help give shape to the questions that follow. Katherine Hayles (1996) in "Simulated Nature and Natural Simulations" differentiates between strong and weak constructivism and the role of the body. The most difficult and she believes the most productive place to locate, is neither contracted inside the body nor unproblematically projected outside it, but at "the cusp between the beholder and the world" (p. 412). I'm also thinking here about the idea that we are "sets of relationships or processes in time" (Evernden, 1985, p. 40). If we are in fields of care then Carol Gilligan's narrative approach to moral development makes much more sense than Kohlberg's stage theory, which followed from Kant's and Piaget's work. There is also the revolutionary work of the late Paul Shepard who took a completely opposite approach to Kant and argued that intimate knowledge and bonding with place and nature was a critical part of human maturity, a stage that is often missed these days.

How would you envision a "maturity-developmental plan"/dream for children that gives them the space (and diverse places) to resist the notion that [as suggested in chap. 8] "mature human understanding is free from nature's leading strings?"

What is the role of the body for you in environmental education, given your critique of reason and constructivism?

DJ: The cases I've seen where this resistance is cultivated are ones where the curriculum topics entrusted to schools are taken up with students as substantive, bodily, image-filled, ancient wisdoms and ways. That sounds a little high-handed, but I really think that many schools have lost a good, fertile, and intellectually sound and vibrant understanding of the *topics* sketched so meagerly in most curriculum guides. Most topics have been stripped down to easily manageable and assessable and monitorable surface features. All the old wisdoms and secret cults and flooded Niles that surround, say, the Pythagorean theorem, have been erased. In school (but not in the living world of mathematics) the Pythagorean theorem has been objectified into a memorizable formula the possession of which (there's that constructivism again) can be tested.

I've been in classrooms where these hidden worlds and wisdoms that surround, say, the Pythagorean theorem, have been allowed to open up and flourish, and where children have been invited into the deep mysteries and relations and diversity and kinship lines that define the world of the Pythagorean theorem as a living place, a living thing, a living inheritance. Kids are transformed, and so, too, are teachers. The work becomes real, the difficulties become bearable, the questions that both students and teachers have become vital, and sometimes heartbreakingly intelligent and wise and unbelievable—all this when they are allowed to go to these vivid places, these vivid topics.

There isn't a whiff, in such cases, of any desire to cut any leading strings but to do precisely the opposite—weave, relate, tether, follow leads, tug and pull, explore, play, suffer, commiserate, and so on. Getting back to your question about maturity, and what you said regarding Paul Shepard's vision in these matters, I suggest that forms of thinking and knowledge that are oriented to and by regimes of constructive dominance (remember, constructivism tells us that we give order[s]) are actually rather petulant and immature, rather frightened and, following Susan Bordo (1988), actually a bit psychotic.

There is great bodiliness suggested here. It is as if the Pythagorean theorem (just to harp on that example further) has, in schools, been stripped to the bone, lost its flesh, lost its eyes and ears, its heat, its desire. It has been effaced—it is no longer a *topos*, it is no longer Greek, no longer part of a European intellectual ancestry, no longer related to the harmony of the spheres or to the shortening of shadows as the summer solstice nears. Putting the Pythagorean theorem back into the body of the world of mathematics at once puts the body back into the act of understanding, the act of learning, the act of ecological sound schooling. All of this is deeply "cusp work," to use Hayles' term, neither interior to a subjectivity nor exterior like some indifferent object. A living person in a living world.

LF: What does this mean for the praxis of environmental education?

I believe that "environmental education" should not be a subdivision of schooling, but should describe the way we educate *altogether*. There has got to be a way to make the learning of, for example, long division, into an *environmental pursuit* into the ways of a place, a topic, an ancestry, housed in communities of knowing and writing and reading, in texts and images, and in learned practice. *All of the topics* entrusted to teachers and students in school can be understood as living fields, living inheritances, living places with ways and relations and interdependencies, *including* (but not restricted to) those topics that usually fall under "environmental education" currently in schools.

If we forget this and turn the topics of education into lifeless, fragmented, indifferent objects, we abandon most of the learning that our children undergo to a degraded, ecologically and spiritually unsound and fragmented view of the life of the world. Just as a bio-system may become degraded by being stripped of its sustaining relations, so, too, the living place of commas in the English language becomes degraded by being stripped of the sustaining relations that make this a living topic in the life of language. I always have my student teachers do meditations on curriculum topics along this line. "How is this a living topic in the world?" has to be asked before "How do I teach this to students?"

Hiving off environmental education into some sort of separate domain, usually under the umbrella of the natural sciences (and, don't forget, their inevitable constructivist logic [this is where I think Kant and Piaget were right, by the way]) abandons most of the human inheritance to antiecological thinking and imagining, and equally abandons environmental education to recycling in the classroom and having a compost heap. Meanwhile, most of what kids learn is abandoned to the dominate egologic of fragmentation and constructivistic command.

So, I think environmental education needs to be how we think of education itself, all of it, in its deepest and most loving and most sustainable sense.

LF: If humans and the more-than-human world meet one another, and come into being in relation to each other how does one represent, in the richest ways possible, the more than human world, and what are the implications of this for education?

Maybe by keeping visible in that representation the limitedness of that representation and potential violence that can ensue if we believe that the representation eats up the thing into its own constructions?

To tell you the truth, I find the term "representation" really creepy, because it keeps in place the idea of knowledge and language and experience as being a "stand in" (representative) for the real thing, a stand in "constructed" by me and therefore a construct that is my property, my product. To push this one step further, if we have in hand (à la Kant and Piaget) the a priori categories of representation, we have in hand the conditions of any possible representation. We have in hand, therefore, the ways in which things in the world are allowed to show themselves, under our command and sway.

Representationalism and constructivism thus go together somehow and they devolve into that awful murk that Arthur Schopenhauer pronounced in the 1850s:

"The world is my representation": This is a truth valid with reference to every living and knowing being, although man alone can bring it into reflective, abstract consciousness. If he really does so, philosophical discernment has dawned on him. It then becomes clear and certain to him that he does not know a sun and an earth, but only an eye that sees a sun, a hand that feels an earth; that the world around him is there only as representation, in other words, only in reference to another thing, namely, that which represents, and this is himself. (Schopenhauer, 1963, p. 63)

Part of the hermeneutic and phenomenological critiques of Cartesianism are critiques of representationalism—"stand-in-ism" and the sort of psychologistic loneliness that it portends, where each of us becomes a Cartesian subjectivity caught in the bubble of its own making.

Again, the hermeneutic critique wants to invert this Cartesian logic. When a child pipes up about, say, the way that colors are mixed around the edges of a Renoir painting, their claims and queries and findings are not constructed "stand-ins" for (i.e., representations of) the entangled topic of 19th-century painting and its troubled, often contradictory ways. Instead, they are moments in which the topic is *present*. Now it isn't fully present, of course, but what is present is no stand-in. It is Renoir that is present, that is appearing, not a stand-in. *How* he is appearing is, of necessity, limited and finite, because Renoir, as a living part of the human inheritance, doesn't just appear here and now and thus. Of course not. No presentation is absolute, but that doesn't mean we've got only stand-ins. Therefore, instead of saying that a topic is represented differently in each child's constructs, we can just as easily say that a topic presents itself differently to each child. Each child will find in that place something irreplaccably different than I might have found if I was there by myself. That child's explorations don't simply help me understand him or her. They also help me understand that this place can be thought of and experienced and articulated differently than I might have thought of, experienced, and articulated all by myself. This place can embrace us both. If we articulate these rich topics well enough as teachers, all of our students can go there and find that that place can take care of them all and can hold their differences together. *This* is why we *gather teachers and students together in a place* in order to learn about its ways, because the topics at hand present themselves differently to each of us (and to our ancestors who have taken up this topic before us), and each of these presentations complements, corrects, expands, and limits the others. The problem with "representationalism" is that I've got mine and you've got yours and that is the end of it. Representationalism that becomes timid of the belief that its constructs have any sway becomes opinionism—this is what I think, but who is to say really? Again, this entrenchment into constructs is an ecological disaster, because we lose any sense of any places where we might meet our limit.

LF: Given that Gadamer imagines "human understanding as vulnerable, de-pendent, immersed in the world," can you say more about vulnerability and moral de-velopment with respect to environmental education?

When I talk to student teachers about imagining the Pythagorean theo-rem as a rich and interesting world of relations instead of as simply an inert and indifferent formula to be memorized and soon forgotten, their first re-sponse is simple. Memorization would be easier to get across, easier to as-sess, simpler, more uniform, easier to measure the success of, and so on. Nobody said that opening up these ecologically profound matters would be a cinch. It is hard work, but there is a certain profit in work's pleasure.

Pursuing these ancestral threads puts us in a vulnerable position of real-izing how, in understanding the deeply human, deeply Earthly life of a topic, we have to realize at the very same time that our pursuit is destined to be outrun. The abundance of the topic outruns our mastery and dominance of it. Such abundance, such outrunning, defines its life as one lived "beyond our wanting and doing." Differently put, the more I learn about the Pythag-orean theorem, the more students' queries I get to explore, the better *it* gets, and the less my own knowledge feels equal to its measure. *It* gets better and my knowing seems increasingly vulnerable and helpless in the face of it.

However, there is another turn here that Gadamer suggests regarding "becoming experienced," say, in the world of Pythagoras. He suggests—I really like this and I am still meditating upon it—that the more experienced we become, the more and more sensitive we become to the subtleties and differences that new experiences bring. This really inverts a whole logic of knowledge as command and mastery and dominion. Gadamer's suggesting that becoming more and more experienced in the ways of a place entails that I'm more likely to be knocked off my feet by a child's unexpected comment or question or the like.

This is a simple idea, in a way. I've got over 200 Duke Ellington CDs—I know my way around this guy's music and recordings. Because of this ex-perience, when I first heard "Blood Count" I nearly passed out! My being experienced opened me up to its newness and the irreplaceable differ-ence it made in how I heretofore understood this man's music. The whole topic "wavered and trembled" (Caputo, 1987, p. 6). My being experi-enced, in this weird way, gave me more command over this place by giv-ing me less command.

I find this now with doing practicum supervision in elementary schools. It is very often almost overwhelmingly abundant in its significance and depth, its beauty and body. Conversely, when I go into classrooms where writing has become rote, where adding has become mechanical, where even memorization is no longer an ancient art, well, it breaks my heart, and the more experienced I become, the worse I feel. The pleasures to be had that are being lost. The idea of caring for the places we inhabit or traverse, ask-ing after their ways and being tactful and thoughtful and hard-working and sensitive and participatory. Our kids are being sacrificed to an image of the topics entrusted to schools as being objects of production and consumption. Let's not forget George Grant's warning, that constructivism has wedded knowledge and production. Schools that have attempted to avoid knowledge as blind and obedient consumption have, in many cases, left this consumptive logic in place. Instead of consumers, children are imagined as constructive producers.

There certainly is some moral sense and sensibility here. What would happen if we imagined children, not as consumers and producers of constructed products of our own making, but as inhabitants in a world that is more abundant than I make of it?

A FINAL THOUGHT

One question that came up during the conversation at the American Educational Research Association conference in Montreal, Quebec, was, in paraphrase, this: Of all the ways that you could have talked about constructivism, why did you construct it this way?

This question is profound in its display of precisely the dangers of constructivism, even though it was intended, I (D.J.) expect, to be rather lighthearted in its pointedness. What occurs in this question is that attention is moved away from *what was being claimed* (again, the topic) and toward *the constructing habits of the one making the claims*. One of the dangers of constructivism is that it allows us to feel warranted in avoiding the issues at hand (in this chapter, colonialism, imperialism, the demanding character of human thinking, the ways in which environmental science is premised on a form of thinking that just might be an ecological disaster). Rather than taking up any of these issues, they are devolved back upon the issuer. My original affront with this question is simple to state: I'm not making this up! Our world is in potential danger from this form of thinking and its ancestries, and believing that we can avoid the *topics* of cautionary tales simply by "subjectivizing" them into the constructs of the author telling the tale is *precisely* the danger of constructivism.

And, just in case this seems far fetched, I was in a Grade 3 class several years ago and told a child, with great delight, that his writing reminded me of Dylan Thomas. I was reprimanded by the teacher: "In this class, we don't impose our views on others. The only thing you have the right to say to a child in such a case is 'Tell me about your writing.' It is about what *he* thinks it's about." Thus the beachheads are set, each of us becomes "the 'god' of your own story" (Melnick, 1997, p. 372), and education becomes either a "monstrous state of siege" (Smith, 1999c, p. 140) between those for us or against us, or a pacifying mush, where all we can do is concede that we each are different and special and unique (see chap. 16 and Jardine et al., 1999).

Preamble 10:
"Within Each Dust Mote ..."

Within each dust mote is vast abundance.

— Hongzhi (*Cultivating the Empty Field*, 1991, p. 4)

This chapter has at its center how interpretive inquiry or hermeneutics operates with a sense of abundance, a sense that relates intimately to Hongzhi's Buddhist invocation regarding the abundance of a dust mote. Simply put, when paid attention to hermeneutically, seemingly simple, everyday events start to bristle with meaning and portend. Hermeneutic research should not begin as do the natural sciences, with the impoverishment of events and the stripping away of alluring connections and suggestiveness. It begins with what is *actually* given in our experience of the world: all my relations. To understand the "truth" of things is to understand how things "empty" into all their relations (see chap. 19). This is the great and difficult breakthrough that names the affinity between hermeneutics and Buddhist thought.

Most research methodologies deliberately begin by severing these nets of belonging, these abundant tethers and leads ("cutting nature's leading strings"—see chap. 8). Hermeneutics begins by pulling on these tethers and following their leads out into ancient worlds of relations, just like Richard followed Dolly on her genomic ambles.

Hermeneutics is squarely focused, not on tradition, but on what happens to us in the face of the arrival of events that reverberate or resound, full of what Gadamer (1989, p. 458) called "summoning." I (D.J.) am just about to go back into an elementary school, and what I will witness is neither simply what I've seen before, nor is it simply new. It is, rather, a meeting *between* the new and the old, the young and the experienced. In such meetings, we can reasonably speak of "the fecundity of the individual case." And, given such fecundity and such "between work," we can reasonably say that hermeneutics is pedagogical at its heart, because it is precisely the abundance or overflow of the new *in the midst of this old and experienced (and often deaf and stupid and violent) world* that is its concern. As Hannah Arendt (1969) articulated so well, the "fact of natality" (1969, p. 177) saves the world from the morality of its creators:

> We are always educating for a world that is or is becoming out of joint, for this is the basic human situation, in which the world is created by mortal hands to serve mortals for a limited time as home. Because the world is made by mortals it wears out; and because it continuously changes its inhabitants it runs the risk of becoming as mortal as they. To preserve the world against the mortality of its creators and inhabitants it must be constantly set right anew. The problem is simply to educate in such a way that a setting-right remains actually possible, even though it can, of course, never be assured. Our hope always hangs on the new which every generation brings; but precisely because we can base our hope only on this, we destroy everything if we so try to control the new that we, the old, can dictate how it will look. Exactly for the sake of what is new and revolutionary in every child, education must be conservative; it must preserve this newness and introduce it as a new thing into the old world. (pp. 192–193)

Chapter 10

"The Fecundity of the Individual Case": Considerations of the Pedagogic Heart of Interpretive Work[1]

David W. Jardine

A former student teacher phoned me in a panic late one August, excited that she had been offered a job in an Early Childhood Education classroom starting the next week and, of course, apprehensive about all that might entail. She phoned, I suspect, as much for reassurance as for advice. Eight weeks later, well into the school year, she phoned again and recounted the experience of going to her new school just days before the children were to arrive.

The principal was not available when she arrived, and she was instructed by the school secretary that her room was "down there, Room 10." She had walked down the hallway to what was to be "her room" and paused. The door was shut and she spoke of this shut door being "imposing," "as if something was going on in there already" that of which she was not a yet part, something to which she did not yet "belong." As she told it, she knew that when she opened that door, somehow, "everything would be different," things would be, in her words "turned around." She sensed that, once she "stepped in," she would be finally "crossing over" from student to teacher: "Once I entered the room, I knew that would be *it*."

We have all had similar experiences to this. In some sense, and to some degree, we all understand what she is talking about. Her tale is familiar, familial, something with which we already have deep, unvoiced kinship (Wittgenstein, 1968, p. 36). In the face of this undeniable sense of kinship and understanding, what is the task of educational inquiry with respect to such an incident? How are we to do justice to this particular

---

[1]Reprinted from "The fecundity of the individual case," by D. Jardine, 1992, *British Journal of Philosophy of Education, 26*(1), pp. 51–61. Copyright © 1992 by Blackwell Publishing. Reprinted with permission.

episode that happened to a particular teacher at a particular time and place, while at once respecting the undeniable kinship we experience in hearing this teacher's tale?

This chapter explores how the interpretive disciplines understand and address the powerful "fecundity" (Gadamer, 1989, p. 38) of such incidents. Understood interpretively, such incidents can have a generative and reenlivening effect on the interweaving texts and textures of human life in which we are all embedded. Bringing out these living interweavings in their full, ambiguous, multivocal character is the task of interpretation. There is thus an intimate connection between interpretation (concerned as it is with the generativity of meaning that comes with the eruption of the new in the midst of the already familiar) and pedagogy (concerned as it is with the regeneration of understanding in the young who live here with us in the midst of an already familiar world) (Arendt, 1969).

It is not simply that pedagogy can be one of the themes of interpretive inquiry. Rather, interpretation is pedagogic at its very heart.

The first section of this chapter is a playful consideration of unvoiced philosophical assumptions underlying those forms of educational inquiry that begin with methodical acts of severance in order to ensure "objectivity" in what they might have to say about such an incident. The next section shows how this incident could be read interpretively, bringing out the difference in the underlying assumptions of such an interpretive reading. The concluding section of this chapter attempts to weave together more explicitly the threads that bind together interpretive research and pedagogy.

THE "ISOLATED INCIDENT" AS THE SUBSTANCE OF INQUIRY

"A substance is that which requires nothing except itself in order to exist" (Descartes, 1640/1955, p. 275). This is a long-standing definition, cited here from Descartes (17th century) but winding its way back into the work of Thomas Aquinas (13th century) and from there, back into Aristotelian metaphysics (3rd century BCE). I cite it here because for much work in educational inquiry, the fundamental given (the root of the notion of "data" as "that which is given or granted") in inquiry is not that original, ambiguously alluring familiarity that first strikes us when we hear this teacher's tale. Rather, what is strictly given is the "isolated incident." The literal text produced by this particular teacher at this particular time in this particular situation—this, severed from all its abundant allure, is "that which requires nothing except itself in order to exist." This is the substance of (some forms of) inquiry. Such abundant allure is henceforth understood to be *subjective*.

Therefore, before we can begin such an inquiry, we must make this incident into something portioned off from anything else except itself. We must begin by systematic acts of severance aimed at retrieving the given ("the isolated incident") out of the amorphous web of interweaving meanings in which it was originally embedded and in whose abundant embrace it first appeared. We must sever any interconnections that are already at work before the methods of our inquiry are enacted. We must (ideally, at least) put out of play any understanding of or connection to this instance that we may have as inquirers. We must suspend any spontaneous familiarity or sense of kinship that it evokes in us, any sort of aesthetic appeal (see Preamble 2) or experiential reminder. We must also put out of play any interconnections we see or suspect between this instance and any other meanings or tales or stories or narratives.

These two acts of severance—this instance from us and our lived familiarity with it, and this instance from other instances—will allow it to become a self-identical substance, something that stands "without us" and without reference to any other incident. Thus severed, it no longer signifies or signals anything beyond itself. It becomes, as far as we know thus far, "an isolated incident," just itself and nothing more. These systematic severances have acted on the assumption (implicit in empiricism) that all that is given is the empirical instance. Therefore, any interconnections or evocations have been *imposed upon it* and these impositions must be put out of play before we can retrieve the integral instance itself. Our isolation of the instance, then, is done against the backdrop of the belief that it is "in fact" isolated. In this way, our methodical severances are not understood as violations of already-existing, real, and vital interconnections. Rather, these severances involve systematically reversing those violating interconnections that have despoiled the actually isolated incident. We have retrieved the integrity of the instance by retrieving the isolated, individual (i.e., not further divisible) case.

This is a fascinating process to which we subject both the instance and ourselves. It is akin to a sort of purification ritual (Bordo, 1988, pp. 78–82) that both we and the instance must undergo. Regarding the instance itself, ambiguous linkages and tell-tale signs and marks of potentially violating interconnectedness are systematically eliminated, producing a sort of virginal, untouched instance. And regarding ourselves, we can no longer approach this instance with the moist and fleshy familiarity with which we began. We must now simply "behold" it with what Alfred North Whitehead named the "celibacy of the intellect" (cited in Fox, 1983, p. 23). We must remain strictly within the parameters of the methods of severance we have enacted, for any other interconnection would despoil or defile the instance we have so carefully and methodically isolated and purified. Our connection to this instance thus becomes gutted. We understand it "from the neck up," uprooted from the dark and original familiarities and kinships that have been put out of play. And, correlatively, the instance itself loses its ambiguous allure and is rendered fully present. Along with the assumption that all that is given is the isolated instance, we find a correlative assumption: The given is equatable with the clear and distinct. Any signs of ambiguity in what is given (in "the data") indicate that we have not yet rid the given of its impurities or not yet controlled for the possible interpenetrations of dependent and independent variables. The isolated instance, if properly isolated, is what it is and therefore can contain no ambiguity. Ambiguity or any other sign of a lack of clarity and distinctness is understood to be nothing more than a problem that needs to be fixed through further purifications and severances. An ambiguity in the data is thus simply the occasion to subdivide the problem and conduct a further study. The given, therefore, is univocal, clear, and distinct. Any entrails of meaning that might have wandered from it off into dark corners or that may have dug deep into our lives and drawn us into unanticipated, illicit interplays have been cut off (see chap. 7).

A more direct and familiar way of putting this process is that, through these severances of the original familiarity in which we were immersed and that drew us in in the first place, we render this instance into an object and, correlatively, render ourselves into a "knowing subject" that has this object, not as something to which we belong and have a kinship or relation, but as something standing over against us. The instance-as-object now no longer fits into a complex fabric of interrelations in which I belong with it, but rather "stands out," isolated from what surrounds it. It becomes "obtrusive, importunate, and demanding of our attention" (Weinsheimer, 1985, p. 5).

From this original severance thus begins a long series of correlative movements between this instance and myself as inquirer. "Subject and object precipitate out simultaneously. Yet even while separate, they remain interdependent, because the breakdown in the world [i.e., the tearing of the instance out of the fabric of familiarity in which it originally lived] corresponds to a breakdown in understanding" (Weinsheimer, 1985, p. 5). Once divested of the original, intimate knowing, I can no longer claim to understand this now severed object. That original allure never was *knowing the object*. It was just subjective.

In this way, "both subject and object are derivative and secondary, in that both precipitate out of the more primordial unity of being at home in the world" (Weinsheimer, 1985, p. 5), a "being at home" bespoken by the fact that I somehow "already understood" what this teacher said before the specific work of rendering it an object of research even began. This precipitated subject and precipitated object "are [both] determined negatively: the knowing subject [now severed from our original senses of familiarity] no longer understands and the object [now severed from its living context] no longer fits" (Weinsheimer, 1985, p. 5). Now "real research" can finally begin.

These fundamental acts of severance and the convoluted sequence of correlative purification transformations in both the object of inquiry and the inquirer give inquiry a peculiar and deliberate anonymity and rootlessness. Once we become severed from the abiding senses of kinship and familiarity and embodied allure that this instance evokes (once it becomes an "object" and we become a "knowing subject"), we are left with clear, univocal, given surfaces both regarding the instance and regarding ourselves. It is transformed into what objectively presents itself to us (i.e., univocal "key terms," or coded words, that can be accurately mapped and charted) and we are transformed into deployable methods that themselves have a clear and univocal character (Weinsheimer, 1985, p. 6). Once these instances of our lives become uprooted from their fitting place in the world and once we become uprooted from our familiarity with the world, inquiry into such (now "objective") instances becomes enamored of frequency and reoccurrence.

The only significance we can glean from these rootless surface readings of the incidents of our lives are from quantities and enumerable surface repetitions. When, for example, we hear a beginning teacher talk about the anxieties of opening the classroom door for the first time and entering in, speaking and writing of the resonant meaning of such an event are foregone in favor of an inquiry into whether a significant number of "respondents" will cite the same experiences, use the same words and concepts, speak in the same terms in their reports. Because we have actively and intentionally reduced this instance to an isolated incident, it becomes essential to collect more and more incidents in order to raise this first incident out of its isolation. An interesting turn of events: We raise things out of their isolation through our knowing. We did not *create* isolation through our methodology. Because we have actively and intentionally restricted ourselves to that knowledge produced methodically, it becomes illegitimate to engage these instances in ways other than simply collecting them. This first instance becomes significant (that is to say, it points to something beyond itself) only insofar as it can now be shown to reoccur in a (mathematically) significant number of other equally actively isolated incidents. Significance thus becomes intimately linked with frequency. More pointedly put, significance becomes mathematized. This instance links up with others only under the watchful eye of this most celibate of disciplines (but see chaps. 3, 5, and 13).

The interest of such a mathematization of significance is not to better understand this instance and its meaning as a feature of human life, but to be better able to control, predict, and manipulate its future reoccurrences (Habermas, 1973). Earlier, we mentioned that, following upon the methodical severances of our familiarity with the world, there is a correlative negative determination of both object (which now no longer fits) and subject (which now no longer understands):

> The cognitive remedies for these twin defects are likewise correlative. The object is disassembled, the rules of its functioning are ascertained, and then it is reconstructed according to those rules; so, also, knowledge is analysed, its rules are determined, and finally it is redeployed as method. The purpose of both remedies is to prevent unanticipated future breakdowns by means of breaking down even further the flawed entity and then synthesizing it artificially. Thus Gadamer speaks of "the ideal of knowledge familiar from natural science, whereby we understand a process only when we can bring it about artificially" (1989, p. 336). (Weinsheimer, 1985, p. 6)

Once these "cognitive remedies" are enacted, we can (within mathematically prescribed limits) predict the reoccurrence of such incidents and therefore we no longer be "taken aback" by such reoccurrence. Such incidents will not allure us again and catch us off guard, with all the disorienting and disturbing consequences that such allure can have. These remedies (recall, produced of the original precipitation of "subject" and "object") prevent the possibility of understanding being provoked by something unwittingly and without methodical anticipation. Thus, "objectification" protects us from dangerous unanticipated (monstrous? See chap. 7) turns that the world may take (this is precisely the strength of such work). It rules out of its considerations unanticipated ("uncontrolled-for") interchanges with the world.

Of course, the methodical attainment of such objectivity does not altogether prevent playful, risk-laden, unanticipated interchanges. They will still occur. However, their occurrence is divested of any claim of or access to truth. Truth and method become identified. It is precisely this identification that the interpretive disciplines work against. Certainly the methods of quantitative research can help us better understand this incident and their assertions can make a claim to truth. The interpretive disciplines suggest, however, that there is a "truth" to be had, an understanding to be reached, in the provocative, unmethodical incidents of our lives, a truth that is despoiled and thus left out of consideration by the methodical severances requisite of empirical work. There is some truth, therefore, in abundance.

AN INTERPRETIVE READING
OF THE INSTANCES OF OUR LIVES

> The term "initiation" in the most general sense denotes a body of rites and oral teachings whose purpose is to produce a radical modification ... of the person to be initiated. Initiation is equivalent to an ontological mutation of the existential condition. The novice emerges from his ordeal a totally different being: he has become *another*. (Eliade, 1975, p. 112)

"I knew when I walked through that door, I would be the teacher. Everything would be different." Perhaps this teacher's words can be read as a retelling of ancient and power-laden narratives of initiation and transformation, "insiders" and "outsiders," thresholds and boundaries, of being turned around in those moments when everything becomes different, of risking self-understanding and self-definition by moving into a new sphere, of repetition and renewal, of the turns and interplays of responsibility and irresponsibility, of the turns from childhood to adulthood.

Interpretive research begins with a different sense of the given. Rather than beginning with an ideal of clarity, distinctness, and methodological controllability and then rendering the given into the image of this ideal (see chap. 8), it begins in the place where we actually start in being granted or given this incident in the first place. It begins (and remains) with the evocative, living familiarity that this tale evokes. The task of interpretation is to bring out this evocative given in all its tangled ambiguity, to follow its evocations and the entrails of sense and significance that are wound up with it. Interpretive research, too, suggests that these striking incidents make a claim on us and open up and reveal something to us about our lives together and what it is that is going on, often unvoiced, in the ever-so commonplace and day-to-day act of becoming a teacher. In this sense, our unanticipated, unmethodical being in the world—this happenstance phone call from a former student and her tale of walking down a hallway and standing by a closed door—can, quite literally in certain instances, make a claim to some sort of truth. Teachers like this story of this student teacher because it "rings true" to the lives they have led. That is, they find it all too familiar, now, as new children burst in on them once again. September.

When this teacher phoned me, her words evoked in me a sense of something already familiar that I did not fully understand, but somehow undeniably "knew." I felt suddenly implicated by her words, as if she spoke about something in which I was somehow already involved and that I somehow already understood but had forgotten or not explicitly noticed. Interpretive inquiry thus begins by being "struck" by something, being "taken" with it—in this particular case, the unanticipated eruption of long-familiar threads of significance and meaning in the midst of a wholly new situation. "Understanding begins ... when something addresses us" (Gadamer, 1989, p. 299). This striking incident called for (Heidegger, 1968) understanding. For all its incidentalness, it aroused and generated a new and fresh understanding of something already understood. We got a glimpse of how very strange the familiar act of becoming a teacher is, how ancient and abundant. It opened up something that seemed "over and done with."

It is at this juncture that the true fecundity of the individual cases comes into play.

This teacher's story is not an isolated instance to which the concept of "initiation" is to be applied, as if "initiation" were already understood, already fixed and closed and definitively defined, and this instance were simply a replica or a copy of it. Rather, what this teacher's story speaks of is initiation—it belongs to initiation and therefore adds itself to what initiation can now be understood to be. But saying that this instance is initiation requires understanding "is" in the manner of *analogia entis:* in the manner of "analogical being" (see chap. 13). Its being initiation does not mean that it is identical in all respects to some pregiven and preunderstood fixed set of concepts (this would make the instance superfluous to this already-established meaning). But neither is this instance simply "nothing except itself," simply different than initiation. Rather, the instance is, so to speak, the generative offspring or "kin" of initiation. It bears a "family resemblance" (Wittgenstein, 1968) to initiation, interweaving with it in ambiguous ways that are not mathematizable into univocal terms that could be simply counted and recounted. For with this teacher's tale, it is not perfectly clear whether we have an unambiguous reoccurrence of some phenomenon, for this tale is not identical to any other instance of initiation (but neither is it simply different). What we have, rather, is exactly what we thought we had: something vaguely familiar, vaguely recognizable, something that bears a "family resemblance" that warrants further investigation.

Thus, the relation between the instance and that to which it seems to bear a "family resemblance" is always in a type of suspense. Interpretive inquiry does not wish to literally and univocally say what this instance finally is. Rather, it wishes to playfully explore what understandings this instance makes possible. There is not a question, then, of whether this instance "really is" an instance of initiation, but whether it is possible to understand it this way and what happens to us if we allow such an understanding. It justifies this approach by harkening back to the fact that it does not take up this instance as an "object" with certain given characteristics. It takes up, rather, as something that evokes and opens up an already-familiar way of belonging in the world, a possible way of being (i.e., "being an initiate"). This instance must be taken up as a "text" that must be read and reread for the possibilities of understanding that it evokes. Interpretation involves "making the object and all its possibilities fluid" (Gadamer, 1989, p. 367). That is to say, interpretation "make[s] the novel [this particular incident] seem familiar by relating it to prior knowledge, [and] make[s] the familiar [what we have already understood 'initiation' to mean] seem strange by viewing it from a new perspective" (Gick & Holyoak, 1983, pp. 1–2). Thus, interpretive work doesn't simply read the instance into a pregiven, closed, and already-understood "past," but, with the help of the instance, makes what has been said of initiation in the past readable again by reopening it to new, generative instances. The abundant ancestries of initiation into teaching become real again, readable again, true again. To the extent that interpretation makes things readable, it is intimately linked up with a sense of literacy.

This particular instance, then, can be understood as bearing forward the phenomenon of initiation, reinvigorating it and thus transforming it, making it fruitful, making it a forebearer, not an "isolated incident." Initiation thus needs the instance to become and remain generative. Put the other way around, without living instances, initiation would no longer be a living feature of our lives; it would no longer be something that concerns us, that provokes us, that entices us. Initiation would no longer be an ongoing, vibrant narrative or story of which our lives and our experiences are an intimate part and to which we belong. It would simply be a lifeless concept or the name of some object that "stands apart" from the life we live, couched in some textbook, an object of indifference.

It is in this sense that the instance is fecund: It keeps the story (of initiation) going, a keeping going that adds to the story and that thereby changes what we will come to understand the already past chapters to have meant. What we have with interpretation is a process akin to having children. The birth of my son transformed me into being a father, and my father into being a grandfather. Paradoxically then, my son regenerated what I have come to understand the course of my life to have already been. He constitutes not simply the addition of one new, isolated element in a chain of events. He constitutes the necessity to rethink the whole chain and each event in it. Thus we can legitimately speak of the "fecundity of the individual case" insofar as it is allowed to wind its regenerative tendrils out into the "old growth" from which it has erupted—insofar, that is, as we do not begin our work by severing precisely these regenerative tendrils of sense.

We end up, here, with one of the most telling features of interpretive work. Initiation is not a given whose features can be simply listed and to which instances can be simply compared. Rather, the relation between initiation and the instance is an interpretive one. The new instance transforms what initiation is, and initiation helps articulate what the instance means. The instance is thus irreplaceable in its particularity, because that very particularity can have a generative, transformative effect that cannot be and does not need to be "duplicated" because interpretive work allows us and requires us to experience it as duplicitous in the first place. It is this resistance of the particular to simple, powerless subsumption (under "themes" and the like) that helps interpretive inquiry from simply being a reiteration of conservative, traditional understandings. Those shared and contested understandings in which we live are called to account by this instance, made to "speak," change, accommodate, and, so to speak, "learn" through this encounter.

If an instance is simply duplicated in all respects over multiple cases, the duplicates add nothing new to our understanding of what initiation is. They will simply confirm its reoccurrence. More simply put, a quantitative study may provide us with irrefutable assurance that the phenomenon of "initiation" is reported to be widespread among beginning teachers (a valuable piece of information in and of itself). But it can accomplish this without opening up and contesting our understanding of what initiation is and what it means as a feature of human life in general and of the practice of teaching in particular. It is this—adding to our understanding of our lives—that is of interest to interpretive inquiry.

We have to be careful here. This "adding to the understanding of our lives" is not a matter of establishing once and for all what certain objective features of human experience are and are not. We cannot fully know once and for all what "initiation" is because, so to speak, it *is not* yet. As something that forms a living part of our shared and contested human experience, we don't fully know what initiation is because we don't yet know what will become of it. And we don't know this because it is still coming. To the extent that we do not know what is to be made of initiation in the future—how it might appear and how those appearances might transform our understanding of what it means to be an initiate—our interpretive relation to this particular instance cannot be oriented toward having some "last word" about it as if it were an "object" that is simply present, that simply stands there before us to be univocally named. "It would be a poor hermeneuticist who thought he could have, or had to have, the last word" (Gadamer, 1989, p. 579). A "good" interpretation, then, is not definitive and final, but is one that keeps open the possibility and the responsibility of returning, for the very next instance might demand of us that we understand anew. Interpretation doesn't keep the possibility of returning open in order to be fair or in order that everyone can have their own interpretation, but because of the nature of the matters at hand—the living human inheritance *is* open (see Preamble 5). This is deeply pedagogical: The next student teacher will return to the origin of the world and take it up again, here, now, in this way, with this face and flesh. This openness and susceptibility to interpretation—this vague familiarity which could have gone so many ways—is the nature of *data* in interpretive work. It is what is given. What is given is that things are still arriving. What is given is that the given contains, of necessity, an absence, a future (see Preamble 15 and chap. 15).

This is one of the reasons that the language of interpretive inquiry (the language, one might say, of this book) can be, for some, so unfailingly annoying, for it purposely struggles against the tendency of language toward literalism and univocal declarations regarding what is and is not the case. Its language tends, therefore, to be more "playful" (see Preamble 3 and chap. 3) and seemingly less serious than other forms of inquiry. It is here that interpretive work can easily fall into puerile excess and narrative and emotional and poetic overload.

Despite its playful appearance, there are serious consequences at issue in the nature of interpretive work and its choice as a "research methodology," especially, I suggest, in education. Failing to keep open the possibility of returning to understand anew is at once demanding of initiation that it no longer be open to the possibility of fecund new instances. It becomes a frankly boring "theme" in a dissertation or in a research study. It renders the abundance of the human inheritance into a manageable and controllable array of fixed (or at least *fixable*) objects that need nothing except themselves and their numerable (quantifiable) "relations" in order to exist. It is equivalent to believing that the new, the young, have nothing to add, nothing to offer, no real work to do. It is equivalent to believing that the human story can go on without renewal and regeneration. It is, in effect, a desire for the death of the child.

We need to ask here the inevitable question: How do I know that this reading I have given this instance is reliable? Hermeneutically conceived, the reading of this instance is "reliable" if the instance begins to become open and lively and vibrant and memorable. That is, as a living part of the human inheritance, a reliable interpretation is one that reads this instance as part of the living human inheritance, that reads it, that is, for its living kinships, its possible bloodlines and family resemblances. How do I know that this is what I'm doing when I'm sitting here, trying to write and think about this event? How do I know I'm not just delusional, spooked by Descartes' demons or black biles?

Well, I don't know all by myself or in advance of the reading and the writing itself. I cannot separate out in advance which features of my reading reveal nothing more than idiosyncrasies of my individual experiences and which features reveal something more—not the teacher's text "in itself," but the binding arcs of meaning in which I, that teacher, and the text belong together—something about the world of teaching, this living thread of the human inheritance. I'm not interested in this instance "in itself," but insofar as I am a teacher and a student of teaching itself. This is the part of the human inheritance in the midst of which this instance struck me in the first place, and that part of that inheritance out into which this interpretation proceeds. It is not an "absolute" interpretation. I cannot separate out in advance and by some pregiven method how the work of Mircea Eliade I read as an undergraduate student as an undergraduate in religious studies at McMaster University, or Johan Huizinga's texts on play, or my own life experiences, will end up having a bearing on my reading of this instance. "This separation must take place in the process of understanding itself" (Gadamer, 1989, p. 296). I can only find out about the revelations and distortions that my life brings to the images haunting that phone call from a student teacher by *working such matters out*. And I have to work these matters out *in public*—in writing, in talking to colleagues, and therefore in letting the distortions of my subjectivity work themselves out into a territory that can comfort. Coming to understand what is true of teaching in the appeal of this instance, what is generous and possible, is only after the fact.

Interpretation thus becomes a movement of shaping and making something of this instance and its human topographies. I have to let my preunderstandings and prejudices and presumptions fully engage this text; I must let them be brought fully into play and therefore risk that they might be changed, embarrassed, even humiliated, in confronting what this teacher's text has to say (Gadamer, 1989, p. 299). I cannot have access to the blind spots all by myself and via an anonymous methodology.

Put more sharply and positively, for interpretation to engage, the text and I must be allowed to "play." And in such play, an unavoidable paradox of interpretive work comes to light. The fact that I happened to have read and remembered Mircea Eliade's work on initiation, the fact that I happened to have been called by this teacher and to have been struck by what she said—all of these "happenstances" made possible the interpretation that will then ensue (Weinsheimer, 1985, pp. 7–8). The interpretation is thus unavoidably linked to me. It is not something produced by a method that anyone could wield. However—and here is the paradox—what the interpretation is henceforth *about* is not me and my past experiences, but that of which I have had certain experiences: initiation. Even though interpretive work is not possible without a living connection to its topic, it is *the topic*, not *the fact of a living connection*, that is the center of interpretive work.

The same can be said of the reader of an interpretive study. If the reader has no living connection to or experience of something like the phenomenon of initiation, the study will be rather meaningless, for it will not address something to which the reader bears any "family resemblance." Again, this is not a matter of readers sharing in some univocal "universal(s)" or "themes" or "old chestnuts" regarding human experience. It is a matter of kinship, and kinships are not housed under universals (see the discussion of cloning in chap. 2 and the discussion of "family resemblance" in Wittgenstein's, 1968, work in chap. 13).

Producing a "reliable" interpretive reading of this instance—"reliable" now meaning one in which those reading the interpretation find the exploration of the topic/topography of teaching provides some insight and comfort and thoughtfulness about their lives—requires living with this instance for a period of time in order to learn its ways: turning it over and over, telling and retelling it, finding traces of it over and over again in what you read, seeing the nod of heads and faint smiles when it is used as an example in a class, scouring the references colleagues suggest, searching my own lived experience for analogues of experience, asking friends if they have experienced anything like this before, testing and retesting different ways of speaking and writing about it to see if these different ways help engage and address possible readers of the work to follow. There is, as mentioned earlier, a creative movement of shaping and forming something in accordance with the ancient arts of writing (in particular, but, as we have all witnessed, this centrality of writing is being overwhelmed). It takes time to dwell with such an incident and allow the slow emergence of the rich contexts of familiarity in which it fits. I can learn the ways of this instance only by taking the time to experience where it "goes," and thereby seeing to what territories and terrains it belongs. This instance is thus not static but rather "leads" somewhere. Time is needed, blind alleys and lots of discarded work are unavoidable, but this time, this temporality, in an important sense, belongs to the instance itself. In spite of my deadlines and desires, very often insight and articulation "takes its own sweet time." Only over this unmethodical course of time does the full fecundity of the individual case come forward. They need to be worried over, mulled, meditated upon, thought about, forgotten, and remembered. As a monk once said, you know something is beautiful if, because of your attention and devotion to it, it begins to glow.

And, some might say unfortunately, "there is no art or technique of happening onto things. There is no method of stumbling" (Weinsheimer, 1985, p. 7). This incident, which gave rise to so much, just happened. For a reliable reading to occur, then, it would never be enough to simply say what I think it means and leave it at that. But neither is it enough to simply turn it back to the "respondent" and ask what she intended it to mean, or whether she intended to mean something about "initiation" or "responsibility" or "becoming an adult" and the like, as if calling out to the author might save us the task of interpreting the text (the idea of "the genius" fits here—see chap. 15). The author's (respondent's) reading of her own story is not the lynchpin of hermeneutic work (as it might be for some forms of "teacher narrative" now gaining ascendancy in educational inquiry), as if the topic at hand is the subjectivity of the one traversing the topic. Rather, "we are moving in a dimension of meaning that is intelligible in itself and as such offers no reason for going back to the subjectivity of the author" (Gadamer, 1989, p. 292). The living, generative, abundant, and even contradictory meaning(s) of the text are at the center, and the game of interpretation is afoot *for us all* in the face of this or any other text. This is the most profound message of interpretive work, whatever its topic: We find ourselves here, engaged in this world of teaching trying to make something of the experiences that happen to us, talking to each other, finding, one hopes, some solace and meaning in such conversations:

> Language ... is by itself the game of interpretation that we all are engaged in every day. In this game nobody is above and before all the others; everybody is at the centre, [everybody] is "it" in this game ["The centre is everywhere" (Nishitani, 1982, p. 146)—see chap. 19]. Thus it is always his turn to be interpreting. This process of interpretation takes place whenever we "understand." (Gadamer, 1977, p. 32)

Interestingly enough, this does not mean that the connection to the author is severed. That student teacher of mine hasn't disappeared in her uniqueness and individuality. It means, rather, that, in the face of this abundant trace line in the world—this "text" she produced—the author is one of us and not in some elite, "authoritative" position. Certainly, the author is in an elite position regarding the experiences she underwent, just as each of us is authoritative regarding what we think and experience and feel. However, once erupted into a text, not one of us holds some authoritative sway over what those experiences and thought might mean, here, in this *world* of teaching. In fact, in this particular case, this new teacher was relieved to discover that her experiences were not just "hers," not just, as she put it "inside my head." She was relieved to find that what she was going through meant something to those with whom she spoke. The expression of her experience into a text thus relieved her of the burden of isolation. She discovered that her experience linked up with long-standing characteristics of human experience and articulation. She discovered that this experience had a character and vitality over and above the fact that she had undergone this experience and the fact that it had been powerful for her. This discovery, as mentioned previously, puts a peculiar spin on the notion of "literacy." Decoding, counting, and recounting the surface signs (of texts, of experiences) is not especially adequate to becoming experienced in the world, knowledgeable in its ways. Rather, as we unearth the signs of life crackling underneath the surfaces, "we ... become more literate [and] we may become less literal, [less] stuck in the case without a vision of its soul" (Hillman, 1989, p. 28). Simply "telling my story" can unintentionally breed a type of literalism/illiteracy by disallowing "a vision of its soul." Such a "vision" would help liberate my story from being just mine (which bears a frightening resemblance to the severances and isolations requisite of objectivity). This is why language plays such a predominant role in interpretive work, for, by its very nature, it serves to raise up the instances of our lives out of the burden of their specificity (Gadamer, 1989; Smith, 1999). It allows us to escape "the compulsive fascination with one's own case history" (Hillman, 1987, p. 7). It makes it possible to see what one is going through as intimately wound up in human life as a whole, a generative "process that is continually internalizing and externalizing, gaining insight and losing it, deliteralizing and reliteralizing" (Hillman, 1989, p. 27). It thus allows us to read our individual lives as fully participant in the shared and contested, generative work of humanity as a whole. Thus, in interpretive work, the author's reading is but one voice among many, perhaps an especially unmindful and unattentive one, perhaps the very one best suited to read this text well. Sorting out this eventuality, as with so much of interpretive work, "depends." Interpretively understanding this teacher's text, then, is not a matter of unearthing her experiences, but of "clarifying this miracle of understanding, which is not a mysterious communion of souls, but sharing in a common meaning" (Gadamer, 1989, p. 292). "What emerges," in opening up a conversation with this instance, "is neither mine nor yours" (Gadamer, 1989, p. 331) but is that "in which" we dwell together—the contours of that original familiarity and kinship that made this instance so telling in the first place. "Understanding is the expression of the affinity of the one who understands to the one whom he understands and to that which he understands" (Gadamer, 1983, p. 48). None of us necessarily knows all by ourselves the full contours of the story each of us is living out, and none of us knows, except in the grimmest of ways, how it will turn out. This is why dialogue and conversation figure so predominantly in interpretive work, as contrasted with the "monologue" of scientific discourse (Habermas, 1973), suitable as such a monologue is to the univocal character of "isolated incidents" and the correlative univocity of the methods deployed by a "knowing subject." We know full well that we are not done with this topic, that we could have proceeded differently, that, had this former student teacher's words been different, it may have required little more than consolation and encouragement, and that the meaningfulness of the conversational text of encouragement has its own ways and means of unfolding. We know something we've always known: This *Spiel* about initiation and about how to do hermeneutics is not for everyone, not a "good" interpretation in some universal sense. It won't last and is not everywhere welcome and does not (*cannot*, by the very nature of the matters at hand) preclude different interpretations from others and in the future. It is, once again, a *living* text, a fecund case.

One problem in doing interpretive work should be clear by now: knowing when to stop in the spinning out of implications of meaning. There are widespread possibilities embedded in this incident and there is no surefire method for guaranteeing that you haven't gone too far and stretched the incident out of all proportion. For example, when we begin to picture this incident as a retelling of the tale of initiation and then couple it with an innocent comment that I have heard from several principals regarding student teachers and beginning teachers, sparks begin to fly: "I like having student teachers in my school because the profession constantly needs new blood." The connection of "blood" with the rite of the initiation of the new ones into the profession (which literally means "those who take to vows," yet another feature of initiation rituals) becomes even more telling when we recall that rites of passage and initiation tend to take place in the spring—the time of Easter (itself a sacrificial blood ritual involving the opening of barriers and allowing the ones outside to come in), of graduation, as well as the time when interviews are often done for school boards seeking "new blood." At the tail end of this sequence, we may have gotten rather "carried away ," but the implications are not meaningless. In spite of the fact that they can easily become too "wild," they are not altogether "unfitting" (the monster still speaks, one might say—see Preamble 7 and chap. 7). The "analogical kinships" of meaning still seem to pertain. The "family resemblances" persist despite being somewhat strained.

The problem of interpretive research, then, is one of withholding the interpretive impulse and developing a sense of proportion and, for me, housing this in the discipline of writing. Again, this is not a method that can be handed over (it is almost impossible to answer a question like "How do you do hermeneutics?"), but is a practice. It is a practice in a strong sense precisely because the incident under consideration and the concrete context of speaking about it (with this beginning teacher in the midst of her anxiety, in casual conversation with a friend, as a topic in a class, as a subject for an academic paper, etc.) will have something to say about what a "good" sense of proportion might be in this case or that. One cannot say, therefore, in general and ahead of time, what the practice of interpretation is like, as if it were a set of rules that needed to be simply applied to an incident independently of the contribution that incident might have regarding what needs to be said (Smith, 1999c). This point, again, bespeaks "the fecundity of the individual case" in the pursuit of understanding.

CONCLUDING REMARKS: ON INTERPRETATION, PEDAGOGY, AND HERMES AS TRICKSTER AND THIEF

Hermes is cunning, and occasionally violent: a trickster, a robber. So it is not surprising that he is also the patron of interpreters. (Kermode, 1979, p. 1)

When Hermes is at work ... one feels that one's story has been stolen and turned into something else. The [person] tells his tale, and suddenly its plot has been transformed. He resists, as one would try to stop a thief ... this is not what I meant at all, not at all. But too late. Hermes has caught the tale, turned its feet around, made black into white, given it wings. And the tale is gone from the upper world historical nexus in which it had begun and been subverted into an underground meaning. (Hillman 1982, p. 31)

There is one further aspect of Hermes that may be worth noting, namely his impudence. He once played a trick on the most venerated Greek deity, Apollo, inciting him to great rage. Modern students of hermeneutics should be mindful that their interpretations could lead them into trouble with the authorities. (Smith, 1999c, p. 27)

It is admittedly rather frightening and disorienting to discover that the incidental story we might tell can have implications of sense that we did not anticipate and cannot fully control. We all know, and have all suffered in our own ways, how this has often meant that others have spoken in our stead and "for our own good" and how, so often as well, someone else might be able to read my own experiences back to me in ways I could have never imagined and that have saved my life.

To say that Hermes is a trickster and a thief is not to say that the one doing the interpretation is Hermes and the teacher I spoke with is the sole victim of the theft of meaning and the subsequent transformations of understanding that ensue. Rather, the playful tricks and turns happened to me as much as to her. It is not as if I could, in the inquiry I pursued, say anything I wanted or do anything I wished. I, too, was "subject" to Hermes' seeming whims, having things collapse without warning, gaining insights at the worst of times and losing them before I could catch them, muttering quite often while writing or rereading what I thought was so clear "this is not what I meant at all, not at all. But too late...."

Pursuing interpretive inquiry is a potentially painful process, because it is not produced of a method that (ideally) will keep everything under control by severing all the tendrils of sense that can pull you in so many different, often incompatible ways. There is a risk involved in such work, a risk of "self-loss" (Gadamer, 1977, p. 51) and the recovery of a sense of oneself that is different (and perhaps not especially "better") than the one with which we begin such inquiries. Its risk is increasing susceptibility to the world, not increasing managerial control.

There is a straightforward sense in which interpretive work is pedagogic: It is concerned with the regenerative and enlivening relationship between the young and the old. It will not abandon the new to some empirical isolation, but will always try to find its kinship there. It is therefore disruptive of fossilized sedimentations of sense, desiring to open them up and allow "the new" to erupt and thus allowing the old and already established and familiar to regenerate and renew itself and find its life again. It is oriented, thus, to "furtherance" (Gadamer, 1989, p. xxiv)—that is, reading what seem like deadened and deadening certainties for their liveliness, their life, their ongoingness (like Richard and his ambles with Dolly—see chap. 2).

But there is a different sense in which interpretive inquiry is pedagogic. The process of interpretation is not the simple accumulation of new objective information. It is, rather, the transformation of self-understanding. Living with this instance and following its ways and engaging my own life and the lives of others in an attempt to understand it has changed who I am and what I understand myself to be. New possibilities of self-understanding have opened up; old ones have been renewed and transformed and rejected. Some other matters have fallen from memory and into a darkness whose measure is hard to know. This is what understanding is like as a human endeavor. We try things, we fail, we succeed, things last for a time, become new again or fade, fit here and not there, will suffice now but maybe not later. What I understand myself, my work, and the lives of my students to be have changed, for better or worse. And, of course, all these understandings cannot now be trumpeted as final, not because of a failure to "research" enough or write enough, but *because of the nature of the matters at hand*. The world *is* interpretable.

These will have to work themselves out over the course of my life and the lives of those I engage. Moreover, writing of this incident is not a matter of passing on information to a reader, but of evoking or educing a different self-understanding in the reader. The goal of interpretive work is not to pass on objective information to readers, but to evoke in readers a sense of the odd abundance in which we live and that we have inherited. Following the entrails of sense that this incident regenerated means, in however small a way, understanding who we are differently, more deeply, more richly. Unlike some work in educational inquiry that begins with a "knowing subject" that is fully in possession of itself ("itself" being defined as the methods it can deploy), interpretive work inevitably begins with a living subject in a living dialogue with the life that surrounds us. "To reach an understanding ... is not merely a matter of putting oneself forward and successfully asserting one's own point of view, but being transformed into a communion in which we do not remain what we were" (Gadamer, 1989, p. 379). In such a case, interpretive work is profoundly pedagogic, for:

> In the last analysis, all understanding is self-understanding, but not in the sense of a preliminary self-possession or of one finally and definitively achieved. For self-understanding only realizes itself in the understanding of a subject matter and does not have the character of a free self-realization. The self that we are does not possess itself; one could say that it "happens." (Gadamer, 1977, p. 55)

AFTERWORD

One more playful turn. "Understanding is an adventure and, like any other adventure, it is dangerous" (Gadamer, 1983, pp. 109–110). Involvement in interpretive inquiry runs the risk of getting quite lost in the flurries of sense that make up our lives. It faces, too, the dangerous insight that, so to speak, "getting somewhere" in understanding one's life is never finished—understanding "always must be renewed in the effort of our living" (Gadamer, 1983, pp. 110–111) and this need for renewal is not an accident that we can fix, but a situation that we must learn to live with well.

In the end, the notion of "initiation" is of especial interest to hermeneutics. Hermes, as mentioned earlier, was a trickster and a thief. He was also a
messenger, a "go-between." Initiation has to do with the rites of passage and
with transformations in how we understand ourselves, and this is precisely
the interest of hermeneutics. Hermes is identified with borders, with
boundaries and with keeping open the gates between one realm and another: "to hear the messages in whatever is said. This is the hermeneutic ear
that listens-through, a consciousness of the borders, as Hermes was wor-
shipped at borders. Every wall and every weave presents its opening.
Everything is porous" (Hillman, 1987, p. 156).

Preamble 11: "Given Abundance ..."

The next three chapters are rooted in the discipline of ecology, but this is meant in a particular way, a way briefly sketched in the previous chapter. Simply put, in schools, ecology is very often identified with "environmental science," which is itself subcategorized under the requisite grade-level appropriate, developmentally sequenced school-science curriculum guides. What is proposed in the following chapter (and in the preceding chapter) is that there is another way to proceed, wherein ecology becomes a way to imagine the very nature of teaching and learning itself. It becomes a way to imagine the curriculum topics entrusted to schools—all of those topics, not just those in the sciences (see chap. 9) as rich and abundant topographies, full of ancient interdependent webs and relations, and full, too, of the turbulent arrival, into the midst of this ancientness, of the young, the new. If this last set of images serves as a viable allegory to the nature of education, then this discourse of ecology can come to be a way to express the nature of education in a way that sidesteps the sort of impoverishment of relations requisite of contemporary schooling.

Under the terrible pall of scarcity—as we have been suggesting, that great imaginary that drives contemporary education—a genuine experience of our earthly lives and the great nets of interdependence, generativity, and abundance that constitute us and the places we inhabit (topographies) becomes envisioned as a scarce resource doled out in timid measure by schools. Great topographies become impoverished topics because of the both imperial and paranoid boundary-fixations that are inherent in regimes of scarcity. The arising of wild energies that threaten to revitalize old questions and breathe new life into the world become feared, corralled, abnormalized (see Preamble 7). Those liminal places (see chap.

7) where there might be a vivid admixture of the well-bounded curriculum disciplines are henceforth considered "out of bounds."

There is, of course, something warrantable here when we look at what has often occurred under the auspices of "the integrated curriculum." Too often classrooms end up with an amorphous mess—an interesting term, being the privative (*a*) of "body" or "shape" (*morphous*). In its worst cases, curricular fragments that are already conceived of in impoverished ways are simply (and often good-heartedly) flung together—"math facts" written on the stomach of a cartoon black-line drawing of a teddy bear (see Jardine, 2000, pp. 69–86), or white cotton balls for gluing on to a photocopied Santa face (see chap. 17), or charts that count various colors of shoes (see Jardine, LaGrange, & Everest, 2004) and so on. Once the life of the curriculum disciplines entrusted to schools has been broken, once scarcity and impoverishment come to hold sway, simply putting such fragments back together in their impoverished condition does not lead to integrity. This does not simply mean that, as the old adage goes, "the whole is greater than the sum of its parts." It means, rather, that, because of the degradation and impoverishment under which schools operate in imagining the nature of curriculum "topics," the parts are no longer parts of a whole.

Wendell Berry, a farmer and essayist from Kentucky, makes a telling point in this regard that helps flesh out Lewis Hyde's (1983) insight that, "given ... abundance, scarcity must be a function of boundaries" (p. 23). Once bounded, once fragmented, we find that:

> Not only is [such] fragmentation a disease, but the diseases of the disconnected parts are similar or analogous to one another. Thus, they memorialize their lost unity, their relation persisting in their disconnection. Any severance produces two wounds that are, among other things, the record of how the severed parts once fitted together. (Berry, 1986, pp. 110–111)

Before attempting to put back together the broken and impoverished pieces of the curriculum, what is first required is a long, sometimes arduous act of remembering what is memorialized in the scar tissues that each discipline bears. Two impoverished pieces do not add up to abundance.

What follows is a chapter that focuses on an idea that is commonplace in the early years of elementary school: the integrated curriculum. As was suggested in chapters 8 and 9, the abundance of earthly things is not a product of our agency. What ecological discourse allows us to imagine is that the integrity and integration of the topographies of the curriculum is not something we have to *do*.

Chapter 11

On the Integrity of Things: Reflections on the "Integrated Curriculum"

David W. Jardine

> *From the pine tree*
> *learn of the pine tree,*
> *And from the bamboo*
> *of the bamboo.*

—Matsuo Basho (1644 1694)

The forest surrounding our house is mainly composed of spruce, pine, poplar, and aspen trees. Two Evening Grosbeaks have taken up strategic positions on a tall pine near the feeder and are swooping down on it in measured flights. Their flights are cut by calls of complaint from several Blue Jays evenly spread through the surrounding trees. In their approaches, they deftly balance the swoops of air and space between them and the feeder, the wind that has picked up, and the way the feeder sways—loosely hung to avoid the cats who watch these events in wide-eyed frustration.

In such a place, it is difficult to sustain the belief, common, for example, in the work of Jean Piaget and his legacy, that we somehow "give" order to what is in itself unorderly experience—"imposing cosmos on the chaos of experience" (Piaget, 1971b, p. xii). The pinwheel display of radiating spruce needles in repeating multiples, the symmetrical curve of branches perfectly shortening to a point clustered with cones, the thatched layers of scales on the spruce cones themselves, spun out in Fibonacci sequences, the rhythmic and orderly and repeated calls of the Jays, the flash of brilliant yellow one finds without fail or effort on the male Evening Grosbeak—all of

this deeply mathematical orderliness is *experienced* as a *given*, and it is tempt-
ing to say that such orderliness is somehow *there*, even if the young child
(imagined in Piagetian theory) cannot yet experience it.

This chapter is a playful exploration of the link between recent, increasing attention to the integrated curriculum and increasing interest in ecology. Exploring this "ecopedagogical" relationship will shed light on an
underlying "turning around" of our understanding of ourselves and our
place on the Earth required by a truly whole, integrated curriculum.

It is almost too easy to consider the integrated curriculum without considering the profound investment that our culture and our profession have
in images of knowledge as disintegration, isolation, fragmentation, and
disconnectedness. Such severances allow for the control, prediction, and
manipulation of discrete curricular content. Such severances make possible
a certain ease of manageability, trackability, mathematized accountability,
clarity of objectives, testability, and the like. It also demands curricular and
pedagogic specialization. Such specialization comes at a tragic cost: "Specialization is ... a way of institutionalizing, justifying, and paying highly for a
calamitous disintegration and scattering out of the various functions of
character: workmanship, care, conscience, responsibility" (W. Berry, 1986,
p. 19). What is forfeited in such disintegration is "the continuity of attention
and devotion without which human life on the Earth is impossible" (W.
Berry, 1986, p. 14). And without such a continuity of attention we can too
easily forget that "no matter the distinctions we draw, the connections, the
dependencies remain. To damage the Earth is to damage your children"
(W. Berry, 1986, p. 106). Thus breaks the spell of imagining children as our
greatest natural resource.

At this juncture, ecology, pedagogy, and the themes of the integrated
curriculum begin to intertwine. The disassembling of curriculum into disparate disciplines is all too akin to the ecologically disastrous and life-
threatening disassembling of our Earth. And these foretell of a disintegration of spirit and character, a certain loss of a sense of where we are, a sense
of the wholeness of our lives, the lives of our children, and the life of our
Earth. We are slowly beginning to see the madness involved in pursuing
considerations of education without at once considering the life of our
Earthly home in the embrace of which the pursuit of education is possible.
Aspiring, for example, to understand the articulate beauty of mathematics
is simply madness without attention to the actual breath required to pronounce such aspirations. I believe that meditation on the integrated curriculum has, trembling near its heart, the wherewithal to pose the terms of the
renewal of our loving and integral attention and devotion.

Integrating the curriculum is not something we must *do*. We do not *be-
stow* integrity and interrelatedness upon things by our efforts. Rather, the
integrated curriculum—the whole and healthy course of things—gains its
integrity insofar as it is an expression of the already existing interconnections of things themselves. If we believe that our task is to bring together

disparate curricular interests and disciplines, we have already granted precisely the disintegration and specialization for which the integrated curriculum was to be the response.

Put in the simplest way with the simplest of examples, it is the integrity and "gathering power" of the pine tree that draws together language, science, mathematics, social studies, art, history, mythology, and on and on. This pine tree poses to us the question of what is required for its continued existence—sun, soil, water, air, and their interdependencies. We can be drawn in by its beauty and form and also by thoughts of its use. It draws our attention to this very page from which you are reading and from here, back to pulp mills and chlorine bleach—kraft processing, and effluent and dioxin and poisoned fish and cancer. It evokes questions of employment and the relations between the scars left by job loss and those made by clear-cutting and subsequent napalming of the land. It stands before us as a sign of continuity and longevity and as a reminder of the fact that certain things can go on without us. It thus can highlight the nature and limits of our "doings"—our deep human needs as well as our consumptive, economically driven desires. It can be the moment at which the assumed ascendancy of human life over the Earth can be raised and that this ascendancy is an assumption of only some cultures, some religions. From the pine tree, learn of the pine tree. But also, from the pine tree, learn of ourselves. It places us in question.

In this way, even such a simple thing as this pine tree comes forward as the nesting point of a vast interconnecting network of relationships and it is the integrity of such a network that bestows integrity on the integrated curriculum. This simplest of examples reminds us of a rich and ambiguous belonging together of things that goes on before and despite our efforts to disintegrate.

We must have a deep integration (a play here on the term "deep ecology" [Devall & Sessions, 1985]) to do justice to this already existing integrity. This pine tree tells of the underlying kinship of all our efforts to understand it: The scattered disciplines themselves belong together in a deeper way than their well-drawn and often viciously territorial boundaries might allow. As Wittgenstein (1968) noted, we can draw boundaries in such matters, but we cannot give such matters a boundary—each discipline echoes a kinship with the whole texture of human endeavor just as each thing echoes a connectedness with all things. Mathematization, for example, is not something we do to this tree; it is something called for by its living symmetry that evokes a mathematical response from us. And this response evokes the symmetry and rhythm and rhyme of poetry that evokes the living rhythm of the breath of the poet (W. Berry, 1983), which depends on this tree for oxygen, itself produced through the rhythm of day and night. Being mindful of these multiple evocations (and resisting the deep-seated desire to violate these connections on behalf of clarity, manageability, and control) defines the "turning around" required by an integrated approach to curriculum.

The belonging together of things is not a function of what we explicitly know: Our living dependencies on the Earth are not equivalent to our objectifiable knowledge of such dependencies. The integrated curriculum puts in perspective, into "place," our efforts to understand. An integrated understanding neither "constructs" nor "consumes" its object but delicately sustains that object while drawing from it; as ecology maintains, the living source must be protected so that we can return.

The inherent tension in such a description of understanding is unavoidable. An integrated understanding has a certain essential ambiguity and difficulty to it, not because its object is vast and complex, but because understanding is a feature of that "object" at the outset. Understanding is an Earthly event to the extent that this pine tree is never simply an "object," but is always also part of the dwelling of which we and our attempts to understand are also a part and it is precisely this generative, ambiguous "wholeness" that must be sustained. An integrated understanding requires keeping open the possibility of returning again and again and again; and this is precisely a description of keeping open the possibility that there will always be new life in our midst (Smith, 1999c), returning again and again. Here again, the themes of ecology, pedagogy and the integrated curriculum intertwine: "This way works at wholeness not in halves but through wholeness from the start. The way is slower, action is hindered, and one fumbles foolishly in the half-light. The way finds echo in many familiar phrases from Lao Tzu, but especially: 'Soften the light, become one with the dusty world'" (Hillman, 1987, p. 15).

The disintegrative desire is deeply rooted. We find voiced in Descartes (17th century), rooted in Thomas Aquinas (12th century), and originating in Aristotle (3rd century BCE) a notion of *substance:* "a substance [i.e., an integral, individual thing] is that which requires nothing other than itself in order to exist" (Descartes, 1640/1955, p. 255). It follows from this that to know an individual thing is to sever its connections with all other things, including the one who knows. Knowledge, in fact, is defined as disconnectedness, objectivity, distance; things are defined as isolated/isolatable objects that stand against us, separate from us; the knower is defined is disinterested, separate, and anonymously methodical.

The integrated curriculum cuts deep into this notion: An individual thing gains its integrity by requiring *everything else* in order to exist; to know an individual thing is to allow that thing to expand into the full, living breadth of its Earthly interdependencies and kinships, including those kinships with the one who knows. Knowledge involves an exploration of already existing kinships and connections done with a considerateness, care, and attention that does not violate those connections. In this way, the image of knowledge that is appropriate to the integrated curriculum is essentially educational. It involves bringing out (*educare*) our living relations to things that now includes those relations educed by our previously severed curricular disciplines.

For example, mathematics does not lose its indigenous integrity. Rather, it gains a different integrity by becoming appropriated as part of our life, as a specialized, exquisite, irreplaceable way of taking up the world that has, within an integrated curriculum, a place here in the interweaving texture of human life. Mathematics becomes no longer a separate, self-enclosed "discipline" but a way of living with things that forms part of our Earthly life, one of its most eloquent gestures. It belongs here with this pine because it is an expression of its living, already existing symmetries, rhythms, and rhymes and because this pine, in kind, gives breath to this expression.

Chronos was known for consuming his children, and many in education have suffered this fate, of time eating up our attention and devotion. Ecology speaks against the image of linearity of time that fits well with the sequentiality, regularity, and discreteness of disintegrated approaches to curriculum. Ecology teaches us that things have their own timeliness and that often the most considerate response to such things, is often waiting, attending, lingering, returning, often for longer or more often than we might desire if left to our own devices. Some things take time and to allow things to come forth in a whole and healthy way requires a peculiar "giving in" to the timeliness of things that goes on without us. Knowing something in an integrated way requires the time to return, perhaps again and again and again, now from this direction, now that. An ecologically considerate response requires time for consideration.

The problem for our educational institutions is that this sense of time is not prescribable, but is inherent in the particular, localized relation between this thing and the time it takes to be learned, and this learner and his or her timeliness. This pine tree thus becomes a sign of the ever-accelerating character of education and the manic pursuit of excellence and mastery that guides a great deal of curricular thinking. It is a sign of our own consumptive desire to be up-to-date in our educational research and a way of considering the relentless proliferation of words and findings and data and theories done with little heed to what is required to sustain such relentlessness.

A final ecopedagogical point: It is precisely the localized diversity of living systems that gives them their sustainability and health and wholeness. It is precisely the multiplicity and diversity of an integrated approach to the curriculum that makes it whole, healthy, and sustainable, allowing multiple "ways in," multiple portals or opportunities for exploration and understanding to arise. Such a curriculum recognizes the rich multiplicity of interconnectedness inherent in any thing and the rich multiplicity inherent in the range of students' interests and experiences. I must conclude by adding that deep integration makes our lives and the lives of our students more ambiguous and difficult and, correctly understood, this is good news. It does not have the clarity and distinctness and quantifiable accountability of discrete curricular content in the same way that a wilderness area does not have the well-fenced rows of a single crop or the vaguely obscene uniformity of a replanted forest. The "wildness" that an integrated curriculum requires gives teachers and students alike the sense that the difficult kinships and interconnections they have come upon are real. Its "wildness" is not disorder but an attentiveness to a deeply inherent order that is not of our own making. We find ourselves in the midst of things. The integrated curriculum can sustain our interest because, quite literally, it is our real interest (from the Latin, *inter esse*, our "being in the midst of things") that is its concern. To the extent that the integrated curriculum orients to sustaining the possibility of our "being in the midst of things," it is essentially ecological at its heart for it essentially speaks, as David G. Smith (1999c) put it, of the possibility of life going on.

Preamble 12:
Settling and Unsettling

Tempo, time, and mood. Wendell Berry named one of his most profound books *The Unsettling of America* (1986). The subtitle, "Essays on Culture and Agriculture," could easily have added "education" as well, because this image of "unsettling" is a rampant and pernicious consequence of the scarcity regimes under which teachers and students operate. This is not the generative "unsettling" that the monster portends, or the vibrant "unsettling" that the young bring with them as portents of "new life in our midst" (Smith, 1999c), what Hannah Arendt (1969) called "the fact of natality." The sort of "unsettling" that is being explored in Berry's work is that which is produced through regimes of scarcity and fragmentation. It is akin, we suggest, to the sort of urban and urbane epistemology that underwrites constructivism (see chap. 9)—untethered postmodern consciousness as named by Usher and Edwards (1994) in the following chapter.

The fragmentary doling out of scarce bits and pieces of various curriculum topics has a profound effect on the tempo, time, and mood of education itself. Wendell Berry's book title does link ideas of the *settlement* of America to the mood of being unsettled. The fragmentation of the curriculum means that any one "topic" that is "covered" cannot be "settled into," because it has been stripped at the outset of its abundant relations. It is not as simple as saying that today's kids have short attention spans (as if this were simply an epistemological or psychological issue; see chap. 5). In a fragmentary world where topics have become impoverished, nothing *needs* prolonged and disciplined work, or any "continuity of attention and devotion" (W. Berry, 1986, p. 32) and, therefore, short attention spans are *precisely* a warrantable response. More bluntly put, blaming kids for short attention spans when the

177

world we present them in schools needs only meager attention in the first place is a deep and terrible irony.

It is here that themes we've touched on thus far start to thread together. Constructivism leads to a pursuit of constructive and productive activity, and when the pieces students are presented with no longer have any ancestry and integrity, all that activity can produce is hyperactivity. If no one of the pieces warrants much attention, multiple pieces simply multiplies attention, but only in terms of frequency and speed and acceleration. Attention doesn't slow down, settle, deepen, ripen, not because it refuses but because *there is no "place" to do so,* there is nothing to settle *into.* Attention starts to skitter. And, of course, such skittering attention leads to the belief that the world is fragmentary. Here is where the insight of constructivism is helpful: If we skitter over things, the only experience we will have of things is that they are impoverished and not in need of settling into.

The following chapter takes up this ecological theme, that, once curriculum is understood in abundance, time slows down, agency becomes "housed" in the abundant work that has already been done and that now needs to be done, instead of being caught in the spell of its own productivity. There is an old pedagogical wisdom, here: "As in love, our satisfaction sets us at ease because we know that somehow its use at once assures its plenty" (Hyde, 1983, p. 22). When it comes to our love affair with the world and its wisdoms, there is plenty and there is no hurry.

Chapter 12

"Under the Tough Old Stars": Meditations on Pedagogical Hyperactivity and the Mood of Environmental Education

David W. Jardine

> *under the tough old stars—*
> To the real work, to
> *"What is to be done."*
> —Gary Snyder, "I Went Into the Maverick Bar"

I

The term "environmental education" can give us pause to consider how ecological awareness, ecological attunement, might be more than simply a particular topic among others in the classroom. It might help us glimpse how it is that *education itself*, in its attention to all the disciplines that make up schooling, can be conceived as deeply ecological in character and mood.

Ecology can provide us with images that help us reconceive the traditions and disciplines of education as themselves deeply ecological communities of relations, full of long, convoluted histories, full of life and lives, traditions and wisdoms that require our "continuity of attention and devotion" (W. Berry, 1986, p. 34) if they are to remain generous, sustainable, and true, if they are to remain *liveable*. For example, mathematics can become conceived as a rich, imaginative place, full of topographies and histories and tales to tell, full of relations of kin and kind, full of deep patterns and powers. Mathematics might become conceived as itself a deeply interconnected, Earthly phenomenon, linked to patterns of breath and bone, bearing kin-

179

ships to patterns of language and song, linked, too, to symmetries etched in stone, to the spiral doings of leaves and to the sun downarching toward *sol stasis* and return.

Ecology can also provide images of what it would mean to talk of the classroom as a real, living community, full of traces of the old and the young, the new and the established and the often difficult conversations between them. Classrooms, too, can become full of a commitment to working out and working through those wisdoms and disciplines and traditions and tales, shared and contested, that have been handed down to us all. It can be a place full, in a deeply ecological sense, of "real work" (Snyder, 1980).

II

> The connections, the dependencies, remain. To damage the Earth is to damage your children. (Wendell Berry, 1986, p. 57)

Ecological awareness always and already involves the presence of our children. Ecology thus always already involves images of pedagogy and the teaching and learning of the tales that need to be told for all of us to live well. As with pedagogy, ecology is always already intergenerational (see Jardine et al., 2003, pp. 115–128).

In this way, we can conceive of disciplines such as poetry, or negative and positive integers, or the histories of this land, as large, generous places, full of relations in which we might learn to live well, adding our work to these places, our memories and voices, our arguments and alternatives and difference. We can now ask of education itself that it:

> [Help to develop] the sense of "nativeness," of belonging to the place. Some people are beginning to try to understand where they are, and what it would mean to live carefully and wisely, delicately in a place, in such a way that you can live there adequately and comfortably. Also, your children and grandchildren and generations a thousand years in the future will still be able to live there. That's thinking as though you were a native. Thinking in terms of the whole fabric of living and life. (Snyder, 1980, p. 86)

Understood in this Earthly, intergenerational way, education (and not just "environmental education" as a subbranch, most often, of science education) has the opportunity, perhaps the obligation, to slow down the pace of attention, to broaden out its own work into the long-standing patterns and places we inhabit and that inhabit us.

It has the opportunity, perhaps the obligation, to take on a mood not unlike ecological mindfulness.

III

> Manic pace is cultivated as a virtue in elementary schools. Teachers getting kids to run from place to place, activity to activity. All noise and no *sounds*.

Quiet is undervalued as only the quiet of straight rows—*made to be* quiet by somebody, not *being* quiet. (Patricia Clifford, a teacher at Ernest Morrow Junior High School)

It is fascinating to consider how, in these ecologically desperate days, just as ecology is heralding the need for a continuity of attention and devotion, our schools are, in so many cases, full of attention deficits (itself a wonderfully co-opted marketing term along with its dark twin, "paying attention"). This is coupled with a sort of hyperactivity that precludes the slowing of pace and the broadening of attention to relations and interdependencies that love and devotion to a place require of us.

This all-too-apt image—"kids running from place to place, activity to activity"—is clearly not a phenomenon that appears simply in elementary schools. Rather, it is endemic to what is now widely described as postmodern culture in North America: an onslaught of frenetic, disconnected, fragmented images and free-floating meanings, a twirling free play of signs and signifiers and surfaces, none of which requires or deserves care or attention, none of which has a strong or vital link to any other fragment. In this flickering place, nothing *pertains* and therefore, of course, we can do whatever we desire. We make all the patterns or connections and they can, at our beck and call, always be undone and redone as we like. Loosed, here, is an image of the human subject as isolated from any deep obligation or complicity or relation to anything. Loosed here, too, is the portent of ecological disaster.

Think, for example, of television channel surfing, or, more recently, "surfing the Net."

If the surface is all there is, then surfing is all that is required.

I can always, as one Grade 7 student put it, "switch" if things get demanding or bog down or become no longer amusing or stimulating.

And, of course, as with surfing, if one loses momentum, if one hesitates for a moment, you're sunk.

Consider this horrible image: "The subject of postmodernity is best understood as the ideal-type channel-hopping MTV viewer who flips through different images at such speed that she/he is unable to chain the signifiers together into a meaningful narrative, he/she merely enjoys the multiphrenic intensities and sensations of the surface of the images" (Usher & Edwards, 1994, p. 11). And, in light of such a subject, the corpus of the world and the traditions we are living out become "part of the emporium of styles to be promiscuously dipped into. It becomes yet another experience to be sampled—neither intrinsically better or worse" (Usher & Edwards, 1994, pp. 11–12).

In this milieu, meaning and significance and connection get reduced to glinting surface stimulation. And since stimulation is inherently always momentary, new stimulation is always needed—new "activities" are always under way. And so we have a common feature of many schools—a relentless rush from activity to activity, all in the name of "keeping the children's interest."

Once this occurs, it is little wonder that panic sets in. And it is little wonder that Wendell Berry (1986) suggests that it is precisely this sort of unsettled panic that makes us excellent consumers of ever more and more activities.

Just as ecology has been suggesting, we find ourselves in schools help-lessly feeding the voracious activity beast, finding ourselves sometimes taken by the exhilarating rush of it all, and finding ourselves unwittingly equating the ends of education with being able, in deft postmodern fashion, to manipulate surfaces to one's own ends and to live consumptively.

IV

Perhaps the "ADD kids" in our classrooms can be understood to be like ca-naries in a mine shaft—warnings, portents, heralds, like the monstrous, transgressive child often is (Jardine, 1994; Jardine et al., 2003, pp. 41–52; see Preamble 7 and chap. 7), that airs have thinned and sustaining relations have been broken and need healing. Perhaps they are signs that education needs to become a form of ecological healing (P. Clifford & Friesen, 1994)—mending "all my relations."

A mending done through the recovery, through our teaching, of the gen-erous wisdoms and patterns of the world.

This is the juncture where education can become environmental in a deep sense. It can be the place where we might slow the attention and broaden our relations to the Earth.

Consider, for example, the deep pleasures to be had in the mathematical symmetries and geometric curves of just this yellow leaf corkscrewing down from a late fall Cottonwood, and how it heralds the arc of seasons and the movements of planets and suns, and the bodily desires for shelter, and how many have stood here like this, stockstill, trying to read the deep patterns and dignities and eloquences of this place:

> I think probably the rhythm I'm drawing on most now is the whole of the landscape of the Sierra Nevada, to feel it all moving underneath. There is the periodicity of ridge, gorge, ridge, gorge, ridge, gorge at the spur ridge and the tributary gorges that make an interlacing network of, oh, 115-mil-lion-year-old geological formation rhythms. I'm trying to feel through that more than anything else right now. All the way down it some Tertiary gravels which contain a lot of gold from the Pliocene. Geological rhythms. I don't know how well you can to do that in poetry. Well, like this for example. Have you ever tried singing a range of mountains? (Snyder, 1980, p. 4)

Consider this reminder that the desire to utter this place up into the eloquences of language and rhyme is itself ecological work, the work of a place, and the work of the breath:

> The rhythm of a song or a poem rises, no doubt, in reference to the pulse and breath of the poet. But that is too specialized an accounting; it rises also in

reference to daily and seasonal—and surely even longer—rhythms in the life of the poet and in the life that surrounds him. The rhythm of a poem resonates with these larger rhythms that surround it; it fills its environment with sympathetic vibrations. Rhyme, which is a function of rhythm, may suggest this sort of resonance; it marks the coincidences of smaller structures with larger ones, as when the day, the month, and the year all end at the same moment. Song, then, is a force opposed to speciality and to isolation. It is the testimony of the singer's inescapable relation to the earth, to the human community, and also to tradition. (W. Berry, 1983, p. 17)

Consider that perhaps our rhyming utterance of this leaffall "leads one to hear an ancient cosmology" (Meschonnic, 1988, p. 93) that is folded into language and breath itself.

   ... so that just this leaf opens countless tales, each one of which is about all the others, each one of which holds and deepens and quiets and places all the others.

   ... the pace of attention slows and broadens and becomes more stable, less frantic. We don't need to speed ahead, to keep up, to crowd and cram the classroom with activity after activity. We can slow and settle and return.

   ... so that just this leaf becomes the portal or opening into a Great Council of All Beings gathering in interweaving relations and suddenly, it sits still, settled, and the whole of things starts to corkscrew around its stillness.

   And then, just in time, Coyote shows up, ready to tweak the nose of such ecological self-seriousness, watching the selfsame:

> ... beautiful little gold coloured Cottonwood leaves floating down to the ground, and they go this ... this ... this ... this ... this, this this this and he just watches those for the longest time. Then he goes up and he asks those leaves "Now how do you do that? That's so pretty the way you come down." And they say, "Well there's nothing to it, you just get up in a tree, and then you fall off." So he climbs up the Cottonwood tree and launches himself off, but he doesn't go all pretty like that, he just goes bonk and kills himself." (Snyder, 1977, pp. 70–71)

But, as we know, "Coyote never dies, he gets killed plenty of times, and then he goes right on travelling" (Snyder, 1977, p. 71), teaching a little lesson on the way, that these patterns of leaves falling are their own, and remember where you are and who you are, and it's getting cold and enough writing and it's time to get the wind kicked up to hot breath walking again.

V

Just as with much of our lives, many classrooms are full of cheap, trivial, laminate-thin hyperstimulants meant to titillate, amuse, or seduce us into wanting more.

   Just as with so many of us, many schools are full of teachers ravaged by the skittering activity that has become their daily work.

Education, environmentally understood, requires that we refuse to participate in this ecological disaster. It requires that we find work to do, for ourselves and our children, that bears some dignity and Earthly discipline—good stories, large fields of thought, that need children to rethink them, that are *that* generous and true.

As always with ecological work, the work begins at home. There is no one left over here to demonize. It is always first *my own* attention and devotion to the world and its ways that is at issue, my own ability and willingness to pursue experiences that deepen as they proceed, and to refuse, when I can, as I can, experience-as-[hyper]activity, experience-as-distraction.

The problem, however, is that healing the flittering of attention that underwrites much of our lives cannot be had quickly or painlessly or finally. Remaining alert, remaining open to new experiences, is always a task to be taken up again, from here, with these children, this year, with these wisdoms of the world.

We cannot do to children what we have not already done to ourselves (P. Clifford & Friesen, 1994). We cannot deepen their wisdom of and attention to the Earth and its ways until we have first taken on the work of this wisdom and attention ourselves.

Preamble 13:
Kai Enthautha Einai Theous

> *There is a peculiar etymological twist involved in the ability to do mathematics. It is the ability to "be at home with." Habilite, inhabitation, being at home with something, being able. And being at home with something is being familiar, having familialness, finding family resemblances and kinships. And the parallel Sanskrit root of "kin" is gen: genesis, genealogy, generativity, generousness. Kin/kindness, generativity/generosity. Kindness and generosity. Affection, freely given.*
>
> —Jardine (2000, p. 32)

Considered out from under regimes of scarcity, understanding tends toward an affection for a certain playfulness and savoriness in language itself. Young children and old poets show us this on a regular basis. Interpretive work (as we saw in chap. 10) does not want to seek out playful and rich language to describe matters that are, "in reality," actually univocal, simple, and straightforward. Interpretive work seeks out such language because it is called for by the abundant nature of the matters themselves. Part of the struggle of coming to understand curriculum in abundance is finding the language appropriate to such abundance.

Again, as seen in chapter 10, the examples we need are often so profoundly mundane as to be invisible. Martin Heidegger pointed this out when he interpreted a fragment from the pre-Socractic philosopher Heraclitus: "*Kai enthautha*, 'even there,' at the stove, in that ordinary place where every thing and every condition, each deed and thought is intimate and commonplace, that is, familiar, 'even there,' in the sphere of the familiar, *einai theous*, 'the gods themselves are present'" (Heidegger, 1977, p.

234). Abundance does not point to something spectacular. To become experienced in the ability to hear the "vast abundance" in a child's simple and
straightforward talk of "higher numbers" is to become attuned to the pedagogical character that such abundance portends.

Chapter 13

On the Ecologies
of Mathematical Language
and the Rhythms of the Earth[1]

David W. Jardine

INTRODUCTION:
ON THE ECOLOGIES OF MATHEMATICAL LANGUAGE

> *Thinking is not a means to gain knowledge. Thinking cuts furrows in the soil of Being. About 1875, Nietzsche once wrote (Grossoktav WW XI, 20): "Our thinking should have a vigorous fragrance, like a wheatfield on a summer's night." How many of us today still have the senses for that fragrance?*
>
> —Heidegger (1971a, p. 70)

How peculiar it seems to consider this passage as offering images of the thinking and language of mathematics. Mathematical language is language at its most civilized, full of explicit rules of order and clear, unambiguous procedures on how to conduct oneself properly. It appears as an unearthly language, born of what Alfred North Whitehead called the "celibacy of the intellect" (cited in Fox, 1983, p. 24). It appears to be fully severed from the messes that moisten our lives and give them an unruly fragrance—"the juice and the mystery" (Adler, 1989).

Mathematics is considered a serious and exact science, a strict discipline, and such images of seriousness, exactness, and strictness often inform how it is taught and how it is understood. It requires silence and neat rows and ramrod postures that imitate its exactitudes. It requires neither joy nor sadness, but a mood of detached inevitability: Anyone could be here in my place and things would proceed identically.

---

[1]Reprinted from "The ecologies of mathematics and the rhythms of the Earth," by D. Jardine, 1994, *Mathematics, Philosophy and Education: An International Perspective, Studies in Mathematics Education, 3* (pp. 109–123), edited by P. Ernest, Copyright © 1994 by The Falmer Press. Reprinted with permission.

Finally, mathematics, in its very exactitude, conjures images of a mute and exacting authority and consequent punishments—"lonely school rooms, where only the sometimes tearful wicked sat over undone sums" (Thomas, 1967, p. 13).

In the face of such persistent images, mathematics has become simply meaningless for some teachers and some children. It often produces little more than anxiety, apprehension, and the unvoiced belief that mathematics is a matter for someone else, for some "expert" who has abilities and understanding that are "beyond me," someone better able to "climb up into their heads" (Le Guin, 1987, p. 10), into this "closed operational system" (Piaget & Inhelder, 1969, p. 278). For many of us, mathematics has become inhuman, lacking humus, lacking any sense of direct presence in, or relevance to, our lives as they are actually lived. It seems that it still is, as it was for the ancient Greeks, a divine science that knows no humility, no place in the moist darkness of the Earth. Hence Dylan Thomas' peculiarly apt pairing of undone sums and wickedness.

In these ecologically desperate times, we are being forced to fundamentally rethink the course we have taken in our understanding of ourselves and our relation to the Earth. We are being forced, in turn, to rethink curriculum in a ray that considers, not simply its idealized possibilities as a "closed operational system," but the real, Earthly conditions under which pursuing such ideals and sustaining such closure are possible.

Wendell Berry (1986) speaks of "the continuity of attention and devotion without which human life on the Earth is impossible" (p. 32). However, ecological awareness begins and remains within a paradox regarding human life. *We can do the impossible:*

> The unnoticeable law of the Earth preserves the Earth in the sufficiency of the emerging and perishing of all things in the allotted sphere of the possible which everything follows and yet nothing knows. The birch tree never over-steps its possibility. It is [human] will which drives the Earth beyond the sphere of its possibility into such things that are no longer a possibility and are thus the impossible. It is one thing to just use the Earth, another to receive the blessing of the Earth and to become at home in the law of this reception in order to shepherd the mystery and watch over the inviolability of the possible. (Heidegger, 1987, p. 109)

"The inviolability of the possible" here is not commensurate with what we can do, assuming "that the human prerogative is unlimited, that we must do whatever we have the power to do. What is lacking (in such an assumption) is the idea that humans have a place and that this place is limited by responsibility on the one hand and by humility on the other" (W. Berry, 1983, pp. 54–55). Human action, human will, can, so to speak, spiral out of order, out of proportion, breaking the analogical threads of kinship that might delimit our prerogative. Our truly sane, human prerogative finds itself interwoven with the Earth and the fundamental dependencies and reliances that "limit" our actions, not to what is conceivable, but to what is sustainable (see chap. 12). We can pursue a vision of our course that in fact works against the ecological conditions of the continuance of that pursuit. We can speak with great aspirations about mathematics curriculum and yet that aspiration, in its ecological assumptions and consequences, can unwittingly work against the actual breath needed to utter it.

Mathematics and mathematics education (not unlike education generally) have dovetailed with Enlightenment visions of human life and human Reason that begin with the (ecologically unsustainable) assumption that humanity is somehow separate from the Earth and that, in acts of understanding, we simply give order(s) to an otherwise unorderly Earth (see chaps. 8 and 9).

This is an assumption that cascades down from Immanuel Kant (1767/1964) ("the order and regularity in [what] we call nature, we ourselves introduce," p. 147), through the neo-Kantianisms of Piagetian theory (where the developing child sequentially imposes cosmos on the chaos of experience [Piaget, 1971a, p. 10]) down through some contemporary forms of constructivism.

Contrary to the hubris that suggests, in its most degenerate and bewildering form, that "[we] make all the patterns" (W. Berry, 1987, p. 5), ecology suggests this: Prior to our deliberate interventions and actions (actions that admittedly make patterns), the Earth and our Earthly lives are *already* full of patterns and rhythms of interdependency and kinship. Human action and human understanding (of which the makings of mathematics are a part) do not make these Earthly relations—mathematics does not make one's heart beat rhythmically, nor does it make the turns of a Blue Jay's call, nor does it make the cycles of breath and day and pine needle arrays. Rather, the makings of mathematics are threaded within a fabric of makings that are always already at work. The makings of mathematics are threaded, in fact, in a fabric of makings the integrity of which must be maintained for mathematics to actually be possible for us to do at all. We rely, for example, on the convoluted intersections of the rhythms of our blood and the rhythms of day and night and the complex rhythms of oxygen-producing ecosystems. Mathematics cannot simply impose its own makings on this fabric of relations as if the Earth must live up to the clarity and distinctness that mathematics demands of itself (this is, in part, the beginnings of an ecological critique of quantitative research; see chap. 10).

The Earth and our Earthly lives—including human understanding and human language and the makings of mathematics—"are bound together by an anciently perceived likeness between all creatures and the earth of which they are made," where "like speaks to like" (W. Berry, 1983, p. 76). Even in the pursuit of mathematics, we are deeply and inevitably *of* this Earth. Rather than envisaging it as giving the world order or imposing cosmos on chaos, an ecologically sane understanding of mathematics sees it as participating in, and bespeaking, an order that goes beyond human wanting and willing—an order to which human wanting and willing must be attentive if it is not to overstep the bounds of its Earthly possibilities. Unambiguous mathematical formulations of symmetrical relations, for example, are akin to the patterns of these spruce tree branches and needles. These mathematical formulations don't make these trees symmetrical.

I realize that it is all too easy, at this juncture, to allow this point to devolve into epistemological and linguistic quarrels—for example, "symmetry is not a feature of the Earth but rather is a concept that we impose on our experience." Rather than enter into these quarrels, I agree with Thomas Berry (1988) when he suggests that ecological insight requires a type of "post-critical naivete." I live here, in the foothills of the Rocky Mountains, and all of my experience, and all of the wisdoms of the peoples who have lived here for thousands of years, tell me beyond any reasonable doubt that this precious place has its own integrities and rhythms and patterns that I did not author or impose and to which I must become attentive if my life here and the patterns that my living imposes are to be sustainable. Through such attentiveness, my living bears a deep nonepistemological and nonlinguistic kinship to the patterns and integrities of this place. I will admit that it is difficult, in our urban(e) age of hyperreflectivity and hyperactivity to experience this kinship and these integrities and rhythms and patterns (the ecological traumas we have created certainly attest to this difficulty). We get caught too easily in worlds of our own making. I will admit as well that, in experiencing the Earth—not just talking about it and understanding it, but walking it and breathing it—we do impose our expectations and constructions and conceptions upon it. But a clarification and developmental sequencing of these impositions does not describe a sustainable ecological starting point for our curricular reflections as much as it describes a profound problem we face in respecting what comes to meet us in our experience as having its own life and integrity. Saying that this leaf or the life of this animal (or the cadences between my heaving breath and the pitch of this hill I am climbing) has no pattern/order of its own and that all we can understand of the Earth are the patterns/constructions we impose on it—this might make a sort of epistemological or philosophical sense. But it points to a way of life that is becoming no longer sustainable, In the area of academia—here, in this chapter—the ecological task is to explore how to take up issues of human knowledge and language (and the inevitabilities of human imposition) in a way that preserves and honors our kinship with the Earth and that resists replacing his anciently perceived sense of kinship and alikeness with quarrels of our own invention. Ecologically speaking, then, rethinking mathematics and mathematics education requires, in part, that we seek out the language that allows like to speak to like in generous and sustainable ways, in ways different from the patriarchal relations of mastery and dominance and imposition that haunt our Enlightenment legacy. It requires reembodying mathematical discourse into a more Earthly discourse, a discourse full of pungent dependencies and ambiguities and relations of likeness and kin and kind, a discourse that is bodily, generative, and "incurably figurative and polysemous" (J. Clifford, 1986, p. 5).

Mathematics has often been understood as the cure for such figurativity and polysemy, a replacement of relations of ambiguous likeness (or, playfully put, relations of "kindness" and, to cite the parallel Sanskrit root to "kin," "generosity") with unambiguous relations of univocal identity/difference. Ecology is telling us that the envisaging of ecological interdependencies and kinships as problems to be cured simply because of their ambiguities and mysteries are itself the source of our ecological despair.

Such a curative response assumes that entities in the world are in reality, separate and distinct "substances" ("a substance is that which requires nothing except itself in order to exist" [Descartes, 1640/1955, p. 255]) and that a language that properly names such a reality is itself full of separate and distinct univocal definitions. Ecology is showing us that this is not the case, and the consequences are dual. Not only does the Earth consist of interdependent nests of kinships and relations and not separate substances that require nothing themselves in order to exist. The language proper to designating such an interdependent Earth is *itself* full of kinships and relations that resist univocal, unambiguous designation. The desire to overcome such resistance spells ecological disaster. In fact, resistance to such "unambiguous designation" (Gadamer, 1989, p. 434) is precisely a sign of the resilience and life of a living system. It is a sign of its abundance.

A similar set of moves away from our Enlightenment legacy can be found Edmund Husserl's phenomenology, albeit in a rather more "epistemologized" version. Phenomenology wishes to describe the deep embeddedness of the "exact sciences" in the life-world, in life as it is actually lived. Husserl maintained that we cannot understand the discourse of the sciences by beginning with the "surreptitious substitution of [a] mathematically substructured world of idealities for the only real world, our everyday life-world" (Husserl, 1970, pp. 48–49). If we begin with such a substitution, the resonances of mathematical discourse that echo down through the "living metaphoricity" (Gadamer, 1989, p. 432) of language and through the deep ecological rhythms and patterns of bone and breath and flesh end up being understandable only as simply a blurring of what is in fact clear, a concretion of what is in fact abstract, a making profane of the sacred, humiliation. Hence the humiliation felt by a Grade 2 child who believes that these undone sums have answers already, without his intervention, and that his intervention has only made things worse. Hence, too, the aura of wickedness that surrounds such worsen, and the subterranean linking of mathematics to sacredness and purity and a linking of the humiliation of undone sums to the sins of the flesh.

Phenomenologically, the reverse is the case. The idealizations of mathematical discourse appear in the midst of the world of everyday life and they are not despoiled by such appearance, but enlivened by being connected back to their living sources. "These are human formations, essentially related to human actualities and potentialities, and thus belong to this concrete unity of the life-world" (Husserl, 1970, p. 170). Mathematical discourse resonates deeply with our humanity understood in its full, fleshy, embodied sense, with our humus and those anciently perceived likenesses that tie the entrails of our humanity out into the Earth in ambiguous relations of kinship and kind. And again, this does not despoil the idealized exactness of mathematics. Rather, it makes such exactness a real, living achievement that erupts out of life as it is actually lived, rather than seeing such exactness as graciously bestowed "from above." Mathematics is not something we have to look up to. It is right in front of us, at our fingertips, caught in the whorl patterns of skin, in the symmetries of the hands, and the rhythms of blood and breath.

GIVING AND DRAWING BOUNDARIES:
A CLASS IN EARLY CHILDHOOD CURRICULUM

> To undergo an experience with language ... means to let ourselves be properly concerned by the claim of language by entering into and submitting to it. If it is true that [we] find the proper abode of [our] existence in language—whether [we are] aware of it or not—then an experience we undergo with language will touch the innermost nexus of our existence. (Heidegger, 1971b, p. 57)

> If we may talk of playing games at all, it is not we who play with words, but the nature of language plays with us, long since and always [see Preamble 3]. For language plays with our speech. It likes to let our speech drift away in the more obvious meanings of words. It is as though [we] had to make an effort to live properly in language. It is as though such a dwelling were especially prone to succumb to the danger of commonness. Floundering in commonness is part of the dangerous game in which, by the nature of language, we are the stakes. (Heidegger, 1968, pp. 18–19)

Years ago, in an undergraduate class in Early Childhood Curriculum, I asked the students the following question: In precisely what sense is 198 a higher number than 56? The initial reaction to this question was silence, followed by scattered bewilderment and confusion. Although the students were becoming somewhat accustomed to this sort of question, the precise intent in asking it was not clear. Some students took the question as an indirect form of accusation—198 isn't "really" higher than 56, so the fact that they may have been using this language is an error to be corrected. Others simply struggled to make explicit what would be meant by "higher." They found themselves caught up in a swirl of interweaving and interconnecting meanings that seemed to resist being "straightened out" in any definitive manner. One student slipped into the language, common to young children, of numbers being "big" and "little." Far from remedying our situation, it simply multiplied the problem, so to speak.

The question then arose: If we don't know precisely what we mean when we use such language, how is it that we can feel confident when we attempt to teach such aspects of mathematics to young children? Implicit here is the reasonable equation of the ability to teach something with knowing what it is that you are teaching. This equation is one that I tend to encourage. However, there is a deeper supposition here that must be addressed. Implicit here, too, is the equation of "knowing what it is you are teaching" with being able to be precise, to be exact and fully explicit, to provide exact, literal definitions and the like. One of the points I hoped to educe with my question was that we *do* know what it means to say that 198 is "higher" than 56, but that this knowing is not definitional, literal, univocal, or clear. It interweaves in unanticipated ways with the young child building a higher and higher tower of wooden blocks, with the fact that we can speak meaningfully of "counting *up* to ten," or with the fact that growing older means growing "up," and growing up means becoming taller, and that the "higher" one's chronological age, the "bigger" one is, and that, for children, importance bears a resemblance to height and age, and so on.

The initial difficulty with such interweavings is precisely this "and so on." Although reflecting on our language can bring forth unanticipated, playful interweavings of experience, it is never quite clear, in following such interweavings, if one has gone too far. After all, is it too much to say that the progression of higher and higher numbers orients to infinity, that is, to God, the most High, and that numbers that fall below the "ground" (below where we stand, below "ground zero") have a dark and negative character? Or is it too much to say that when counting higher and higher quantities, we must keep track of them by consistently bringing them back to Earth, back to base, so that we use "base ten" as a way of preventing the pile from spiraling upward out of sight, out of hand, a way of keeping them at our fingertips (our digits)? that we organize higher and higher quantities into groups that we can handle, into "handfuls," into "tens?"

Clearly these examples "go too far," but they are not meaningless simply because they cannot be resolved into some univocal meaning that would bind them together under some unambiguously nameable identity. These examples are not *identical* to each other, but neither are they simply *different*. Rather, they all describe the same *kind* of thing. They are *like* each other:

> As in spinning a thread, we twist fibre on fibre. And the strength of the thread does not reside in the fact that some one fibre runs through its whole length, but in the overlapping of many fibers. Don't say "There *must* be something common" ... but *look and see* whether there is anything common to all. For if you look at them you will not see something that is common to *all*, but similarities, relationships, and a whole series of them at that. To repeat: don't think but look! We see a complicated network of similarities, overlapping and crisscrossing: sometimes overall similarities, sometimes similarities of detail. I can think of no better expression to characterize these similarities than "family resemblances." (*Familienahnlichkeiten*). (Wittgenstein, 1968, p. 32)

Such relations of likeness and kind-ness/kinship and family resemblance are, as these metaphors suggest, full of generativity and life. It seems that new possibilities, new relations, new likenesses simply keep coming (in a way akin to how new children, with new ideas and formulations and experiences and questions, keep arriving in the mathematics classroom). It is never quite clear just what the parameters are for this kind of phenomenon. Each new example, each new interweaving thread or fiber, reopens the "kind" to new permutations and possibilities, and each new permutation has a cascade effect, rattling through each instantiation, giving it new relations. For example, when I used this phenomenon as an example in a graduate class, a colleague suggested that this whole array of relations becomes inverted if we consider ordinal instead of cardinal numbers. This suggestion is no simple additive to the list given earlier (like some discrete substance that needs nothing except itself in order to exist). This suggestion arrives *already bearing its own relations*. But more than this, it moves indiscretely through this list, bearing and generating relations as it proceeds. It inverts the bodily metaphor and ushers in images of "ground" and "grounding/foundations," where "what comes first" is now visible as "the Rock." God, the most High, is also "Number One."

Not only does this new suggestion regenerate the living character of the whole list cited previously. It lets us see that there is something incorrect about speaking about the *whole* list without hesitation and caution. "The whole," in this case, is never simply given, not because we have not worked hard enough on the list, but because of the way in which *there is* a "whole" (see Preamble 5, and chaps. 5 and 11). "The whole" is not something that can simply be univocally designated independently of the interdependent nest of threads that make it up. The inherent ambiguity of the list is thus not an accident that must be fixed. Rather: "There is quite a bit of 'give', 'flexibility', indeterminacy or vagueness right within the concept itself: with the result that the meaning remains essentially incomplete, so underdetermined that it cannot be clearly understood until further reference is made to some mode or modes of realization" (Norris-Clarke, 1976, p. 67). The meaning of "higher and lower numbers" is not separate from its instances, like some ghostly "idea" that could be univocally named independently of the difference and resistance that those instances portend. If we recall Wittgenstein's threads of family resemblances, the "kind" being named here *is* its diverse instances, and there is no independent, overarching "family member" that can fully speak for the rich diversity of all the rest of the family members and thus render them silent. To fully understand the kind, we cannot revert to some foreclosing, overarching pattern (some patriarchal voice that can simply impose itself on the rest of the members of the kind) without heeding the generative difference that each member makes to what we understand the whole family to be. Understanding in accordance with this idea of family resemblance not only requires "running up and down the known range of cases to which it applies, actually calling up the spectrum of different exemplifications, and then catching the point" (Norris-Clarke, 1976, p. 68). It also requires more than this. It requires conceding the fact that the point that is thus caught remains susceptible to the fact that that ranging is not over. The point (the "nature" of the family resemblance) will inevitably need to be caught anew (see Preamble 8).

This is not to say that abstraction, clarification, generalization, and definition are impossible. We can produce and name an "overarching pattern" that binds all these cases together and that names what we anticipate "the whole" to be. However, there is another sense in which "the whole list" is never given. Not only are we always in the midst of working through the diversity of exemplifications in order to "catch the point," there is always another instance just about to arrive. The full meaning of "higher and lower numbers" is always in a state of generative suspense. Its full and final meaning is always "yet to be decided" (Gadamer, 1989, p. 333). We cannot say once and for all what the relation of kind are in an embodied sense of number, because we can never know what might come of it in the future as new cases arrive and require us to run down the range of cases anew. This is why such insight is deeply pedagogical. (See chapter 10.) The young child who stretches out her arms and says "I have a miiiiiilion stickers at home!" shows us, in the raising of her voice, in the stretching of her arms and the word, that the issue of an embodied sense of number is not a closed, given issue, but an open, yet-to-be-given one. In order to understand "the kind," we must proceed, not with foreclosing impositions of our constructions upon it, but with "a consciousness that must leave the door ajar" (Hillman, 1987, p. 154), open to the arrival of that which outstrips our constructions and goes beyond our anticipations.

The strength of Wittgenstein's thread of family resemblance is thus not simply in the *overlapped* fibers, but in the *overlapping* of fibers. As with relations of kinship and family resemblance, the "kind" exists only if new kin keep coming. Put differently, it only exists if the kind remains open to the arrival of the new that will renew and transform it and open it again. The kind exists, therefore, only if it resists precisely that sort of foreclosure demanded of unambiguous designation: The kind needs the next case to remain living and vital and to avoid closure and calcification.

Thus, "the kind" does not simply apply to the case and represent it. Rather, the case enters into the flesh of the kind and makes "waver and tremble" (Caputo, 1987, p. 6) what we have heretofore understood the kind to be. "Kinds" are therefore always and necessarily "yet to be decided"—"the whole list" is never simply a given to be univocally named. Suggesting that the whole is never simply given suggests an image of education itself: that our already established understanding of the world is never established and fixed once and for all, but is necessarily open to the arrival of the young. More strongly put, it suggests that such regenerative arrival is somehow essential to our understanding of the world if that understanding is to remain vital.

This suggests an ecologically delicate matter: It is not only that children need the already established curriculum in order to understand their course. This is certainly the case. As with a vibrant ecological system, already established, "old growth" protects the young by protecting the living conditions under which such new growth can be nurtured. This is the strength of the ties that bind and the reliability and integrity and strength of the "kind." However, to pursue this ecological metaphor, in its character as a *living course, our already established course needs children in order for it to remain alive and invigorated.* An ecosystem that forecloses against the regenerative arrival of the young is unsustainable. Once the curriculum becomes calcified into static rules and regulations—univocal, unambiguous designations—it becomes closed to the arrival of the new. It becomes ungenerous and un-kind. In such a "closed operational system," the next child will, in fact, make no real difference, like those undone sums, where anyone could be here in my place and where my doing of these sums leaves them untouched and untransformed. Worse yet, the next child can be nothing but an annoyance, like so many classrooms where the boundaries of the curriculum and the objectives of the lesson plans are already set and the arrival of the child can only replicate this curriculum and meet these objectives exactly (identity) or despoil them (difference). Ecologically speaking, both of these extremities are unsustainable because both extremes (including the Romantic visions of "each individual child" [see chap. 16]) are premised on cutting the threads of family resemblance.

It is precisely the sense of security that comes from the fixing of boundaries that many teachers desire. As Wendell Berry (1987) notes, such boundaries can at once provide a sense of security and be profoundly disruptive: Just as they bring under control what falls inside the boundary, what is left outside the boundary is henceforth understood to be simply out of control. From the point of view of univocal designation, the ambiguous, "living metaphoricity" of language begins to appear as simply meaningless or chaotic. We can, from such a premise, falsely believe that our task in teaching is to somehow "conquer" the "wilderness" by imposing order on it. As Alice Miller (1989) has noted, the challenges to closure that children bring to the classroom can become envisaged as nothing more than wild(er)ness and unruliness. No longer are children understood as our kin or our kind, and no longer is the task to bring out these relations of kind between us and with the Earth. We need not listen to the unvoiced experiences they have already undergone before our concerted efforts at "taming" them. They are not envisaged as ecological beings who are caught, with us, in an already working nest of relations. Rather, they become simply separate objects to be controlled and manipulated in imposed relations of dominance and mastery, because they are little more than threats to the security of the boundaries we have set. Teaching thus becomes a "monstrous state of siege" (Smith, 1999c, p. 140) between the old and the young. Once the bonds of kinship and relations of kind are broken, both the old and the young become understood only in their worst aspects. Out of relation to the vivifying arrival of the young, the old becomes harsh, static, foreclosing, and unforgiving: The senatorial aspect of age as the passing on of wisdoms becomes mere senility. Out of relation to the old wisdoms of the world that protects and nurtures them, the young no longer provide generativity and renewal, but become simply puerile, cut loose, abandoned.

The telling point in this class demonstration about higher and lower numbers is that even in the use of terms like "higher" and "lower," we already understood what each other was talking about without aspiring to the boundaries and securities of univocity and exactness. The kinships that bound us together were visible as already at work, so to speak, *before we knew it*. As Ludwig Wittgenstein (1968) noted, we can draw a boundary around these experiences and concepts, "but I can also use [them] so that the extension of the concept is *not* closed by a frontier" (p. 33). Regarding the desire we may have to define "higher," to draw a boundary or frontier, Wittgenstein rather playfully says "that never troubled you before when you used the word" (p. 33). The attempt to bind discourse to a central, singular, unambiguous designation reflects only a practical and circumstantial exigency and we become troubled only when explicitly called upon to produce a boundary around such a center: "If someone were to draw a sharp boundary I could not acknowledge it as the one that I too always wanted to draw, or had drawn in my mind. For I did not want to draw one at all. His concept can then be said to be not *the same* as mine, but akin to it. The kinship is just as undeniable as the difference." (Wittgenstein, 1968, p. 36). And, as Wittgenstein further notes, I can *draw* boundaries or frontiers matters, but I can never *give* such matters a boundary (p. 33). In its lived, lively usage as a mathematical term, the term "higher" resonates in an untroublesome way, beyond the idealized frontiers that we *can* draw, but *cannot* give. We were not compelled, in that Early Childhood Education class, to declare in the end that either 198 "really" *is* higher than 56, or that it *is not*, even though such declarations might have made us feel more secure and more in control. Perhaps this is why a student teacher said recently, when she realized that the topic of her lesson might be one with which the children were already vaguely familiar, "Wait! I'm not ready!" This is the beginning of a recognition that life goes on beyond our earnest intentions and actions as teachers and that this familiarity/family resemblance that the child brings has its own reliances and securities and strengths that we share with them, not identically, but in relations of kind. These family resemblances describe an ecological strength that we share with them: a common fortitude in which both take comfort. It is the first glimmerings of a precious realization so essential for student teachers to undergo, that understanding erupts out of life itself, and not simply as a response to an act of teaching and therefore, that teaching must first and foremost attune itself to what is already at work in our lives and the lives of the children we teach. And this, in turn, is the beginning of a precious ecological realization that the Earth and our Earthly lives have an integrity to which our acts and intentions must become attentive so as not to violate this integrity in the name of univocally designated lesson objectives, curriculum mandates, and the like.

Part of the purpose in asking this question to these student teachers, then, was to help them see that what goes beyond their control and master is not simply chaos and that they can rely on these already working relations in which they dwell with children in relations of "kind-ness." In a peculiar way, mathematics in its fleshed out sense, is something that just happens. In walking down the stairs, the 2-year-old child's life is already pacing out mathematics in the rhythms of his steps, the cadences of his breath, and the recurring patterns of his mother's laughter.

CONCLUSION

> Every word breaks forth as if from a centre and is related to a whole through which alone it is a word. Every word causes the whole of the language to which it belongs to resonate and the whole world-view that underlies it to appear. Thus, every word carries with it the unsaid. The occasionality of human speech is not a causal imperfection; it is, rather, the logical expression of the living virtuality of speech that brings a totality of meaning into play, without being able to express it totally. (Gadamer, 1989, p. 458)

> The rhythm of a song or a poem rises, no doubt, in reference to the pulse and breath of the poet. But that is too specialized an accounting; it rises also in reference to daily and seasonal—and surely even longer—rhythms in the life of the poet and in the life that surrounds him. The rhythm of a poem resonates with these larger rhythms that surround it; it fills its environment with sympathetic vibrations. Rhyme, which is a function of rhythm, may suggest this sort of resonance; it marks the coincidences of smaller structures with larger ones, as when the day, the month, and the year all end at the same moment. Song, then, is a force opposed to speciality and to isolation. It is the testimony of the singer's inescapable relation to the earth, to the human community, and also to tradition. (Berry, 1983, p. 17)

> Rhyme leads one no doubt to hear in language a very ancient cosmology. Rhyme is not only an echo from word to word. Arrangement for arrangement, the order of language evokes and mimes a cosmic order. In realizing itself, rhyme is tuned in to [this cosmology]. Rhyme and meter are praise. An indirect theology. (Meschonnic, 1988, p. 93)

A 7-year-old friend of my son came to visit us years ago, and I told him about the pond in our neighbor's field. The spring runoff had created a slough about 8 feet deep. After discussing that it would be over his head if he fell in, over my son's head, and even over my head, he asked: "If a hundred-year-old man stepped in it, would it be over his head too?"

I answered, "Yes, it's *that* deep."

I told this tale to a mathematics education colleague and he said, "Isn't it cute when kids get things so mixed up?"

If we lose a sense of interweaving kinships inherent in this tale, the ways that relations of bodily height and importance and age and depth "rhyme analogically" (W. Berry, 1983, p. 75), the way that this tale has a deep "analogical integrity" (W. Berry, 1989, p. 138), we not only lose a sense of our kinship with this child. We also lose a sense of kinship with ourselves. We become cut off from our own Earthly being and mathematics becomes a disembodied, inhuman discipline, full of my colleague's harsh condescensions of "cuteness."

One of the purposes of the class described earlier was to begin to reinvest these students in the reliabilities of their own fleshy, mathematical being such that they can begin to hear, not only children, but their own breath and bearing of kinship with children and with the Earth. This child's pond tale carries with it its own reliable patterns that do not need our constructions and impositions, but simply our openness and care and attention to what is *already at work* in its bearing and grace.

After our exploration of mathematical language in this class, most students said that they were having more difficulty with language than before. The work they did in this class was not meant to make their lives *easier* but to begin to help them become at ease with the real difficulty, the real claim that language makes on us. Some have described how this experience has made them more careful in their language, more attentive to the lessons and themes that our language and the language of children have to offer. For some, however, it induced a sort of temporary paralysis, rendering them silent, speechless, fearful, in some sense, of the unvoiced and unintended implications of meaning that issue with every word. In the long run, this silence might be a good sign. Out from under the noisy clatter of tricks and techniques they have mastered, they may have come upon their silent kinship with children.

If the discipline of mathematics were as unEarthly and pristine and self-enclosed as it often announces itself to be (if it could *give* itself a boundary, and not merely *draw* one), there could never be any "new ones" among us. It is precisely a loving attention to these "new ones" (an act in attunement to the openness and generosity of "the kind") that defines our special task as teachers.

How peculiar it still seems to consider all this as offering images of the thinking and language of mathematics. But when the 3-year-old child announces that he or she is going to "count all the way up to ten!" and we hear the rising pitch of voice that squeaks higher and higher, literal-minded and disciplined and exacting mathematicians will already understand what has been said, even though such understanding belies the unambiguous designations to which they may be professionally accustomed.

Preamble 14: Abundant Webs

Given the arrival of new information and communications technologies under regimes of scarcity, a sense of hypothetical abundance holds sway. One Web-crawl (lovely image!) search-item entry-click instantly, effortlessly, yields *thousands,* maybe even *millions* of "hits." Any possible topic hypothetically outruns any possible effort. And so, new information technologies do not simply make "accessible" that which used to be "scarce." On the contrary, if the regime of scarcity is left in place, they have the potential to aggravate that sense of scarcity by *relocating it.* Given new information technologies, we no longer have an issue of a scarcity of "resources" in the classroom. There is no "lack" of possibility. Now that we have access to millions of possibilities at the click of a mouse, what becomes scarce is our ability, our time, our lives. We can search every "hit" *if we want to,* but our sense of our own wants has become weirdly unrecognizable. If I am interested in exploring a particular topic that I might want to introduce in the classroom, what holds such explorations in place in the face of *millions* of "easily accessible" possibilities? What becomes scarce is the very possibility of my own efforts at taking up such possibilities. And, as Wendell Berry has demonstrated, once I "buy into" this, I become an excellent consumer of that which promised to *relieve* (but in fact simply aggravates) such panic: one more program, one more hyperlink, one more new gadget. Just like old medicine shows, we become convinced of our illness by those very people who just happen to have on hand the remedy we need, a remedy that, of course, must, of necessity, lead us to need something more from their snake-oil wares.

There is nothing new here at all. It is just that we get reminded again of Ivan Illich's (1972) insight, that the main thing that we learn in school is that we need more school. He did prophesy that perhaps something like "educational webs" (p. v) might have some hope in outrunning the degrading scarcity reach of institutionalized schooling. We've yet to reach a point where we know of the truth of this prophesy. Many happily hold to the prospect that "the Web" might hold a key, but unless the spell of scarcity is broken, simply adding new information and communications technologies into the web of that spell does not bode well for pedagogy.

What new information technologies have portended is a sense of expanding possibility coupled with an inverse proportionally decreasing sense of ability and agency. If regimes of scarcity are left at work in the classroom, the arrival of new information and communications technologies simply accelerates matters. Given scarcity, it is the productive and constructive surveillance abilities of subjectivity that is in question, its "genius" if you will (see chap. 15). Thus, as millions of possibilities arrive in ever expanding webs, subjectivity becomes aggravated into pursuit and into an ever-expanding sense of its own incapacity. Scarcity is relocated in subjectivity—I haven't done enough, need to do more, need to be more productive, more active, and this becomes life-long (learning), where restlessness and unsettledness hold sway. What results is hyperactivity and epistemological obesity.

Understood in abundance, the arrival of new information and communications technologies can be experienced as a sort of freedom and spaciousness, wherein I can lay down the burden of being the constructor, owner, or manager of a place, a topic. However, thoughtfully cultivating this sort of experience is not a technical matter, because, by their very nature, technical matters are wont to side-step issues of cultivation. As we discussed in chapter 2, an ever-expanding sense of what we can do if we want to (abundance reduced to a sort of technical and hypothetical proliferation) cannot help us answer the question of what we want do to or of what might be best. As discussed in chapter 7, the character of abundance is an ethical issue. "No learned or mastered technique can save us from the task of deliberation and decision" (Gadamer, 1983, p. 113). Given a million "hits," we still have to consider what might be best. Thus, in this turn, where Internet abundancies threaten to overwhelm us, a sense of our own agency and ability has to be rethought. No longer can it be tethered to a galloping chase after finality and mastery and dominion (see Preamble 8 and chap. 8). As the Buddha said, something has to "let go" if we are going to learn how to experience the abundance of the Web (see chap. 19).

Chapter 14

"If You Want To": Inquiry and the Arrival of New Information and Communications Technologies Into the World of the Classroom

David W. Jardine
Sharon Friesen
Patricia Clifford

The arrival of new information and communication technologies (ICTs) in the lives of teachers and their students, student teachers and those involved in teacher education, means much more than simply the arrival of new ways to provide the same old news. These new technologies demand that educators rethink the nature of their work and the forms of collaboration and communication that are proper to this work.

The arrival of new ICTs in schools has tended to take the following form: Courses in the integration of ICTs are siloed as specialty topics divorced from curriculum, policy, and pedagogy. Students are sent "down the hall" to "computer labs" to learn keyboarding or the ins and outs of various program and/or software possibilities. Treated in this isolated way, the teaching and learning of ICT becomes squarely and simply a technical matter. And the same pedagogical form frequently appears in teacher education practices—student teachers are either taught "computer courses" geared for educators (how to start a Web page, how to do a slide show, how to use PowerPoint, how to do Web searches, and so on) or are taught how to "integrate" new ICTs into their university and practicum classes.

The difficulty we have encountered with this image of the place of ICTs is not only that it lends itself to an image of education that is no longer viable (education envisaged according to an industrial model of production, consumption, and delivery). There is another, more odd and pernicious thing going on that is, we suggest, of vital pedagogical importance.

We have witnessed elementary and high school students, as well as student teachers, classroom teachers, and faculty of education teachers and researchers, becoming swept up in a phenomenon that could be called "if you want to." This phenomenon is widespread in places where education and ICTs meet. The logic of this phenomenon is simple and very ordinary and familiar. ICTs are presented as follows: "If you want to create a web page (or cut and paste a document, or insert a picture into your work, or divide your presentation into two columns, or import sound-bites into a presentation, or, or, or …) here is how it is done." What begins to occur here is that a wider and wider array of technical possibilities are opened up while, at the same time, this wide array becomes less and less tethered to any strong *pedagogical purpose*. In school, I can learn how to insert a picture into a document without ever learning anything about why you might do such a thing, what good it can do, and what harm, why the work might require such a thing, whether the discipline involved (say, mathematics) has use itself for such ICTs, and so on. With regard to education and ICTs, all I'm often taught is *how to insert the picture*. The only other thing that seems to come with this know-how is an odd and sudden pedagogical abandonment. Now that I know how to insert such pictures, I'm on my own: not simply "if you want to do such insertions, here's how," but "go ahead and do such inserts if you want to."

The possibilities that new ICTs have opened up will not help us answer the sorts of questions we start running into at this juncture. These questions are not technical questions regarding what we can do, but ethical questions regarding what would be a good thing to do. Just because I can insert a picture into this document you are currently reading does not in any way mean that it's a good idea.

The arrival of powerful ICTs has faced educators with a dilemma: these technologies themselves cannot address the issue of what good work might look like, both inside and outside the classroom. And the more possibilities that ICTs open up, the more this ethical question gets aggravated—a question regarding what is best to do, why one course of action might be preferred over another. Such technologies "will never prevent us from doing anything we are able to do" (Gadamer, 1989, pp. 196–197), but neither can they help us decide what to do. They will not help us answer questions such as "Having the ability and desire to know, how and what should we learn? And, having learned, how and for what should we use what we know? One thing we do know is that better solutions than ours have at times been made by people with much less information than we have" (W. Berry, 1983, pp. 54–55).

We believe that, as educators, these are *precisely* the sorts of questions that need to be asked regarding new ICTs. Interestingly enough, these questions can be addressed only by thinking through what we believe about those living disciplines *about which* we want information and about which we wish to communicate. The full paradox is this: ICTs cannot help us with this, and, at the same time, they are radically transforming both *what* and *how* we think about curriculum topics themselves.

THE LOGIC OF FRAGMENTATION AND ISOLATION

We have found a powerful parallel to this fragmented, isolated, "technical" arrival of ICTs in our schools. ICTs are not the only things that are "siloed" and taught in ways that are divorced from any sense of how knowledge might operate in the living disciplines of, say, mathematics or poetry or chemistry. It is commonplace for teachers to break up each of the living disciplines that form the human inheritance into easily deliverable bits and pieces that are doled out to students in ways that can be efficiently managed and controlled. This industrial image of education has turned some classrooms into a version of an assembly line. And, under the auspices of educational psychology, teachers choose from these fragments activities that are geared and targeted to each individual student's abilities, grade level, or developmental level. As with ICTs, it is commonplace to fragment students' learning into developmental sequences, isolated activities, and grade-level curriculum expectations. Once the work of students is thus fragmented, the work of teaching becomes one of trying to keep up and manage what becomes an ever-expanding and ever-accelerating array of individual differences and an ever-expanding array of isolated demands. In this light, ICTs become one more thing to do, one more thing to get "covered."

In this light, the most common types of questions that student teachers ask is "What about the students who are having trouble?" "What about the students who are finished in a flash?" "What about the child who barely speaks English? who has a short attention span? who hates math? who is having trouble at home, who is bored, overstimulated, not working at grade level, has an Individual Program Plan?" Attempts by educators to outrun the differences that present themselves in any particular classroom are exhausting, confusing and, sometimes, nearly hopeless, especially with increasing classroom sizes, decreasing assistance in the classroom, and the social, economic, and cultural pressures that are now ordinary in Canadian schools. If we now add ICTs into this mix and leave in place the "if you want to" logic that has driven their arrival, teaching with any sense of sanity and composure becomes nearly impossible. ICTs become, as David Smith once put it so eloquently, "one more damn thing" that needs to be done by teachers already overburdened with the weight of many other worlds.

Or, even worse, ICTs become taken up simply as the technical means to deliver a form of pedagogy that has been untransformed by their arrival. Isolated worksheets, all form-fitted to individual differences, can now be delivered and marked at the speed of light. Meaningless repetitive practice and drills can be self-correcting and geared to ever-narrowing student

needs (all in the name, of course, of individualizing and differentiating curriculum to serve the special needs of each individual student).

The main characteristic of this scenario in our schools has been one of *acceleration:* Not only are teachers, administrators, and students inundated
with an ever-multiplying set of demands. Into this setting are introduced
ICTs, which are (it sometimes seems deliberately) designed to become
out-of-date and in need of replacement or evergreening—"keeping up" becomes the clarion of such a pedagogy based on fragmentation and isolation,
and the promises of technology become imagined as cures to precisely the
sorts of panics that they have helped cultivate. Just like the old fourth-edi-
tion-of-the-textbook hucksters of old, how often have we been promised,
now, that "This new computer program, this new hardware or software (or
color printer or scanner or firewire do dah) will cure all your ills." Worse yet,
with new ICTs we can (if we want to) place in the hands of our children the
means of their own self-isolation, self-monitoring, and self-correction. This,
of course, is all done in the name of "freeing" them somehow and doing
right by their individuality. What we have freed them for, in such cases, is
the cultivation of the unsatiable desire for new and flashier gadgets without
any growing sense of place and possibility or of real, substantial work. We've
abandoned them to the belief that their wants are enough, and if they want
to, they should "go for it."

STEPPING AWAY FROM THIS LOGIC

We have found it essential to step away from this logic, in classroom practice, in our theorizing about education, and in attempts to think through
the work of student teacher education. The arrival of new ICTs cannot and
should not be expected to hold itself in check. And neither is it pedagogically sound to abandon our students to the consumptive and insatiable logic
of "if you want to" as an adequate form of pedagogy. As educators, we are
called upon to reimagine our work—with classroom students, teachers, student teachers, administrators, those involved in professional development—in ways that cultivate a new sense of what it means to be an active,
creative agent in the work of schooling, how to become "stewards of the intellect" rather than mere dispensers of knowledge. To interrupt this logic of
isolation and fragmentation is the step toward what we are calling an inquiry
stance, and the development of this stance, paradoxically, has been encouraged by the arrival of new ICTs.

Because of the widespread arrival of ICTs in North America, both in
many homes and in most classrooms, our students have already, so to
speak, "skipped school." Many students are already able, with much more
facility than many of the adults that teach them, to find online a tumultu-
ous amount of often undigested, often brilliant work on any possible topic
that might come up in school. Our students are already experiencing a
world that is much richer, much more difficult and challenging, much

more alluring and full of adventure than the version of the world made available in many classrooms.

We believe that it is essential to cultivate a vision of education that is able to sustain the sometimes overwhelming arrival of ICTs into our lives and into the work of stewarding the intellect in this burgeoning "information age."

It is this inevitability that, in part, has led us to something much older than these new technologies: inquiry. Inquiry begins by imagining the topics into which we might invite our students as living topographies, living places full of their own worldliness, diversity, relations, multiplicity, history, ancestry, and character. Rather than beginning with the common educational impulse to fragment and subdivide these living fields, inquiry begins with questions aimed at getting in on the conversations that constitute that life. Here is a simple example. Recently, a student teacher talked about how he was approaching the topic of "percentages" with a Grade 6 class. He noted that, in this particular case, he did what is very common in education: He started scouring resources to figure out *how to teach this topic*. At a certain point, however, he remembered an adage about inquiry: The first questions to ask in an inquiry are not how to *teach* such a topic. Rather, the questions are more like this: What *is* "percentage?" What is it that matters about this topic as it is lived in the world? How did we come to have such a topic in our world? Why would we want to pass along such a topic to our students? Where does it belong in human experience? How is it and can it be understood, shown, represented? Where does it appear and how, in what guises, to what ends?

Once he started to ask himself such questions, whole families of relations and ancestries began to appear—the idea of "per hundred" (per cent) as a common denominator, a common standard; the founding of this idea on "base ten" and issues of place value; images of cents and centuries and centurions and decimals and decimation (the effective technique of domination of the Roman Empire, where every 10th person was killed in order to establish order in a newly-taken-over town). Once he got over the all-too-common spell of "How do I teach this?" and turned his attention to the topic, the topography of the inquiry itself, the ancestors and their questions and their work began to show up. In an inquiry, the guiding question becomes "What are the living questions for which 'percentages' might be a good answer?" (a buried version of the ethical questions that arrive with new ICTs).

By allowing himself the time to enter into this sort of topographical meditation, he began, so to speak, to learn his own way around this phenomenon. He began to let himself become experienced in this place. There is a wonderful etymological twist that is at work here. To become experienced means "to learn your way around," that is, to have ex-*peri*-ence (as in the term "perimeter"—the "measure" [meter] of "around" [peri-]).

To become increasingly more experienced, however, does not mean to have any final, definitive knowledge, such that further, new experiences (e.g., the ones brought forward by students in a Grade 6 classroom) become

less and less necessary, less and less possible, less and less interesting or relevant or pleasurable. In this foreclosing version of "becoming experienced,"
students' troubles become increasingly annoying and the "experienced person" becomes more and more cynical or condescending toward those newly
arriving in some territory. This is the old saw about "the expert" and why we
find such a notion so troublesome in education. It seems to bespeak a "know
it all" impatience and a grim sort of finality.

In stark contrast to this, in inquiry, "becoming experienced" in something means quite the opposite:

> "Being experienced" does not consist in the fact that someone already knows
> everything and knows better than anyone else. Rather, the experienced per-
> son proves to be, on the contrary, someone who ... because of the many expe-
> riences he has had and the knowledge he has drawn from them, is
> particularly well-equipped to have new experiences and to learn from them.
> Experience has its proper fulfillment not in definitive knowledge but in the
> openness to experience that is made possible by experience itself. (Gadamer,
> 1989, p. 355)

The "expert" can be portrayed as the one who already knows and therefore
as the one who is ready to simply dispense what they know to those who do
not know, at a moment's notice, and with great ease and confidence. The experienced person, on the contrary, is someone who is ready for new experiences *because of* the experiences they have already undergone.

Having himself entered into the great human conversations that constitute this phenomenon of "percentages," this student teacher has cultivated
in himself the ability to take up the differences that different students might
now bring to this inquiry.

Once he had explored for himself this topography of "percentages," this
student teacher realized that the ancestors faced a real, living question in
the world for which "percentages" was a real, living response. He had
opened up a space of genuine *inquiry*, where this topic had become a living
topography and not just a meaningless fragment among others to be delivered to students as one more thing to learn. And, as he then noted, this is
precisely the question that the students in his class now faced in coming to
learn about percentages: What are the sorts of questions in the lives of students for which percentages might be the response? Or, as students often
ask their teachers, "Why are we learning this?" If all we have examined for
ourselves is how to teach percentages, this question is simply baffling.

Interestingly enough, therefore, in an inquiry, the ancestors and the children show up *at the very same time* and *in the very same way*, demonstrating that
inquiry is a necessarily *intergenerational* enterprise (Jardine et al., 2003, pp.
115–128). And here is the lovely twist. Doing an inquiry into percentages is
not simply a good way for this student teacher to prepare himself to teach it.
Doing an inquiry *with* his Grade 6 students into the nature of percentages is
precisely a pedagogically sound way for this student teacher to *teach* per-

centages. The question now is, how might we invite our Grade 6 students into this wonderful place we have come upon and whose ways we have walked?

Too often, percentages is understood as an isolated curriculum fragment, one more thing to be taught by teachers and mastered by students. Understood as such, ICTs can be used, if you want to, to perhaps deliver a fun game about percentages that would help students learn about it and test their knowledge, perhaps in cooperative games they could play. And we could give students self-testing banks of questions that they could go through and hone their skills. If you want to.

When we understand percentages as a long, complex inheritance that forms the basis of an inquiry, with all its substantive questions, images, and threads, in the midst of all the ancestries and inheritances and appearances of this phenomenon of percentages, the ethical question of the proper place of ICTs can now be asked. It can now be asked because we are becoming familiar with the territory within which deciding about the place and importance and appropriateness of ICTs might be soundly asked: What good, for example, might inserting a picture into an assignment do in order to aid in the understanding and communication of percentages and their ways?

With this shift, the arrival of ICTs takes on different character. This arrival is now *held in place* by questions that are not themselves technical: What does this place require of us as teachers and learners? What place do ICTs already have in the life of this living discipline? What role can they have in helping us sustain real conversations about our collaborative work? It is this sort of imagining that inquiry demands of educators, especially now, when new information technologies are ready to break apart the old, fragmented, school-bound versions of knowledge that will no longer do.

Preamble 15:
The Abundance of the Future

The topics entrusted to teachers and students in schools are not abundant only insofar as there is a wealth of tales that have been told, stories that have lingered or been erased, multiple past threads to be unraveled and explored, and so on. More than this—and much more vital to pedagogy—is that *the story is not over*. The story is still being unfolded. As we see in the following chapter, as part of the human inheritance, we find that any (table of) content(s) has at it an empty chair, awaiting and anticipating arrival.

Understood in abundance, the knowledge, skills, and attitudes listed in the curriculum guides are not fixed and final and given and meant simply to be delivered. Rather, such matters are, by their very nature, susceptible to a future (new questions, concerns, evidence, applications, transformations, additions, reinterpretations, explorations, occlusions, discoveries, happenstances, and so on) that is *still arriving. That* is what it means to call mathematics or poetry or biology or writing a *living* discipline. It doesn't simply mean that there are lots of old books, old ancestors, and fixed canons of wisdom that students must simply accept as given and finished and final. It means that this still-arriving, yet-to-be-decided future will have something to say about what we have understood these old books, these canons, these wisdoms and ancestors to mean. In such a light, Anh Linh's work (and the work of her teachers and fellow students and the work of the authors of that chapter, and the thoughts and actions of those reading that chapter) *adds itself* to that ongoing, living conversation. In understanding a contour of the living discipline of mathematics, we take part in something that abounds beyond the bounds of our own efforts and, in such partaking, we keep such matters open to question, susceptible to the future. That, we suggest, is what

good teachers spontaneously do—they keep the world(s) open to the arrival
of the young, and they teach the young the ways of such worlds. And, to spin
this again, we learn from the young what might become of this world, because they always bring with them the questions that we could have not
asked without their arrival. Simple, in its own way. To experience such
abundance—to experience, paradoxically, how a curriculum topic goes beyond my experience of it—is an experience of its truth.

The following chapter is rooted in some ordinary events in an extraordinary classroom. It provides an exploration of one of the ways in which regimes of scarcity intercede in our attempts to understand what is going on
when something wonderful happens. As with Anh Linh and Richard, so
too with Nathan—the arrivals of their insights and questions and work are
often pathologized, not into the troublesome monster that falls behind
and doesn't understand, but into that other monstrosity that has invaded
educational discourse under regimes of scarcity: the genius. If the troublesome questions of the "gifted" child are handed back to them as "their
property" (e.g., "he's very special"), they count as no gift at all. What has
been given has been given back.

In Jennifer's classroom, the troublesome, breathtaking work of Nathan in
this Grade 1 classroom was graciously taken up. Coincidentally, during this
school year, Jennifer was taking a class on hermeneutics, and she found that
Nathan's work proved Gadamer's *Truth and Method* to be disturbingly accu-
rate regarding the metaphysics of "the genius," and how this metaphysics
forecloses on the possibility (the necessity!) of interpretation and therefore
abandons pedagogy to the lamentations of constructivist interiority (for the
genius becomes the "origin" [see chap. 4] of the constructive forming of the
work of genius). Once Nathan's (and all the other children's, and the
teacher's, and all the books') insights are each drained back into the subjectivity that gave rise to them (the generative "genie" that produced them), the
topic at hand—in this case, the world of Van Gogh—is emptied of its abundance. That abundance is "deposited" inside the doings/producings/con-
structs of individual subjectivities. The topic, consequently, becomes just the
sort that can be dealt with in schools: impoverished. What emerges in the
next chapter is a different sense of "myself" than some isolated genie who
magically "brings" abundance to the world.

Chapter 15

Filling This Empty Chair:
On Genius and Repose

David W. Jardine
Jennifer Batycky

I

I [Jennifer] listened to many classes about hermeneutics, and after each class I seemed to be filled with the same feeling of confusion. It was not so much a confusion about what hermeneutics was, but more a perplexed feeling about how this style of inquiry was going to impact my life as a teacher. From what I initially gathered, in some sort of "magical" way, something remarkable from the life world of the classroom would simply present itself to me. It seemed that my role would be to take up this particular event and care for its message, so that the beauty of its dailiness was gently uncovered and honored. Well, I certainly had no intention of holding my breath and waiting for the hand of the curriculum god to tap me on the shoulder, delivering a profound message! As a teacher, I felt so tangled up in the everydayness of the classroom, I wondered if I could ever step far enough out of the situation to see and hear the possibilities that presented themselves daily. By the middle of October, I had resigned myself to the fact that everyone in my graduate course had received a special message from Mercury, except for me.

Wednesday, October 28th, 1998. My plan for the morning was to provide the children with an opportunity to apply their imagination and skills to a descriptive writing passage. Rather than simply "teaching" all about what descriptive writing entails, I decided to select an art reproduction and share my own writing about it. My intention was to draw upon our collective background experience with art and use that as a springboard to create beautiful writing. Since the beginning of the year, the walls of the classroom had been filled with reproductions of the works of Van Gogh, Gauguin, Monet, Manet, Matisse, and several others. Available, too, was a large pile of smaller, 8"-×-10" reproductions that children could take to their work areas and ponder. Daily, we would sit in front of large reproductions and talk about them, how they made us feel, made us think, and we learned of the lives of these artists, their troubles and successes. As I read my own paragraph based on Van Gogh's painting of a bedroom, I could instantly sense a connection between myself and the children. I remember thinking "This is going to be a great lesson."

One of the first student books I picked up to read was Nathan's. He had written two pages on the image of Van Gogh's chair:

> *The sad and lonely chair sits alone in a cold and empty room. The only warmth is a little smokeless pipe. So as the chair sits alone with still only a little warmth, the chair waits for something. But what is it? It still waits for the moment, that moment that the chair thinks will never come. The brick floor gives a chill in the air. The chair still sits by the door, waiting for the moment. But the door doesn't budge. Days pass, but everything is still. Still as a rock. So everything goes like this day after day after day. This goes on and no-body sits on the chair. Nobody even notices the chair and that's how it will stay.*

When I read Nathan's passage, I felt a chill up my spine, knowing that the chair was waiting for Van Gogh to return from the field in which he shot himself. During the weeks that followed, I shared Nathan's writing with colleagues both at my own school and in the system. I also shared it with friends and family members because I didn't want this event to simply be held under an awful educational gaze. Each time I shared his writing, I was met with a stunned look, followed by always well-meant comments that always seemed to dismiss this gift Nathan had given us:

> *"Nathan is so thoughtful. He always says the most amazing things."*

> *"What grade did you say you teach?"*

> *"You are so lucky. I could never do that with the children in my class. They just aren't capable."*

> *"Nathan is really gifted. He really ought to be tested."*

> *"Well, how are you going to extend this child's learning now? Perhaps he should have an opportunity to take his own writing and create his own picture."*

How should I extend Nathan's learning? How absurd! The real question that Nathan's writing presented me with was about my own learning being extended. For days I carried his book and picture around with me; to my home, to meetings, around the school ... just wondering what to do next. I found myself tempted to sit Nathan down and drill him about why he wrote what he did about Van Gogh's work and what it meant. Thank goodness I refrained, because, upon reflection, I realized that asking Nathan about his own work in this way was not going to give me the answer or the questions I was looking for.

In almost all of the responses to Nathan's writing no one could find a way to speak of the work he produced: What does this writing tell us about this painting and what we ourselves may have failed to see, to feel, to understand? about the loneliness and sadness and isolation and emptiness that Van Gogh often hides under such colorful images? about our beliefs as teachers about children's ability to even express such things?

What also became troublesome were questions like these: Would Nathan's writing have been this rich if he had no images to build from, to rely on, if we had not pursued and practiced, with the whole class, how to respond to such works with care and thoughtfulness, if we had not deeply explored the worlds that these painters evoked and how they offered us a new vision of our own world, if we had not listened to what each other said about the paintings we were looking at? Most responses to Nathan's work failed to respond to his work. The reason for this is that many people tried to start with Nathan himself. I realized that the only way that I could take care of Nathan's writing was to start with the world opened up by Van Gogh's work, because that is what his writing is about.

By the way, when David [Jardine] came into the class later that week, I asked Nathan to read his work to him. Nathan had been reading passages from Van Gogh's letters to his brother, and we had watched portion's of Sister Wendy's Story of Painting, *a charming and moving video series on the history of art (http://www.tpt. org/BTW_folder/Sept/wendy.html).*

They went out into a quiet spot in the hall, and after reading his work to David, Nathan said: "He's buried next to his brother, you know."

II

Empty chairs had been a feature of van Gogh's thinking since childhood. The memories that crowd behind this single image are connected with deep mournfulness, with thoughts of the omnipresence of death.... His own chair, simple and none too comfortable, with his dearly-loved pipe lying on it, stands for the artist himself. We may well be tempted to recall the pictorial tradition that provided van Gogh with his earliest artistic impressions. Dutch Calvinism sternly insisted on an iconographic ban that prohibited all images of the Holy Family except symbolic ones: the danger that the faithful might be distracted by the beauty of the human form had to be avoided at all costs. Thus Christ could be represented by a "vacant throne." (Walther & Metzger, 1997, p. 8)

Thus, too, Van Gogh himself, not just his death but aspects of his living, can be represented by his room, by the place he has inhabited—the pipe, the chair, the modesty of the surroundings, the colors that speak of Arles (unlike, say, the dark muddiness of *The Potato Eaters*, 1885, which places its inhabitants so differently, in hues and colors that seem to place them right into the ground out of which their meal has come).

Jennifer had her Grade 1 students doing "self-portraits" this same year as Nathan arrived, not by literally drawing pictures "of themselves," but by drawing pictures of their rooms, the spaces they live within. She also introduced me to a wonderful, disorienting book called *Room Behaviour* (1997) by Rob Kovitz. From the back cover:

Room Behaviour is a book about rooms. Composed of texts and images from the most varied sources, including crime novels, decorating manuals anthropological studies, performance art, crime scene photos, literature and the Bible, Kovitz shapes the material ... to create an original, fascinating and darkly funny rumination about the behaviour of rooms and the people they keep.

Those room portraits that the children did, like Van Gogh's painting, were akin to portraits of "vacant thrones"—portraits of spaces that a non-portrayed "subject" (for lack of a better term) inhabits. But this is not quite correct—"the subject" *is* portrayed, but the portrait is *of* a particular *sort* of subject. These are not portraits of an isolated, autonomous, egocentric "I myself" that somehow sits at the center of any inhabitation, but of a "self" that issues up out of and leaves traces within an inhabitation, a "keep," up out of and into a world of voices and relations and ancestries and kin, of colors and palettes and hues, images and tales, up out of places, memories, and topographies and even up out of the most ordinary, everyday objects that we find ourselves surrounded by. The "self" that these "room-portraits" portray is, so to speak, an ecological (nonsubstantial, unable to exist by its self) "self," not an isolated "I."

So the vacant throne, the empty "room portrait" somehow *is* the self, but now treated as empty of a self-existence independent of its Earthly relations. (This interpretive thread is, of course, *not at all* in line with the Dutch Calvinist idea of "the vacant throne." On the contrary, what we are pointing to here is a way of loving the world and its places and loving our own straggly emergence into being who we are.)

These Grade 1 room portraits thus provide a simple critique of Cartesianism and its belief in the logical precedence of an abstract, empty, worldless "I am," in favor, instead, of an inhabitation that is the Earthly self's keep and an "I" that grows up out of its sojourns in the world.

This Grade 1 venture highlights the oddness of many curriculum guides that go through a sequence like this: me, me and my family, maps of our classroom, our neighborhood, our city, our city past and present, the province, and so on. These sequences presume that what is somehow most immediate in the life of the child is his- or herself and that curriculum should radiate, so to speak, "outwards" from there. This, of course, is totally unsupported, both by developmental theory (see Jardine, 2006; Piaget, 1952) and by the common sense we develop by living around children and carefully listening to what they are saying to us about these matters. As Kieran Egan (1986, 1992) shows so well, the worlds of imagination and mythology and great stories of places and people far away are much more *immediate, compelling,* and *understandable* than is the abstraction "myself." Children are much more drawn to, capable within, and articulate about large, troublesome, ancient, venturous, living, imaginal "spaces" of Impressionist painting (see chap. 17), the allure of old geometries or Pythagorean cults, the spell of trickster tales (e.g., Jardine, Clifford, & Friesen, 2003; Lensmire, 2000), or the age-old troubles of time and its telling (to name a few, clearly limited examples), than they are within the cramped and literal-minded enclosure of "myself."

"Myself" doesn't simply disappear in ventures into such alluring, difficult places, only its metaphysical (i.e., nonexperiential, disembodied, uninhabiting, hallucinatory, ideational, logically consistent but ecologically insane [Bordo, 1988]) sense of enclosure. This "myself" is experienced as issuing up out of the course of the experiences, not that I *have* (*Erlebnisse;* see Gadamer, 1989, pp. 60–70) but that I *undergo* (*Erfahrung;* see Gadamer, 1989, pp. 240–262) in and through the world. This world in which I undergo or suffer experiences is not just inhabited and formed and fashioned by myself and by and within my own(ed) experiences, but is always and already experienced, articulated, and inhabited. It has always and already been formed and fashioned by shared and contested inheritances, voices, and ancestries, up out of which I must slowly and continually "find" myself becoming who I am. I am surrounded by a "multifariousness of voices" (Gadamer, 1989, p. 295)—and not just up out of the human inheritance but all Earthly calls and keeps.

Even these late autumn birds locate, form, and fashion this worldly "I am" (Jardine, 2000) in ways far "beyond my wanting and doing" (Gadamer, 1989, p. xxviii)—here, spotted by these Pine Grosbeaks "before I know it" and whether I have a "lived experience" of it or not (differently put, this is a way to distinguish between phenomenology and hermeneutics).

In just this way, this "world" of Impressionist paintings is *already long since inhabited* before Jennifer, her Grade 1 class, or I arrive. Therefore, because this world is not simply "our experiences" or "our constructs," or "our meanings" or "our perspectives," entering this world requires some measure of giving ourselves over to *its* "wantings and doings" (Gadamer, 1989, p. xxviii)—*its* measure of what it wants of *us*. It helps form and fashion who we each become in venturing through it. That is to simply say, we *learn* from it. But now, learning does not just mean that there is a subjectivity who now has, as some interior possession, new information. Rather, it means that each one of us who ventures to this place becomes someone who, in different and multiple ways, has come to know her or his way around (*ex-peri*) this place—someone "experienced" in it. The experiences undergone are experiences *of the place* and not simply and only and obviously experiences somehow "of" the experiencer. Simply put, Nathan's words are *about* Van Gogh and self-portraits and rooms and loneliness and dying. They are *of* Arles and Theo. They invoke the muddiness of *The Potato Eaters* (even if Nathan never *meant* to refer to it or to the Dutch Calvinists portrayed in it).When we take his words to be *about Nathan* (which, as teachers, we surely must do as part of our obligation to him), we have changed topics. We have, so to speak, "switched rooms" by now taking these words out of the worlds they invoke and re-placing them into Nathan's life and biography and psychology,

This frail, contingent, finite, emergent, dependent "self," then, slowly finds and forms itself in and through its inhabitations, through the "rooms" that are this self's keep. But here, the possessive case is still misleading because each individual self (whatever this exactly now means) does not simply possess its keeps but is also kept by them. The character (*Bildung;* see Gadamer, 1989, p. 9 and following) of this emerging self is dependent, at least in part, at least to some terrible extent, upon the company it keeps.

It is no accident, however, that we find such talk so odd and disturbing. We have inherited a great and variegated and sometimes contradictory faith in individuality, autonomy, freedom, independence, genius, creativity. We are suckers for talk of courage and heros, partly because we have grown up into the inhabitation of and under the auspices of the European Enlightenment and its faith in an off-stage, disembodied Reason. Immanuel Kant (1794/1983) named any sense of Earthly dependence a form of "immaturity":

> Enlightenment is man's emergence from his self-imposed immaturity. *Immaturity* is the inability to use one's understanding without guidance from another. This immaturity is *self-imposed* when its cause lies not in a lack of understanding, but in a lack of resolve and courage to use it without guidance from another. *Sapere Aude!:* "Have courage to use your own understanding!"—that is the motto of enlightenment. (p. 4)

We need only courage and resolve, to lead the way with a Reason conceived as not "of" the world but as the seat of judgment before which the world can be forced to give witness:

> A light broke upon the students of nature. They learned that reason has insight only into that which it produces after a plan of its own, and that it must not allow itself to be kept, as it were, in nature's leading-strings, but must itself show the way with principles of judgement based on fixed laws, constraining nature to give answer to questions of reason's own determining. Reason ... must approach nature in order to be taught by it. It must not, however, do so in the character of a pupil who listens to everything the teacher chooses to say, but of an appointed judge who compels the witnesses to answer questions which he had himself formulated. While reason must seek in nature, not fictitiously ascribe to it, whatever has to be learnt, if learnt at all, only from nature, it must adopt as its guide, in so seeking, that which it has itself put into nature. (Kant, 1787/1964, p. 20)

Reason is thus conceived as broad, empty "forms" of thinking that, when applied to things, form and fashion them and demand of them that they "shape up" (it is from this philosophical juncture that Jean Piaget developed his notion of "cognitive schemata" [see Jardine, 2006, and chap. 8]: hence, of course another kind of a "vacant throne [as] a symbol of [a] judgement and power" [Walther & Metzger, 1997, p. 8] that is "out of this world," unkept in or by the frailties of our Earthly human countenance [see Jardine, 1992b]).

And, unless we miss this point, Kant does suggest that our immature sense of dependence is *self-imposed*.

III

Consider, then, another take on something oddly both akin and radically different from "the vacant throne." Jacques Derrida (& Ferraris, 2001) is speaking to the question of the difficulty of his own writing and an image arrives:

> One does not always write with a desire to be understood—that there is a paradoxical desire not to be understood. It's not simple, but there is a certain "I hope that not everyone understands everything about this text", because if such a transparency of intelligibility were ensured it would destroy the text, it would show that the text has no future [*avenir*], that it does not overflow the present, that it is consumed immediately. Thus there is the desire, which may appear a bit perverse, to write things that not everyone will be able to appropriate through immediate understanding. There is a demand in my writing for this excess ... a sort of opening, play, indetermination be left, signifying hospitality for what is to come [*avenir*]. As the Bible puts it—the place left vacant for who is to come [*pour qui va venir*]. (pp. 30–31)

Here, the place left vacant with bread and wine at the Seder table, waiting for Elijah to arrive, does not bespeak someone who has *left* but someone who is *coming*. As with "the vacant throne," it represents someone who is not here, who is not a given, not present, but this absence is now not a once-present and now vacated Self that is elsewhere and still governing, like some Cartesian "I am" or some Husserlian "transcendental subjectivity" that experiences itself as "above this world" (Husserl, 1970, p. 50). This empty chair now stands for *a future that has yet to come* (avenir). The futurity represented by the empty chair is not a given, not "frozen" (Loy, 1999; Smith, 2000), not "foreclosed" (Smith, 1999c) but "yet to be decided." What will become of me, what will become of this work I am producing—all this is still coming, is not yet settled, and no amount of hurry or anxiety or effort will outrun this eventuality.

This is what is "given": this empty chair.

In this light, the empty chair, like the Grade 1 room portraits, portrays an inhabitant who *has a future*, who is always yet-to-be-itself, yet to fully and finally arrive. So even Nathan's lamentations over Van Gogh's empty chair and the impending sense of loss and death it portends points to the fact that here we are—who would have thought?—over a century later and half a world away, experiencing Van Gogh's suicide and the work signs he left of his life, and the room portrait trace of his leaving. Van Gogh has died and has no future. But imaginally speaking, here we are, still living out the work he left. Not unlike Nathan himself, what Van Gogh's work will turn out to be is still yet-to-be-decided and it is being decided anew right here, right now, in this Grade 1 classroom.

Just to complicate matters further, not just this "self" but these "keeps" are *themselves* not frozen or foreclosed or finished. They are not givens but are "open for the future" (Gadamer, 1989, p. 340). The places we venture

with (or without) children in (and out of) school—spelling, reading, mathematics, poetry, art, biology, chemistry, philosophy, Dutch Calvinism, Impressionism, writing, hermeneutics, ecology, and so on—are continuously
becoming constituted and understood and inhabited differently. They are,
so to speak, *living* places or spaces or rooms (or, if you will, "living disciplines") that form part of our living Earthly inheritance, and as such—as *living*, that is, as susceptible to the future—we "must accept the fact that future
generations will understand differently" (Gadamer, 1989, p. 340). When
Jennifer surrounded her classroom with prints of Van Gogh, Monet,
Matisse, Picasso, she was providing her class with a "roomy," generous
topic/topography (see Gadamer, 1989, p. 32) whose full meaning is, in its
very temporal, finite, contingent nature, still being decided. There is not yet
any final word on this place of Impressionism and Van Gogh, even though
much has been said. Our only option, then, is finding ways to *get in on this
conversation* and to speak in ways that *keeps the conversation open* to being
taken up anew (Smith, 1999c). To paraphrase a phrase of Derrida's (&
Ferraris, 2001, p. 32), this topic still has an empty chair at its table of con-
tents. It is still "open" to question, to debate, to transformation, to being understood differently, becoming ignored or forgotten, or to perhaps even
becoming despised again as Van Gogh and his works once were.

IV

The Austrian art historian Hans Sedlmayr gives the title "The vacant throne"
to the final chapter of his essay in cultural criticism, *The Loss of the Centre
[Verlust der Mitte]*. Sedlmayr writes: "In the 19th century there was an altogether new type of suffering artist: the lonely, lost, despairing artist on the
brink of insanity." Van Gogh's chairs constitute a metaphor of the crisis of the
entire century. (Walther & Metzger, 1997, p. 9)

This line of argument is also found in Gadamer's (1989) concern over the
image of the artist as a mad or tortured genius who has no place in the
world and whose works thus became like "vacant thrones." Under such an
image: "Whenever one 'comes upon' something that cannot be found
through learning and methodical work alone—i.e., whenever there is
inventio where something is due to inspiration and not methodical calculation—the important thing is *ingenium*, genius" (Gadamer 1989, p. 54).
Under such a logic, we don't look to the works and what they have to say to
us, but to the creator, the one who has generated this work, its "genius"
and what the work has to say about this creator-genius ("Nathan is really
gifted. He ought to be tested"). We look for the "origin of the work of art"
(Heidegger, 1971a, 1972a) in a subjectivity, some great, off-stage "I am"
that has uttered the work into existence, sometimes seemingly *ex nihilo*. In
this light, Van Gogh's paintings are *all* "vacant thrones" that point to the
off-stage creative, gifted genius from whom they have issued and who is,
somehow, their "reason" for being.

One of the greatest and most troublesome gifts that Hans-Georg Gadamer's work *Truth and Method* (1989) offers us as educators, a gift in part inherited from his teacher Martin Heidegger, is a disruption of this discourse of "the genius." Much of the early part of this work is dedicated to unearthing how, through what he calls the "subjectivization of aesthetics" (Gadamer, 1989, pp. 42–81), any sort of human production (the *work* of an artist like Van Gogh, or the *work* of a burgeoning author and art connoisseur such as Nathan) had become reduced to a sort of "subjective production" that is available only through the equally subjective reactions or responses of a viewer, reader, listener, and so on. (This tendency is what Edmund Husserl identified in his *Logical Investigations* [1902/1972] as "psychologism" and to which his phenomenology—which greatly influenced Gadamer's work—was a response.) Nathan's description of Van Gogh's work and Van Gogh's work itself are both understood, under such a logic, as subjective creations that point, most immediately and fundamentally, *to the subjectivity who produced them.* Worldly works are therefore understood as "creations" that are comprehensible only insofar as we unearth or re-create the "creator" of the work (this was, according to Gadamer [1989, p. 187 and following] a central desire of Schliermacher's [1768–1834] version of hermeneutics, where understanding the work of a creator-genius, in fact, understanding any historical inheritance, becomes a matter of "congeniality"—a matter, one might say, of "like-mindedness").

In Nathan's case, rather than approaching his work and the worlds it opens up, and thus encountering him becoming himself *in the midst of* and *in the keep of* and *in relation to* these worlds, we pursue a type of subjective, psychologistic attribution of talents, backgrounds, skills, proclivities, likes, dislikes, or gifts. We want to fill the empty chair by metaphysically positing a presentable, knowable, assessable, given, self-identical generator of the work from whom the work gets its original/originary (see chap. 4), authoritative/authorial (Jardine, 1992c) bestowal of meaning, its *mens auctoris*. Thus, under the metaphysics of genius, we call out to the author to save us from the task of interpreting the questions that the work itself places *us* under.

Likewise, our responses to this painting or these words have themselves become subjectivized. Just think of how epistemologically timid we have become. I might suggest that Nathan's description of Van Gogh's work is wonderful, but, under the metaphysics of genius, all I am actually reporting about is myself—my responses, my thoughts, my perspectives, my opinions, my experiences. Under the metaphysics of genius, we are not drawn out of ourselves into a worldly meditation with each other about a world that is already full of a "multifariousness of voices." Rather—and not disingenuously meant and not exactly false either—we get a commonplace educational adage, "Nathan is so thoughtful." The next most commonplace adage is "You are a really experienced teacher who loves art. I could never do that." In this latter case, the metaphysics of genius is attributed to the teacher instead of the child, thus keeping in place the inability to explore—or to see the worthwhileness or even, sometimes, the *possibility* of exploring—the work itself and the worlds it might portend.

Under the metaphysics of genius, to understand the work, then, is, to some extent, to *turn away from the work itself* toward its creator through a de-coding of the author's intent or meaning or desire or experience or background circumstances or "knowledge, skills, and attitudes" (all versions of the *mens auctoris*). This, of course, recapitulates a much older metaphysic: that the world itself, in all its rich array, is understandable, venerable, worthy of our attention, only insofar as it is understood as a sign of God's creative beneficence. All things are only *ens creata*, and, under this gaze, becoming enamoured of any worldly thing in and for itself or in terms of its mundane, Earthly inhabitations is a form of fallenness and a source of potential deceit, deception, seduction, or betrayal. Hence an old argument that the Church has long since had with the advent of modern science: Figuring out the worldly causes of worldly things is a vacuous and pretentious enterprise. Why? Because, in their deepest reality, all worldly things are "vacant thrones" pointing to the one great off-stage Creator (which becomes recapitulated in the Enlightenment's capitalization of Reason). And, to the extent that humanity is made in God's image, we, too, although in much more contingent and mundane ways, are both the crown of the *ens creata* **and** are ourselves creators of works (see chap. 2): *ingenia*—all of which, again, becomes recapitulated in the Enlightenment's vision of Reason (see chap. 8).

Even though it appears that we have arrived in a place that is quite arcane, traces of this phenomenon are rampant in education. To understand this gift that Nathan has handed us requires handing it back to him. It's *his*. Doing anything else, under the metaphysics of genius, would simply involve imposing our own views on his, robbing him of his voice and replacing his *ingenium* with ours. But then here comes the constructivist horror hidden in the metaphysics of genius—"the old mythology of an intellect which glues and rigs together the world's matter with its own forms" (Heidegger, 1985, p. 70). This pernicious phenomenon is at work for many "qualitative researchers" who tie themselves in knots taking transcripts back to their "authors" for checks on what the words mean *to the author*, all in a valiant effort to not "impose" on the transcripts their own "forms." It is at work, therefore, in the desire of many "qualitative researchers" to report to us what their participants mean (somehow imagining themselves as the "representatives" or "stand-ins" for their absent participants [another appearance of a "vacant throne" in a transcript that now the qualitative researcher attempts to fill?]). Under this same metaphysics of genius, researchers become perpetually caught in the epistemological dead-end: "I can only tell you what I thought the participant meant when I took their transcript back to them with *my* interpretation of what it means and heard them say this about what I said they said." Even the sad and impossible question that some will ask ("How many times should I take it back?") bespeaks the spell of the metaphysics of genius.

And it is clearly at work in the profound silence Jennifer encountered from those who read Nathan's words. All in all, we hide a deep desire for the author to come fill this chair that has been left empty before us.

We can't believe, perhaps, that this chair has been left empty *for* us.

V

[Martin] Heidegger shows that the work of art [and, in his later work, Earthly things and even words themselves] [are] not merely the product of an ingenious creative process, but that [they can be] *works* that [have their] own brightness in [themselves]; [they are] there [*da*], "so true, so fully existing." (Gadamer, 1994, pp. 23–24)

The chair waits for something

The brick floor gives a chill in the air

Days pass, but everything is still

nobody sits on the chair

Nobody even notices

This work has been recited because returning to it helps dislodge a final feature of the metaphysics of genius by introducing a phenomenon that does not make an appearance under the metaphysics of genius: the worldly repose of things.

Having been through the twists and turns of this chapter, I now experience how both Van Gogh's painting and Nathan's writing have each become much more fulsome and troublesome and provocative and substantial than they initially were. Each of them has become, so to speak, "stronger" and more robust than either would have been without the appearance of the other. This is a version of the "art of strengthening" that Gadamer (1989) suggests defines a true conversation: "[It] consists not in trying to discover the weakness of what is said, but in bringing out its real strength. It is not the art of arguing (which can make a strong case out of a weak one), but the art of thinking (which can strengthen ... by referring to the subject matter)" (p. 367). In fact, unexpectedly venturing into this world of Impressionist painting once again in this Grade 1 classroom, having been in this place many times before, facing Nathan's words and the reappearance of Van Gogh and this cascade of empty chairs and vacant thrones and dreams of rooms and habitations, I'm struck again by how incommensurate to this Earthly place is my knowledge and experience of it (a first beginning of an ecological humiliation of "constructivism," wherein the limits of my own experience are experienced). In fact, the more I experience of this place, the more often I find my way around it, the more threads of referentiality and ancestry and dependence and kin that I can muster, the more incommensurate my knowledge and experience become.

Put the other way around, the more often I venture to this place, the more experiences I have of it, the better *it* gets.

This is, in fact, a rather ordinary thing: The more we learn and experience about a particular artist or composer, or about a painting or piece of music, the more often we return to a piece of wilderness in all its various seasons, the more we pay attention to the cycles of Pine Grosbeaks and their tethers to weather and sun, the more often we arc together circle-segment cross-hatches in the bisecting of angles (see chap. 5), the more deeply do we experience the fact that these things have lives of their own, "beyond my wanting and doing" (Gadamer, 1989, p. xxviii), beyond my "rigging and gluing" (Heidegger, 1985, p. 70).

Therefore, as my experience-of-this-place grows, I come to realize more and more deeply a profound ecological point: *This place is not just here for me.* It does not just "face this way," so to speak. It "stands-in-itself." It has its own "repose":

> The existing thing does not simply offer us a recognizable and familiar surface contour; it also has an inner depth of self-sufficiency that Heidegger calls "standing-in-itself." The complete unhiddenness of all beings, their total objectification (by means of a representation that conceives things in their perfect state [fully given, fully present, fully presented, finished]) would negate this standing-in-itself of beings and lead to a total levelling of them. A complete objectification of this kind would no longer represent beings that stand in their own being. Rather, it would represent nothing more than our opportunity for using beings, and what would be manifest would be the will that seizes upon and dominates things. [In the face of Van Gogh's work, or Nathan's] we experience an absolute opposition to this will-to-control, not in the sense of a rigid resistance to the presumption of our will, which is bent on utilizing things, but in the sense of the superior and intrusive power of a being reposing in itself. (Gadamer, 1977, p. 226–227)

There is an empty chair, not just facing here, inviting, welcoming, waiting, but also on this table's hither side.

This is where the notion of the metaphysics of genius really begins to hit home pedagogically. When Jennifer chose to surround her Grade 1 children with works of the Impressionists, she understood that this world, this space, this place, this "room" has its own repose and part of the work of the classroom adorned with these works became to introduce her students to their repose. This is the great and necessary pretense of an experienced teacher: Even though these children may not at the outset experience the repose of this place, their teacher is experienced in this place. They have come to know their way around, which means that they have experienced for themselves that this place stands-in-itself and has a repose that is worthy of children's (and teachers') attention. An odd and pedagogically familiar faith follows here: As a teacher, I know that, if the right work can be done *here*, with *these* students, within all the frailties of *this* classroom, *this* year, that repose just might come forward and show itself in all its myriadness and generosity and openness and undecidedness:

> All things show faces, the world not only a coded signature to be read for meaning, but a physiognomy to be faced. As expressive forms, things speak; they show the shape they are in. They announce themselves, bear witness to their presence: "Look, here we are." They regard us beyond how we may regard them, our perspectives, what we intend with them, and how we dispose of them. (Hillman, 1982, p. 77)

This strikes another ecological blow to the metaphysics of genius and the confidences of constructivism: that things might regard us beyond how we may regard them. That even in those times in which we force the witness to give answer to questions of our own determining, we are being witnessed as well, beyond our own determination.

As the previously cited passage from Gadamer suggests, this experience of repose is not simple, familiar, nor easily had. Repose is not a "surface feature" that is simply lying there, somehow out in the open and immediate and obvious. The appearance of the living repose of things *requires something of us*. An experience of repose has to be *cultivated*.

Ecologically, this is such a simple point. It takes no time, patience, effort, learning, work, or love to simply use this place for our own ends or to experience this place only in light of our own "wanting and doing" (Gadamer, 1989, p. xxviii), our own ingenious "rigging and gluing" (Heidegger, 1985, 70), our own effortful "seizing and dominating"(Gadamer 1977, pp. 226–227). It does, however, take time and effort and work and love and patience and learning to come to experience this place in its repose. Experiencing this place in its repose—say, this place of Impressionist paintings—is experiencing that it stands there in ways that no amount of our experiencing, however ingenious, can fill.

Preamble 16:
Covering the Curriculum

Over and over again in our experience as a teachers of "curriculum methods" courses and as practicum supervisors in elementary school settings, we have witnessed student teachers assailing themselves, their colleagues, their cooperating teachers in school placements, and those in their teacher education programs with a horrible vision of "the curriculum" as something that has to be variously submitted to, followed, taught, covered, committed to memory, shoved in a drawer, or accounted for in meticulous detail in the practice of teaching young children.

Here is a thesis we have been presuming all along in this book. If we begin by "entrusting ourselves" (Gadamer, 1989, p. 378) to the great abundance of the topics/topographies of the world and allow the work we do with children to become full of deep ancestral relations, full of old wisdoms and places for new insight, full of rich, rigorous, real work, instead of time-filling "school work," full of discipline and care and attention to things, then the curriculum as bare-boned in the curriculum guides will be spontaneously, pleasurably, and (comparatively) easily "covered." If, however, we begin within the scarcities and dryness and impoverishment of those very same curriculum guides, this will never necessarily lead us to the deep intellectual pleasures of learning, the deep intellectual pleasures to be had in our living in the world with children. The movement between the mandated curriculum and the disciplines and beauties of the world it bespeaks is a one-way street.

It is very difficult to learn to "read" curriculum guides as thresholds into abundant worlds. One stumbling block in this regard is how overwhelmed student teachers get when they begin by thinking about the vast array of students in their care. The proliferation of needs and differences does not lead to or add up to a sense of abundance but a sort of paralysis. This paralysis seems to find its relief in breaking down the abundance of a particular topic in light of the differences students bring to the classroom. Just imagine, then, developmental differences, gender differences, racial differences, socioeconomic differences, skill-level differences, differences in past experiences, different likes and dislikes, strengths and weaknesses, expectations and hopes and desires and on and on. Once this myriad of "difference" is let loose, it becomes quite understandable why Hannah Arendt (1969, p. 186) spoke about "the onslaught of the new."

In light of our understanding of curriculum in abundance, we suggest precisely the opposite course of action, one that can be named but appears quite odd in today's educational climate: Begin by ignoring the differences that students bring to the classroom.

Chapter 16

The Individual Student

David W. Jardine

> *It is not at all a question of a mere subjective variety of conceptions, but of [this topic's] own possibilities of being that emerge as it explicates itself, as it were, in a variety of its aspects.*
>
> —Gadamer (1989, p. 118)

In pursuing curriculum in abundance, it is vital to inquiry to choose a topic of inquiry that is rich and generous and abundant enough to embrace all of those who venture into it. Rather than breaking up a topic/topography into developmentally appropriate "bits," inquiry leaves the topic/topography intact and finds ways that we can all venture into it *with* our differences. By beginning with this image of rich, living topographies as the places where we come across our students in an inquiry, many of the commonplaces of educational discourse take on a new and invigorating emphasis.

One such change of emphasis is around this commonplace truth that we have inherited from constructivism: Each individual student will make sense of his or her venture in her or his own ways. As the saying goes, each student "brings to" this topography different backgrounds, experiences, skills, interests, likes and dislikes, hopes, boredoms, learning style, family troubles, previous school experiences, and so on. Each student, so to speak, "constructs" an understanding of the venture from his or her own point of view. What can happen if we follow the logic of this commonplace is that each of us can be imagined as somehow "having" one of a whole "subjective variety of conceptions" of whatever topic is on hand.

In an inquiry, this commonplace about the "individual student" doesn't disappear. Constructivism isn't simply and easily just *false*. Rather, its truth must be treated carefully.

Certainly each individual student develops his or her own understanding of the topography that is ventured into (geometry, say, or Ancient Greece, or the ways of punctuation in the *grammarye* of English). However, this sentence requires a particular *emphasis:* Each individual student develops his or her own understanding *of the topography*. That is to say, understood in abundance, each individual student's understanding in this venture is treated as an understanding *of* (i.e., belonging properly to) *the place* and not simply *of* (i.e., belonging properly to) *the individual student*. Each student's voice and work and knowledge and questioning is located, therefore, not in their "genius" (see chap. 15) but rather "in" the abundance of the topic of which they are giving a voice, the place in which their work appears, what it is they have knowledge of and questions about. It is treated *pedagogically* rather than *pathologically*.

In a classroom where the idea of curriculum in abundance holds sway, the task is to take up a particular student's question as a way of opening up to conversation and question the rich possibilities *of the repose and truth of the place*, rather than a way of opening up the "glue and rigging" of the genius who asked the question. Simply put, how might this individual student's question help us see something *about the place* that might have been lost or forgotten or occluded but for this question? What is their question true to? What is it true of? The multiple, various, and differing questions and experiences that each individual student brings forward are treated, not as an aggregate of a "subjective variety of conceptions" that each belong to each individual, but as openings and enrichments and articulations and cultivations *of* "[the topic's] own possibilities of being." Each person's work is therefore taken up as adding itself to the richness of the place that we *all* find ourselves living in.

This is why Gadamer (1989, p. 40) suggests that such living topics undergo an "increase in being" because of our ventures. As our understanding of a topic increases, *the topic* gets better and better, richer and richer, more and more constituted by hidden histories and ancestries and voices that had been forgotten or ignored (see the treatment of the idea of the "repose" of things in chaps. 15 and 19).

Part of the undeniable task of being a teacher is that there are times when it is pedagogically necessary to take up an individual student's questions about a topic as helping us see something *about the individual student*. I am suggesting that we are far more able to see something about the individuality of a student in the process of that student inquiring, in the presence and the witness of others (both those in the classroom and those whose ghosts still inhabit the territory in question), into a rich, living, generous topography that can allow such differences to show.

Preamble 17:
The Face of "The Real World"

We have seen, in many of the preceding chapters, how the rich and abundant character of the living human inheritance is not an especially easily and simply available and obvious property of things as we experience them day to day. Day to day, North American culture (in particular) has succumbed to the impoverishment requisite of regimes of scarcity and abundance has been replaced by numbing and violence-inducing parades of untethered, accelerating, postmodern "spectacles" (Dubord, 1995) and titillations. It takes time and, we've found, deliberate bloody-mindedness to cultivate the sort of quiet attentiveness that would allow the abundance of things to show itself.

This is, of course, an ecological and spiritual point as much as it is a pedagogical one. If I go out into the forest surrounding my house with my three dogs, no wildlife will appear, but that occurs, at least to some mysterious extent, because of *how* I ventured. I can't simply point to the forest as being bereft, say, of deer. To this odd extent, constructivism has something to teach us (see chaps. 8 and 9). Without practiced slowness and stillness and repetition and thoughtfulness and return, cultivating our being experienced in this world simply won't happen (see chap. 16). Abundance may not be a consequence of our "wanting and doing" (Gadamer, 1989, p. xxviii), but it may be that its appearance asks something of us. It takes work to work.

Christmas. In elementary schools, just like Halloween, this seasonality portends little more than sugar fixes and the running out of certain colors of construction paper. Frantic Santa faces need to be sent home, and all that is wrong with "art" in the arts of elementary school become blatantly obvious.

When you think of the great brilliance and resilience and colorfulness and beauty and proportionality and emotionality of art, the impovershments that ravage schooling become terribly obvious. Most people don't experience the great and abundant arcs of relations that are lost in the meager memorization of the Pythagorean theorem. But those black-line masters of snowmen and bells and Xmas trees become the scarcity-induced inverse of "even there the gods are present" (see Preamble 13). As we see in great detail in chapter 19, such black-line masters are like objects in hell. They are *horrible,* and we need to treat them as monsters sent to warn us of great danger (see Preamble 7).

Just a reminder. The works that illustrate the following chapter were done by children in kindergarten and Grade 1, but they are the result, not of "genius" and "creativity" alone, but of long hours and detailed and loving attention, and from the care and attention of a teacher who had done her own work of composing herself in the face of the rushes of schooling.

Many teachers and student teachers love the *idea* of abundance, but some of them balk at the work it takes, not realizing that the work they are doing running around trying to outrun scarcity is already overwhelming. We are audacious enough to believe that at least the work of abundance has some scholarly and spiritual integrity to it. Many teachers and student teachers tell us that they will try this idea of abundance "later on," after they've got "a few years under their belts."

Tanya Graham, the kindergarten and Grade 1 teacher in whose class these works were shaped (see also chap. 18), did not wait. More frighteningly, almost every single student teacher we have known who decided to wait, out of the thousands we have supervised over decades of experience, never returns. Once the spell-panic of scarcity catches hold, its grip is near-deadly and so mesmerizing that abundance soon seems, like we've suggested, impossible in the face of "the real world."

Sorry to say that the face of this real world is a black-line Santa face.

Chapter 17

Staying Within the Lines: Reimagining What Is "Elementary" in the Art of Schooling

David W. Jardine
Tanya Graham
Annette LaGrange
Hanne Kisling-Saunders

> *When I [Tanya] first announced to my friends and family that I was hired to be a kindergarten teacher the response that I got was somewhat disturbing. For the most part, everyone commented on the "cuteness" of kindergarten. Others asked me about my ability to finger paint, wipe noses, and tie shoes. Such comments speak volumes about how people view young children and their teachers.*

I

With Christmas approaching, the laments of the student teachers in our undergraduate Early Childhood Education methods classes were almost inevitable. Practicum was starting and the photocopied black-line Santa faces, all ready for coloring and gluing, were already beginning to appear, an appearance as consistent as the disappearing of red and green construction paper through school system supply cupboards.

We had wonderful, difficult discussions in our class about these Santa faces. Where do they come from? What do they tell us about our images of children, of teaching, of the work of schooling, about art, about creativity, about visual literacy, about craft, about the returns of light into the world that Christmas portends, about the nature of "the gift" (Jardine et al., 2003, pp. 211–222) as an image of teaching and learning, about the Europeanness of our schooled presumptions?

We talked about how deeply disappointing are some of the taken-for-granted practices inside elementary schools and about how the deep (and both shared and contested) disciplines and traditions and ancestries of human life so often and so seemingly easily become black-line-mastered in the practices of schooling. Many of the "activities" these student teachers confronted contained no body, no richness, few real pleasures. The students spoke of a sort of strangulated "thinness" to a lot of schoolwork, and a sense of seemingly deliberately holding back the beauties and difficulties of the world that we and our children readily experience outside of schools.

We quarreled over where our image of "the basics" in elementary education actually comes from, and what this has done to our ability to imagine the fullness of the human inheritance(s) we are entrusted to pass on to our children.

We commiserated over our own experiences of such Santa faces and the wisps of cotton balls stuck on our fingertips and having too much glue, and precisely what sorts of satisfactions and disappointments we ourselves had felt over doing such things ourselves as parts of our own schooling.

We talked about how easily young children are willing to trust the teacher's images and understandings of the world and therefore, how many children, even by Grade 1, have already come to "enjoy" such "art activities." We talked, therefore, about the difficult position of the beginning teacher who is sometimes faced with children who are already inculcated into a thin and hyperactive version of "schooled activities" (see chap. 12).

In a horrible turn of events, children's enjoyment of such activities can be too easily offered as an adequate pedagogical case for their continuance. Worse yet, such enjoyment can sometimes be offered as an adequate reason for dismissing (as "theoretical") any critical consideration of what such activities actually portend about the lives of our children and our lives with them in schools. Such critical considerations can be simply seen as speaking against children's enjoyment or against the confident voice of "practical experience": "I've taught for years and *my* kids really like it!"

One thing we settled on in our class is that no one could quite remember or decide precisely *whose* "black lines" these actually are. Their origins have faded from view. Such activities seem to be perpetuated in schools, year after year, in the midst of a sort of personal and cultural amnesia. They seem to just *happen*, with no rich or satisfying pedagogical trace lines attached. They have become, in a strange sense, unaddressable, mute, authorless, anonymous, impersonal, almost automatic in their regular, yearly appearances. However, it is ironic that, given such anonymity and impersonalness, attempts to question them and their nature and place and prevalence in our schools often seems *profoundly* personal, like a vaguely offensive affront to the genuine good-heartedness of teachers and to their generous willingness to share all they have with student teachers. As one teacher attested, nearly in tears, during a Professional Development Day when one of the authors raised questions about the thinning out of much of the world's beauties in our elementary school classrooms: "I've been doing the sorts of things you described for years, and I don't think that I've ever actually *harmed* a child." This was clearly a courageous statement that attests to the personal and emotional depth of our mutual, often unvoiced and unnoticed and unquestioned investment in the taken-for-granted, well-meant practices of schooling. It is unfortunate, however, that, in the face of this courageous admission, none of us could find how to continue what was a thoughtful and difficult conversation about weak practice. In the end, what can start out as personal courage can end up as a sort of public cowardice on *everyone's* behalf.

II

In light of our conversations about Santa faces, our curriculum class began to talk at length about wanting children to understand the deep, delicious, disciplined character of the world. Our talk was organized, in part, around a passage from David G. Smith's (1999) brilliant and often frightening essay "Children and the Gods of War":

> It is as if young people ask for, above all else, not only a genuine responsiveness from their elders but also a certain direct authenticity, a sense of that deep human resonance so easily suppressed under the smooth human-relations jargon teachers typically learn in college. Young people want to know if, under the cool and calm of efficient teaching and excellent time-on-task ratios, life itself has a chance, or whether the surface is all there is. (p. 139)

We played with Smith's images of "thinness" and "surfaces" by looking at the thin plastic "wood veneer" surfaces of the desks we were using at the university. They are flat and easy to keep clean and clear of any traces of anyone having been here before (or after) us; they require little care, little attention, little notice, and they refuse any attempt at cultivating a sense of craft, relationship, memory, obligation, or commitment; they resemble wood, but they are fake, they are cheap. They are not interesting or memorable or important or worthy of note. Nothing can especially *happen* over them. In fact, they are designed so that little will happen. They will simply eventually "break" and be replaced by equally thin, nonstick surfaces; and all this will happen without our remembering, without our having to directly suffer such passing.

All of this is terribly akin ("kinships" [see chap. 13], as we all know so well, don't portend just good news) to black-line Santa faces: Little will happen, it's just an "activity" with a lesson-planned date-time-place-rationale-objectives-materials-plan-closure-assessment-follow-up that will simply eventually "be done" (usually in about 20 to 40 minutes) and sent home and be replaced by the next worksheet activity.

We talked of how exhausting it is to surround ourselves with a world that not only does not *need* "[ours or our students'] continuity of attention and devotion" (W. Berry, 1986, p. 34), but is precisely designed to *prevent* the necessity, even the *possibility* of such attention and devotion (see chap. 19). We spoke of ecological issues of disposability, immediacy, distraction, consumption, and what we and our children become when this is what we surround ourselves with (Jardine, 2000). We toyed, then, with how surrounding ourselves with such disposability produces a sort of "unsettledness" (W. Berry, 1986; see Preamble 12) which, in consequence, not only produces a sort of experiential acceleration (because nothing especially requires much care and attention [see Jardine, 2000]) but also aggravates a sense of "lack" and "want" (Loy, 1999; Smith, 1999a, 1999b) that then pushes us into even more (eventually itself unsatisfying) consumption.

One student called out "life-long learning!" and we all initially laughed over a peculiar sort of shock of recognition. This phrase no longer sounded like simply or only good news. And, as with the teacher mentioned earlier, none of us have ever meant any harm with such a phrase. However, suddenly, under its surface charm lay questions as yet unposed.

We eventually bumped up against Martin Heidegger's (1977) contention that, in surrounding ourselves with such a thin, consumptive surface world, *we ourselves* become "disposable," part of a "standing reserve" (p. 111) in the service of, in our case, the machinations of schooling. After all, with this photocopied black-line Santa face, what difference in the world does it make that *this* child filled it in and did such gluing and coloring? *This* child is simply one of a long line of thousands and thousands of children who have given themselves over to the replicating continuance of the anonymous appearance of such black lines year after year. Not only does the worksheet become an object of producing and consuming; children become producers and consumers and, worse yet, a great deal of their time in schools, their *lives* in schools, are consumed with momentary, eventually unrewarding "activity." *Children themselves*—because they are, after all, spending an enormous part of *being* a child in school—*become produced and consumed,* oddly bought and sold. Think, for example, of the rank-order postings of school achievements, or how grade point averages determine a student's marketable saleability to a university or a good job.

We then took up Smith's challenge, "Is this odd, fractured array of surfaces all there is?" It was clear when students reflected on their own elementary school experiences and on the nature of many of the classrooms in which they were placed as student teachers, that fragmented, thinned out, and isolated bits and pieces are often what counted for "the basics" in elementary schools. We then asked: Is there some way of speaking about age, character, memory, inheritance, ancestry, work, discipline, and care as themselves "basic" to the living disciplines with which we are entrusted as teachers? Are the things we taken-for-grantedly surround ourselves and our children with in schools worthy of attention? Do they *call for* (Heidegger, 1968) something more than a surface-gloss, momentary "activity," a momentary "distraction?"

These, of course, are very tough questions.

   Therefore, when we ask, following David Smith, whether "life itself has a chance," we are never speaking *solely* of the life and experiences of the child or *solely* the life and experiences of the teacher. We are speaking, as well, for example, of art as a *living* discipline, that is, as a discipline full of lives, in which there is some life, some vigor and character, a discipline in which a child might find their own liveliness able to live itself out in the presence of a whole, living world of relations and traditions and shared and contested ancestries.

III

Students in our university curriculum class spoke of still somehow wanting to keep the children "together," within a bounded space of work, working, somehow, "on the same thing" or in the same place, together, somehow. We talked of how these Santa faces perhaps were designed to fulfill such promise: They are a "parameter" of sorts, circumscribing the work, making it vaguely topical and seasonal, giving a sense of boundedness and clarity, circumscribing and limiting choices and demands. However, students consistently report that when they are in classrooms where such activities are commonplace, it feels, as one student teacher put it, "more like a 'classroom management class' than an 'art class.'" Moreover, students reported

FIG. 17.1. After "The Scream" by Edvard Munch (Grade 1).

that, during such activities, time always seems to be running out (typical of
the time of the machine, the time of production and consumption, as
Wendell Berry [1983] suggests). There is, with such activities, a sort of
built-in franticness and distraction, even a low-level near-panic (see Fig.
17.1). Several students in such elementary school settings reported witnessing four, five, once even up to eight different hand-out photocopied
"activities" occurring in a Grade 1 classroom *before morning recess.* We spec-
ulated as to whether the demands of schooling (e.g., the wonderfully cryp-
tic and monstrous "covering the curriculum") created the need for such
"activities" or whether these are two beasts feeding off each other, each
finding in the other its excuse to continue unquestioned.

We agreed that if that franticness and panic is all that "staying within the
lines" can mean, we'd rather not. We wanted "something else."

What has happened in many elementary school classrooms is that the
stupefying character of black-line Santa faces have sometimes been replaced with what could be understood as their equally abstract opposite.
Rather than beginning with anonymous, authorless, impersonal black-line
masters, classroom work is organized around the personal, authorial, creative, unique individuality of each child. Each child thus becomes, theoreti-

FIG. 17.2. "Roses"
by August Renoir.

cally at least, their own "master." As is so often the case in educational theory and practice, we find ourselves riding another pendulum (Throne, 1994) by simply inverting the situation we despise.

In rolls "the metaphysics of the genius" (see chap. 15) where each unique child becomes an artist, an author. We find ourselves standing helpless before the generative uniqueness of each child (Arendt, 1969; Jardine et al., 1999), declaring "you're the 'god' of your own story" (Melnick, 1997, p. 372). And, in such declaration, we declare ourselves unworthy or unable to do anything but "facilitate" their creative urges.

IV

At the first round of parent–teacher interviews in October, one of the parents commented while viewing her child's work, "I just can't believe what these kids are capable of! This isn't colouring, this is actually drawing. You [Tanya] gave them a blank piece of paper and they did this? I can't believe it!." To be honest, I think that this is somewhat sad, that this is so unbelievable to a parent. I mean, why shouldn't a child be capable of this? But then again, I didn't just "give them a blank piece of paper." Our water-colour project involved viewing and critiquing art work of the Group of Seven and practising the blends and bleeds of colour on different papers. I believe that this

FIG.   17.3.   After "Roses" by August Renoir (Grade 1).

provoked the children into thinking about possibilities for their own works and thus helped them to begin developing their own internal "lines."

Instead of being read weakly, "staying within the lines" can point to the sensuous, immediate presence of the materiality of a real, living world that roils within the bounds of a particular style of art or the (debatable) limits and (equally debatable) generosities of a particular living tradition, or the work of a particular artist, or the intensity of a particular creation, like Vincent van Gogh's *Café Scene at Night* (1888) (see Fig. 17.4).

Just a reminder. The children whose work is found in this chapter are from kindergarten and Grade 1. These children have carefully studied such paintings and the lives of those who made them. They played with moist workings of watercolor paint on different papers, or the pulls of wet chalks and dry chalks, absorbencies. They measured the spatialities had with moving Leo—Leonian tears of papers placed apart, leaving emptiness—forms in between things. They practiced layering colors. They labored over imitating "the masters," not in order to be mastered by them, but in order to feel the labors of the works that surrounded them and to learn some worldly limits, and how the limits of Matisse draw out of them different things than the limits of Renoir (see Figs. 17.2 and 17.3), open them to different worlds of relations and interrelations, different demands and desires and possibilities. They rested over lovely books with lovely illustrations and learned the intimacies between reading the text and reading the pictures.

FIG. 17.4.   After Vincent van Gogh's "Café Scene at Night" (kindergarten).

They *practiced these arts* over long periods of time, developing, each in their own way and within the limits of their own lives and experiences, a feel for the various materialities of these worlds, these odd, debatable inheritances. They experimented in class with the pulling of a horizon line downward or upward, invoking the Greek ghosts of proportionality and figure that will arise again in the Grade 6 mathematics class and beyond. They sketched out the lives of different artists—hatreds of women found in dancing ballerinas with the master-artisan always picturing himself full of distain and distance—listening to their own words being read out in the classroom and speaking with their parents about the inevitability of the nude form that they'll be encountering. Now the children were surrounded, not only with large prints of the work world of the Impressionists, but with their own work gathered on walls together because each child had journeyed, so to speak, to the same rich, contested topography, the same rich, contested "place."

Suddenly, there are "lines" everywhere, but they are not solid, they are not uncontested or unambiguous, they are not "givens," and they are not always straight and linear. Instead of keeping children "together" within the bounds of the abstract black lines of a Santa face (or abandoning them to its abstract opposite of "uniqueness"), children can be kept "together" within the more sensuous, more ambiguous, more tangled, more rich, more compelling, more variegated, more demanding, more disciplined lines of a particular, located, encultured, historical, image-filled, worldly inheritance. However, the sense in which children are now "together" is such that they must *enter into the ongoing, living conversations that constitutes such inheritances*. They must enter into the "real work" (Snyder, 1980) of this world because this world *is* its real work; it *is* its "gathering and collecting" (Gadamer, 1989, p. 106) intergenerationally, through time, in a located and specifiable history and place. Their individual presence and witness to such inheritances becomes visible as *essential to the living character of those inheritances*. In fact, "only *in* the multifariousness of such voices do [such inheritances] exist" (Gadamer, 1989, p. 284).

Suddenly, these children were no longer alone, neither with their own Santa face that seemed to arrive from nowhere except school, nor with their own "creativity." They found themselves *together* in a place with a highly contested, rich, alluring shape and history and character. With these experiences in hand, a whole part of the world opened up for the children, a free-but-limited range of possibilities, avenues to be explored. It is as if the children had been ushered into a "place" that had character and that allowed and housed and took good care of certain possibilities that are now free to explore and transform, to refuse or take up, to expand or imitate or combine or break apart.

Rather than squelching creativity, the techniques and terminologies and visual literacies they learned helped form and shape and solidify and protect and open up their creativity to possibilities and limits that cannot be found within the subjectivizing metaphysics of creativity and genius

(Gadamer, 1989; see chap. 15). Instead of this Romantic image of creative genius, children's creativity was able to be strongly held in the embrace of the world and was able to *present itself* through such holding, such embrace. Through these limited, within-the-lines creations, the difference and delicacy of each child's hand and eye and heart became visible. Moreover, and this cannot be emphasized too strongly, these differences became visible *in relation to each other*, and *because of* these relations. The "field of living worldly relations" into which the children and teachers were ushered allowed and provided for (a wide range of) difference. These art worlds were strong and resilient and contested enough to hold the full range of different children together in relations of kind, so that the fields of their differing, living relations could be *worked out* and not just *worked on*. Here, in this place, each child just might *make a difference* and not just *be different*.

This child still stands in a long line of thousands who have brought forward, for example, Van Gogh's work and world, but now, it is a *bloodline* full of characters and faces and histories and questions and contestations and vigorous debates and tales to tell and different takes on the tales that have been told or left unsaid. One wonderful example, given the cultures of the children in these particular classrooms, was Van Gogh's (and Europe's) late-nineteenth-century "orientalism." The work these children were entering into was rich enough and real enough that such a debate became possible because of it.

The practicum students in the Early Childhood Education class agreed: *This* is a strong (albeit rather frightening at first glance, rather intimidating) sense of "classroom community," where we gather together *in* our differences *over* something worthy of our attention. The trouble is, of course, that this by itself leaves as yet unaddressed questions of what is worthy of our attention.

V

We've just returned from taking another group of practicum students to the school and again, a similar response not yet noted: the unanticipated, bewildering, sensuous *pleasure* of experiencing such works. That first reaction was nearly autonomic: a gasped intake of breath, and the immediate desire to look more closely, to remain here, to go back and forth, to let the bewilderment settle in and to let the realities of what they are seeing take hold. All the students admitted that these children's works are *beautiful* (see Fig. 17.5). This is *good work*.

It might have been theoretically possible, sitting there a wee bit stunned in the school hallway, to enter into some ethical or epistemological quarrel, and raise claims of "how do you know it is good work?" or "what is good work?" or "who is to say?", but that sensuous first moment was undeniable, even though we might be able to *think* our way out of its demand and its address.

FIG. 17.5. After Claude Monet's "Waterliles" (kindergarten).

END BIT

Perhaps it is because this is my [Tanya's] first "official" year of teaching, that I find the preceding questions and the hundreds of other similar questions swirling in my mind to be challenging, frustrating and inspiring all at once. At the same time, I feel fortunate to have all of these seemingly endless, complex questions to ponder, rather than believing in simple answers.

Back in our practicum methods class, a student teacher remarked, partly in amusement, partly in confusion and disgust, that she had been handed *the very same black-line master of Santa's face* some 18 years before, in her own ECE class.

Three classes later, she brought in her own Santa face, browned from age, missing some cotton balls, pulled from a box in her mother's basement.

Preamble 18:
Murmuring Over Texts

Elementary school teachers and student teachers are all well familiar with the practice of scribing young children's stories so that their ideas and images and visions can be captured in texts that they are not yet fully able to produce of themselves. This is, of course, an ancient practice, full of ancient tales to be told of its nature and limits. Dictators and scribes, cuddled in candle-lit *scriptoria,* murmuring over texts and their illumination. Ivan Illich's (1993) wonderful discussions of how silent reading was once simply incomprehensible and how the silencing of reading lead to a very different understanding of ourselves and of the nature of understanding itself (Illich & Sanders, 1988) are well worth reading.

The most interesting and most difficult task, however, is remembering such matters. The practice of coming to learn to read and write is not merely an impoverished set of "skills" to be practiced only by the young. Such wrist-cramping practice belongs in the midst of a great and abundant living inheritance and, as we have been suggesting all along, in order to *teach* such matters in abundance, we need to find ways to place the efforts of young children back into the living comfort of all of their relations. We have witnessed, over and over again, in classroom after classroom, what pleasures even the youngest children take in realizing that their work, although perhaps the work of a child, is not childish work. In the effortful taking up of the great inheritances of reading and writing, they are taking on a great tapestry that has been handed to them. They are not alone, they are not simply stuck within the confines of their own abilities, their successes and failures are not private property but belong in worlds of work. To recall a passage from Wendell Berry (1989) with which we started this book, "where is our

245

comfort but in the free, uninvolved and finally mysterious beauty and grace of this world that we did not make, that has no price, that is not our work? Where is our sanity but here? Where is our pleasure but in working and resting kindly in the presence of this world?" (p. 21).

Herein lies a preambling thread that we have not yet explicitly teased out. The great abundances that surround and house and care for and comfort those curriculum topics entrusted to students and teachers in schools are not the philosophical and speculative property of *adults*. They are the living character of the world(s) that children are inheriting. Learning that the Latin term *monere* underwrites the idea of monsters is not a philosophical and theoretical game played by adults. It points toward a *teaching practice*. Finding out, right in the midst of kings and queens and knights and dragons and castles, that almost no one could read or write in such times is, we suggest, a classroom practice, because it is in the nature of the place that young children are raised that their learning to write and their fascination with dragons has this character.

Curriculum in abundance, therefore, must be understood "in practice." Otherwise it becomes nothing more than an exercise in cleverness and knowledgeability.

When I (D.J.) discovered Quintilion's recommendation of the use of ivory letters for young children to handle, or the ninth-century equivalent of alphabet strips (see later discussion), these things were, of course, brought into the classroom as ways of surrounding and making abundant that alphabet strip taped to each child's desk. And here is the great difficulty, posed once again. There is no label on those alphabet strips saying "look here for further inherited threads of significance." All that can be "prescribed" by the image of curriculum in abundance is that, when student teachers enter a classroom, "the centre is everywhere" (Nishitani, 1982, p. 146). Or, as Gadamer (1989, p. 458) put it, "*every* word breaks forth as if from a center."

More on this in the final preamble and chapter. For now, a sojourn into what breaks forth from the work of the scribe in a Grade 1 classroom.

Chapter 18

In His Own Hand: Interpretation and the Effacing of the Scribe

David W. Jardine
Tanya Graham
Sharon Friesen
Patricia Clifford

I

As an early childhood educator, the heart of my [Tanya's] philosophy is the belief that young children are highly capable and intellectual learners who have a right to a school experience that is respectful of their curiosities, worthy of their time, and mindful of their place within the larger human context. It is this belief that drives me in my daily work. It is this belief that causes me to question over and over whether or not I am creating an environment and a program that sings in concert with my beliefs. I am thankful for this continuous drive that I feel to build a larger story with the children. Without it, I believe that I would allow myself to sink into a routine of habit and superficiality and in turn lose the very essence of my being as a teacher.

As I have attempted to bring the children into deep and meaningful conversations, I have recently felt the needs of one particular little boy weighing on my heart. For 2½ years I have had this little boy sitting in my room while we have explored descriptive writing, symbolism, rich literature, art, and poetry. Rarely has he engaged in conversation or even demonstrated interest in what we talk about. His eyes wander around the room; he appears to be interested in and distracted by everything except what we are taking up. During this entire time, I have struggled with questions from both myself and colleagues: "How does this *work for Darren?" "Does Darren have an opportunity to join in* this *conversation?" "Why don't I just bring it down a couple of notches so that it will make sense to him?" "Where should I start with Darren?"*

The final question, was perhaps the one that kept me up most nights when I first met this little boy. After all, where could I start? He didn't know his alphabet, he couldn't write, making marks on paper was a challenge, and he was barely talking. A part of me kept asking, "Where should I start in order to fix him?" Nothing that I knew could fix him—none of the new or old methods. He was not progressing in the area of reading or writing. There were no books to which I could turn; really there were few specialists who could offer anything that Darren would respond to without wrapping him up in labels and languages that made everything his problem. This was a whole new landscape and it was up to me to find the way to navigate.

If I truly believe that all children deserve a program that is respectful of their curiosities, worthy of their time, and mindful of their place within the larger human context, then I had to believe that this was true for Darren as well. I began to realize that I had to start with "Darren the person" rather than "Darren the problem," the nonreader or nonwriter. My goal had to transform from "fixing Darren" to "respecting his place and his learning within the larger story." I had to start with him in his landscape not mine. I had to let what he showed me of himself to be true, to be telling and real, not just a failure of my own expectations. I had to look beyond his scrawls and his inability to demonstrate his knowing in the familiar ways that other children demonstrate theirs. Instead of fearing the uncertainty of this landscape through which Darren travels and fencing him in with a steady diet of "fixer activities," I had to trust that my starting point with Darren could and should be no different than that of other children.

I would, as I have always done with other children, bring to his landscape what I have learned about the world myself: rich, and meaningful literature, powerful questions, and beautiful art. I knew that he would appear not to listen, not to be moved as the other children appeared to be moved. I was even prepared for the withdrawal that he would show. However, I held the unrelenting belief that perhaps I was planting a seed, one that just might (or—can we admit it?—just might not) grow and blossom.

Darren's reading and writing, of course, would remain a concern and a goal. This sample—"In my dreams there were aliens" from his journal, written in his own hand, attests to this fact (see Fig. 18.1).

However initially disturbing such journal entries might first appear, how could I possibly suggest that I know from evidence like this the full extent of Darren's participation in our class and our conversations? It has been amazing how easily and forcefully such journal work can set nods and knowing glances. But I know that this journal entry and others like it are not enough.

Perhaps my own images of what participation should look like were stifling my ability to see David's involvement, his knowing, his experiences. I was looking for those well-known signs of involvement: the raising of a hand, the nod of a head, the sharing of a personal story.

When the class was asked to create their own poetry in their writing books, David created the following poem through a scribe:

The hot sun is like the Mojave Desert.

The sun is a beautiful colour of gold.

FIG.   18.1.   In   my
dreams   there   were
aliens.

The mountain peaks are covered

With a small double wizard of snow.

I walked across the bridge

And smelled the trees.

The mountain has purple shadows on it.

The wind is blowing just a little bit.

A fat mountain is right in front of me, it's huge.

Both these traces of Darren's work—the hand written journal entry and the scribed poem—came into terrible focus when I recently attended a morning workshop on children's writing, and all of the talk was pointedly in favor of "starting where the child is at." The suggestion was made, over and over again, that we always "gear down" what we do as teachers "to the child's level."

So later that afternoon, a group of student teachers ended up in my classroom, and I showed them the two pieces of work and asked "What does it mean to start from where Darren is at?" Some of the initial reactions were so familiar. Even though all the students agree that the poem was wonderful and that the journal entries were "a concern," the main question that arose again and again was over the scribed work: "Yes, but did he actually **write** *this or did someone write it for him?"*

II

When we recently scanned Web sites using the term "scribe" as our search item, we ended up with several hundred references to the practice of "scribing" in a wide variety of language arts programs, classrooms, and textbooks—mainly dealing with how it is done and why it is done and describing, sometimes in great detail, precisely how such a practice worked in a particular school setting.

However, none of these "hits" dealt especially with *what it is*, to scribe for another. All of them treated this notion *as if* "what it is" either is somehow obvious or is simply what we intend it to be. As is frequently the case in the emergence of seemingly "new" educational practices, scribing is treated *as if* it appeared just now, out of nowhere, with no relations or attachments or consequences or shared and contested ancestries and images other than the ones we might generously intend in practicing language arts well in our schools.

As we've come to expect, education is most often interested in *how to do it* and *whether it works*.

This absence of the question "What does it *mean*, to scribe for another?" is both not unexpected and, for us, full of interpretive portent. As James Hillman and Michael Ventura suggested in their lovely, disturbing book *We've Had a Hundred Years of Psychotherapy and the World's Getting Worse* (1992), North American culture in general (and, we add, educational theory and practice in particular) is almost exclusively interested in *practicing* ideas (such as "scribing" for children in schools) but has little or no interest in *entertaining such ideas*—holding them, so to speak, "between," and stopping our rush to practice for a moment to consider this inheritance we've been handed, out from under the auspices of producing, out from the rush of "doing."

Interpretation requires stopping and letting all the ancestries, voices, and relations that are hidden in this simple, obvious "practice" of scribing come forward and have their say.

"Scribe," interpretively understood, is thus not simply the name of something done in schools. It is not just a "good idea" according to either implicit or explicit criteria, and therefore either recommendable or not recommendable for practice in the classroom. It is also the first word of an allegory (Gadamer, 1989, pp. 70–81), a long and convoluted and sometimes contradictory tale full of a "multifariousness of … voices" (Gadamer, 1989, p. 295). It is only if we risk reading our way through this tough, ambiguous allegory that we might come to understand how its images are silently working themselves out "beyond our wanting and doing" (Gadamer, 1989, p. xxviii) in the lives of teachers and children and schools. It is this unintended "beyond" that is the territory of interpretation:

> Every word [like the word "scribe"] breaks forth as if from a centre and is related to a whole, through which alone it is a word. Every word [like the word "scribe"] causes the whole of the language[s] to which it belongs to resonate. Thus ["scribe"] ... carries with it the unsaid, to which it is related by responding and summoning. (Gadamer, 1989, p. 458)

The term "scribe," to be interpretively entertained, must be allowed to summon up the world(s) to which it belongs. "Understanding begins when *something* addresses *us*" (Gadamer, 1989, p. 299): To interpret means to attempt to respond to this summons, this address, to find out what *it*—this world of implication—is asking of us, to find out how it—this world of implication—defines *us* beyond how we may define *it*. To interpret means to find out that, even in our innocent use of the term "scribe" in schools, we are summoning up worlds of implication without necessarily intending to. And, as a *living* allegory, our readings of how our taken-for-granted practices might belong to this allegory *add themselves to what the allegory then means*. By interpreting, we "further" (Gadamer, 1989, p. xxiv).

To entertain interpretation, therefore, is to entertain the possibility that the agency of inquiry—its motive, its movement, its demand—lies outside of the command of the knowing subject and the methods it might wield. Things *show themselves:* "Look, here we are" (Hillman, 1982, p. 77). Interpretation requires learning to "entrust ourselves to what we are investigating to guide us safely in the quest" (Gadamer, 1989, p. 378). And, through such entrusting, our own tales of scribing add themselves to this bloodline. Our tales become its begats.

III

From the *Alberta Learning Document on Testing and Achievement: Guidelines for Scribing:*

Use of Scribes

If a scribe is approved to assist a student during a test, the following procedures apply.

A scribe may assist in recording the student's answers. A scribe may not improve a student's response by rewording or otherwise changing the student's answer. The student's response must be recorded with no change of any kind.

Scribes may not:

- provide suggestions or interpretations of any kind

- correct grammar

- make any changes to the student's response unless directed to do so by the student

A scribe may not read a test to a student. Audiotape versions of the test or readers may be provided for this purpose, if previously approved by the superintendent. The school jurisdiction is responsible for the appointment of a scribe and for any expenses incurred.

Parents or other immediate family members may not serve as scribes or readers for their child.

The scribe must adhere to the *Achievement Test Rules,* as described in the Policies section.

A test administered by a scribe shall be given in a separate writing area so that other students are not disturbed.

The scribe must sign his/her name at the end of the student's work.

The principal will record in the appropriate section of the test booklet or answer sheet that a scribe assisted the particular student.

Note: Scribed papers are not marked for conventions, or in the case of functional writing, for content management. Students' scores are pro-rated.

From Blake Morrison's (2000) *The Justification of Johann Gutenberg:*

[In] the scriptorium, we also sometimes sang hymns, among them an Ode to All Our Labours, whose rhymes I grew to hate:

> Unless we scribes this book enhance
>
> By writing in God's hand,
>
> The words will lack his governance
>
> And never breathe or stand.

With what solemnity we sang of this. But I had seen the obscenities written in margins by scribes, blistered and chilblained, whose endurance had run out. For what is noble in copying? The act is mechanical. If a monkey could be trained to copy the Bible, would its version be less holy than a monk's? I do not think so.

Our masters in the scriptorium urged us to be neat and self-effacing. But in all my time there I never saw two hands the same. Because they could not put their names or be given credit, the scribes like to parade themselves in other ways—with flourishes, blots, curlicues, misspellings and other marks of distinction. As a reader, I resent such intrusion. I like the relations with an author to feel private; I think he does too. I hold him in my hands, and he takes me into his confidence, and neither of us wants a third to come between. Print is better that way, because self-effacing. It makes the script undistinctive. It takes all "character" out of the characters. It is oblivious, as no man's hand can ever be. What I learned in the scriptorium is that the scribe is a meddler. And I began to think how to stop his meddling. (Morrison, 2000, pp. 44–45)

IV

It was more than profit that drew me to vellum. I loved its springiness to the touch. Its velvet nap. The whiff of animal still hanging about it, as though when reading or writing you were living inside the beast. I loved the blood-veins running there, under the ink. I loved the brown-white, brown-white run of the pages in a vellum book, since however long soaked in lime-water, and whatever sharpness of blade is used to scrape it, and no matter what creature it has come from (calf, goat, pig, sheep, deer—with smaller books, even squirrel), hairside will always be darker than fleshside. I loved all this as a boy with a goosequill in a scriptorium. (Morrison, 2000, p. 210)

If I were able, I would write it myself. But my hands being shaky and my eyes half-blind, I have hired a scribe to do it for me. Anton sits with me, transcribing my impressions as fast as they lept out of my mouth. He has been told to set down each word I speak, even those just now spoken of him. For though to see his own name may discompose him, these words do not compose them selves. And though humility may be a virtue, to be effaced, as I know myself, is a painful wound. I will not play that game, Anton. Without you, this manuscript cannot exist. Without you, there is no hope of making it a book. Let your presence be admitted here—you are Anton, not Anon.

Be careful, then, you do not skip or nod. Nor must you leave words out or write them twice over, as scribes are wont to do. My invention sought to correct such error—in metal, books should read as God intended. But for drafting this testament I put my trust in your ear and hand. Be sure, then, you copy me in good faith. (Morrison, 2000, pp. 4–5)

As these passages from Blake Morrison's compelling novel *The Justification of Johann Gutenberg* attest, writing, even carefully scribing the words of someone else is not as much a technical, anonymous act that the previously cited *Alberta Learning Document* might have us believe. In fact, that government document makes scribing sound precisely like what was so feared about Johann Gutenberg's new invention:

"The Bible! You plan to make the Bible as well?"

"I have considered it."

"The Bible, to have authority, must be written by monks, not by some heretic machine."

"With my press, it will look as though a monk has written it."

"But it will be counterfeit, the work of an engine. And God does not inhabit an engine." (Morrison, 2000, p. 160)

It is especially interesting, in the images that the Ministry provides online, that *family members* especially not be scribes for their kin. Ideally, once familial ties have been severed, the hand of the scribe becomes "undistinctive" (Morrison, 2000, p. 44). It must "take all character out of the characters" (Morrison, 2000, p. 45). And, in perfect parallel, as the scribe loses all familial relation to the student—all distinctiveness and character—the one scribed for becomes "abandoned to their own devices" (Arendt, 1969, p.

233), cut off from all their relations. Both scribe and student become anonymous in the face of a presumed realm of "meaning" that is to be anonymously handed on with no inhabited hand involved. Reading and writing thus no longer occur "as though you are living inside the beast" (Morrison, 2000, p. 210) of our Earthly blood relations.

(We might playfully say then that "living inside the beast" is living with our kin, in their full difference and diversity "inside" the living, often contradictory, ambiguous, and "multifarious" [Gadamer, 1989, p. 295] human enterprise of writing, of reading, of meaning, of expression, of understanding. Handwriting, for Darren, is not just a problem that he has. It is also a place that he has in this enterprise, a place *here, with* us.)

However, Blake Morrison's Gutenberg is convinced that scribing by hand—perhaps even under the auspices of the Alberta Ministry of Education—is unable to attain such undistinctiveness and lack of character, and this novel illuminates the great conflict inherent in this inability. It may be that Gutenberg's printing press effaces the obscene, bestial interferences of the scribe's hand. However, as the character of Gutenberg finds as the novel proceeds, scribing by hand is an act that requires faithfulness and trust and a certain embodied discipline and attention. It is an act that cannot be effaced, cannot become anonymous.

In the cloistered Scriptorium, the monk's hand works in the *Imagio Dei*—the monk's hand is inhabited by God. And, even in the more mundane cloisters of classrooms or examination rooms, where it is our children who are at stake in our practices, the scribe's hand clearly maintains a trace of the body labors and the love involved, and the sense of natural affection, kind-ness, where hands become inhabited by long ancestries, relatednesses, and bloodwork. Could we have ever been delivered "a small double wizard of snow" without some love and attention and alertness and readiness and trustworthiness in the hand of the scribe? Don't these scribed words flesh out more than the hands of the scribe and more than the interiors of the one scribed for?

Let's get brutal about this: Given Darren's admittedly troublesome handwriting, would a teacher who, from such evidence, believed that he wasn't very able, be able to hear this poem at all, as something worthy of attention, as something worthy of scribing? Is *this* part of the startle response hidden in student teachers' queries ("Yes, but did he actually *write* this or did someone write it for him?")? That not only did we not expect this from Darren, given what we've seen of his handwriting, but that we realize, to our horror, that, given his handwriting, *we might not have listened to his stories if we had been his teachers*? This is not *at all* about the practice of scribing itself, but about our own humiliation in the face of what we may have too quickly presumed was our task as teachers with children in our care.

As a wonderful illustration of *The Scribe* by Hieronymus Bosch attests, scribes like those pretended to in the *Alberta Learning Document* cited earlier are equally objects of potential ridicule as they attempt to cleave relentlessly to the letter, to the literal, all bloodhoundedly droopy-eared and penpointedly-mouthed, skating squinty-eyed from place to place so as not to miss a thing. An image not unlike Friedrich Nietzsche's "inverse cripples," where we become (crippled by) what we most desire (see Smith, 1999c): ears so long and so ready for listening that they trip up and encumber and distort, a bill so crooked for writing that speaking is impossible, attention so skating, so necessarily surface-fleeting (don't think, don't stop, don't entertain, don't interpret, don't teach, don't learn, don't read, don't be suggestive, don't correct, don't breathe) that our kinships are gone, and we become like Gutenberg's machine, soulless, uninhabited, unhospitable, full of wariness and paranoia instead of attention and love, bereft of flesh and relations, all in the name of fairness and objectivity. To be "fair" in this techno-mechanical sense, we must scribe what "the child him- or herself" dictates and nothing more. Being true to these children is being detached, mechanical. We must simply write down what the child says verbatum—where "verbatum" has itself shed all its ancestries of the Verbum and Word debates that once raged through Scholasticism (see, e.g., Lonergan, 1997).

As we become scribes for the Ministry of Education, the children for whom we scribe must become *dictators:* autonomous individuals who have some sort of hidden life independently of the living, intergenerational body of work that surrounds and holds us all in the living practice of reading and writing and the difficult ways of the hand. Perhaps it is therefore a good idea that the Ministry of Education does not allow family members to scribe for each other. At least with those students who are not familiar and familial, who don't expect trustworthiness from us and love, we can feign and fake such independence. As the student becomes a dictator, something, too, becomes of us. We fail to listen with love. We fail to enter into conversation. We examine, as if our child were an object and as if reading and writing did not draw us together inside the body of the beast.

V

I learned the torture of working: cramped wrists, swollen elbows, aching back, thumb and fingertips scalded by constant pressure on the quill. But I was taught new disciplines: how to rule a page to perfection; how to pare a quill and slit a nib, how to illuminate in different colours until a text looks to be spiked with gems. The ink was made from oak apples—gall nuts—crushed and soaked in rain water, then stirred with a fig stick in green vitriol till it turned gummy and black. The quills came from geese, the left wing-pinion curving best to sit in a right hand. It was here, too, that I learned the ways of vellum—how calf-skin rubs smoother than goat, how ink sticks better to the flesh side, and so on. (Morrison, 2000, pp. 42–43)

Not incidentally, most of the *remaining* readily available Web site "hits" around the idea of "scribing" are deeply religious in character, involving, most often, candlelights and calfskins and inks and the handiworks of rabbis, *Schules*, monks and monasteries, the character and necessities of proper ascendants and descendants in the curlicues of illuminated manuscripts, the cloisters of Scripture and the Scriptorium and the bloody handwork knowledges of the absorptivity of certain blood-veined vellums.

We can all imagine children in rows, "cramped wrists, swollen elbows, aching back, thumb and fingertips scalded by constant pressure" doing rows and rows of lower- and uppercase *R*'s (lower and upper, of course, the descendants of Gutenbergian arrangements of upper and lower cases full of print-type letters), with ascendants and descendants still at issue.

Those commonplace elementary school pages of properly formed letters taped to children's desks remind us of the burning body labors that make the training of the hand in writing such an urgent phenomenon. This is a deep body memory that we all have, having been schooled with rows of *O*'s and *B*'s and *A*'s. We were not just learning to write. This was not the only schooling occurring. The training of the hand dovetails with the training of the wilful beast of the rough child body. The training of the hand is an allegory of the coming to command and coming to properly control the body's sinfulness and fallenness.

Incidentally, those in Early Childhood Education can easily imagine classrooms full of young children with their fingers in the air tracing out air letters as a form of artful practice. And we can also remember those store-bought or homemade sandpaper letters and numbers that young children could play with, running their hands over the rough surfaces to help ingrain the body movements and ways of the hand necessary to writing (see, e.g., Piechowak & Cook, 1976, p. 98).

A student teacher recently asked whether such "sandpaper letters, textured fabrics, and sponge letters" are a good idea for kids:

> I quite approve of the practice of stimulating children to learn to play by giving them ivory letters to play with, the sight, the handling, and the naming of which is a pleasure. As soon as the child has begun to know the shapes of the various letters, have these cut, as accurately as possible, upon a board so that the stylus may be guided along the grooves. By increasing the frequency and speed with which the child follows these fixed outlines, we shall give steadiness to his fingers. (Quintilion, circa 85 CE, from his first volume of *The Art of Oratory* [cited in Illich, 1993, p. 9]).

This is obviously an odd and impractical response. It is part of the annoying character of interpretation. It is intended, following Hillman and Ventura, to make it possible to entertain this idea, not just practice it.

It can easily seem that interpretive work is simply a joke meant to interrupt and complicate and sometimes humiliate the ordinariness and straightforwardness of that student teacher's question: "Are these a good idea for kids?" Why do this, then? Because it re-places the idea of the sensuous tracing of letters back into the body of a long-lived beast, back into all its relations, back into all the multifarious voices that make it a living, breathing question for us, here, in the confines of school, in the presence of *this* child and what she or he asks of us. Thus re-placed, such tracing of letters becomes full of character and distinctiveness. As with scribing itself as a living inheritance, letter tracing now arrives "trailing [all the] dark and chaotic attachments" (Hillman, 1987, p. 123) that make it what it is, not as a dead object, but as a living inheritance. It also makes our task one that is more complex than simply training the hands of children: We are also always handing on an inheritance the child's participation in which is essential to its life. Who would have imagined that Quintillion was an ancestor who not only might have something to teach us, but might have, beyond our knowing, *already handed down to us a teaching in the very ordinariness of these sandpaper letters in Early Childhood Education.* Who would have thought, as well, that hidden in the very ordinariness of those one-page letter-formation blackline masters hide old ghosts that haunt us "beyond our wanting and doing" (Gadamer, 1989, p. xxviii), ghosts that just might have something to say to us about what we understand to be so obvious.

But again, why do this? Why not just "use" these things if the kids like them and they help and be done with it? We suggest that treating these matters interpretively makes the act of teaching more sensuous, more pleasurable, more generous, more serious, and more full of a sense of kinship with the children we teach and with those who have come before us in this great, difficult task. Recall, earlier, where we suggested that, in an interpretive treatment of these matters, handwriting, for Darren, is not just a problem that he has. It is also a place that he has in this long-standing enterprise, a place *here, with* us. He is no longer simply the object of our attention (an attention always aimed at "control, prediction and manipulation" [Habermas, 1973]). He is now *one of us* and, often more disturbingly for some of our student teachers, we, too, are some of us. We, too, are *in* the enterprise of reading and writing and meaning and expression and understanding, along *with* the children we teach. *Of course* we are all not doing identical work in that enterprise. Of course we don't all have equal skills, desires, fears, masteries, previous experiences, practice, and so on. Nevertheless, treating these matters interpretively means making it possible to engage with our children as fellow travelers, not only as objects to be controlled, predicted, and manipulated.

VI

Brother Erhard loved my hands especially, which he though, being dexterous, were "gifts from God." When we were sent some Biblical text to copy, I would take infinite care over the spacing, the angles, the depths of the ascenders and descenders. And at the end, mine would be the paper brandished in class.

"Here, boys, look at the beauty of the script," Brother Erhard would say. "Regard the elegance of the strokes. It is more like a woven tapestry than parchment. This is a hand guided by God." (Morrison, 2000, p. 5)

Clearly Darren's hand, at 6 years old, is not yet so guided, and it is equally clear that part of our mandate as teachers is to help Darren develop his dexterity. But there is something else at work here. Consider, from Alberto Manguel's *A History of Reading* (1996):

The inventor of the first written tablets may have realized the advantage of these pieces of clay over the holding of memory. Tablets did not require the presence of the memory-holder to retrieve information. Suddenly something intangible ... could be acquired without the physical presence of the message giver; magically, it could be imagined, noted, passed on across space and beyond time. Since the earliest vestiges of prehistoric civilization, human society had tried to overcome the obstacles of geography, the finality of death, the erosion of oblivion. With a single act—the incision of a figure on a clay tablet—that first anonymous writer suddenly succeeded in all these seemingly impossible feats. (pp. 178–179)

Is this part of the fear behind the question *"Yes, but did he actually* write *this or did someone write it for him?"*, this magic, that the message can be acquired without the physical presence of the message giver, and in such a way that the message giver is oddly erased from view? Where exactly *is* Darren in this transcribed poem? And can we, knowing of the love and care of his teacher, ever surely say that this poem is strictly somehow *his*? Or is there some mild accusation here, that maybe the teacher *did* "write" it and not just "scribe" it? If it is the product of Darren being encouraged to tell what he knows, is it not, then, as the product of encouragement, not "[him] actually" but also somehow another "someone?"

Writing is meant to *disappear*. But this erasure is too horrible to imagine. If writing is meant to disappear, so are writers:

The writer was a maker of messages, the creator of signs, but these signs and messages required a magus who would decipher them, recognize their meaning, give them voice. Writing required a reader.

The primordial relationship between writer and reader presents a wonderful paradox: in creating the role of the reader, the writer also decree's the writer's death, since in order for a text to be finished the writer must withdraw, cease to exist. While the writer remains present, the text remains incomplete. This uneasy relationship between reader and writer ... is a fruitful but anachronistic [one] between a primeval creator who gives birth at the moment of death, and a post-mortem creator, or rather generations of post-mortem creators who enable the creation itself to speak, and without whom all writing is dead. From its very start, reading is writing's apotheosis. (Manguel, 1996, pp. 178–179)

It was said I hated scribes and my invention would dig their grave. This last, as Anton knows, is a wicked lie. They are our nameless ghosts, condemned to a purgatory of oblivion, while those whose words they copy enjoy immortal fame. (Morrison, 2000, p. 205)

So again, what is the urge to see traces of the hand that wrote? Is it centrally a refusal to allow the possibility that the writing might stand without its creator, in spite of its creator, as something subject to being read? This is the helplessness of the written word worried over by Plato in the Phaedrus:

You are father of written letters. But the fact is that this invention of yours [writing] will produce forgetfulness in the souls of those who learn it. They will not need to exercise their memories, being able to rely on what is written, calling things to mind no longer from within themselves by their own powers, but under the stimulus of external marks that are alien to themselves. So it's not a recipe for memory, but for reminding that you have discovered. (Plato, *Phaedrus*, trans. 1956, p. 275)

It was worrying still to Hans-Georg Gadamer in his *Truth and Method*. Writing, Gadamer (1989) notes, is as Hegel suggested: an attempt to "make memory last" (p. 391), but the memory that lasts is embodied, not in the body that has written in its own hand, but in the text that has shed the body of the writer in favor of the body of the work itself, in favor of *what is said* and *what such writing says to those who read it*. The writer, even the scribe, is thus meant to be *effaced*. This is again a hint of the heat behind the question "Yes, but did he actually *write* this or did someone write it for him?" If the writer's troubled handwriting is effaced in scribing, what is left is a poem that, precisely because of the *absence* of the writer, is *meant for us*.

Rather than us being in a position to judge Darren's handwriting, it is we who become subject to question with the scribed poem: What, in heaven's name, are we to do with this poem? Are some of the images in it as good as they seem to be? Where *is* Darren "at," as they say in the workshops? What is the compulsion to "gear down?" And then what of our own humiliation at suspecting that this sort of imaginal presence should not be possible in such a student? As the writer becomes effaced in scribing, we ourselves come forward as the one's who are now *addressed*.

VII

Darren, this lovely child who signaled in some of the student teachers visiting him an ill-at-ease, not-enough-experience sense of "trouble"—Darren is not effaced by the transcribed poem, even though his handwriting difficulties might temporarily be occluded. Neither is his scribe, his teacher, effaced. What is effaced here are the security and presumed (or, with student teachers, "hoped-for-in-the-future-when-I-have-learned-enough") certainty of our own next pedagogical gestures.

We are cast out of the familiar role of readiness to help, to rescue, to fix, to repair. Those Mojave images don't exactly need to be *fixed*. They aren't a *problem*. However, these images do require that we come to face a certain humiliation: Why did we ever imagine that such a thing was *not* possible? Why are we so very surprised?

What becomes effaced then, is a certain "gap": between the first face of Darren as a presence in the classroom (drifting attention, slightly clumsy, always asking unexpected questions, troublesome handwriting at the beginning of the year, and so on) and the undeniable presence of the imaginal worlds he inhabits and articulates, if given the opportunity. The "portal" in this case is a scribe full of readiness, relatedness, trustworthiness, love, and expectation. In Morrison's novel, Johann Gutenberg was not possessed of an untrained hand but of old and failing hands. Once so able to write in ways inhabited by God, he is now unable himself to write at all, and he entrusts himself to a young boy-scribe: not to Anon, not to just anyone and no one (the Alberta Ministry's version of "the scribe"), but to Anton, someone whose hands he trusted.

So the great lesson here is that when our attention falls to Darren's handwritten work, we witness not only the child's troubles, but also our own panics and our own desires to intervene and fix. As the scrawls and misformed letters become our object, we ourselves become something appropriate to such witness: purveyors of a lack of skill and technique. We become, as professionals, fully able to act, to help, to remedy, to repair, to intervene, with all the energies requisite of setting things right. And even if we fail in this, and can't understand what to do, in place already are vast regimes of assessment tools, specialists and, if tragically necessary, the grand admission of well-researched failure in the face of this child's problems. In our concerns for his handwritten work, we already know what the future of this work can possibly be because we have, in a great technical-rational project, laid out in advance of this particular child's efforts, the architecture of a possible future: developmental stages in the sequential achievement of the ability to write and scribe for oneself.

The only thing up for grabs, here, is not what the future will hold but simply whether, how, or when Darren will achieve the future we have already planned for him (a planning to which, of course and of necessity, *he is not party*—a whole other sense in which the child is effaced by school itself and the particular sorts of technical attentions it brings to bear). With this piece of writing, therefore, there is no future, because it is already here, already oddly "out of our hands" (this *is* the sequence, no matter how we might intervene on Darren's behalf), already laid out and fated. Darren's own progression into what we already know in advance is thus an accident. It is not an accident in the sense that we have no hand in his training. It is an accident in the sense that Darren's particular progress can make no difference to what we already understand the essential character of writing development to be.

This is what David G. Smith (2000), following David Loy (1999), calls "frozen futurism," a future in which there in fact is no future.

With the transcribed poem, the situation is more fulsome and ambiguous. It seems to invite. It seems still somehow undecided what will come of it:

> Here I am tempted to say that my own experience of writing leads me to think that one does not always write with a desire to be understood—that there is a paradoxical desire not to be understood. It's not simple, but there is a certain "I hope that not everyone understands everything about this text", because if such a transparency of intelligibility were ensured it would destroy the text, it would show that the text has no future [*avenir*], that it does not overflow the present, that it is consumed immediately. Thus there is the desire, which may appear a bit perverse, to write things that not everyone will be able to appropriate through immediate understanding. There is a demand in my writing for this excess … a sort of opening, play, indetermination be left, signifying hospitality for what is to come [*avenir*]. As the Bible puts it—the place left vacant for who is to come [*pour qui va venir*]. (Derrida & Ferraris, 2001, pp. 30–31)

For Darren's poem, we are not prepared and there is a future, but now that future appears *as* a future, unfrozen: "an open horizon of as-yet-undecided possibilities" (Gadamer, 1989, p. 289).

What does this mean? It doesn't only mean that we weren't expecting this quality of work from this child. It also means something more fearsome. What, pray tell, are we properly to do? The transcribed poem breaks apart our decided, frozen, distanced gaze, draws us into its orbit, halts our helpful resolve and our measured relationships to "children and their needs." It is *our* need that comes forward.

With Darren's poem, we have a terrible futurity to face, of what might come of his compelling imaginal ability (especially because we know something of what he has in store in schooling).

This does not mean that we are somehow in favor of simply ignoring Darren's handwriting. That would be pedagogically irresponsible. The issue of starting "where Darren is at," however, is not whether one piece of his work—the scribed poem or the journal entry—is more reflective of his "actual" ability. Not only can either one be granted this status by the school's knowing gaze. We could also just as easily say that these pieces have nothing to do with one another: One is a matter of physical dexterity and manual practice, and the other is an issue of imagination, creativity, and composition.

The purpose of all this interpretive focus on "the scribe" is not to demean the terrible troubles we face in the face of Darren's pencil scrawls. They are, undeniably, troublesome. However, now these scrawls *and our troubles with them* can appear in a vast and generous topography of work, a place full of possibility, futurity, arrival, hospitality, spots left empty, alluring us to go on. Now there is a place where our troubles with his handwriting might work themselves *out* and might cease to be simply something to work *on*. Now they can appear back *in relation* to stories told and transcribed, back *in relation* to communication and its nature, limits, and difficulties, back *in relation* to the mixed messages of the ear that hears and the hand that writes and the eye of reading.

END BIT

> *The stars are beautiful*
>
> *Stars are little pieces of fire*
>
> *Stars are good*
>
> *Stars drop and turn into fire from the sky.*

As can been seen from the handwritten piece in Fig. 18.2, Darren's handwriting is coming along. And, thus far at least, the future of his imaginal

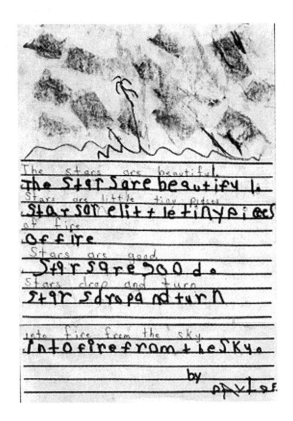

FIG. 18.2.   Stars are beautiful.

abilities is still open, and stars, as little pieces of fire, can still charm and draw us in. As can be seen, too, from this piece of his work and the one pictured near the beginning of our chapter, the scribe's hand still appears, now bypassing our abilities to decode his handwriting itself, and moving, instead, to what he means to say, asking him to read it to us and placing, in a loving and legible hand, a scribing of his work that will help us not lose what he has imagined to write in his own hand. "Making memory last" (Gadamer, 1989, p. 391) in such a way that there is a future.

So interpretive work can itself be seen as a way of attempting to remember the strange topographies that underwrite the most ordinary of events. Little wonder that interpretation takes an interest in the scribe. We've only scratched a few surfaces here. The good news is that in a couple of days, we get to meet Darren again for another year of his life in this tough old enterprise of writing.

Incidentally, check the scribe's handwriting in Darren's earlier poem about aliens, and Darren's own handwriting in the later piece about stars and fire. It seems that Darren just might be imitating the distinctiveness and character of the hand of a scribe he trusts.

> *I was thinking that perhaps the true beauty in my scribing for Darren lies in the fact that together we are creating a piece of work which otherwise would have had no past or future—it would have been lost to time within Darren's mind—put aside to make room for more "important" school stuff. Without the technical (my recording of it) there could exist no reader, and yet had the focus been the technical Darren would not have been freed enough to express his imagination thus there would be no need for a scribe. Perhaps the beauty of scribe-creator-reader relationship is that they are in essence inseparable in a sense symbiotic. Together, the scribe and creator (in this case teacher and student) are weaving words that will speak to a future of readers—words that perhaps would never have been heard were it not for a historically based act of the hand—scribing. I get goose bumps when I think of the analogy of the Bible. Would we ever have known God were it not for the work of scribes? Would we ever have known Darren without the hand of a scribe? I would argue that Darren spoke to us through my hand—my hand was the tool that Darren moved and through his work we were all moved.*

Preamble 19:
On Emptiness and Abundance

We've been having some odd conversations recently about what it is that our work is bringing us to after all these years. We are ending this book with a difficult and rather wild chapter that takes up the idea of abundance by exploring the Buddhist image of emptiness. There is much more to be said later about what this might mean about curriculum taken up in abundance. For now, we have a few parting thoughts.

What is it that so many student teachers and teachers have found so comforting and yet initially terrifying about this idea of curriculum in abundance? In order to have the time and energy to practice this idea (for it is a practice and it does require practice), you have to repeatedly "let go" of something. You have to let yourself venture and, inevitably, you have to let yourself venture *again*. Gadamer has noted how this necessitates, over and over again, a "momentary loss of self" (1977, p. 51). In fact, he goes so far as to say that this sort of experience involves, of necessity, a sort of "suffering" (1989, pp. 356–357), an "undergoing" (*Erfahrung*). In fact, he goes as far as to say that "experience is experience of human finitude. The truly experienced person is one who has taken this to heart" (1989, p. 357). The idea of abundance leads to a deep experience of the limitedness of human life, this life, my life.

We've experienced this over and over again. As new topics arrive, the whole process must start anew. We're going to have to be patient and alert all over again, here, now, in this place, over this topography, with this topic and these children, this fall, as I (D.J.) go back to supervising student teachers in an elementary school. As Gadamer (1989, p. 307 and following) put it so well, interpretation is always application. That is to say, understanding curriculum in abundance always has to be practiced as the understanding of the abundance of *this*. Interpretation must always "entrust" itself to the object of its affections. You don't really know ahead of time that, for example, scribes are going to show up and call for some "continuity of attention and devotion" (W. Berry, 1986, p. 32) from us. Who would have thought that Dolly the sheep would still charm us, that tree shadows would have caught a boy's attention at recess? To understand curriculum in abundance is to understand that, well, things happen and that these happenstances can be invitations if they are treated well.

It is little wonder that James Hillman (1987) can produce such lovely work that tethers together interpretation and the ancient mythological image of the Wound:

> In an encounter, the lacuna, the weak place … gives the opportunity. *Perception of opportunities requires a sensitivity given through one's own wounds.* Here, weakness provides the kind of hermetic, secret perception critical for adaptation to situations. The weak place serves to open us to what is in the air. We feel through our pores which way the wind blows. We turn with the wind; trimmers. An opportunity requires … a sense … which reveals the daimon of a situation. The daimon of a place in antiquity supposedly revealed what the place was good for, its special quality and dangers. The daimon was though to be a *familiaris* of the place. To know a situation, one needs to sense what lurks in it. (p. 161)

The more one practices this meditation of curriculum in abundance, the more susceptible one becomes to its call. You become experienced, one might say. More alert to the weak places of portent.

But there is something more here, something the three of us have just recently named and can't quite follow up yet with many words—that this experience of the "letting go" of a topic out of its self-containedness and fragmentary and impoverished isolation—its "emptying" in the Buddhist sense, into the abundance of all things—seems to ask us to experience a sort of death.

Odd to find abundance in such a place. But it only seems odd under regimes of scarcity, which convince us that death comes when scarcity and lack overtake us. Buddhism teaches, on the contrary, that it is precisely a sense of lack and the terrible, exhausting and, in the end, hopeless attempt to "fill" this sense of lack that is the great Ignorance.

Chapter 19

Unable to Return
to the Gods That Made Them[1]

David W. Jardine

> *The sound of water implies … the eye and the ear of a recluse attentive to the minute changes in nature and suggests a large meditative loneliness, sometimes referred to as sabi: the sound of the water paradoxically deepens the sense of surrounding quiet.*
> —Shirane (1996, p. 51)

Late May, foothills of the Rocky Mountains, and the banks of the Elbow River are starting to shift again under the weight of water and the billow of spring runoff. Funny how the banks and shores and waters and airs have, once again, in this mysterious perennial arc, attended each other so perfectly. *Not one stone,* however meticulously small, is anywhere at all except exactly where it should be, perfectly co-arising in a big, goofy Alberta Sunblue Grin of interdependence.

Things have warmed up enough that you can start to smell the pine trees. Evening Grosbeaks and Pine Grosbeaks and Red Crossbills. Sickly new apsenleaf sour smell. I remember these smells. *But this is not quite right.* This place has taken perfect care of a bodily remembering that I had since forgotten. This place spills my own most intimate memory out into an Earthbody greater than this sheath of skin.

Memory, here, alludes to a deep mutuality with this place. I remember these smells, then, but not singlehandedly.

A mating pair of Harlequin Ducks in a bit of a stillpool on the far shore up against warm cliff faces.

We've been spotted!

But we'd already been spotted by the aspensmells. Not the Great Alertness of this duck eyeing. But still *there.* A felt awareness of being placed by

---

[1]Reprinted from *Unfolding Bodymind: Exploring Possibility Through Education* with permission from Holistic Education Press. <https://great-ideas.org> 802-247-8312.

this place into place in a way I could not have done alone, could not have even imagined.

How can it be that none of these things is ever elsewhere than *precisely* where it is, following the silent mysteries of the ways of water and steepness and volume or the tangled clutters of bushwillowy roots that hold just like *so*, with their long trailing underground reddish rootedness through loose gravel shoals holding as fast as is possible and no faster? How is this possible, that their attentions to all their relations are so acute?

Some have endured this winter's end.

Some have passed and got pushed up onto silty bars or edges alongside a downed age-old spruce whose banksoils failed and in such failure did precisely what was possible. There can be no grieving here except for that sweet fact that all life is One Great Suffering, One Great Undergoing, One Great Passing.

In the presence of such a fact, there is the fragile beginnings of a release from the odd self-containedness, the odd, desperate, and understandable holding-on—holding ourselves away from the fact of suffering—that we humans have hallucinated as self-identical substances.

As René Descartes says in his "Meditations on First Philosophy" (1640/1955), "a substance is that which requires nothing except itself in order to exist" (p. 255). An ecological nightmare, this simple step of envisaging that the reality of something, its "substance," is what it is independently of everything else, any of its relations, any of its sufferings. So clearly the great Cartesian task of understanding the substance reality of any thing is the great task of severing its relations and forcing it to stand alone under the colonizing gaze of objectivism (Jardine, 1992a, 1998; see chap. 8), a gaze that demands of things that they "shape up" and conform to the logico-mathematical certainties that modern(ist) science demands of all things. This is one more step along a path (Jardine, 1990, 1998), inherited by Descartes from Thomas Aquinas and before him, Aristotle, toward what biologist E. O. Wilson has named the new era: Nemozoic, the Age of Great Loneliness.

But this is not the loneliness of a great, empty (*sunyata*) spaciousness full of dependent co-arisings (*pratitya-samutpada*). It is not the meditative loneliness of *sabi*, which is aimed at the increase of such releasing spaciousness around the restlessness paranoia of any seemingly isolated thing (think, e.g., of Chogyam Trungpa's [1988, p. 44] "restless cow" image of meditation and the meditative task of making its meadow larger and larger and richer and richer "so that the restlessness becomes irrelevant").

Rather, this is the venerated Protestant-Eurocentric-Neo-North American Loneliness of Individuality, of one's self existing estranged of all its relations (like some independent, immortal soul caught through some awful accident in the messy, bloody, dependent squalors of the flesh). Following from such a sense of estrangement, we then demand such isolationism of Earthly things if they are to be properly and substantially understood, thus reproducing our own loneliness in all things. A perfect example is an isolated "math fact" on a Grade 1 worksheet: $5 + 3 = \_\_$, isolated from the "x" that would make it sensible (Jardine et al., 2003, pp. 133–136), isolated from subtraction that would make it meaningful, memorizable, but never especially memorable. A horrible little thing—one more "wanting and doing" (Gadamer, 1989, p. xxviii)—that only needs to be *done*. Little wonder that a Grade 7 boy recently told me that he used to want to get his mathematics questions correct "because if I do, I won't have to do anymore."

I have never heard a more damning condemnation of what schools can sometimes (seemingly unwittingly, witlessly) do.

In beginning to release ourselves from such self-contained holding-on, we necessarily begin to release ourselves to suffering, to undergoing, to experiencing each thing (even things like [seemingly] isolated math facts) as in the Earthly embrace of every other, one Great Dharma Body, turning, wheeling. It is little wonder we rarely pursue such release and enjoy the full consequence of its sweet and sensuous spell, because this spell portends our own suffering, our own shit and piss mortalities.

This is the sweet agony of interpretation: Every thing thus begins to appear as a luscious, spacious, standing-in-itself moment of repose in the midst of a great and heralded topography of relations and dependencies and belongings. With the grace of interpretation, we begin to stand in the vertigo of the movement of "opening," of "clearing." And yes, even that little math fact that seemed so lifeless, so inept, so isolated, so unmemorable, starts to howl with the "multifarious … voices" (Gadamer, 1989, p. 284) of all its lost ancestors.

More fearsome yet is the glimpse we suddenly get that this previously seemingly isolated little math fact *is* that multifariousness, and to the extent it is presented to our children as an isolated "fact," understanding its real, Earthly *facere*, its real "makeup" is no longer possible at all.

We can only understand this riveredge in the middle of its attunement to and thereby witness of the waters and skies that it has endured. It *is* its endurances, just as we are ours, just as the Pythagorean theorem is the attentions it has deservedly endured in order to have come down to us thus (the real mathematical question to ask of the Pythagorean theorem is thus not "how do you do it?" but "how has it come to be entrusted to us?" and "*now* what are we going to do?").

Thus I become visible, here, too—"[my] self in its original [Earthly] countenance" (Nishitani, 1982, p. 91). Spotted, smelling aspens and also sniffed on passing winds *even if I don't know it*. In the midst of all these things "claiming, *but not requiring* [my] witness" (Hillman, 1982, p. 78).

Spring moon crouched here near river vents that breathe when waters roll over rocks and capture oxygens from airs above.

These places of song, where rivers sound. Perfectly so, just like the arcs of rock and the drumskins of waters over white turbulences allow.

In places like this, the old Zen adage finally makes some sort of sense, some deeply bodily sense in the wet middles of this deep Earthbody: that if this twirl of dust bootkicked up off the path did not exist, *everything* would be different.

Suddenly, this odd crown of human consciousness gets turned around, turned inside out, caught in the giddy belly giggle of how wonderfully ridiculous is this dribbling trail of words.

This is, of course, the great *converse* that is at the center of a true conversation, that we are turned around: addressed, not simply addressing ("Understanding begins when something addresses us. This is the first condition of hermeneutics" [Gadamer, 1989, p. 299]), claimed (Gadamer, 1989, p. 127), not simply making claims, spotted, witnessed, not simply bearing witness: "not what we do or what we ought to do, but what happens to us over and above our wanting and doing" (Gadamer, 1989, p. xxviii). This animate upsurge of the worldbody (not precisely an "unmotivated upsurge" as Merleau-Ponty suggested in an early work [1964, p. xiii], but an upsurge surely beyond the horizon of merely human motivation) is one of the greatest and most fearsome insights of David Abram's beautiful work (1996).

No. Perhaps the greatest and most fearsome is the moment of knowing I am this Earthbody *and nothing besides.*

My consciousness that turns this attention here and there is not different in kind from the lure that pulls these flowerheads to face the sun.

Sit squat in the open forest arc. Spending my passing days listening to the eerie auditory spaciousness of Grosbeak whistle echos off the foothill to the west.

The ear of the other animal was always already open and even though I'd forgotten to listen, I've been heard.

I sit flower-headed facing Sun.

Pulled now, beyond my wanting and doing, into an effort, these words, at airbubble rockcast riversinging.

I

The unnoticeable law of the Earth preserves the Earth in the sufficiency of the emerging and perishing of all things in the allotted sphere of the possible which everything follows and yet nothing knows. The birch tree never oversteps its possibility. It is [human] will which drives the Earth beyond the sphere of its possibility into such things that are no longer a possibility and are thus the impossible. It is one thing to just use the Earth, another to receive the blessing of the Earth and to become at home in the law of this reception in order to shepherd the mystery and watch over the inviolability of the possible. (Heidegger, 1987, p. 109)

The thing is, I've been living under a hood of depression and distraction and exhaustion for the past months. Somehow, somewhere, I've lost track of the things that might sustain my life, sustain this writing, this *entheos*, things like stomping along this riveredge and feeling my breath surge up again out from under winter's dark dip.

How is it possible to forget such things? Worse yet, how is it possible to forget such things *again*? No sense pretending that this hasn't happened before, feeling a bit like a dirty little math fact caught in perpetual self-isolation. Loneliness. So here are the riverbanks and waters remembering all their living relations exactly, remembering the pitch of aspen smells, with an exquisiteness and a relentlessness and an inviolability that is sometimes almost terrifying, and I'm left, goofing again, forgetting again, tumbling again.

Thank the gods at least that Hans-Georg Gadamer (1989, pp. 15–16) reminded me that the dialectic of memory and forgetting is part of what constitutes the building of character, what constitutes the great and terrible human enterprise of becoming *someone*. This is why the first part of his *Truth and Method* speaks so often of *Bildung:* I become someone because of what I have been through, what I have endured in losing and gaining, in remembering and forgetting, in venture and return.

Thank the gods, too, that he was able to admit out loud that "every experience worthy of the name" (Gadamer, 1989, p. 356) involves suffering. It involves opening ourselves to the open-ended sojourn of things, their ongoingness and fragilities and sometimes exhilarating, sometimes terrifying possibilities and fluidities (interpretation "makes the object and all its possibilities fluid" [Gadamer, 1989, p. 367]). This is central to the arguments in his *Truth and Method:* that experience (*Erfahrung*) is not something we *have;* it is something we *undergo*, and, to put it more intergenerationally, something we just might *endure.* It therefore has to do with duration, with what lasts, and therefore with what can be cultivated, taken care of: Experiences worthy of the name are not interior mental events had by a selfsame subject, but are more like places that hold memory, topographical endurances (like these riveredges) full of ancestry and mystery and a complex, unrepayable indebtedness. Full of dependencies, full of "it depends," full of dependents. And more, experience therefore links with my own endurance, what I can live with, which, in part, means where I need to be, in what "space," (in what relations) to endure.

That, of course, is why these last months have been so humiliating coupled as they have been with a forgetting of what I need to endure. The question seems to be, again, how could I have forgotten this, again?

It may be, however, that such Earthbound forgetting is inevitable as may be having to endure such forgetting again and again.

This gives human experience the character of a journeying (another meaning buried in *Erfahrung*), becoming someone along the way, but never in such a way that suffering is simply overcome or finished, but only in such a way that, perhaps even for a moment, the stranglehold of consciousness may be gracefully interrupted by the dusty world and the unanticipated plop and peep of an American Dipper off a midriver rock.

So here's the rub. Forgetting these things that sustain me is akin to Martin Heidegger's terrible idea, cited in the long passage earlier, that we can somehow sometimes do the impossible. Human will—our "wanting and doing" (Gadamer, 1989, p. xxviii)—with all its consequent unEarthly Cartesian dreams of an Earth full of isolated substances, isolated "objects" bereft of relations, can push us beyond the allotted sphere of the fleshy, Earthly relations we need to sustain us, into doing things that overstep the allotted sphere of the possible and are thus impossible.

We can, that is, work against the conditions under which our work might be actually accomplishable.

I can, like this darkening winter mood, "not be myself."

And even though I may then still be on Earth, I can act out of a forgetting of this given, this gift, worldless mumbling a soft cocoon of merely words that have lost their sensuous spells, their fleshy referents, their hum and rattle on the breath.

II

> All things show faces, the world not only a coded signature to be read for meaning, but a physiognomy to be faced. As expressive forms, things speak; they show the shape they are in. They announce themselves, bear witness to their presence: "Look, here we are." They regard us beyond how we may regard them, our perspectives, what we intend with them, and how we dispose of them. (Hillman, 1982, p. 77)

So what of those odd things we often surround our children with in schools? Odd objects that have lost their body, their richness, their rigor, their recursiveness, their relations (Doll, 1993)? Objects that seem to have no ancestors, no place, no topos, no topographies, no lives, objects that might be memorizable but not memorable, that don't bear remembering, that don't require our suffering the journey of coming to understand them and therefore coming to understand ourselves differently having understood them?

What witness to such things bear on us and our doings? Not "what do we have to say about them" but "what do they have to say about us."

(Spotted!)

Many of the things our children are surrounded with in school are simply isolated activities (simply our own "wanting[s] and doing[s]"; Gadamer, 1989, p. xxviii) instead of places to go full of their own wantings and doings, places to inhabit, places to take care of and cultivate, places the traveling of which might require us to become someone in the presence of others who travel with us and in the presence of this place that itself will shape our character (Jardine, 2000).

Many of the things we all surround ourselves with are unable to show their suffering, their care, their relations, their topographies.

Consider this Styrofoam cup I'm just about to throw away. It is produced as part of a standing reserve (Heidegger, 1977) for something else (just like math facts are produced as part of a standing reserve for the accumulation of marks and grades). It (and from here on, we're speaking of the Styrofoam cup but also imagining at the same time the frantic little do-its of mad math minutes) is so disposable (so without position or place, without composure, one might say), that any relations of it or to it cannot be cultivated, chosen, cared for, remembered, enjoyed, either by us or by anything else that surrounds it. I cannot become composed around such a thing. There will be no mourning at its loss or destruction. It does not show its having-arrived-here and we have no need to try to remember such an arrival. All trace of relations and endurance are gone. In fact, it does not endure. It does not age.

It breaks.

In fact, it is produced deliberately in order to *not* hold attention, *not* take on character, *not* arouse any sense or possibility of care or concern. *It is deliberately produced in order to not be remembered*. It is deliberately produced of forgetting. It is *Lethe*. It is lethal.

It is what we use so that our ability to remember the care and suffering that constitutes the interdependencies of the Earth (and therewith the possibility of remembering our own suffering) is not visible and seems to be not necessary. But worse, it *"is" in such a way that care is not even possible*.

It is impossible.

And, to the extent that our human life and this great Earth life is constituted by the attentiveness and suffering of all its relations (Heidegger's, 1962, understanding of care as *Sorge* and his insistence, along with Gadamer's, 1989, on our "finitude"), to that extent, this Styrofoam cup is impossible, even though *there it is*.

So the problem with such things—and therefore the problem with surrounding ourselves and our children with such things—is their impossibility. Human will has produced something that has spiraled out of the order of relations. The problem with the disposibility of this cup is not simply the products or by-products of its manufacture or the nonbiodegradability of what remains of it after its use (this is ecological consciousness at its most literal-minded). The deep ecological problem with it is that it is unable to be cared for and living in its presence therefore weakens, undermines, or occludes our ability to see how our lives and this Earth are constituted by such suffering. (And, too, the problem with the disposability of isolated math facts is that they are unable to be cared for and living in their presence therefore weakens, undermines or occludes our ability to see how we might understand mathematics as a living place, a living inheritance with which we have been entrusted, full of its own hidden agencies that live "beyond my wanting and doing [Gadamer, 1989, p. xxviii], and therefore that can, potentially, release me from my [schooled] isolation out into a *world* of relations.)

This Styrofoam cup becomes a perfect example of a Cartesian Substance: something that is bereft of any relations. This Styrofoam cup thus stands there in the world "by itself," as an object produced of bereaving. But it also promises to help us get over our sense of loss through a relentless, ever-accelerating stream of consumptiveness: one faceless, bodiless, placeless, careless cup after the other (just like one faceless, bodiless, placeless, careless schooly math activity after the other), all bent to the satisfaction of our "wanting and doing" (Gadamer, 1989, p. xxviii).

And then, of course, we excuse the existence of such cups by pointing to our own convenience, never once suspecting that our sense of convenience has been manufactured by and is now housed in the very cups that use our sense of convenience as their excuse. And, just as evidently, we inundate our children with relentless streams of one activity after the other and excuse it by referring to their short "attention spans," never once suspecting that many of the things they are inundated with in schools *are not worthy of attention,* because they have been stripped of their imaginal topographies (their living "ecologies," we might say). We thus become caught in producing rushed, impossible activities to service the very attentions we have violated through such production. A *perfect* image of knowledge-as-consumption-and-production, knowledge as a scarce resource, and school as commodified exchange processes bent on producing consumers in a forgetfulness of the original given, the original gift (Jardine et al., 2003, pp. 211–222; what Matthew Fox [1983, p. 23] called "the original blessing," of the Earth). Because, in such an economy of consumption, "time [itself] is always running out" (W. Berry, 1987, p. 44), the only hope, in the midst of such a rush of activities, is not slowing down and opening up rich fields of relations. Rather, hope is found only in *accelerating the rush* (Jardine, 2000; see chap. 12) in a grand eschatological race for the End Times: a time when wholeness will be achieved once all the scattered bits and pieces of the curriculum are finally, finally "covered." These impossible, consumptive, isolated, never really satisfying bits and pieces thus always leave us looking longingly for the last days when all will be redeemed and we can finally rest, assured. Differently put, our relentless consumptivism is premised on a desire for it to end in the full satisfaction guaranteed of our "wanting and doing."

III

In the summer of 1998 I taught a course on hermeneutics at the University of Victoria, and we spent our last class considering James Hillman's "*Anima Mundi:* Returning the soul to the world" (1982). There is a certain point in this essay where the image of an object cut off from all its relations is brought up, an object unable to return to the gods that made it, an object unplaced. In our class, I offered up the image of a fragment of Styrofoam cup buried 10 feet underground in some long-forgotten dump site.

Darkwormyness. The roiling relief of decays, where all things begin to return to the gods that made them, begin to empty out from their illusion of self-containment into all their relations. And then, right in the midst of these rich, dark, moist underworlds, these rich sufferings, this dry brightlit brightwhite self-contained, "clear and distinct" (Descartes, 1640/1955), full present, unreposing, utopian thing, unable to let go of its self, unable to find its lost relations (excuse the Heideggerianism, but unable to *world*).

Oddly impossible, having overstepped something unutterable, now condemned, it seems, to never re-turn, never to con-verse, never to breathe out into its topography.

Hillman (1982) says that this image of an object that has "no way back to the Gods" (p. 83) is precisely an image of a "figure in Hell" (p. 83).

IV

In *Truth and Method* (1989), Hans-Georg Gadamer insists that "Youth [and, of necessity, anyone new to anything] demand images for its imagination and for the forming of its memory. [We must, therefore] supplement the *critica* of Cartesianism with the old *topica*" (p. 21). The "*critica* of Cartesianism" are essentially methodological and procedural. As Martin Heidegger (1972b) has noted, in this fulfillment of the modern age, "the matters at hand become matters of method" (p. 66; see the meditations on method deployment found in chap. 8 and consider how focused beginning teachers become on issues of "method"). Once this Cartesian inheritance is enacted in schools, isolated, anonymous, disembodied, clear and distinct, methodologically reproducible and assessable math facts become understood as more "basic" than the troublesome, roiling, ongoing, irreproducible, ambiguous, highly personal, and bodily engaging conversations we might have with children and colleagues about living mathematical relations. Ideologically, under the hood of Cartesianism, such living conversations blur and despoil and contaminate and desecrate what is in fact objective and certain and self contained.

"We are living out a logic [of fragmentation and isolation] that is centuries old and that is being worked out in our own lifetime" (Berman, 1983, p. 23). Against this modernist logic, Gadamer insists that understanding and its memorial formation require the productive supplementation of topographical imagination, thus placing what might have seemed to be isolated "math facts" back into the sustaining relations that make them what they are, that keep them sane, that make them rich and memorable. "The old *topica*" is thus essentially, not methodological but substantial, full of smells and names and faces and kin, full of ancestral roots and ongoing conversations and old wisdoms and new, fresh deliberateness and audacity and life. It is also necessarily and unavoidably multifarious, contentious, ongoing, intergenerational, and unable to be foreclosed with any certainty because, for example, as a *living* discipline, mathematics endures. Therefore, topographically-hermeneutically-ecologically "understanding mathematics" means going to this living place and getting in on the living conversation that constitutes its being furthered.

Understanding is thus not method: It is *learning to dwell in the presence of this riveredge, or learning to dwell in the presence of Pythagorean proportionality* and, under such witness, becoming someone because of it.

V

As unhidden, truth has in itself an inner tension and ambiguity. Being contains something like a hostility to its own presentations. The existing thing does not simply offer us a recognizable and familiar surface contour; it also has an inner depth of self-sufficiency that Heidegger calls "standing-in-itself." The complete unhiddenness of all beings, their total objectification (by means of a representation that conceives things in their perfect state) would negate this standing-in-itself of beings and lead to a total levelling of them. A complete objectification of this kind would no longer represent beings that stand in their own being. Rather, it would represent nothing more than our opportunity for using beings, and what would be manifest would be the will that seizes upon and dominates things. [By this riveredge] we experience an absolute opposition to this will-to-control, not in the sense of a rigid resistance to the presumption of our will, which is bent on utilizing things, but in the sense of the superior and intrusive power of a being reposing in itself. (Gadamer, 1977, pp. 226–227)

The project of hermeneutics requires that we strive to "overcome the epistemological problem" (Gadamer, 1989, pp. 242–264). The healing art of interpretation is not concerned simply with knowing things differently than Cartesianism allows. Rather, it requires that we strive to "break open the *being* of the object" (Gadamer, 1989, p. 362) we are considering. Things, taken up interpretively, *exist differently* than the logic of self-containedness and self-identity allows. The healing art of interpretation is thus first and foremost *ontological* in its movement.

Living things in this world *are* all their vast, ancestral, intergenerational, Earthly relations. *This* is the greatness and power of their "repose." They *are* all the ways, all the voices, that have handed them to us, a great and vast receding spaciousness, where "beings hold themselves back by coming forward into the openness of presence" (Gadamer, 1977, p. 227). This riveredge *is* all its relations sounding outwards into all things and back and forth in the cascades of generational voices faded and to come. It isn't first some thing and somehow "then" in relation (which gives rise to "the epistemological problem"). "Only *in* the multifariousness of such voices does it exist" (Gadamer, 1989, p. 284). And it resists objectification—it "holds itself back" in repose—because it is unfinished. It is open to the endurances and sufferings to come that can never be fully or finally "given." "The whole" is never given (Gadamer, 1989, p. 38) and it is therefore never fully present or presentable or representable (this is the great "critique of presence" that Heidegger initiated as a critique of the Being of things, not an epistemological critique).

And, if the whole is never simply given, health is never given. Healing and wounding, like memory and forgetting, like *sol stasis* and return, are never done. Again, suffering, endurance, furtherance:

This ultimately forces an awareness that even [a simple thing like a twirl of dust kicked up from the path, or a seemingly isolated math fact, or the seem-

ingly pristine givenness of the Pythagorean theorem] possesses its own original worldliness and, thus, the centre of its own Being so long as it is not placed
in the object-world of producing and marketing. Our orientation to [such
things, unlike our orientation to the object world] is always something like
our orientation to an inheritance. (Gadamer, 1994, pp. 191–192)

The act of understanding such things is not a matter of utilizing or control
or making fully present and objective or making completely clear. It is the
act of participating in the work of "handing down" (Gadamer, 1989, p. 284)
such things. However, we must also cultivate in ourselves the ability and the
desire to adamantly *refuse* (Jardine, 1994b) some inheritances, those that
toy with impossibility and despoil our ability to dwell in the suffering of
things (that despoil our ability to *experience* [*Erfahrung*]). We must refuse the
leveling that violates the deeply ecopedagogical repose of things.

So even when a young child simply counts up to ten, to *understand* such an
event means to allow ourselves to experience (*Erfahrung*) how they are
standing with us in the middle of a great human inheritance, a great human
endurance, full of arcs of ancestry and memory that define mathematics as a
living discipline. This is one of us, one of our kind, one of our kin, counting
out in an act that is of a kind with the measured pacing of birdcalls heralding
the sun's arcing higher and higher.

Under such an image of our work as educators, the task of learning the
ways of a place like mathematics becomes akin to the task of becoming native to a place, developing:

> … the sense of "nativeness," of belonging to the place [see the detail with
> which Gadamer (1989, p. 62) deals with the idea of understanding-as-be-
> longing and the relationship between belonging (*Zugehörigkeit*) and hearing
> (*hören*). I'm quite sure that our coauthor of Preamble 7, who is deaf, will have
> something to tell us here that we could not have imagined ourselves]. Some
> people are beginning to try to understand where they are, and what it would
> mean to live carefully and wisely, delicately in a place, in such a way that you
> can live there adequately and comfortably. Also, your children and grand-
> children and generations a thousand years in the future will still be able to
> live there. That's thinking as though you were a native. Thinking in terms of
> the whole fabric of living and life. (Snyder, 1980, p. 86)

Thus it is that there is a great kinship between hermeneutics, ecology, and
pedagogy. They are each, in their own ways, concerned with returning us to
our suffering and to the suffering we must undergo to understand our place
in this great Earthly inheritance, full as it is with both riveredges and the
graceful beauty of Pythagoras—these two now no longer different in kind,
both understood as finally able to return to the gods that made them.

END BIT

"Understanding is an adventure and, like any adventure, it always involves
some risk" (Gadamer, 1983, p. 141). In fact, *"understanding proves to be,"* not

a method but an *"event"* (Gadamer, 1989, p. 308), a moment of the fluttering open of the meticulous co-arisings that repose around any thing.

This is what hermeneutics understands as "truth": *Alethia,* the opening of what was previously closed (and therefore, like the necessary dialectic of memory and forgetting, the necessary closing off of things as well, part of the "hostility towards full presentation" that Gadamer alluded to earlier), the remembering of what was forgotten (*Lethe* as the river of forgetfulness and our living in the wisdom that "only by forgetting does the mind have the possibility of seeing things with fresh eyes, so that what is familiar fuses with the new. 'Keeping in mind' is [thus] ambiguous" [Gadamer, 1989, p. 16]), the making alive, the livening up, of what was dull and leveled and therefore deadly (lethal) and morose.

As for me, I'll sit here a bit, near solstice, facing Sol's perennial highpitched summer stasis over the Tropic (the *tropos,* the "turning") of Cancer. From now on, the shadows will be shortening, but I've heard, somewhere, that something stays the same.

References

Abram, D. (1996). *The spell of the sensuous: Language in a more-than-human world*. New York: Pantheon Books.

Adler, M. (1989). "The juice and the mystery." In J. Plant (Ed.), *Healing the wounds: The promise of ecofeminism* (pp. 33–41). Toronto: Between the Lines Press.

Alberta Learning Document on Testing and Achievement: Guidelines for Scribing. http://www.learning.gov.ab.ca/k_12/testing/achievement/ach_gib/sec5_accom.htm.

Alberta Junior High Science Curriculum Guide, revised 1990.

Aoki, T. (2005 [1990]). Sonare and videre: A story, three echoes and a lingering note. In William F. Pinar & Rita L. Irwin (Eds.), *Curriculum in a new key: The collected works of Ted T. Aoki* (pp. 367–376). Mahwah, NJ: Lawrence Erlbaum Associates.

Arendt, H. (1969). *Between past and future*. London: Penguin Books.

Baker, L. (2000, August 30). Pope opposes human cloning. *Calgary Herald*, p. A20.

Berman, M. (1983). *The reenchantment of the world*. New York: Bantam.

Berry, T. (1988). *The dream of the earth*. San Francisco: Sierra Club Books.

Berry, W. (1983). *Standing by words*. San Francisco: North Point Press.

Berry, W. (1986). *The unsettling of America*. San Francisco: Sierra Club Books.

Berry, W. (1987). *Home economics*. San Francisco: North Point Press.

Berry, W. (1989, March). The profit in work's pleasure. *Harper's Magazine*, pp. 19–24.

Berry, W. (1999). Thy life's a miracle. *Wild Duck Review*, 5(2), 1–4.

Berthoff, A. (1981). *The making of meaning: Metaphors, models and maxims for writing teachers*. Upper Montclair, NJ: Boynton-Cook.

Block, A. A. (2004). *Talmud, curriculum, and the practical: Joseph Schwab and the Rabbis*. New York: Peter Lang.

Bly, R. (1988). *A little book on the human shadow*. New York: Harper & Row.

Bordo, S. (1988). *The flight to objectivity*. Albany: State University of New York Press.

Bowers, C. A. (2006). *The false promises of constructivist theories of learning: A global and ecological critique*. New York: Peter Lang.

Britzman, D. P. (2003). Practice makes practice. [revised edition.] Albany: State University of New York Press.

Calasso, R. (1993). *The marriage of Cadmus and Harmony*. New York: Knopf.

Caputo, J. (1987). *Radical hermeneutics*. Bloomington: Indiana State University Press.

Carpenter, W. B. (1886). *Principles of mental physiology*. London: Kegan Paul.

Casey, N., & Fellows, M.. (1993). *This is mega-mathematics!* Los Alamos, New Mexico: Los Alamos National Laboratory. Also available at http://www.c3.lanl.gov/mega-math/menu.html.

Cayley, D. (1992). Introduction. In I. Illich. & D. Cayley (Eds.,), *Ivan Illich in conversation* (pp. 1–57). Toronto: House of Anansi Press.

Chua-Eoan, H. (1991, August 12). The uses of monsters. *Time*, p. 27.

Chwialkowska, L. (2000, August 4). Court allows patents of life forms: Human beings not included in landmark decision. *National Post*, p. A1.

Clifford, J. (1986). On ethnographic allegory. In J. Clifford & G. Marcus (Eds.), *Writing culture: The poetics and politics of ethnography* (pp. 98–121). Berkeley: University of California Press.

Clifford, P., & Friesen, S. (1994, October). *Choosing to be healers*. Paper presented at the JCT Conference on Curriculum Theory and Classroom Practice, Banff, Alberta, Canada.

Connelly, M., & Clandinin, D. (1988). *Teachers as curriculum planners*. Toronto: O.I.S.E. Press.

Cook, F. H. (1989). The jeweled net of Indra. In J. Callicott & R. Ames (Eds.), *Nature in Asian traditions of thought: Essays in environmental philosophy* (pp. 213–239). Albany: State University of New York Press.

Crary, J. (1990). *Techniques of the observer: On vision and modernity in the nineteenth century*. Cambridge, MA: MIT Press.

"Critics Sound Alarm Over 'Master Cell' Technology." (2000). http://www.netlink.de/gen/Zeitung/1998/981106.htm.

Daignault, J. (1992). Traces at work from different places. In W. F. Pinar & W. M. Reynolds (Eds.), *Understanding curriculum as phenomenological and deconstructed text* (pp. 195–215). New York: Teachers College Press.

Derrida, J., & Ferraris, M. (2001). *A taste for the secret*. Cambridge, England: Polity Press.

Descartes, R. (1955). *Descartes selections*. New York: Scribner's. (Original work published 1640)

Devall, G., & Sessions, B. (1985). *Deep ecology*. Salt Lake City, UT: Peregrine Books.

Doll, Jr., W. (1993). *A post-modern perspective on curriculum*. New York: Teachers College Press.

Doll, W. (1993). Curriculum possibilities in a "post"-future. *Journal of Curriculum and Supervision, 8*(4), 277–292.

Dubord, G. (1995). *The society of the spectacle*. San Francisco: Zone Books.

Dyson, F. (1996). The scientist as rebel. *American Mathematics Monthly, 103*(9), 800–805.

Egan, K. (1986). *Teaching as story telling: An alternative approach to teaching and curriculum in elementary schools*. London, Ontario: Althouse Press.

Egan, K. (1992). The roles of schools: The place of education. *Teacher's College Record, 93*(4), 641–645.

Eliade, M. (1968). *Myth and reality*. New York: Harper & Row.

Eliade, M. (1975). *The quest: History and meaning in religion*. Chicago: University of Chicago Press.

English, F. (1999). *Deciding what to teach and test: Developing, aligning and auditing the curriculum*. Thousand Oaks, CA: Corwin Press, Inc.

Evanson, B. (2000, August 4). Decision nothing to fret over, experts say. *National Post*, p. A6.

Evernden, N. (1985). *The natural alien: Humankind and environment*. Toronto: University of Toronto Press.

Feyerabend, P. (1999). *Conquest of abundance: A tale of abstraction versus the richness of being.* Chicago: University of Chicago Press.

Foucault, M. (1999). *Abnormal.* New York: Picador.

Fox, M. (1983). *Original blessing.* Santa Fe, NM: Bear and Co.

Friesen, S. (2000). *Reforming mathematics in mathematics education.* Unpublished doctoral dissertation, Faculty of Education, University of Calgary, Alberta, Canada.

Friesen, S. (2003). E-mail correspondence from the Galileo Educational Network Association (GENA). http://www.galileo.org.

Friesen, S., & Stone, M. (1996). Great explorations. *Applying Research to the Classroom 14*(2), 6–11.

Frum, D., & Solomon, E. (2004, January 18). Interview. On the Canadian Broadcasting Company program *Sunday Morning.*

Gadamer, H. G. (1977). *Philosophical hermeneutics.* Berkeley: University of California Press.

Gadamer, H. G. (1983). *Reason in the age of science.* Boston: MIT Press.

Gadamer, H. G. (1989). *Truth and method.* New York: Continuum Press.

Gadamer, H. G. (1994). *Heidegger's ways.* Boston: MIT Press.

Gadamer, H. G. (2001). *Gadamer in conversation: Reflections and commentary* (R. Palmer, Ed. and Trans.). New Haven, CT: Yale University Press.

Gardner, H. (2000). *Intelligence reframed: Multiple intelligences for the 21st century.* Toronto: HarperCollins Canada/Basic Books.

Gick, M., & Holyoak, K. (1983). Schema induction and analogical transfer. *Psychology, 15,* 1–2.

Glieck, J. (2000). *Faster: The acceleration of just about everything.* New York: Vintage Books.

Grant, G. (1998). *English-speaking justice.* Toronto: House of Anansi Press.

Gray, J. (1998). *False dawn: The delusions of global capitalism.* London: Granta Books.

Greene, M. (1988). Philosophy and teaching. In M. C. Wittrock (Ed.), *Handbook of research on teaching* (3rd ed., pp. 479–503). New York: Macmillan.

Grumet, M. R. (1988). *Bitter milk: Women and teaching.* Amherst: University of Massachusetts Press.

Habermas, J. (1973). *Knowledge and human interests.* Boston: Beacon Books.

Haraway, D. (1997). *Modest_Witness@Second_Millennium. FemaleMan_Meets_OncoMouse: Feminism and technoscience.* New York: Routledge.

Hayles, K. (1996). Simulated nature and natural simulations: Rethinking the relation between the beholder and the world. In W. Cronon (Ed.), *Uncommon ground: Rethinking the human place in nature* (pp. 409–425). New York: Norton.

Heidegger, M. (1962). *Being and time.* [Trans. J. Macquarrie & E. Robinson.] New York: Harper & Row.

Heidegger, M. (1962). *Being and time.* New York: Harper & Row.

Heidegger, M. (1968). *What calls for thinking?* New York: Harper & Row.

Heidegger, M. (1971a). *Origin of the work of art.* New York: Harper & Row.

Heidegger, M. (1971b) *On the way to language.* New York: Harper & Row.

Heidegger, M. (1972a). *Poetry, language and thought.* New York: Harper & Row.

Heidegger, M. (1977). Age of the world picture. In M. Heidegger, *The question concerning technology* (pp. 115–154). New York: Harper & Row.

Heidegger, M. (1985). *History of the concept of time.* Bloomington: Indiana University Press.

Heidegger, M. (1987). Overcoming metaphysics. In M. Heidegger, *The end of philosophy* (pp. 84–110). New York: Harper & Row.

Henderson, M. (2000, October 4). Infant's cells harvested to save critically ill sister. *Calgary Herald,* p. A2.

Hillman, J. (1982). Anima mundi: Returning the soul to the world. *Spring, 40.*

Hillman, J. (1987). *Puer papers*. Dallas, TX: Spring Publications.

Hillman, J. (1989). *Healing fiction*. Barrytown, NY: Station Hill Press.

Hillman, J., & Ventura, M. (1992). *We've had a hundred years of psychotherapy and the world's getting worse*. New York: HarperCollins.

Hirshfield, J. (1997). *Nine gates: Entering the mind of poetry*. New York: HarperCollins.

Holding, J. (1991). *The investigations book*. Cambridge, England: Cambridge University Press.

Hongzhi, Z. (1991). *Cultivating the empty field: The silent illumination of Zen master Hongzhi*. San Francisco: North Point Press.

Huebner, D. E. (1999). *The lure of the transcendent*. Mahwah, NJ: Lawrence Erlbaum Associates.

Husserl, E. (1970). *The crisis of European science and transcendental phenomenology*. Evanston, IL: Northwestern University Press.

Husserl, E. (1972). *Logical investigations*. New York: Routledge & Kegan Paul. (Original work published 1902)

Hyde, L. (1983). *The gift: Imagination and the erotic life of property*. New York: Vintage Books.

Illich, I. (1972). *Deschooling society*. New York: Harper & Row.

Illich, I. (1973). *Tools for conviviality*. New York: Harper & Row.

Illich, I. (1992). *In the mirror of the past: Lectures and addresses 1978–1990*. New York: Marion Boyars.

Illich, I. (1993). *In the vineyard of the text: A commentary on Hugh's* Didascalicon. Chicago: University of Chicago Press.

Illich, I. (1996). *The right to useful unemployment and its professional enemies*. New York: Marion Boyars.

Illich, I. (2000). Disabling professions. In I. Illich, I. Zola, J. McKnight, U. Caplan, & H. Shaiken (Eds.), *Disabling professions* (pp. 11–40). New York: Marion Boyars.

Illich, I., & Cayley, D. (1992). *Ivan Illich in conversation*. Toronto: House of Anansi Press.

Illich, I., & Sanders, B. (1988). *ABC: The alphabetization of the popular mind*. Berkeley, CA: North Point Press.

Inhelder, B. (1969). Some aspects of Piaget's genetic approach to cognition. In H. Furth (Ed.), *Piaget and knowledge: Theoretical foundations* (pp. 9–23). Englewood Cliffs, NJ: Prentice-Hall.

Irwin, R. L. (2003). Towards an aesthetic of unfolding in/sights through curriculum. *Journal of the Canadian Association for Curriculum Studies, 1*(2), 63–78. Available at http://www.csse.ca/CACS/JCACS/V1N2/essays.html 16 pgs

Jardine, D. (1988). Play and hermeneutics: An exploration of the bi-polarities of mutual understanding. *Journal of Curriculum Theorizing, 8*(2), 23–42.

Jardine, D. (1990). On the humility of mathematical language. *Educational Theory, 40*, 181–191.

Jardine, D. (1992a). "The fecundity of the individual case": Considerations of the pedagogic heart of interpretive work. *Journal of Philosophy of Education, 26*(1), 51–61.

Jardine, D. (1992b). Immanuel Kant, Jean Piaget and the rage for order: Hints of the colonial spirit in pedagogy. *Educational Philosophy and Theory, 23*(1), 28–43.

Jardine, D. (1992c). Naming children authors. *Readings in Canadian Literacy, 10*(4), 53–61.

Jardine, D. W. (1992d). Reflections on education, hermeneutics, and ambiguity. In W. F. Pinar & W. M. Reynolds (Eds.), *Understanding curriculum as phenomenological and deconstructed text* (pp. 116–127). New York: Teachers College Press.

Jardine, D. (1992e). *Speaking with a boneless tongue*. Bragg Creek, Alberta, Canada: Makyo Press.

Jardine, D. (1994a) The ecologies of mathematics and the rhythms of the Earth. In Paul Ernest (Ed.), *Mathematics, philosophy and education: An international perspective, studies in mathematics education* (Vol. 3, pp. 109–123). London: Falmer.

Jardine, D. (1994b). "Littered with literacy": An ecopedagogical reflection on whole language, pedocentrism and the necessity of refusal. *Journal of Curriculum Studies, 26*(5), 509–524.

Jardine, D. (1994c) Student-teaching, interpretation and the monstrous child. *Journal of Philosophy of Education, 28*(1), 17–24.

Jardine, D. (1995). "The stubborn particulars of grace." In Bert Horwood (Ed.), *Experience and the curriculum: Principles and programs* (pp. 261–275). Toronto: Kendall/Hunt.

Jardine, D. (1997). "Their bodies swelling with messy secrets." In T. Carson & D. Sumara (Eds.), *Action Research as a Living Practice* (pp. 161–166). New York: Peter Lang.

Jardine, D. (1998). *"To Dwell with a Boundless Heart": On Curriculum Theory, Hermeneutics and the Ecological Imagination.* New York: Peter Lang.

Jardine, D. (2000). *"Under the tough old stars": Ecopedagogical essays.* Brandon, VT: Psychology Press/Holistic Education Press. (Volume Four of the Foundations of Holistic Education Series Catalogue No. 4177)

Jardine, D. (2006). *Jean Piaget: A primer.* New York: Peter Lang.

Jardine, D., & Abram, D. (2001). Afterword: All knowledge is carnal knowledge: A conversation. In B. Hocking, W. Linds, & J. Haskell (Eds.), *Unfolding bodymind: Exploring possibility through education* (pp. 325–333). Brandon, VT: Psychology Press/Holistic Education Press.

Jardine, D., Clifford, P., & Friesen, S. (1999). "Standing helpless before the child." A response to Naomi Norquay's "Social difference and the problem of the 'unique individual': An uneasy legacy of child-centered pedagogy." *Canadian Journal of Education, 24*(3), 321–326.

Jardine, D., Clifford, P., & Friesen, S. (Eds.). (2003). *Back to the basics of teaching and learning: "Thinking the world together."* Mahwah, NJ: Lawrence Erlbaum Associates.

Jardine, D., LaGrange, A., & Everest, B. (2004) "In these shoes is the silent call of the earth": Meditations on curriculum integration, conceptual violence and the ecologies of community and place. In D. Flinders & S. Thornton (Eds.), *The curriculum studies reader: Essential contemporary readings* (2nd ed., pp. 323–330). New York: Routledge.

Jardine, D., & Misgeld, D. (1989). Hermeneutics as the undisciplined child. In M. Packer & R. Addison (Eds.), *Entering the circle: Hermeneutic investigations in psychology* (pp. 259–273). Albany: State University of New York Press.

Joseph, G. (1991). *The crest of the peacock: Non-European roots of mathematics.* New York: Penguin.

Kant, I. (1964). *Critique of pure reason.* London: Macmillan. (Original work published 1787)

Kant, I. (1983). What is enlightenment? In *Perpetual peace and other essays.* Indianapolis, IN: Hackett. (Original work published 1794)

Kermode, F. (1979). *The genesis of secrecy.* Cambridge, MA: Harvard University Press.

Kliebard, H. (2000 [1975]). Metaphorical roots of curriculum design. In W. F. Pinar (Ed.), *Curriculum studies: The reconceptualization* (pp. 84–85). Troy, NY: Educator's International Press. [Originally published in Pinar (Ed.), *Curriculum theorizing: The reconceptualists* (pp. 84–85). Berkeley, CA: McCutchan.]

Kovitz, R. (1997). *Room behaviour.* Toronto: Insomniac Press.

Lawlor, R. (1982). *Sacred geometry.* London: Thames & Hudson.

Le Guin, U. (1987). *Buffalo gals and other animal presences.* Santa Barbara, CA: Capra Press.

Lensmire, T. (2000). *Powerful writing, responsible teaching (critical issues in curriculum)*. New York: Teacher's College Press.

Linnaeus, C. (1707–1778). http://www.ucmp.berkeley.edu/history/linnaeus.html.

Lonergan, B. (1997). *Verbum: Word and idea in Aquinas*. Toronto: University of Toronto Press.

Loy, D. (1993). Indra's postmodern net. *Philosophy East and West, 48*(3), 481–510.

Loy, D. (1999). *Lack and transcendence: The problem of death and life in psychotherapy, existentialism, and Buddhism*. New York: Prometheus Books.

Manguel, A. (1996). *A history of reading*. New York: Penguin.

Melnick, C. (1997). Review of Max Van Manen and Bas Levering's *Childhood secrets: Intimacy, privacy and the self reconsidered. Journal of Curriculum Studies, 29*(3), 370–373.

Merleau-Ponty, M. (1964). *The phenomenology of perception*. London: Routledge.

Merleau-Ponty, M. (1971). *Signs*. Evanston IL: Northwestern University Press.

Meschonnic, H. (1988). Rhyme and life. *Critical Inquiry, 15*, 90–107.

Miller, A. (1989). *For your own good: Hidden cruelty in child-rearing and the roots of violence*. Toronto: Collins.

Minh-ha, T. (1994). Other than myself/my other self. In G. Robertson, M. Mash, L. Tickner, J. Bird, B. Curtis, & T. Putnam (Eds.), *Travellers' tales: Narratives of home and displacement* (pp. 9–26). London: Routledge.

Misgeld, D. (1985). Self-reflection and adult maturity: Adult and child in hermeneutical and critical reflection. *Phenomenology + Pedagogy, 3*, 191–200.

Morrison, B. (2000). *The justification of Johann Gutenberg*. Toronto: Random House of Canada.

Nandy, A. (1987). *Traditions, tyranny and utopias*. Delhi, India: Oxford.

National Post, Friday, August 4, 2000.

Negroponte, N. (1996). Where do new ideas come from? *Wired* [online]. Retrieved July 2, 2000, from http://www.wired.com/wired/archive//4.01/negroponte_pr.html.

Nishitani, K. (1982). *Religion and nothingness*. Berkeley: University of California Press.

Norris-Clark, W. (1976). Analogy and the Meaningfulness of Language About God: A reply to Kai Nielsen. *The Thomist, 40*, 176–198.

Orr, D. (1992). *Ecological literacy—Education and the transition to a post-modern world*. Albany: State University of New York Press.

Palmer, P. (1998). *The courage to teach: Exploring the inner landscape of a teacher's life*. San Francisco: Jossey-Bass.

Pappas, T. (1989). *The joy of mathematics*. San Carlos, CA: Wide World Publishing/Tetra.

Peters, M., & Humes, W. (2003). Editorial: Education in the knowledge economy. *Policy futures in education, 1*(1). Retrieved June 14, 2004, from http://www.triangle.co.uk/pfie/.

Piaget, J. (1952). *Origins of intelligence in children*. New York: International Universities Press.

Piaget, J. (1962). *Play, dreams and imitation*. New York: Norton.

Piaget, J. (1965). *Insights and illusions of philosophy*. New York: Meridian Books.

Piaget, J. (1968). *Genetic epistemology*. New York: Norton.

Piaget, J. (1969). *The child's conception of time*. New York: Basic Books.

Piaget, J. (1970a). Piaget's theory. In P. H. Mussen (Ed.), *Carmichael's manual of child psychology* (Vol. 1, pp. 703–732). Toronto: Wiley.

Piaget, J. (1970b). *Structuralism*. New York: Harper & Row.

Piaget, J. (1971a). *Biology and knowledge*. Chicago: University of Chicago Press.

Piaget, J. (1971b). *The construction of reality in the child*. New York: Ballantine.

Piaget, J. (1972). *Judgement and reasoning in the child*. Totowa, NJ: Littlefield, Adams.

Piaget, J. (1973). *The psychology of intelligence*. Totowa, NJ: Littlefield, Adams.

Piaget, J. (1974a). *The child's conception of the world.* London: Paladin Books.
Piaget, J. (1974b). *The language and thought of the child.* New York: Meridian Books.
Piaget, J. (1977). The mission of the idea. In H. E. Gruber & J. J. Vonech (Eds.), *The Essential Piaget* (pp. 26–37). London: Routledge & Kegan Paul.
Piaget, J., & Inhelder, B. (1969). *The psychology of the child.* New York: Harper & Row.
Piaget, J., & Inhelder, B. (1998). *The child's conception of space.* New York: Library Binding.
Plechowak, A., & Cook, M. (1976). *Complete guide to the elementary learning centre.* West Hyatt, NY: Parker Publishing.
Pinar, W. F., Reynolds, W. M., Slattery, P., & Taubman, P. M. (1995). *Understanding curriculum.* New York: Peter Lang.
Plato. (trans. 1956). *Phaedrus* (W. G. Helmbold & W. G. Rabinowitz, Trans.). New York: The Liberal Arts Press.
Plato. (1968). *The republic of Plato* (A. Bloom, Trans.). New York: Basic Books.
Polanyi, K. (2001). *The great transformation: The political and economic origins of our time.* Boston: Beacon Press.
Polanyi, M. (1967). *The tacit dimension.* London: Routledge & Kegan Paul.
Prakash, M. S. (2004). The beginning of justice: Ending global education and the assumption of scarcity. Retrieved June 10, 2004, from www.ed.uiuc.edu/EPS/PES-Yearbook/93_docs/PRAKASH.HTM.
Ransom, J. S. (1997). *Foucault's discipline: The politics of subjectivity.* Durham, NC: Duke University Press.
Remarks by the President, Prime Minister Tony Blair of England (Via Satellite), Dr. Francis Collins, Director of the National Human Genome Research Institute, and Dr. Craig Venter, President and Chief Scientific Officer, Celera Genomics Corporation, on the *Completion of the First Survey of the Entire Human Genome Project* (2000). Retrieved June 2005 from http://www.whitehouse.gov/textonly/WH/New/html/genome-20000626.html.
Ross, S. (1999). *The gift of kinds: The good in abundance.* Albany: State University of New York Press.
Schattschneider, D., & Walker, W. (1982). *M. C. Escher Kaleidocycle.* Norfolk, England: Tarquin.
Schon, D. (1983). *The reflective practitioner.* New York: Basic Books.
Schon, D. (1987). *Educating the reflective practitioner.* New York: Basic Books.
Schopenhauer, A. (1969). *The world as will and representation.* New York: Dover.
Sendak, M. (1988). *Where the wild things are.* New York: HarperCollins.
Serres, M. (1983). *Hermes: Literature, science, philosophy.* Baltimore, MD: Johns Hopkins University Press.
Shirane, H. (1996). *Traces of dreams: Landscape, cultural memory and the poetry of Basho.* Stanford, CA: Stanford University Press.
Siefe, C. (2000). *Zero: The biography of a dangerous idea.* New York: Viking.
Sister Wendy's Story of Art. (n.d.). http://www.tpt.org/BTW_folder/Sept/wendy.html.
Sizer, T. R. (2004). *The red pencil: Convictions from experience in education.* New Haven, CT: Yale University Press.
Smith, D. (1999a). Economic fundamentalism, globalization and the public remains of education. *Interchange, 30*(1), 93–117.
Smith, D. (1999b). Globalization and education: Prospects for postcolonial pedagogy in a hermeneutic mode—Introduction. *Interchange, 30*(1), 1–10.
Smith, D. (1999c). *Pedagon: Interdisciplinary essays in the human sciences, pedagogy and culture.* New York: Peter Lang.
Smith, D. (2000). The specific challenges of globalization for teaching and vice versa. *Alberta Journal of Educational Research, 46*(1), 7–26.
Smith, D. (2003). On enfraudening the public sphere, the futility of empire and the future of knowledge after "America." *Policy Futures in Education, 1*(3), 488–503.

Smith, D. (in press). Troubles with the sacred canopy: Global citizenship in a season of great untruth. In G. H. Richardson & D. Blades (Eds.), *Troubling the canon of citizenship education*. New York: Peter Lang.

Snyder, G. (1977). *The old ways*. New York: New Directions Books.

Snyder, G. (1980). *The real work*. New York: New Directions Books.

Stiglitz, J. (1999). Public policy for a knowledge economy. Remarks at the Department of Trade and Industry Center for Economic and Policy Research, London, January 27, 1999. Available at: http:///www.worldbank.org/html.extdr/extme/jssp012799a.htm.

Stiglitz, J. (2002). *Globalization and its discontents*. London: Allen Lane.

Stoler, A. L. (1995). *Race and the education of desire: Foucault's history of sexuality and the colonial order of things*. Durham, NC: Duke University Press.

Sumara, D. J. & Davis, B. (1998). *Unskinning curriculum*. In W. F. Pinar (Ed.), *Curriculum: Toward new identities* (pp. 75–92). New York: Garland.

Test tube tech may save child. Reuters (2000). http://www.wirednews.com/news/print/0,1294,39224,00.html.

Thomas, D. (1967). Reminiscences of childhood. In *Quite early one morning* (pp. 3–21). London: Aldine Press.

Thomas, D. (1985). The torpedo's touch. *Harvard Educational Review, 55*, 220–222.

Thompson, W. I. (1981). *The time falling bodies take to light: Mythology, sexuality and the origin of culture*. New York: St. Martin's.

Throne, J. (1994). Living with the pendulum: The complex world of teaching. *Harvard Educational Review, 64*(2), 195–208.

Trungpa, C. (1988). *The myth of freedom and the way of meditation*. Boston: Shambala Press.

Turner, V. (1987). Betwixt and between: The liminal period in rites of passage. In L. Mahdi, S. Foster, & M. Little (Eds.), *Betwixt and between: Patterns of masculine and feminine initiation* (pp. 3–22). Peru, IL: Open Court.

Usher, R., & Edwards, R. (1994). *Postmodernism and education*. London: Routledge.

van Manen, M. (1991). *The tact of teaching*. Albany: State University of New York Press.

von Humbolt, W. (2000 [1793–1794]). Theory of Bildung. In I. Westbury, S. Hopmann, & K. Riquarts (Eds.), *Teaching as a reflective practice: The German didaktik tradition* (57–61). [Trans. By Gillian Horton-Krüger.] Mahwah, NJ: Lawrence Erlbaum Associates.

Wallace, B. (1987). *The stubborn particulars of grace*. Toronto: McClelland & Stewart.

Walther, I., & Metzger, R. (1997). *Vincent van Gogh: The complete paintings*. New York: Taschen.

Warner, M. (2000). *No go the bogeyman*. New York: Vintage Books.

Weatherford, J. (1988). *Indian givers*. New York: Fawcett Columbine.

Webber, J. A. (2003). *Failure to hold: The politics of school violence*. Lanham, MD: Rowman & Littlefield.

Weinsheimer, J. (1985). *Gadamer's hermeneutics*. New Haven, CT: Yale University Press.

Wilde, S. (1996). *Awakening care: A possibility at the heart of teaching*. Unpublished master's thesis, Faculty of Education, University of Calgary, Alberta, Canada.

Wilensky, U. J. (1996). Making sense of probability through paradox and programming: A case study in a connected mathematics framework [online]. Retrieved July 2, 2000, from http://www.tufts.edu/~uwilensk/papers/paradox/lppp/msppp.html.

Williams, W. C. (1991). *The collected poems of William Carlos Williams* (Vol. 1, 1909–1939). New York: New Directions Books.

Wittgenstein, L. (1968). *Philosophical investigations*. Oxford, England: Blackwell.

Author Index

Subject Index